CIPIÈRES

Community and Landscape in the Alpes-Maritimes, France

David Austin, Rosamond Faith, Andrew Fleming and David Siddle

Edited by David Austin

WINDgather
PRESS

Windgather Press
is an imprint of
Oxbow Books, Oxford

ISBN 978-1-905119-99-8

A CIP record for this book is available from the British Library

This book is available direct from

Oxbow Books, Oxford, UK
(Phone: 01865-241249; Fax: 01865-794449)

and

The David Brown Book Company
PO Box 511, Oakville, CT 06779, USA
(Phone: 860-945-9329; Fax: 860-945-9468)

or from our website

www.oxbowbooks.com

*Front Cover: Taken from an undated and anonymous poster
for an annual fête in Cipières.*

Printed in Great Britain by
Short Run Press, Exeter

This book is dedicated, with great love and affection, to the memory of Anthony Lewison without whom this would not have been, and to Nora Lewison, his constant support.

Contents

List of Figures

Acknowledgements

The authors would like to thank first and foremost the members of the Lewison family: Anthony who initiated, inspired, assisted and supported us all; Nora, his wife, a scholar and specialist in her own field, who cherished and advised; and Jeremy who inherited Anthony's love of Cipières and his house there which he kindly let us use and who has maintained a constant interest in our progress. Both Jeremy and his brother Kim have also generously supported us by assisting with some of the costs of production and we are immensely grateful.

We would like also to acknowledge our great debt to the people of Cipières who must have thought we were mad, especially Jean-Claude Ruas and later mayors of Cipières as well as their staff who facilitated our access to archive and landscape alike. We would also like to acknowledge the very important work done by David Garrioch in helping Anthony Lewison to organise and index the archive of records held in the Mairie at Cipières, as well as his transcription and analysis of the 1750 cadastral *déclaration*.

We wish also to record the vital support of those who gave us important resources to enable the completion of our work: the Ministère de la Culture, Préfecture de la Région de Provence-Alpes-Côtes d'Azur, Direction Régionale des Affaires Culturelles, Service Régionale de l'Archéologie; the University of Wales Lampeter; and the University of Liverpool.

We are also grateful to the Director of the Observatoire du CERGA (Centre d'Etudes et de Recherches Géodynamiques et Astronomiques) for access to its property on the Plateau de Calern and for unpublished data on climate.

Many individuals have helped us with practical assistance and expertise, too many to name all individually. However we would like to acknowledge particularly the help of Catherine Ungar, Nigel Hepper, Susanna van Rose, Michael Allen, John Crowther, Matthew Johnson, Quentin Drew, Todd Trethowan, Jessica Bone, Greg Stevenson and a host of students from Lampeter.

We want to thank also Frank Bremar, Claudine Dauphin and other colleagues from CEPAM (Centre d'Etudes Préhistoire, Antiquité et Moyen Âge) in Sophia-Antipolis who have given us assistance (and shown considerable patience) in the long, slow process of gestation. We wish also to thank Martine Regert for all her assistance in the final stages of production.

PREFACE

A Brief History of the Cipières Project

David Austin and Andrew Fleming

When the London solicitor Anthony Lewison, the founder of our project (Figure 1), first came to Cipières in August 1960, after negotiating the narrow, tortuous road from Gourdon, there were still elm trees in the *place* at the centre of the village, providing shade for the Cipièrois in the heat of summer. Members of his family recall the general 'sleepiness' of the village in those days, its rough road surfaces, the water shortages in summer, the throwing of rubbish onto an unsavoury tip just below the road on the north side of the château. There were only two working farms; sheep were still kept in one or two of the village houses, in basement-level byres, and it was still possible to buy milk directly from the farm. In those days laundry was done in the communal wash-house, reached by descending a long path from the north side of the village. Anthony and his wife, Nora, were immediately attracted to the general ambience of Cipières – the warmth and sociability of its inhabitants, the evocative decrepitude of the

FIGURE 1. Anthony Lewison looking over La Combe from Le Gros Pounch
PHOTOGRAPH: DAVID AUSTIN

surrounding agrarian landscape, the sense of an old way of life slipping away. Anthony was particularly intrigued by the corbelled shelters on the plateau, especially after reading an editorial in *Antiquity* by the archaeologist Glyn Daniel which suggested that they might have prehistoric origins.

There were many ruined or neglected properties in Cipières, and in 1962 the Lewisons purchased a stable with a hayloft and converted it into a much-loved second home. Over subsequent years, others began to move in – a few old Cipières families, as well as outsiders – families from northern France and from England. They brought plenty of work for local builders. Soon, spreads of red roof-tiles were to be broken by sun-terraces with bright parasols and flowers in hanging-baskets; within the houses, power showers, microwaves and dish-washers now whirred and hummed in respectfully constructed settings of rural simplicity. Anthony Lewison resolved to find out more about the history of Cipières and its landscape, beginning in 1973.

Discussions with the mayor, M. Jean-Claude Ruas, revealed the existence of a considerable archive of communal village documents dating back to the 16th century. They lay untouched and virtually forgotten. Anthony persuaded the mayor to let him have a basement room in the Mairie, and set about sorting, conserving and classifying the archive ready for use. Lewison also discovered a series of magnificent IGN aerial photographs and ordered a set of enlarged copies which became a critical research resource. These photographs provided immediate overviews of an archaeological landscape of a richness and complexity unsurpassed in most parts of Europe. By the early 1980s, Lewison was seeking and obtaining advice and help from other researchers – environmental archaeologists, historians, soil scientists and a botanist; these early contributions[1] to the project's work formed a preliminary resource for the team that was to undertake the main programme.

From the mid-1980s until Anthony's death in the summer of 1993 at the age of 72, the pace of research quickened. He began to publish accounts of his work – a detailed survey of the corbelled shelters in the regional archaeological journal,[2] and an account of the historic context of the relict landscape and its agrarian systems for *Antiquity*.[3] He started working with Catherine Ungar, an anthropologist living near Nice and, with her, published a brief study of the Plateau de Calern.[4]

In 1985 Anthony made contact with David Austin, a landscape and settlement archaeologist who had worked on the medieval and early modern periods in Britain, notably in upland areas, and David Siddle, an historical geographer interested in population, land use and social organisation, especially in Alpine Europe. In 1986 both made their first visits to Cipières. With their encouragement, Anthony prepared a brief overview of his initial work for the regional Institute of Prehistory and Archaeology,[5] and an article on the creation of cadastres in *Landscape History*.[6] Enlisting the help of Andrew Josephs and Sabine Verhelst, he extended his work on field monuments and documents and his scholarly work was awarded the degree of Master of Philosophy of the

University of Wales Lampeter for a thesis entitled *A village and its territory in southern France: a study in upland archaeology.*[7]

By 1990 the project had been joined by John Crowther, soil scientist and geomorphologist, Nigel Hepper, a research botanist and Andrew Fleming, another landscape archaeologist with extensive upland expertise in prehistory as well as later periods. Inevitably, each scholar had his/her own research agenda, but we were also immensely attracted by the idea of developing a project that would be fully inter-disciplinary (as opposed to multi-disciplinary); that is to say, aims, objectives and working practices would be agreed after intensive discussion involving all members of the team. In 1988 and 1989 Austin, Crowther and Lewison carried out an inter-disciplinary study of one doline (153/163) and a long valley, La Combe, on the plateau. In 1989, preliminary results were presented at the 10th International Meeting of Archaeology and History, entitled *Archéologie et Éspaces*, held in Antibes. Two small-scale seasons were undertaken in 1990 and 1991, with further exploratory work on the plateau and on the buildings of the village.

Given the range of skills and expertise available together with the volume and complexity of the archaeological data and the documentary archive, it was clear that sustaining the project on a more systematic basis would require substantial funds. Three major, but unsuccessful applications were made to British research funding agencies – to the Leverhulme Trust in 1987 and 1990, and to the Economic and Social Science Research Council in 1991. The failure of these applications led inevitably to a loss of momentum, and several members withdrew from the team, unable to proceed without access to the resources they needed. Crowther was restricted to a relatively small amount of sampling; Hepper published his study of the sub-Alpine flora independently.[9]

Just before the autumn field season of 1993, Anthony Lewison died. He was much mourned by his colleagues on the Project; we continue to miss his intellectual curiosity, boundless enthusiasm and generosity of spirit. It was a poignant occasion in September of that year, therefore, when we hosted the exhibition which Anthony Lewison and David Siddle had worked so hard to organise. Held in the chapel of St Claude on the edge of the village and entitled '*De Temps Immémorial: Les Cipièrois*', the exhibition was seen by many villagers, as well as visitors from all over the world.[10] Towards the close of our fieldwork in the same year, we held a one-day conference in the church to introduce some of our ideas, methods and results to an audience which included not only the villagers, but senior colleagues from the region.

1993 could be said to inaugurate the third phase of the project, following the slow initial build-up and then the intense activity of the late 1980s and early 1990s. Fortunately, funding was now offered by the Ministère de la Culture, Préfecture de la Région de Provence-Alpes-Côtes d'Azur, Direction Régionale des Affaires Culturelles, Service Régionale de l'Archéologie. They supported the second 1993 season and continued to support us in 1994 and 1995.[11] These resources, enhanced by student field classes funded by the University of Wales

Lampeter, enabled the team to continue in the field, and carry out a small excavation.[12] The bulk of the fieldwork in this period occurred in the Baoume de Brun where Austin undertook extensive detailed archaeological mapping of one *quartier* on the plateau, developing the methodologies and modes of interpretation which could be integrated with the documents in the archive. Siddle at the same time used the same remarkable documentary source to analyse the patterns of population, land use and economy, particularly from the 15th century onwards. During this period Fleming worked on the relationship between the Cipières-Caussols road (mostly on the Plateau de Calern) and the agrarian landscape through which it passed. Using analytical principles in part derived from this work, in 1999–2002 he returned to the plateau, mostly in the *quartiers* of Les Baumettes and Le Rouré, with the objective of 'reading' the landscape. At this stage the project was joined by Rosamond Faith, a medieval historian already working on regional landholding and settlement associated with the abbey of St Victor at Marseille. Her work completed the package, since she was able to research the earlier evidence which concerned the origins and development of the village and commune of Cipières. Thus the team was complete and the tasks of analysis and writing began.

CHAPTER ONE

Setting the Scene

Andrew Fleming, David Austin and David Siddle

The challenge presented to a group of British landscape archaeologists, historians and geographers was as much intellectual as it was about dealing with a very different Mediterranean upland landscape. In broad terms we aspired to the kind of narrative espoused by the Annalistes *and have attempted to produce a strongly interdisciplinary and holistic account of one community. The landscape itself offered a rich, if enigmatic, array of material with some very distinctive topographies. It was a landscape we learnt to experience through long hours of fieldwork, seeing it as much through contemporary eyes, its very recent past of decline and its more hopeful present-day regeneration. Although we have, in a scientific sense, classified these topographies, for ease of description and analysis, we have also retained a strong sense of the wholeness of the community and the actions of people within it. In this respect we were blessed by the existence, alongside a rich archaeology, of a large archive of documents created by many centuries of Cipières' inhabitants and still, quite remarkably to British eyes, retained in the* Mairie *of the village. This has enabled us to populate the material world with a rich assortment of people, families and activity.*

1.1. The intellectual challenge

Andrew Fleming

By the early 1990s a team of experts,[1] both British and French, was committed to the development of interdisciplinary research strategies and methodologies and was poised to engage with the remarkable relict landscape and rich documentary archive of the commune of Cipières.

The insights and conceptual frameworks deployed by French scholars in their work on the rich and varied history of their own countryside have been absorbed by many British landscape historians. Concepts like *la longue durée* and *l'histoire événementielle* are familiar to us; we understand the strength and potential of the *Annales* perspective. Many of us have read Le Roy Ladurie's *Montaillou*; our understanding of the nuanced concept of *pays* is such that we do not usually waste time trying to find an equivalent English word. Nevertheless, it will be obvious, to a French reader, that our account of the landscape history of this French upland commune reflects, at least to some extent, British traditions of fieldwork in landscape archaeology and writing landscape history. This is entirely understandable; at the outset, we were interested in seeing how far we could apply the methods and approaches of the British school of landscape history to a French Mediterranean countryside. As a matter of fact, since the beginning of the project, differences between British and French approaches have come to seem less significant, especially with the publication of works like Christine Rendu's *La Montagne d'Enveig* (2003) which in many ways represents the sort of final publication to which we would have aspired, had our project been better funded.

From the outset, we wanted to embrace a rare opportunity of pursuing an interdisciplinary agenda. While landscape historians usually like to stress the importance of interdisciplinary discourse in developing narratives of the landscape history of a particular locality, this ideal is all too rarely achieved. Moreover, in France national or regional overviews have tended to predominate, at the expense of more holistic treatments of particular localities. Our approach aspires to generate diachronic accounts of human and environmental interaction both for a locality and for that locality in its region. It is distinguished by the significant use of a rich heritage of archival and secondary historical sources. These have been deployed to support, extend or challenge hypotheses of landscape interpretation. This interdisciplinary approach (always an ideal in the mind of our patron, Anthony Lewison) represents a dynamic interaction which has emerged slowly over the years as our researches have progressed.

The archaeological and documentary records at Cipières are rich. They have given us a great deal to discuss, in evenings by the hearth or in more formal seminars, or out in the fields together, tramping through dolines and along ancient trackways, or crouching over the pages of an ancient cadastre. In theory, such an embarrassment of riches should help us to create 'thick description', perhaps developing an *Annales*-type narrative. In practice, however – and perhaps paradoxically – this very complexity has defeated our best efforts to bring archaeological and written sources together to create a seamless narrative; the order which we have chosen for this book represents a compromise. We hope that our major themes will emerge, as we attempt to achieve an interaction of archival sources and landscape evidence to allow much closer interpretation of phases and qualities of changing occupation. In the context of our detailed work in the landscape, in the village and in the archive, our debates over philosophical approaches, appropriate methodologies and emergent narratives have been stimulating and, we hope, productive.

1.2. Encountering Cipières

Andrew Fleming

Cipières is located in the Alpes-Maritimes, some 30 km north-west of Nice and about 10 km NNE of Grasse – though straight-line measurements of distance are meaningless in this rugged terrain (Figure 2). The river Loup, which forms part of the commune's boundary, runs east and then turns abruptly south to enter a deep, spectacular limestone gorge; the village is perched on a shoulder, high above, and to the SW of, this change of fluvial direction (Figure 3). From the village, the river is invisible; it lies far below, shrouded in thick deciduous woodland. The village stands about 750 m above sea level, its houses with their red-tiled roofs clustered around and just below the rock on which a medieval castle once stood (Figure 4). This rock is now occupied by its post-Revolution replacement, *Le Château,* a massive 19th century pile whose visual

FIGURE 2. Location map
DRAWING: DAVID AUSTIN

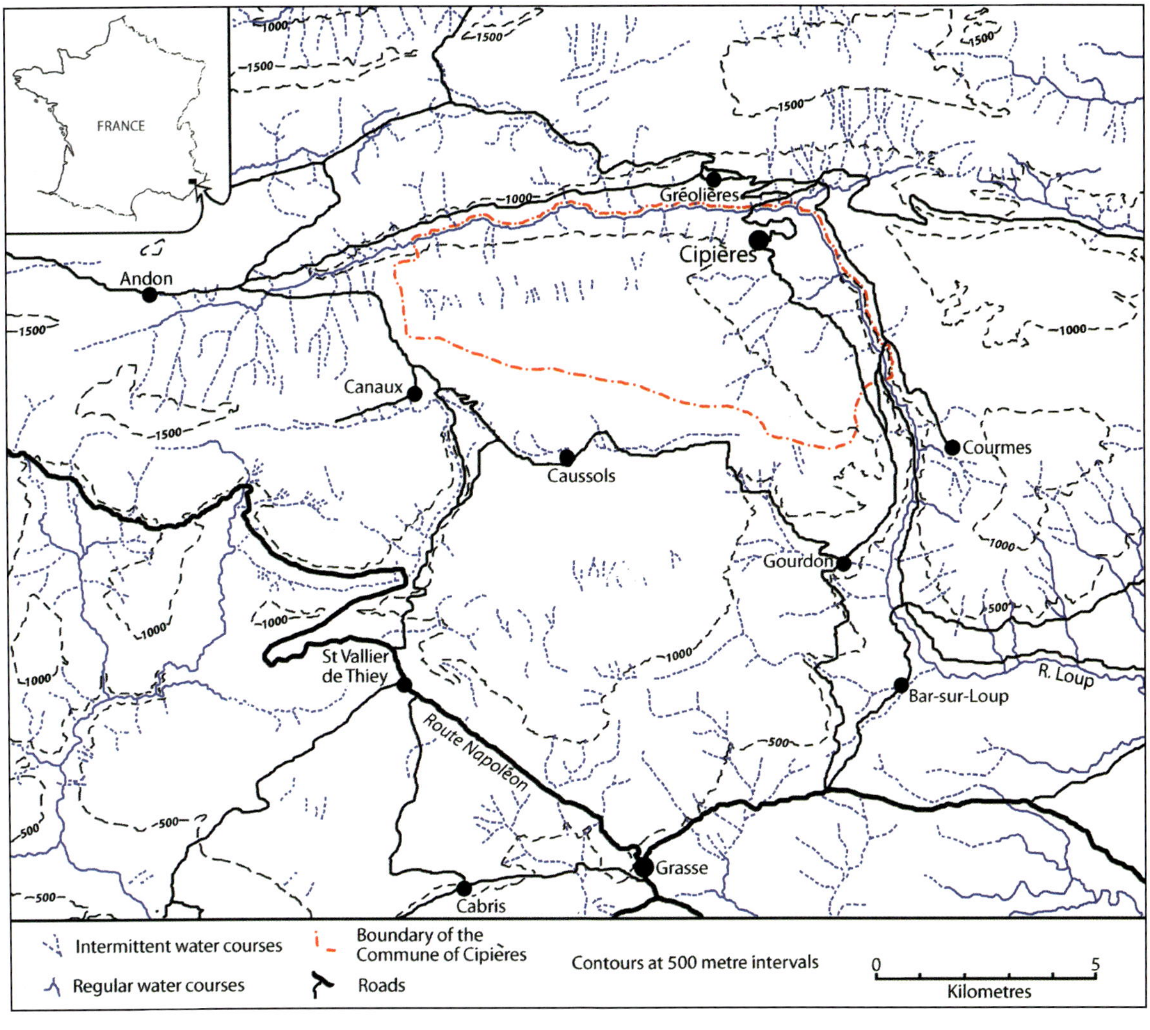

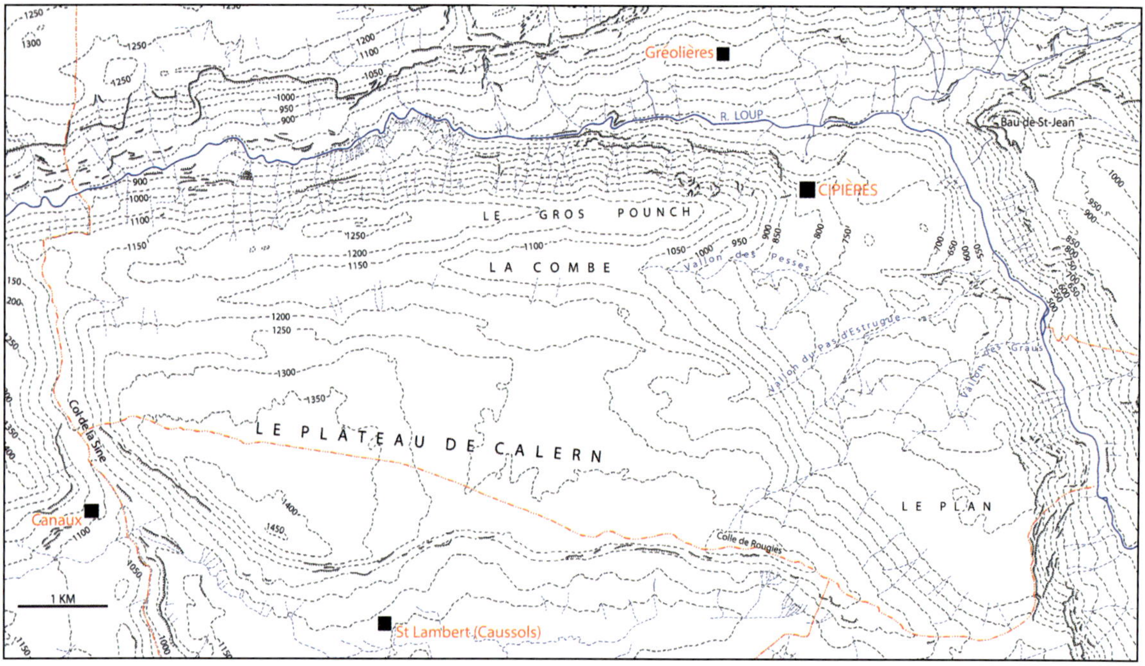

FIGURE 3. Physical map of commune
DRAWING: DAVID AUSTIN

dominance is in inverse proportion to its architectural merit. The core of this classic 'perched' village is formed by narrow streets shaded by long runs of tall houses joined together, the occasional gaps created by houses disused and partly demolished (Figure 5). Sometimes an unassuming façade is broken by an immaculately carved doorway, dating, as its inscribed date indicates, from the time of Montaigne – evidently a time of pride and prosperity (Figure 6). In the centre, just below the large yellow church with its wrought iron bell-cage, lies the village *Place,* a sunnier, more open space with a central fountain – though the name of the café, *Les Ormeaux,* reminds us that there were once great elm trees here, offering deep and welcome shade in summer.

South again from the *Place* runs *La Bourgade,* another narrow street, flanked by unbroken rows of tall houses. The Bourgade leads out to the chapel of St Claude, as well as a scatter of modern houses, one and a half farms, and much of what remains of the farmed land of the commune. Around the village, mostly to the south, lies the best land; there are rich pastures sometimes dusty and yellowing, sometimes lush and green, and a few freshly-ploughed arable fields, tucked in and sometimes half hidden among sinuous lanes and pine-shrouded hills (Figure 7). But one can also see abandoned fields, walled and terraced, reclaimed by woodland and scrub. Great piles of cleared stone may be glimpsed through the trees (Figure 8). But if agriculture is in decline, the village itself now prospers. The tiled roofs of Cipières have sun-terraces set into them, the *terraces tropeziennes* – the architectural signature of the many relatively leisured inhabitants of Cipières who do not have to make their living from this stony terrain. At weekends, visitors and tourists arrive from the densely-populated

4

5

6

FIGURE 4. The château and the village from the south-west
PHOTOGRAPH: ANDREW FLEMING

FIGURE 5. La Bourgade en fête
PHOTOGRAPH: ANTHONY LEWISON

FIGURE 6. A 17th-century dated doorway
PHOTOGRAPH: ANTHONY LEWISON

coastal belt to the south. Sometimes the woods echo with gun-shots and the baying of hunting-dogs, and the *Place* is packed with off-road vehicles. But usually Cipières is a quiet place. Perched the village may be, but it is overshadowed to the west by the flanks of the Plateau de Calern, some 500 m higher than the village, and if they are to see the last light cast by the setting sun, the *Cipièrois* must look north, up to the crags and screes of the Cime du Cheiron, 1000 metres above them (Figure 9). For we are in the Pré-Alpes. To the north, and at much the same level on the opposite side of the Loup valley, one can look across to Gréolières, a village with much the same character as Cipières itself; yet Gréolières-les-Neiges, a little further north, still only 1400 m above sea level, is a ski station, surrounded by characteristic Alpine scenery.

Cipières may exude a quiet, half-abandoned air. But all things are relative, as one will discover on climbing the dusty road which leads west, up to the high limestone Plateau de Calern. Place-name scholars[2] tell us that this name, along with that of Caussols, comes from an ancient, pre-Indo-European word **kal*, meaning 'stone' – a suggestion which is not hard to believe. On Calern the silence is often palpable; yet all around are the signs of a once heavily-used landscape (Figure 10). Occasionally, one encounters a *bergerie* still in use. The sheep, watered from a rock-cut cistern, are usually kept in one large sheep-house walled with stone, with a low, tiled roof, pitched at a gentle angle and supported by beams held up by stone pillars standing within the building. The shepherd's simple accommodation is now rarely used, since four-wheel drive vehicles make overnight stays unnecessary (Figure 11).

Nowadays this is mostly a land for walkers and hunters in the season. The

7

8

9

10

austere, higher summits are mostly found towards the west of the plateau, but there are also extensive grassy plains. The more obvious indicators of limestone country are the dolines, depressions caused by subterranean collapse and enfolding zones of grass and deeper soils. Some dolines look like deep, almost circular self-contained craters; others are shallower and more open – three or four of them side by side, separated by narrow rock sills (Figure 18). There are also one or two caves, and 'pot-holes' with vertical sides; these are *baumes, baoumes or baumettes* (*baoumo, baumitos* in the 16th century). Most of the dolines are clear of trees and scrub, mainly as a consequence of sheep grazing; a few are enclosed with temporary fencing for a day or two, to allow more concentrated grazing and manuring. Tree cover on the plateau is dominated by spreads of pine and box. However, the deciduous trees and shrubs which grow at lower levels are also seen here (Figure 12). Hazel is the only one which might be described as reasonably common; however, oak, elm, ash, lime, field maple, wild apple (eaten and enjoyed by one of us), pear and cherry are all to be found here, as well as several common shrubs. Juniper and box also grow on the plateau, the latter sometimes in extensive and conspicuous patches. Deciduous trees and bushes are often most conspicuous where young saplings escape browsing by deer – especially on bare limestone pavements dissected by 'grykes' – fissures containing small, deep pockets of soil. These deciduous species

FIGURE 7. Land around the village with the chapel of St Claude in the distance

FIGURE 8. One of the great revetted stone-piles near the village amongst the regenerating shrub and woodland

FIGURE 9. View towards Cime du Cheiron from the top of Anthony Lewison's house on the Rue du Coulet

FIGURE 10. General view of the worked landscape of the Plateau de Calern.

PHOTOGRAPHS: DAVID AUSTIN

left: FIGURE 11. A *bergerie*
PHOTOGRAPH: DAVID AUSTIN

right: FIGURE 12. A deciduous tree on Calern with our field vehicle incongruously parked next to it
PHOTOGRAPH: DAVID AUSTIN

below: FIGURE 13. The old *lavoir* on the north side of the village
PHOTOGRAPH: DAVID AUSTIN)

protect one another, a thicket of wild rose allowing young trees to flourish. There are areas of scrub, notably in some of the smaller dolines, providing cover for deer and wild boar, whose traces are obvious, especially when they run through the grassy vegetation on the doline floors, and leave behind the fresh orange–brown scars of their foragings.

The Plateau de Calern feels like the roof of the world. On a clear day, the distant hills of Corsica may be seen from its southern edge. And if one can screen out the drone and rumble of jet aeroplanes flying north from Nice–Côte d'Azur airport, the plateau is ordinarily a quiet place, the sussuration of the insects broken only occasionally by the tinkle of sheep-bells, the pistol-crack of broken wood as deer break cover, the distant voices of a pair of walkers following a footpath, their way marked by bright flashes of paint on stone. Sometimes, one notices the evidence for present-day farming: a set of sheep-pens; a Landrover parked outside a distant *bergerie*; a broad tract of rocks polished by 800 hooves when a flock rushes over them. Elsewhere, one may encounter beehives, row upon row of them. Probably the plateau is at its most silent in winter, when it is blanketed by snow and visited by few. But the weather can be harsh in summer too, with torrential rain and horrendous storms of thunder and lightning which may prove fatal to a human caught in the wrong place at the wrong time. Evidence of the destructive power and soil-moving capacity of torrential flows of water is everywhere. Yet, in normal conditions permanent water is hard to find; the place where the community did its washing, on the north side of the village just below the castle, feels like a veritable oasis (Figure 13).

The silence of the Plateau de Calern is all the more dramatic for the ubiquitous evidence of sustained human work and activity. There are numerous corbelled shelters *(bories),* intact or in various stages

FIGURE 14. A ruined *borie* with Anthony Lewison standing next to it
PHOTOGRAPH: DAVID AUSTIN

of collapse (Figure 14); there are walled enclosures and roofless buildings; there are terraces – some neat, high and uniform, grouped together in well-defined 'fields', others much more primitive and variable in character, or forming sets of small 'steps', climbing the courses of dry stream-beds which only carry water sporadically. The floors of the dolines are often edged by ruinous walls which partially enclose their precious, deep-soiled floors. One comes across abandoned *aires,* carefully paved threshing-floors. Cairns (*claps*) and piles of cleared rock dominate some parts of this landscape. These vary from small, low, circular heaps of stone, long since reduced to angular chippings by the action of rain, snow and frost, to long parallel lines of piled stones which run along the upper edges of rock strata lying at varying angles to the horizontal. Their mimicry of the geology is at first sight disconcerting for the archaeologist, but

FIGURE 15. A marker in the Calern landscape
PHOTOGRAPH: DAVID AUSTIN

we have shown that they usually represent not frost damage but rather deliberate clearance. The really large stone piles of the type common near the village of Cipières do not usually occur on the main plateau, though there are a few of them there. In these 'fields', the cairns seem to occupy as much land as the areas between them. There are also zones of thin soil and bare rock, with small clusters and piles of stone indicating casual quarrying. As one's eyes become attuned to the landscape, one spots more and more way-markers – or boundary-markers, perhaps – an upright stone, perhaps two or three together, prized from bedrock and set on end, sometimes white-washed (Figure 15). Some are set in lines across the land; and sometimes the hill-tops are crowned by more prominent chunky rectangular cairns. For the landscape archaeologist, these surface features are utterly absorbing, offering the enticing prospect of developing a narrative based upon demonstrable chronological depth.

1.3. The geography of the landscape

David Austin

Cipières lies just to the south of the Cime du Cheiron (1778 m) at the eastern end of the Castellan Massif of the French Pré-Alpes, an area also called the Pré-Alps de Grasse. The region is dominated by east–west ridges, resulting from the fold axes still forming in the Alpine mountain-building period, and by deeply-intersected river valleys, cutting down through the succession of Jurassic, Triassic and Cretaceous limestones which have locally ridden over younger series (Figure 16). The bulk of the surface rocks are, therefore, Middle Jurassic Oxfordian,

left: FIGURE 16. River Loup gorge
PHOTOGRAPH: DAVID AUSTIN

right: FIGURE 17. Solution-weathered outcrops
PHOTOGRAPH: DAVID AUSTIN

consisting predominantly of hard friable limestones and softer, soapier dolomites, interleaved in tilted beds averaging about 40 cm in depth. These surfaces have been subjected, during the uplift period, to sub-aerial weathering processes, leaving characteristic solution-weathered outcrops of the base rocks (Figure 17). Intense downpours of heavy rain have constantly washed down the fines from these processes, leaving, in different locations, bare surfaces, incised pavements (*lapiés*), scree and deep deposits of silt, depending on specific slope characteristics and the nature of exposure. Nowhere are the deep silts more apparent than in the karst depressions of varying shape and size which litter the landscape. These are of two main types: dolines (Figure 18) which are funnel-shaped and, today, usually flat-floored; and uvulas (Figure 19) which have formed where dolines have merged by dissolution or collapse of the intervening structures. All this leaves a mountain

FIGURE 18. An example of a doline at the southern edge of the Plateau de Calern
PHOTOGRAPH: DAVID AUSTIN

FIGURE 19. An example of an uvula on the Plateau de Calern with a circular enclosure incorporating a ruined *borie*, and an *aire* just above it and to the right
PHOTOGRAPH: DAVID AUSTIN

FIGURE 20.
A. Storm over the Cime de Cheiron carried on the Mistral
PHOTOGRAPH: ANTHONY LEWISON

B. Boiling up for a Mediterranean storm over the excavated enclosure in Baoume de Brun
PHOTOGRAPH: DAVID AUSTIN

C. Fair weather for field work with Andrew Fleming (left) and Greg Stevenson checking survey material
PHOTOGRAPH: DAVID AUSTIN

mass alternating between steep slopes and relatively flat but broken terrains. On the plateau, geological factors control the nuances of local landforms. Layers of rock may form horizontal beds running around the sides of hills and dolines. But they may also be stacked at 45° to the horizontal, forming linear ribs at the ground surface, and separated by long clear strips where soil has accumulated; or they may sometimes be fully on edge, at 90° to the horizontal. There are also small zones of limestone pavement.

The regional climate, and its immediate expression, the weather, is a strong influence here (Figure 20). The Cipières skies are affected by two major climatic systems: the continental with its dry air to the north and west, bringing the Mistral which can blow for days out of the Rhône valley; and the Mediterranean with its moist winds to the south, including the Scirocco which can carry dust particles from the Sahara. Modern figures for rainfall and temperature are marked by sharp and irregular fluctuations caused by sudden extremes and very localised events. Storm deluges of 50 mm or more can occur in one place and not another, particularly during the summer months when temperatures can also be subject to strong Mediterranean influences and equatorial superheating. The summer temperature means, recorded at the altitude of the village, show maxima rising in July and August to the higher 20°s centigrade, while in the winter they are about 10° when snow is an erratic occurrence and does not linger for longer than a week. At the level of the plateau, by contrast, the winters are much harder with snow sometimes remaining into May; and the minimum temperatures can be well below zero for long periods.[3] Needless to say spring usually comes to the high ground as late as May; around the village, early flowers will be showing in April. On the plateau, winter begins in October, although it can still be reasonably mild in the village for several more weeks. This of course is the situation today. Over the thousand and more years covered by our narrative there have been significant changes in climate.

The only constantly flowing surface water here is the River Loup, deep at the bottom of its gorge (Figures 3 and 21). Otherwise, apart from the periods of storm when sudden streams rip down the flanks of the mountains in ravines and gullies and pools stand momentarily in the dolines, water usually disappears below ground into the caves and underground channels of the karst Jurassic limestone. It resurges on beds of impervious clay over the lower Cretaceous rocks which outcrop in the sides of the Gorge du Loup, at an altitude about 100 m below the village. Here the precious resource of water was collected, and managed by the officers of the community for centuries in the village *lavoir* (Figure 13). Above this line – in the village and elsewhere in the commune – water was either stored in cisterns gathering rain from the roofs of buildings, or, much more rarely, recovered by wells tapping the underground and vadose channels in the bedrock (see Figure 222).

FIGURE 21. River Loup
PHOTOGRAPH: DAVID AUSTIN

Extremes of weather and the movement of water are constant and destructive forces here. Freeze–thaw processes threaten the permanence of stone walls and corbelled roofs, especially on the plateau. The climate constantly promotes erosion, which produces and moves the soils of commune and region. These soils are primarily fine-grained silts and clays derived from the basal limestone and dolomites. They tend to be full of fractured and dissolving stone fragments of varying sizes (Figure 22), except at the bottoms of slopes, especially in dolines and uvulas, where rapid solifluction in the violent rainstorms has led to the accumulation of the fine fraction only. As soon as browsing livestock, introduced by humans, reached critical stocking densities, or when farmers started to clear the natural woodlands, the rate of translocation of soils must have increased dramatically, causing a great release of soil, much of

FIGURE 22. Soils are primarily fine-grained silts and clays derived from the basal limestone and dolomites, full of fractured and dissolving stone fragments of varying sizes
PHOTOGRAPH: DAVID AUSTIN

which would have ended up in the dolines and rivers. From then on, humans had to conserve soil on cultivable slopes as best they could, and retain plants for the grazing of animals. For more recent times there is clear evidence of such agricultural regimes, involving the retention and husbanding of soils. Perhaps, however, the most constant human intervention has been the clearance of stone and the creation of extensive areas of stone piles. As a consequence the soils have become lighter, thinner and more susceptible to air and water transportation. Add to this the persistent leaching of organic material and fine fractions downwards through the karst geology and we have a picture of the interminable effort required to keep the land fertile and in good order. This was to some extent easier on the flatter and more sheltered areas of the zone near the village.

It seems impossible to reconstruct the character of the native woodland of the region. The names of the *quartiers*, which must go back at least to the later Middle Ages, refer to beech, Mediterranean oak, lime, and ash; field observations allow us to add elm, hazel, field maple, and wild apple to this list. Once the trees had been cleared, and a more severe erosion regime had set in, the production of crops and the maintenance of grazing and economically useful plants was dependent on the efforts of humans, using current agrarian technologies and applying traditional skills and knowledge. Our efforts to understand the traditional ecology at Cipières have to confront the fact that the present-day vegetation results largely from reversion and decay of agrarian management.[4] Today only certain flat fields and broad terraces in the area near the village, as well as odd patches of ground elsewhere, are maintained in a regular way under the plough. Few vegetable or grain crops are grown; grass for grazing and hay predominates. Some of these fields display a species-rich carpet of flowering plants in the spring (Figure 23). It is the ubiquitous *garrigue* which epitomises the decline of farming; woodland, now mostly pine, is regenerating, particularly on the slopes (Figure 24). On the slopes near the village, especially on the north and east sides down towards the river, the dominant impression is of the woodlands overwhelming the disused fields and terraces, as may best be seen looking northwards from the village towards the similarly abandoned fieldscapes of its neighbour Gréolières (Figure 25). Here and there a few patches of market garden or grass are still maintained, but they have the superficial appearance of clearings in the forest (Figure 8, above). Some lopped trees or pollards do survive: they are sporadic now in the area of the village, but more abundant on Le Plan; they recall the traditions of meticulous husbandry which once exploited and conserved all available resources (Figure 26). Once saffron was grown in the village, and there are traces of former lavender cultivation in one or two of the plateau dolines. Up to a couple of hundred years ago, vines were tended close to the village, although absolutely at the limit of their range; no one makes the attempt today. The *garrigue* is not entirely unproductive, however; its tightly-packed hardy grass clumps, aromatic herbs, orchids, bulbs and wide variety of rock plants provide enough 'bite' for the two main village flocks to flourish, especially when their diet is supplemented from the cultivated pastures still to be seen around the few surviving *bergeries* (Figure 27). The *garrigue* is also appreciated by bee-keepers, who sometimes bring several dozen hives onto the plateau in summer.

So Cipières and its immediately neighbouring villages occupy a distinctive zone: a high limestone shoulder which lies at a higher altitude than the warm, low-lying villages of the Loup valley and the Vence area to the south, and below the more 'alpine' zone of Cheiron, Gréolières les Neiges and le Plan de Peyron to the north. Within this liminal region, communities have sought out zones of nutrient-receiving, deeper soils; on steep slopes they constructed terraces. Places like Coursegoules and Canaux, to the east and west of Cipières, profited mostly from extensive basins of good, relatively deep-soiled land, although at the former there were also terraces behind the village. While just to the south, the

FIGURE 23. Fields near the village display a species-rich carpet of flowering plants in the spring
PHOTOGRAPH: ANDREW FLEMING

24

25

26

27

FIGURE 24. Garrigue and pine growth
PHOTOGRAPH: DAVID AUSTIN

FIGURE 25. Woodland down the valley sides below Gréolières
PHOTOGRAPH: DAVID AUSTIN

FIGURE 26. A pollarded tree on the Plateau de Calern
PHOTOGRAPH: ANDREW FLEMING

FIGURE 27. Sheep grazing in a doline
PHOTOGRAPH: ANDREW FLEMING

settlement of Caussols is dispersed around an open, wet and fertile plain below the scarp slope of Calern, but with extensive stonier lands as well. By contrast, the territory of Gréolières, just north of Cipières, consists largely of a hillside of south-facing terraces (Figure 25) which once supported two villages, one, Hautes Gréolières, abandoned in the later middle ages. Not far from Gourdon one may observe the opportunistic exploitation of quite extensive areas of relatively good land in the zone around and to the west of the 12th century chapel of St Vincent. This activity was obviously more extensive in the past. What apparently distinguishes Cipières from other communes in the region is the fact that a greater proportion of its territory is located on high upland, notably the Plateau de Calern. Although the exploitation of dolines, uvulas and other limestone features has certainly been practised in neighbouring communes, Cipières is exceptional in that a lot of its valuable land was distributed in discrete parcels of varying size on a high plateau where agrarian success depended on close adaptations to a more diverse suite of limestone terrain forms than would be encountered in most other areas in the locality. Although much of this land is of low value, there are numerous deep-soiled nutrient-receiving dolines and

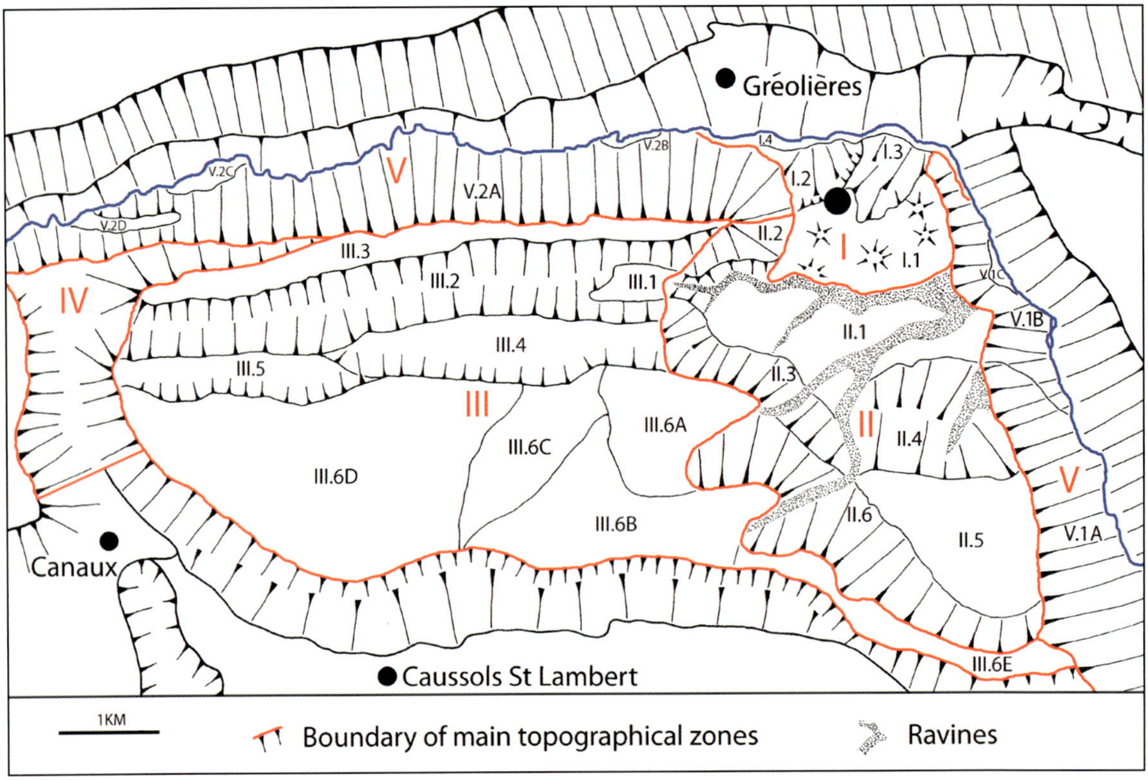

FIGURE 28. Topographical zones

DRAWING: DAVID AUSTIN

uvulas on the plateau, while the suites of terraces on the slopes remind us of what might be achieved, given the appropriate input of labour.

Our description of the commune's physical geography (Figure 3) breaks the space down into a number of topographic zones, which, although not discrete, can be regarded as distinct by anyone moving around and using the landscape, even today (Figure 28). Humans, however, experienced these zones, not in the form of maps drawn from above, as we must represent them here, but on the ground, responding to slope, elevation, land use, pathways and other cultural and environmental factors. The analytical viewpoint is constructed, therefore, from the imagined perspective of the medieval Cipièrois themselves – that is, from the village outwards, much as the dendritic pattern of tracks and paths radiate out on the first cadastral map (Figure 29). We should acknowledge that there would have been other viewpoints – notably those of outsiders. For the traveller from Grasse and the south, the sight of the massive escarpment of the Plateau de Calern would have provided an unforgettable first glimpse of the Cipières landscape. The occupants of La Pinée, at the far west end of the commune, would have had a different perspective. From the villagers' perspective, which we prefer to emphasise here, it would have been the upper windows of their houses, perched on a narrow outcrop of rock, which offered the favoured view, overlooking their best land to the east and south (Figure 30).

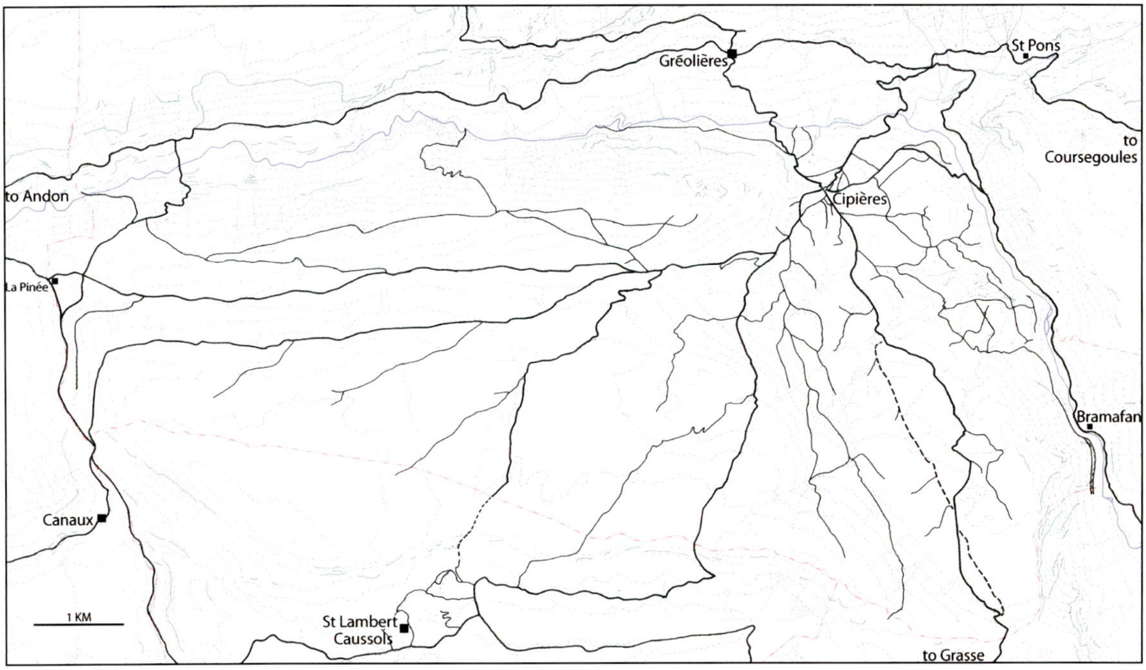

FIGURE 29. Routes and roads from the 1842 cadastral survey
DRAWING: DAVID AUSTIN

FIGURE 30. The village perspective
PHOTOGRAPH: DAVID AUSTIN

Moving out from the village, we may begin (Figure 28) with the basic division which we know was also meaningful to the first makers of cadastres in the 16th century: that between the eastern 'lower' lands (major zones I and II) and the western 'plateau' lands (III), with the adjunct of La Pinée (V) in the far west. Excluded from these are the almost inaccessible steep slopes and crags of the Loup gorge (IV) to north and east, which are now densely wooded and carry few signs of human intervention other than small areas on slightly benching land. Each of these major areas has been divided into sub-zones which are numbered in a sequence which broadly reflects their closeness to the village.

In the descriptions which follow, most of the names chosen for the zones and sub-zones are those of *quartiers* marked on the 1842 cadastral map (Figure 31). Some of these are effectively co-terminous with the topographic zones. Figure 28 ignores the legal bounds of the commune, which diverge from the essential topography in places, most notably on the Plateau de Calern a significant proportion of whose southern edge now lies in the adjacent commune of Caussols. This is a consequence of the break-up of the feudal lordship which once controlled both communities, together with Gréolières. We have tracked the *quartier* names within the documents and have used etymology to interpret their meaning in English (Appendix 1). Most of the names relate to physiographic features, vegetation and personal names. The documents demonstrate that some of these names were already in existence by the 14th century. They also suggest that most of the names were relatively stable over time, but there is also evidence that the *quartier* boundaries were not necessarily fixed or stable (see Chapter 3 on Baoume de Brun *quartier*). It is also noticeable how small and closely packed the *quartiers* become near the village, a sure indicator of competition for good, accessible land.

The eastern shoulders and benches of the commune's terrain are the community's 'lowland' (Figure 28, I and II) and are separated from the plateau by a consistently steep slope, whose dominant name at the southern end is La Faye (II.6); although its appellations to the north (II.2 and II.3) are more varied and inchoate. This slope drops nearly 400 m in height over a distance of less

FIGURE 31. Names of *quartiers*

DRAWING: DAVID AUSTIN

FIGURE 32. The dividing 'wall' of La Faye
PHOTOGRAPH: ANTHONY LEWISON

than a kilometre and runs from the Gros Pounch in the north to the edge of the plateau's main scarp in the south-east corner (Figure 32). The slope was itself once heavily cultivated (except to the south), often with impressive and complex terrace systems, especially at the north end in the Vallon des Pesses, which provides the main access onto La Combe and the plateau from the village. Thus the slope of La Faye formed a major physical boundary between the western plateau and the eastern 'lower lands' which were its most productive and extensive agricultural resource, readily accessible from the village. These eastern lower lands can be divided into two main parts: those areas near the village, including the slope down to the river (I), and more distant lands to the south, which rise in a series of benches towards La Faye (II).

Close to the village, the landscapes (I) significantly contain the only consistently surface-flowing water in the commune, especially a spring and stream just to the north of the village, latterly contained within a *lavoir* (Figure 13) and a well to the south at Le Puit. In this major zone we have identified four discrete sub-zones draped over a shoulder of land and dropping down, from north to south, about 300 m in vertical height over a distance of just over a kilometre. Immediately to the south of the village, and a little below it, is the flattest of the zones containing the best agricultural land, as well as a few prominent hillocks (I.1). Since this landscape is so packed with sub-divisions of space (such as La Croix), it has no single identifying name; we came to call it simply the 'lands near the village' or 'the Bench' because of the broad flat alp on which it all sits (Figures 7, 8 and 33). Here the stone piles are enormous, revetted constructions and tell of many episodes of cultivation and clearance (Figure 34); here too was the best of the lord's demesne, and the bailiff's house (Le Puit; Figure 35).

North of the village there are three smaller sub-zones, structurally part of

33

34

35

36

37

38

FIGURE 33. Zone I.1: 'The lands near the village'
PHOTOGRAPH: DAVID AUSTIN

FIGURE 34. Zone I.1: Revetted stone pile
PHOTOGRAPH: ANTHONY LEWISON

FIGURE 35. Zone I.2: The bailiff's house at Le Puit
PHOTOGRAPH: DAVID AUSTIN

FIGURE 36. Zone I.2: The flat fields and terraces of Le Verger
PHOTOGRAPH: ANTHONY LEWISON

FIGURE 37. Zone I.3: Maurenc and Matheron
PHOTOGRAPH: DAVID AUSTIN

FIGURE 38. Zone I.2: The old route down to the river
PHOTOGRAPH: ANTHONY LEWISON

the Gorge du Loup, but gentler in gradient than elsewhere, and these are of the greatest significance in understanding how the landscapes of the commune functioned. The slopes to the north of the village, Le Verger (I.2) are the gentlest; in fact they descend in a series of benches, with areas of former flat fields and terraces (Figure 36) interlaced with old pathways (including the ancient road to Gréolières), leading down to the river (Figure 38), and past the *lavoir*, the primary source of water for the village. To the east is the more broken and more steeply sloping ground of Maurenc and Matheron (I.3) also heavily cultivated (Figure 37), and finally there is the narrow band of flatter, alluvial, flood terraces along the river floor (I.4) with its mill(s), *foulon*, meadows and bridge. This complex of functions was essential to the processes of village life, and this area, today largely overgrown with trees, probably contains some of the oldest landscape features in the commune.

To the south of these lands close to the village is a terrain (II), which rises as broad benches, by another 300 m in height, to the foot of La Faye. Again, with no single identifier, we came to call this 'the bench'. Moving southwards away from the village, the first sub-zone (II.1) consists of broken ground with small patches of relatively flat land, each with its own topographic names and separated by the slopes of two dry valley systems which run from the west down the slope of La Faye and eastwards across this piece of landscape to merge on the edge of the Gorge du Loup. These two systems, both containing well-built and high terrace complexes, consist of the Vallons de Maupas and de Pesses in the north and the Vallons de la Crous, des Pourcelles and du Pas d'Estrugue in the south, and so we have come to call this area 'Les Vallons'. The western side of this landscape (II.2 in the north and II.3 in the south), the steep slope dividing zone II from the plateau lands to the west, was more lightly terraced, especially on its lower, more soil-rich ground. To the south of Les Vallons is a broad sub-zone with a variety of names at the centre of which is Les Près (II.4, Figure 39), consisting of terrain sloping relatively gently southwards, broken by deep dolines and intersected by the lesser dry valley of the Vallon des Graous (Figure 40). This area has a very complex series of agricultural landscapes still visible, but they are being rapidly colonised by regenerating woodland (mostly pine and box) and garrigue scrub. To the south again is a relatively flat bench with extensive remains of fields and terraces on the sides of deep dolines, known as Le Plan (II.5, Figure 41). Finally to the west of this is the largely barren slope of La Faye (II.6), heavily denuded by erosion.

The Plateau de Calern (III) may be regarded as the community's 'upland' and can be read as a series of linear spaces running from east to west, following the pattern of the main escarpments of the region. The principal approach to the plateau from the village is by the ancient track leading south-westwards, skirting the western edge of La Croix and climbing steeply up the Vallon des Pesses (Figure 42). At the top of this valley lies La

39

FIGURE 39. Zone II.4: Les Prés
PHOTOGRAPH: ANDREW FLEMING

40

FIGURE 40. Zone II.4 Les Près
PHOTOGRAPH: ANTHONY LEWISON

41

FIGURE 41. Zone II.5 Le Plan
PHOTOGRAPH: ANTHONY LEWISON

42

43

44

45

Combe, a long, narrow, deep depression which is geomorphologically part of the same karst structure as the Vallon des Pesses itself. At the eastern end of the Vallon, at an altitude of 1070 m, is a flat area (III.1) known as Valarouvo (perhaps the older name for La Combe). It contains fields, enclosures and *bergeries* and a major junction of tracks and paths, both ancient and modern (Figure 43). From here the ground drops away a little onto the floor of La Combe itself (III.2). This long, narrow valley, which runs almost the full length of the plateau, has a lush, green floor demarcated by low cross-walls serving often as low terraces following the undulations of the ground surface. This is a ribbon of good land, a deep deposit of silt and soil nowadays still cherished for the quality of its grazing. The northern slopes, L'Adrech de la Combe, display ruined terraces, particularly towards the bottom and down the usually dry drainage gullies which scar the mountainside. The slopes up the southern side of La Combe (L'Hubac de la Combe) are as steep as L'Adrech, but not as high, and are much more thickly covered with terrace systems of various ages and degrees of construction (Figure 44). At the top of L'Adrech de la Combe is the long, isolated ridge of the Gros Pounch (III.3), whose northern edge plunges down to the gorge of the River Loup, 1000 m below. Rising to an altitude of nearly 1270 m, the Gros Pounch provided a narrow bench of land, gently sloping southwards, containing the remains of many former fields and terraces. On the south side of La Combe, L'Hubac rises onto a relatively level bench,

FIGURE 42. Zone III.1: Vallon des Pesses
PHOTOGRAPH: ANTHONY LEWISON

FIGURE 43. Zone III.1 Valarouvo
PHOTOGRAPH: DAVID AUSTIN

FIGURE 44. Zone III.2: La Combe from Valarouvo with L' Adrech and L'Hubac in view
PHOTOGRAPH: DAVID AUSTIN

FIGURE 45. Zones III.3 and 4: Vaumeillane and Le Teil with Le Gros Pounch beyond
PHOTOGRAPH: DAVID AUSTIN

divisible into two distinct blocks, the eastern known as Vaumeillane and Le Teil (III.4; Figure 45) and the western as L'Agrémourié (III.5; Figure 46). This bench is dominated by several large dolines and uvulas, which have been formed into extensive well-grassed fields. Rising from here (and part of zones III.4 and 5) is the final slope up to the top of the Plateau de Calern: known as Le Rouré, it is now largely covered in scree with few traces of cultivation, and is best considered as part of the bench in whose *quartiers* it was included (Figure 47).

The high plateau itself (III.6) is broken terrain, with many dolines and uvulas which have been intensively farmed at various times. The intervening areas have been extensively, but more intermittently, altered under various agricultural regimes to be described in detail later. It is possible to divide the plateau into five further sub-zones. The nearest to the village, entered by a track climbing via the Vallon du Pas d'Éstrugue, is Le Calernet (III.6A), which is dominated by long strip-like fields following the tipped limestone joints of the underlying geomorphological structures (Figure 48). Le Calernet forms the lower part of the long dip slope of the plateau, the higher part of which is Les Baudillons to the south (III.6B) dominated by an almost regular pattern of dolines of many sizes (Figure 49). To the west of both Le Calernet and Les Baudillons is a significant fault line visible on the surface as a series of linked dolines and uvulas trending south-west to north-east, where the dominant *quartier* name is Les Poumeirès (III.6C, Figure 50). To the west of the fault, the plateau has been less intensively cultivated in the past. Apart from La Pinée, this is the land which feels furthest

FIGURE 46. Zone III.5: L'Agrémourié
PHOTOGRAPH: ANDREW FLEMING

FIGURE 47. Zones III.4 and 5: Le Rouré
PHOTOGRAPH: DAVID AUSTIN

FIGURE 48. Zone III.6A: Le Calernet
PHOTOGRAPH: DAVID AUSTIN

FIGURE 49. Zone III.6B: Les Baudillons
PHOTOGRAPH: DAVID AUSTIN

46

47

48

49

left: FIGURE 50. Zone III.6C: Les Poumeirès
PHOTOGRAPH: DAVID AUSTIN

right: FIGURE 51. Zone III.6D: Calern
PHOTOGRAPH: DAVID AUSTIN

from the village in terms of both height and length of journey: this is La Plaine de Calern (III.6D) which rises gently to a height of 1450 m on its southern, scarp edge and is also dominated by dolines (Figure 51). At the eastern end of the plateau, there is a thin ribbon of high ground above La Faye and Le Plan – the Colle de Rougiés (III.6E), surmounted by a prehistoric enclosure. The southern and western edge of the plateau is a high impressive scarp with many cliffs and crags overlooking its lower slopes, which have a series of ancient settlements on them, all within the commune of Caussols (Figure 52).

To the far west of these main topographic zones lies a piece of landscape which looks as if it has been grafted, as an afterthought, onto the commune of Cipières. La Pinée (IV) has, perhaps, never contained more than the single farm which is visible today. It is set in the centre of a narrow perched glacial valley hemmed in by the cliffs of the Plateau de Calern and the equally impressive structures of the Sommet de Canaux to the west. Access from the village of Cipières to this piece of good, flat countryside today is by way of either Caussols or Gréolières, and it was probably always farmed and used as a semi-detached, discrete unit. So also were the small, isolated pieces of cleared ground lying on

FIGURE 52. Caussols and the scarp edge
PHOTOGRAPH: DAVID AUSTIN

small benches (V.1C, 2B, 2C and D) just above the River Loup, surrounded by the crags and the steep slopes of its gorge on the eastern (V.1A and B) and northern (V.2A) edges of the commune.

These are the topographic names and zones which lie within the administrative boundaries of the commune today. However, documents in the *Mairie* suggest that Cipières was once larger. Figure 53 is abstracted from a larger compilation which identifies all the places named in the documents (Appendix 1). It shows a number of places which we are not as yet able to find within Cipières; some can be clearly identified with places on the north and west banks of the River Loup which are now in the Communes of Gréolières and Courmes (Figure 54). The loss of these locations was not sudden, but seems to have been the result of gradual erosion over several centuries. It is difficult to escape the impression that the attribution of this land may have been somewhat ambiguous, perhaps dating back to land tenure arrangements which functioned when Gréolières and Cipières were all part of the same lordship in the Middle Ages.

Crossing these landscapes, and fanning out from the village, there was once a rich dendritic network of roads and tracks, some of which are now way-marked footpaths (Figure 29). Many of these *chemins* and *carraires* were dual-purpose;

FIGURE 53. Names now not identifiable within the bounds of Cipières

Suggested Location	*Lost after 1731*	*Lost after 1630*	*Lost after 1539*
Pont Serane, Gréolières			Lybaque desserane
Bramafan, Courmes			Bramafan
			Gravierros
			Le Noyer
		Broquet	
Les Cabanes, Courmes		Cabanos	
Cavillore, Courmes?		Cavillore	
		Caupre, Cauquans, Cauquadis	
La Coulete, Les Fouques, (adjacent) Gréolières		Various Collets, inc. Collet de lau Fouquet	
		Pons de Guiol	
		Tranquat	
Le Foulon, Gréolières?	Lon, Laune	Valalone	
		Vallon Daubout	
		Veilho	
		La Gast	
		Baume de Merle, Myroland	
		Roche de Teyt	
At or near Les Vignes, Gréolières?	Vignes, Vignasse	Vignondrado	Paume de Vignan
	Baud de la Galle		
	Blaus		
	Boullegue		
	Gallis		
	Gardettes		
	Gratte Loups		
Plateau le Sambue, Courmes	Sambouretta		
	St Anthoine		
	Tousque		
	Pré Long		

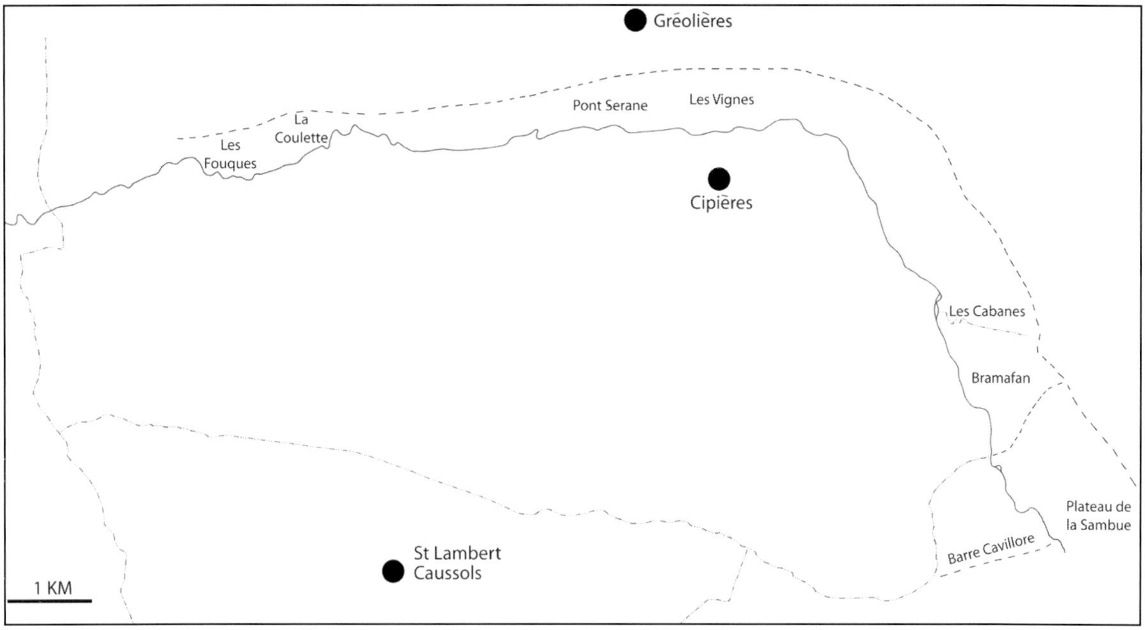

FIGURE 54. Parts of the former territory of Cipierès now in other communes
DRAWING: DAVID AUSTIN

they led to other villages or hamlets, such as Caussols or Canaux, and also gave access to all exploitable areas of the commune. They were supplemented by a few roads which led only to fields and pastures, and eventually petered out – such as the *Chemin des Baumettes* or the *Chemin de la Clapoua.* A few of the commune's roads have been altered out of all recognition – widened by bulldozers and surfaced with chippings; they are used by tractors, and the jeeps of hunters and the teams which maintain the strings of mighty electricity pylons which stride across the commune. Whatever their present state, many of the routeways display a recognisable range of common characteristics, which may vary along any particular route. These roads are often defined by walls – sometimes well-preserved but often ruinous – which are usually integral with the fields or enclosures through which they pass, although occasionally, on the plateau, roads pass through zones of unenclosed open pasture. When a road climbs a steep slope, which it does by selecting a variable mix of long inclines, zig-zag courses and hairpin bends, it becomes clear that it has been deliberately engineered to run along a narrow, revetted terrace produced by a 'cut and fill' technique. A few of these roads contain patches of metalling, and transverse sill-stones which helped to drain the surfaces and minimise the damage caused by frost-heaving and erosion (see Figure 221). Roads of this type can be found outside the commune of Cipières – for example on the road which leads south from Caussols, up to the Col du Clapier. One has a strong impression that many of these roads were installed at much the same chronological horizon, and that they have been mostly deteriorating ever since, along with the agricultural landscape through which they pass.

From the perspective of the Cipièrois, the most vital roads were probably those leading to Grasse – south over Le Plan and the Col de la Faye, and then via Gourdon, or south-west over the plateau and via Caussols (not always the recommended route in winter). Grasse, famous producer of perfume, was a medieval creation, but became quickly the centre of a *viguerie*, a feudal territory ruled by a vicomte, and the region's administrative and market centre towards which Cipières has always been drawn. As such, Grasse had a pivotal part to play at the heart of an upland region through which the difficult routes between modern France and Italy ran. In physical and cultural terms the region has thus always been in a potentially disputed boundary zone, whose identity was never assured until the consolidations of national frontiers in the last 200 years.

1.4. The archive

David Siddle

To the untrained eye much of the Cipières landscape presents itself as a desolate wasteland of rough pasture, grykes and rocky outcrops crossed by a few meandering sheep tracks. The previous sections tell us how the insights of the landscape archaeologist can breathe life into this wilderness, showing us how such a landscape, now empty of people, may be rich with the signs of past activity. Here across the plateau as well as benches and slopes below there are possible patterns which seem to reveal the rich life of a community long since lost. What stands revealed is a patchwork of fields and trackways, stone shelters and sheep folds and a scatter of clearance piles, border stones, and the broken terraces which tessellate the barren hillsides. Obviously such reconstructions are fraught with the difficulties of attribution. How and when where such landscapes created? Archaeological excavation can reveal evidence to support such mind's eye theories of landscape archaeology but in areas where opportunities for excavation are scarce and the product less than revealing, these past landscapes must always remain opaque, full of rheumy uncertainties.

This, then, is the silent landscape; yet it almost groans with the labours of the men and women who created it, stone upon stone.

It seems a long way, physically and conceptually, from the Plateau de Calern to the shaded streets of Cipières, where peasants and labourers once stood patiently in line, awaiting the moment when their names and legal status would be inscribed on parchment or paper in the same sort of way as Pieter Brueghel the Younger depicted in his famous painting 'Rent Day' (Figure 55). Little did they know how much of their business would survive for the curious historian several centuries later. In fact, the evidence of a documentary archive can prove invaluable. A supporting raft of documentary evidence might include ancient maps with old field boundaries, the records of land use value and transfers, family records. All these can be related to the evidence from the field.

Fortified by this opportunity a more hopeful scenario can now begin to emerge. It is one in which field scientists, archaeologists and historians can consult, using archival evidence to test their theories. It would be nice if things

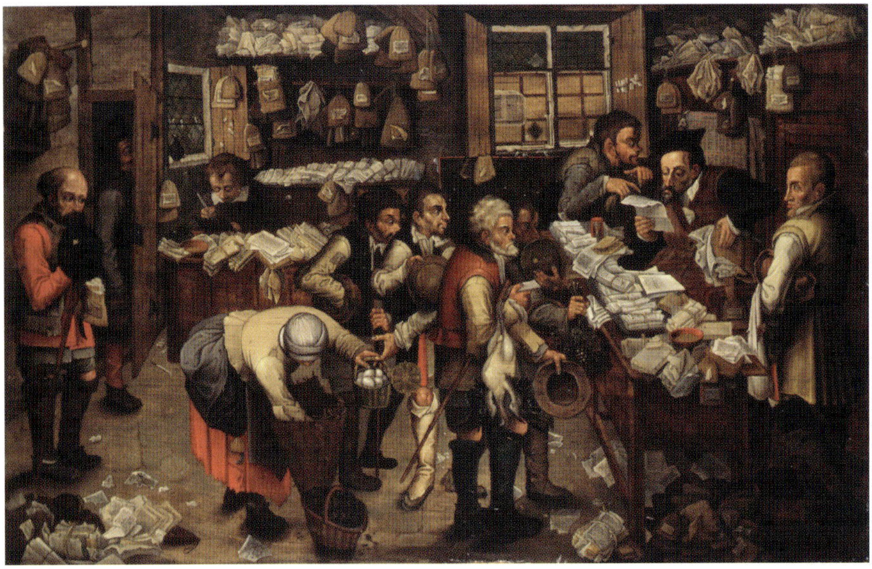

FIGURE 55. Pieter Brueghel the Younger: *Rent Day*
PRINTED WITH KIND PERMISSION OF NORWICH CASTLE MUSEUM

were so televisually simple. This more ideal agenda can just as easily break down because of the fragmentary nature of archival evidence. Indeed the historian approaches a local documentary archive for the first time with some of the same sense of trepidation and excitement that our field working colleagues confront a landscape which is new to them. Our historian is indeed fortunate if any of the potentially relevant material exists and even more fortunate if it has been not only been sorted, classified and properly boxed by trained archivists but also deposited in a safe place, generally in the fireproof buildings of administrative offices (Departmental Archives) designed as repositories. The miscellaneous piles of documents scrambled in age and condition which more normally greets the rural historian in France, has so often been thrown into the back of cupboards or onto the floors of dusty insect and rat infested lofts, or into damp basements. Clerks and officers of modern administrations just like those of the past, have concerns for the present, with only a hint of a sense that there may be some sort of virtue in not consigning material which is becoming ever more remote in time, to the fire and the tip. So often, even this scrambled evidence does not survive more than a generation or two. What is more, the happen-chance of village fires, floods, wars and the duplicity of those with reasons to see records removed or destroyed reduces the numbers of useful sources still further. So, more often than not, those facing an apparently fascinating landscape, rich in the potential for recreating a historical ecology, are left frustrated by the tattered fragments of documentary evidence, often heaped like shards of broken pottery in an excavation which has been inadvertently turned over by a mechanical digger.

For us it has been a different experience. The documentary evidence of the Cipières village archive began life as one such dusty pile which survived by chance. But it not only extended over six centuries but was collated, catalogued, boxed and stored in a dry room within the mayor's office by a trained historian and a lawyer familiar with the forms and language of legal transactional records (David Garrioch and Anthony Lewison) and assiduously preserved by mayor Ruas. French archivists will bemoan (and they have!) the fact that the classification does not follow the national framework. So, our referencing system will appear unusual to those familiar with catalogued French archives. But at least it is complete and in good order. The treasure trove revealed by this Herculean task which extended over a number of years in the eighties, allowed the group of scholars eventually engaged in this project to think of a full reconstruction of the history of community. Suites of information cover the minutes and accounts of the village council in unbroken sequence from 1557 to the present day (Figure 56). They are complemented by a rich set of time-slice information: inventories of people, land and animals for purposes of taxation which extend from the 13th to the mid-19th century. Perhaps the most significant of these are the eight land and property taxation registers (cadastres) for the years 1531, 1610, 1630, 1640, 1727, 1750, 1791 and 1842 which allow us not only to point to critical moments in the developing history of the community and its use of its lands and built

FIGURE 56. Document types and the date ranges they cover

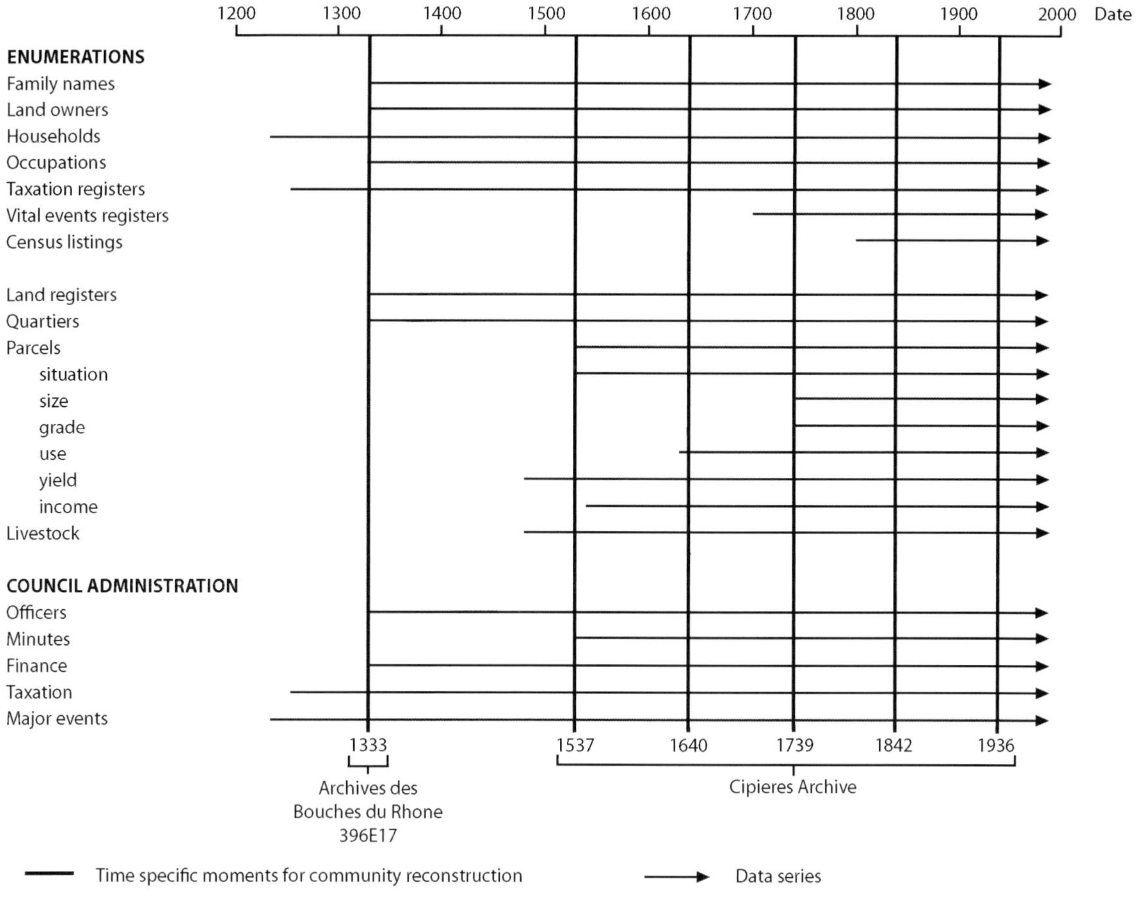

environments, but trace the transmission and transmutation of property up to the point of the rapid decline of the village as an active community after the 1842 cadastration, when the long transaction between those who lived off the land 'from time immemorial' and those who wished to exploit it had come to an effective end. Unfortunately, unlike the great cadastrations in Savoy and Piedmont in the 1730s, no maps survive (or were drawn) to support the catalogue of use and value which previous cadastres provide. Ironically this mid-19th century record is the time of our first cadastral map of land taxation. It has to be said that this was an important constraint.

In addition to such sources we have been able to use the evidence of the registrations of births, marriages and deaths interactively to develop insights into the family and demographic history of the community and to measure ways in which such evidence is played out in the history of the landscape, at least for the eighteenth century. There are obviously gaps and lacunae, the inadequacy of death registration for example, which prevents a full family reconstitution, and the limitations of the surviving notarial and court records which breathe more life into a transactional existence, of conflict and its resolution and of decision making and the evidence of interaction between families.

Rich sequences of evidence congregate around dates and periods which mark Braudelian *événements* within the *longue durée* which underlie the temporal scale of our evidence. These include the flurry of recording activities surrounding the traumas of exposure to the Austrian wars of the 1740s and the Revolutionary period which marked the end of that century and started the next one.[5]

It has also been possible to tie our sources to those which are to be found in the regional archives in Grasse and Nice, Mouans-Sartoux and Marseille. This is particularly valuable for the earlier periods when local sources do not survive *in situ* and to help us to understand the wider regional context. Important transfers of notarial documents (wills, contracts, agreements) help us to complement 18th century sources towards the possibilities of thick description.

All these sequences of source made it truly possible to enter into a dialogue with landscape archaeologists on many if not all the issues raised in this book. Our attempts to present the excitement and interest of our frequent passage between landscape and document, as well as the agonising hard thinking, conflict resolution, cheerful compromise our work together has involved were eased by the products from the vineyards of Provence. What went into this process of bringing the languages of several academic discourses together over a period of more than 20 years of work was punctuated by the accidents of busy lives, other scholarly concerns and the saddening death or departure of members of our team. These may or may not be evident in the text. But we have tried to form a narrative which is suffused by the evidence of this interaction and the ways in which it informed our thinking. We have done this while explicitly allowing each other the freedom to develop our own modes of working and our own languages within the overall discourse. Some may think of this as a post-modern enterprise and certainly this mode of thinking has been liberating.

CHAPTER TWO

An Outline Early Chronology and an Account of the Village's Morphology

David Austin and Andrew Fleming

The community of Cipières is located high in the Pré-Alpes de Grasse in a landscape only sparsely occupied until the Middle Ages and probably mostly associated with transhumance and through routes. Some of its neighbouring communities probably had more signs of settlement at least in later prehistory and the Gallo-Roman period. The major settlement and agrarian event was the influx of settlers and lords in the early Middle Ages and the eventual creation of the village in a process known as 'incastellamento' *in Mediterranean regions. Although little archaeological work was done in the village itself during this project, we did closely examine its morphology and produced a sequence of development until the first cadstral mapping of 1842.*

2.1. An outline early chronology

Prehistory and Protohistory

Andrew Fleming

The work of the Cipières Project has focussed on the later medieval and post-medieval periods, and little more than a sketch of the earlier history of the commune is offered here. Conventionally[1] the protohistoric period starts with the Copper Age/Bronze Age *c.* 2100 BC, followed by the Bronze Age (*c.* 1800–700), the Hallstatt Iron Age (*c.* 700–450 BC) and the La Tène Iron Age (*c.* 450–30 BC). Antiquity comprises the Gallo-Roman period (1st centuries BC and AD), the Roman (1st–5th centuries of the Christian era) the Late Roman (5th–6th centuries) with the Middle Ages lasting from the 6th century to 1492. Thereafter it is the Ancien Régime to 1790 and the Modernity of the Republics to the present day.

The Neolithic and much of the Bronze Age in our region are represented only by a few finds of artefacts in caves and rock shelters, sometimes associated with burials; occasional burial mounds or cairns; and sporadic surface finds.[2]

For the Iron Age numerous high-altitude hillforts and defended enclosures (the term which perhaps best translates *enceintes*) have been found in our region.[3] Although one or two of his identifications may be questionable – notably his site on le Gros Pounch – Brétaudeau lists 4 sites for Cipières, 7 for Courmes, 8 for Caussols, 10 for Gréolieres, 14 for Gourdon and 21 for Coursegoules; Brétaudeau's maps show an evenly-spaced scatter of such sites on the plateaux of Caussols and La Malle.[4] Although material from the Bronze Age/Iron Age transition (*c.* 700 BC) has sometimes been found on these sites, Early Iron Age finds are conspicuous by their absence, and there is a tentative consensus that many *enceintes* were constructed and first occupied in the Middle or La Tène Iron Age, deserted around the start of the Christian era after the Roman conquest of *c.* 14 BC but quite frequently re-occupied in the Roman period and later. In our research area, there are three *enceintes* which make use of the near-vertical southern scarp edge of the plâteau de Calern for defence and also overlook the plain of Caussols – the Castellaras de la Colle de Rougiès, la cote 1334 de la Colle de Rougiès, and Le Gazoduc.[5]

At two of the other defended sites, La Troubade and La Bergerie du Montet (Gourdon), there are complex and extensive settlement sites nearby which are believed to be contemporary with them. La Troubade (Figure 57), with its remarkable and complex rectilinear plan of walled yards and rectangular buildings covering approximately one hectare and set on what is now limestone

FIGURE 57. La Troubade
PHOTOGRAPH: DAVID AUSTIN

pavement, has been claimed to have 'proto-urban characteristics' which might justify calling it an *oppidum*.[6] Arguing from sporadic finds, del Fabbro has suggested that the 'main village' at Troubade was first occupied in the 6th century BC with occupation continuing into the Roman period. La Bergerie du Montet, a comparable settlement, first reported by Brétaudeau,[7] has been partially excavated quite recently.[8] Here the rectilinear buildings, which included a granary containing the remains of carbonised cereals, were set on an array of terraces, with two internal walled 'streets'. The earliest occupation of the site apparently occurred around the middle of the 2nd century BC and lasted until the abandonment of the site around the beginning of the Christian era. The second major period of settlement at La Bergerie du Montet spanned the period from the late 1st century AD to the early 3rd century, though there were also traces of later occupation lasting until the 6th century and the site was also used by medieval lime-burners. One of the most interesting aspects of these two sites is that although the settlements are not, strictly speaking, 'defended', nevertheless at each 'a modest enclosing wall follows the most strategic course around the edge of the site'.[9] This foreshadows the layouts of much later towns and villages in the region, notably at Cipières itself where below the château (cf. the defensive enclosures at La Troubade and La Bergerie du Montet) the nucleated settlement with its internal streets was 'defended' by '*le barry*', presumably never more than a line of contiguous houses (see below).

Our region also contains a few examples of the mysterious and recently-recognised Rectangular Summit Structures (*SQS* or *Structures Quadrangulaires Sommitales*).[10] These structures, built of crude stone blocks in 'cyclopean' style and usually not more than 10 × 10 m in size, are sometimes free-standing and sometimes integrated with *enceinte* walls (where they should not be confused with 'bastions'). They are tentatively and roughly dated to the 5th–2nd centuries BC. Their purpose is not clear; they may be cult sites. According to Salicis[11] there are two SQS at Gourdon, two at Gréolières, and one at L'Adrech (Caussols).

Antiquity

Andrew Fleming

As we have seen, there were numerous *enceintes* to the north and east of Cipières, on the other side of the Loup, and during the Roman period a road ran along the Loup valley north-west from *Vintium* (Vence); Roman milestones survive at Coursegoules, Gréolières (where one of them has been 'Christianised') and Andon. Roman funerary monuments have been found at Andon, Le Bar sur Loup, St Vallier de Thiéy and St Cézaire sur Siagne, and at Chateauneuf de Grasse there was apparently an important *villa rustica,* inhabited from the 2nd century BC to the 5th or 6th centuries AD.

It seems then that there were vigorous communities in these uplands in the Middle and later Iron Age, constructing numerous hillforts and defended enclosures, and that the descendants of these people continued to occupy the area in Roman times. The shoulder of high ground to the west of the Loup which was later to be occupied by the nucleated village of Cipières does not, however, seem to have produced any notable finds from protohistoric or Roman times. Our team has not attempted to search the small wooded hills in the area around the village (zone I), and it is possible that discoveries remain to be made here. On the other hand, the name Cipières apparently derives from *cippus* – a standing stone (marking a boundary)[12] and it may be that in early times the area was somewhat neglected, being relatively high, remote land far from the perception of the inhabitants of the Grasse region, and from the point of view of regional communications, on the wrong side of the river Loup.

The Early Middle Ages

David Austin

The same could be argued for later historical generalisations about change within the *longue durée* of our community. This includes the other myths of the 'troubled Dark Ages' and the 'transformations of the year 1000' (or 'beginnings of feudalism' as it was once called). In terms of regional history this is the period stretching from the ragged failure of Romanitas in the 5th and 6th centuries, through the various acquisitions of power by Visigoths, Franks, Lombards and Saracens, to the late 10th and 11th centuries when the Dukes of Burgundy assumed the title of Count of Provence.[13] The full details of the historical sequence and a debate on the meanings of terms to be found in the documentary sources can be found in Rosamond Faith's discussion in Chapter 5 and David Siddle's in Chapter 6. What follows here focusses on the bare elements of the sequence and an introduction to terms and concepts which relate specifically to the discussion about the morphology of the village. These are also picked up later in the monograph.

At the beginning of this period some of the Roman towns of the region, such as Vence, Antibes and Frèjus, continued as seats of bishops and small trading communities, but in a much reduced form, while others were completely abandoned, such as Glandèlves, near Entrevaux. Out in the countryside, as Rosamond Faith indicates, it is possible to argue for a similar abandonment of the Roman villae, although the term remained in use in the early sources to identify territories 'containing a range of farms and settlements'. Some of these continued in existence, with the addition of semi-fortified refuges,[14] including one high on the side of the Loup Gorge in Cipières (Figure 58), and Christian chapels (later expressed in surviving Romanesque architecture) such as St Hermentaire at Draguignan and possibly St Lambert at nearby Caussols. At the same time, a few of the native Ligurian strongholds in the mountainous areas (see above) may also have been occupied throughout the period and perhaps new sites added. In cultural terms the history of towns, *villae* and strongholds

FIGURE 58. The refugium in Cipières
PHOTOGRAPH: ANTHONY LEWISON

should probably be seen as having a tendency towards cultural elision at a time when higher orders of authority had little influence on the ground in upland terrains like the Arrières Pays around Cipières.

This elision brought about a class of site known most frequently in the early documents as *castrum,* a term which probably included a number of different types of site, but which is frequently found in the records of later village communities in the area. We have to be a little careful in using the documents and applying the terminology, however, since the word '*castrum*' is also used for the village-castles of the 12th and 13th centuries. This has caused some debate among scholars: there is a body of opinion that identifies the *castrum* directly with the fortified village itself throughout southern France and Aquitaine and sees them as integral with their castles where they exist.[15] In Basse-Provence, however, Lagrue[16] in the same set of essays, argues for a more subtle progression of meaning over the three transformative periods of time identified by Poly:[17] from an early fortification of very fragmented localised authority (usually an isolated, often hill-top enceinte) in the 10th and early 11th centuries, replacing the former unfortified *villa*: through a transitional phase when parishes are being redefined and authority is still distinctly localised from 1040–1090 when the word is still usually attributed to the isolated enceintes as well as early castles; finally, to the *incastellamento* village of the 12th century.

Locally, Planel,[18] for example, believed there is in reality a detectable horizon of change in the use of the word at some stage in the early 11th century. Poteur[19] believed that the *castra* were the early castles and that the architectural changes into classic high medieval building types came later. Planel agrees with Poteur that villages post-date the *castra* or castles. Beyond these locations of authority in the regional, largely dispersed landscape, there must also have been many individual undefended farms or small hamlet clusters, but they are almost impossible to detect archaeologically. This issue of the *castrum*, its relationship to the developing castle and the settled landscape is discussed further by Rosamond Faith in Chapter 5.

One other documented element which has a bearing on the physical appearance of early villages is related at Cipières, for example, to the engagement of an important Benedictine monastery. Lèrins was given a *mansus* in Cipières in the 11th century,[20] but what this implies in terms of architecture and landscape is unclear. Contemporary evidence from elsewhere suggests that it may have been a substantial and coherent estate entity with a single residence and farm at the centre, perhaps the *villa* of other documents in Provence.[21] Such a site remains to be found in Cipières, although even this single documentary reference is nonetheless likely to be a further indicator of a pre-village, more dispersed settlement pattern.

As elsewhere in Provence this period was transitional and some of the elements that are essential to the process of village formation began to come together.[22] One strand of this is that the private chapels in the countryside, many of which had been created by local lords, were being drawn into the Gregorian reform of the parochial system and put under the nominal authority of bishops in the resurgent urban centres, although the influence of the former patronage remained strong. The new parochial churches were often in this period put next to or inside the *castra* of the local lords and there are signs, in turn, that these were beginning to be transformed into feudal castles, sometimes on the same sites, but often in new locations.[23] This new architecture had also started to appear in the towns in the wake of the often violent imposition of authority by the Burgundians. Outside of the towns the earliest castles, those of the later 11th century such as Cagnes les Hauts, Hautes-Gréolières and perhaps even Cipières itself, seem to have been placed on high and isolated locations, although some moved later to lower slope positions. These adjustments of powerful architecture seem, on current research, not to have had much immediate impact on the layout of social space in the subordinate communities. This may be because the regional lordship of the Burgundians, apart from being the vehicle of general west European changes in élite architecture and design, may have put very little effort into replacing or reforming the older, local power brokers among their mountain communities. However, in the next century this Burgundian relationship failed and at the same time we find rural settlements being transformed into the forms we can still find in the landscape.

The later Middle Ages

David Austin

From the early 12th century, the region was being brought into the emerging pattern of medieval organisation and power identified as 'public' and fully feudal by French scholars. The specific regional motor of that change was the shift in authority, following disputed succession, to Raymond Bérenger, of the house of Barcelona, during the period between 1112 and 1125. This seems to have been followed by the imposition of a more regular form of feudalism in the relationship between local lords and the Count. By 1160 all the regional lords of eastern Hautes-Provence had sworn fealty, even the inhabitants of the Castellanes pays who remained troublesome into the 13th century.[24] This was consolidated administratively from 1166 when *baillies* and, later, *vigueries* were imposed following the joining together of the Counties of Provence and Catalonia under Raymond Bérenger V.[25]

At this time there are clear signs, in the chronicles and manorial documents, of alterations to local lordships and changes in the lineages of their ancient holders, carried out often in the context of minor warfare. This was the case in Cipières which became part of a single sub-infeudated lordship together with Caussols and Gréolières held by the Lords of Grasse, Princes of Antibes.[26]

The most spectacular aspect of the contemporary transformation was the extensive creation of nucleated villages and their associated landscapes, although the specific processes by which this occurred are unclear and may have differed significantly in date and circumstance from place to place. These processes should not, however, be seen as separate from those which created the larger, urban nucleations at broadly the same time. In a local dispute, for example, in the 12th century, between an adherent of the house of Barcelona and the members of an older local dynasty, the regional see was transferred from Antibes to Grasse. Here a local fortified *castrum* was transformed into a castle, a cathedral added and a town planned outside its enceinte. This rapidly became the centre of administration for the region and its principal market.[27]

Elsewhere in the region two distinct mechanisms of village formation appeared: the secular and the ecclesiastical. This divide seems to be related to the increasing control of ancient parochial centres and their related landholdings by the church, particularly the Benedictines. As a result of this, local secular lords were creating other churches close to their castles under their direct patronage. Perhaps simultaneously or perhaps as separate and subsequent events, they also established tight nucleations of houses and gardens laid out along narrow streets and frequently within light fortifications (*incastellamento*) which might have been either distinct enceintes or little more than the continuous line formed by the blank back walls of terraced houses facing into the village itself. These nucleations and their defences, often in elevated, protected locations (the classic *villages perchés* of the region) were usually integrated closely with the castle. In other places the Benedictine and other ecclesiastical seigneurs also created these compact villages and they often today still carry the name of the saint to which the parish church was dedicated, such as St Auban or St Vallier du Thiey. It is very likely that Cipières itself fell into the first category of secular holdings, although it is very uncertain what role Lèrins had in the whole proceeding.

All of this seems very neat and closely related to the arrangements of feudal power in the region, but the truth is that we are very dependant on a few documented cases, and in no specific instance does the actual process of village creation become apparent. Architectural inferences are drawn substantially from fragments of churches and castles, since few vernacular buildings of the Middle Ages appear to survive and those that do are late and often élite in some way. Even in these cases of fragmentary Romanesque architecture the specific relationship with their surrounding villages is very obscure. In archaeological terms, excavations conducted on a sufficient scale are very rare and extremely problematic in relation to the dating of their earliest deposits. At Rougiers (Var) which is one of the most extensive excavations ever conducted on a village in Europe, the creation of the fortified castle and village complex, perched on the edge of sheer cliff, is clearly identified as belonging to the later 12th century.[28] By the end of the next century the village and castle were already in the throes of abandonment with final desertion in the 15th century.

Other factors need, however, to be taken into account. It is clear, for example, that the whole business of making villages continued into the 13th century and beyond. Planel cites an inquest of 1252 as the last date at which new settlements seem to appear in the regional records.[29] Villages also appeared as the result of some very specific circumstance of power and authority. At Gréolières just across the valley from Cipières, for example, there were two medieval villages barely 500 m from each other.

Elsewhere it is by no means clear that nucleation involved everybody in the parish, lordship or community concerned, and in some cases a village seems never to have been created. At La Faye and Le Mas, for example, in the 13th and early 14th centuries there are references to outlying farms and separate *mansi*.[30] Indeed at Cipières itself the modern farm of La Pinée at the far western end of the commune looks to be the survivor of one such holding, isolated on its island of good soil. At Caussols, just to the south of Cipières, although there is a small deserted site near the church, there appear also to have been other medieval farms and holdings scattered along the valley below the Calern escarpment, perhaps a reflection of pre-feudal dispersed arrangements. This lack of coherent solidarity by all involved in the social relations of local communities at this time may also be found at Gourdon, another Cipières neighbour. Here there is a classic village perché, clustered around its castle and church, but out in the fields about a kilometre to the north there is a Romanesque chapel, with hints of a small settlement around it, which appears to have been the original parish church. If so, then for a while at least, part of the church hierarchy kept its physical and ideological distance from the dominant processes of village creation within the community.

Individual cases like this raise the issue, familiar to all scholars of the medieval village, of how in human terms they came to be created.[31] Over the period of this debate, once nationalistic models of ethnic creation had been abandoned whether in Britain[32] or France,[33] a number of critical questions have arisen, all germane to the processes of analysis and patterns of interpretation we have followed in the Cipières Project. Was village creation simply the result of acts of outright seigneurial coercion or were they a contract between peasant and lord in which the fear of external threat was a binding force greater than the workings of internal power and conflict? Could they even be the result of peasant and freeholding initiatives, perhaps mimicing the fashion for agrarian and social reform to be seen among their neighbours?[34] Were the villages themselves the result of single acts of planning? They appear to be so from morphological analyses, but this may be no more than our own academic procedures of reduction to simple and comprehensible patterns and coherent narratives:[35] perhaps, by contrast, their evolutions were gradual, piecemeal and non-linear.[36] As a final example of the kinds of questions we need to address in a study like this, we can ask: did village creation involve only rearrangements of existing populations or was there, as in contemporary town creation, some form of induced inward migration? In any one region, like the one being considered here, the answer is that probably all the possibilities implied by these questions were happening and that from community to community all of them may have had their influence to different extents at different times.

In addition to all this, at the level of the specific village, another factor must also be considered. Often because, in the case of strongly nucleated villages, we are looking at such physically coherent remains, there is a strong temptation for us to believe that the people who lived within them had similarly coherent and exclusive senses of identity, allegiance and presence. It is important to remember, for any period we are studying, that this itself was highly variable from class to class, from family to family and from individual to individual and changed through time, through the seasons, through life cycles and through generations, something explored by both David Siddle and Rosamond Faith in their chapters on social formations and population. So, even in the clear case of physical agglomeration, like the *villages perchés* of Provence, the human artefact which is the village is really, under close scrutiny, a moving mass like a colony of bees. Community in this sense is a complicated and often fugitive concept, impossible to put a fence around and study in isolation.

We must also take into account the fact that the act of village creation was a phenomenon occurring all over Europe between the 10th and 13th centuries. The particular identifier in the plan is the making of adjacent properties which physically separate and break up extended family, clan and tribal arrangements of space into smaller units more appropriate to the nuclear or stem family. In the documents this shift is represented by the introduction of assessment for individual, named heads of household who now must answer for service, render and tax rather than the kins and their elders. This may, in one way, be seen as part of the drive by centralising states to break the powers of the local brokers which are vested in the bonds and relationships of kinship (including the allodial relationships with local lords). The material analogue of this new social structuring is the house itself in the individually marked and bounded piece of ground within the nexus of the village and the community. But it may be more than analogue and the new spatial arrangements may have been created consciously to enable the differentiation of people and the identification of their new patterns of obligation. This is all, of course, a huge generalisation and there are thousands of exceptions throughout Europe, of which the uplands provide many examples, especially in the more peripheral and resistant societies. In some places the old way of render and farm is maintained almost to the end of the period and in others the village never appears. In yet others the kin is never broken, retaining its authority as the source of local well-being and the counter-state, being 'our thing'. Where Cipières itself sits in all this will be explored later by Rosamond Faith.

Nevertheless the village phenomenon is general and we must acknowledge that part of the process of change lies outside any simple consideration of region or place. It is part of a new attitude to management among the élites, encouraged by the shifting ideologies of the Church during the same period. This is found in the documents which stress personal redemption and responsibility and the authority of the state backed by the hierarchy of the church itself. Documents from Carolingian capitularies onwards also begin to proscribe the systems of good management to be found on the well-run estate. Another, probably even more difficult, question for this period is: what impact did the change to the village have on its surrounding landscape? We must admit that some of the impetus for this question comes from our British experience where the introduction of the village from the tenth century onwards was linked with the simultaneous creation of communal open fields and intermingled strip farming. This was not simply a matter of tenure or lordship, since it meant the physical creation of whole new landscapes on a massive scale. Was the experience of *incastellamento* similar? As in Britain, the documents tell us nothing, but in some places, e.g. San Vicenzo al Voltorne[37] we do know that the movement of late antique and early medieval settlement locations from dispersed estates onto hill-tops involved migration away from older fields on valley floors towards terracing on slopes and greater emphasis on pastoralism. This may have been limited to locations where valley systems were nearby and fell within the compass of the later village territories and in more mountainous terrains such as Cipières such change may not have been possible. However, it must still be reasonable to assume that the massive social upheaval that the village represents was probably accompanied by adjustments also in the physical management and organisation of the economic means of life and modes of production. This is an assumption we will take forward into the morphological analysis which follows.

2.2. Village morphology

David Austin

Methodological context

It was quite late in fieldwork that we came to consider the village itself. In a densely occupied place such as Cipières there is little opportunity for intervention. In addition, by the time we came to study it, there were very few houses which had not been affected by modernisation. Our primary tool, therefore, was the historical geographers' technique of morphological analysis of the settlement plan. In recent years, under the influence of historical geography, morphological studies have further developed the methodologies and justified the sequential arguments for the retrogressive analysis of whole landscapes, particularly as found on early maps.[38] Such studies have been applied especially to the study of historic villages, towns and field systems, attempting to isolate the forms laid down at the point of origin: morphogenesis.

There is now a firmly embedded belief in European scholarship that communities identifiable as units from early documents can be assigned to the structured, especially the regular, spaces as seen on cadastral and other maps of the Enlightenment age, despite being separated by several centuries.[39] The excavation of deserted medieval settlements seems, in general terms, to confirm the antiquity and origin of the forms identified in this way. In conjunction with archaeology and medieval history, there has, as a consequence, developed an argument for proposing the widespread introduction or re-introduction of nucleated forms in Europe in the Carolingian and post-Carolingian periods, stretching from the later 8th or 9th to the 13th centuries. However, the particular characteristics of tightly-packed adjacent tenements, whether burgages or tofts or maisons, laid out in planned units which are so much the hall-mark of high medieval living, appear in abundance largely from the later 9th century onwards peaking in the 11th and 12th centuries. This appears to coincide with the emergence of the systems and phenomena of feudal and manorial power, of the structures of urban corporate life, and of the definition of the heritable household, its head and its land as the unit of production and assessment. This coincidence is taken as an argument for causal linkage, attributing the new patterns of physical life to the introduction of new patterns of authority and tenure. The remarkable aspect of this event is its almost universal appearance across large parts of Europe and, perhaps even, the world at almost the same time.

This kind of analysis in Britain has resulted in a complex system of taxonomy and explanation, which has been articulated most forcibly in the work of Roberts and Wrathmell.[40] The appearance of nucleated forms is shown, in their work, not to be universal across England, but to occur in significant zones, especially when plotted against the persistence of earlier dispersed forms of settlement. The historical meaning of this is unclear, but similar comprehensive mapping is still to happen in France, although individual regional and individual settlement studies have recently been published.[41] There is an awareness here that in France there are variations from region to region in the nature and expression of nucleation and these seem to have some cultural coherence which can be related in broad terms to cultural pays. However, there are patterns larger than the regional pays and one long recognised is *incastellamento* itself. It is a Mediterranean phenomenon, marked out by elevated locations and densely packed housing and properties, originally constrained by fortifications or enceintes. Where they exist they seem also to contain the vast bulk of occupied housing in their territories to the detriment of the surrounding countryside and they often contain both small castles of their seigneurs and parochial churches. Most scholars see these as deliberate, consciously designed creations of the late 11th and 12th centuries, in other words part of the Europe-wide phenomenon which brought planned villages and complex agrarian practices to a large number of emerging feudal states. In this chapter I shall endeavour to identify the processes of analysis, which have produced three speculative maps of what the plan of the village may have been at key stages of its existence. Given what has already been said, it is important to remember that the further back in time we go the more speculative it all becomes, and that we do tend to see simplicity of form rather than complexity, perhaps as a consequence of our intellectual processes rather than because it is a 'truth' about the past.[42]

The first consideration of a place is the ground on which it stands. The modern village of Cipières has two contrasting aspects. One is from the north (Figure 59), the *village perché*, high above the Gorge du Loup from where it can be identified as a, lower, extension eastwards of the great ridge of the Gros Pounch (zone II.1). This, northern aspect is emphasised in modern perception,

FIGURE 59. Village from the north
PHOTOGRAPH: ANTHONY LEWISON

FIGURE 60. Le Saffranier
PHOTOGRAPH: DAVID AUSTIN

top: FIGURE 61. La Bourgade

middle: FIGURE 62. La Place

bottom: FIGURE 63. View of the village from the south with church and château dominating the skyline'

PHOTOGRAPHS: DAVID AUSTIN

under the influence of Romantic tourism and the Picturesque, by the road which has been driven along the cliff edge, looking across the gorge to the village of Gréolières and its impressive terrace systems climbing up the side of the Cheiron massif. The other, southern, aspect (Figures 2 & 23) is the one with which the villagers themselves have been, and continue to be, more familiar. A village of densely packed houses is terraced along a low, east–west ridge and pours down its flanks into a dry valley (or uvula) sheltered by another low hill to the south. Part of the uvula was called Le Saffranier (the saffron grower) in the recent past, but its older name is Le Coulet (Figure 60). To the west is the upland massif of the Gros Pounch and the Plateau de Calern, while to the south and east are the relatively flat lands of broad dolines and dry valleys which constituted some of the best arable land of the community.

Nowadays there is much modern development, which has expanded the village itself and blurred the edges of its form with many dispersed properties. The various modern approaches to the village, whether by car or on foot find their circuitous route up steep slopes and along the contours on modern and ancient terraces. Today the main entrance by car is through La Bourgade (Figure 61), a narrow street on the south side of La Place (Figure 62). One main road comes from the north across the Gorge du Loup and the direction of Gréolières, Coursegoles and Vence, and the other from the south along the edge of the Gorge and from Gourdon and Grasse. Both of these roads are very recent and the old routeway system is now part of a network of well-signed footpaths. Most of them are so narrow and steep that only pedestrians or donkeys with, at best, sledges or small carts, could have found their way along.

On the highest point of the village, and dominating its profile against the sky, is the rigidly rectangular shape of the château, so much altered in the modern era that its medieval

form in the morphology has been almost entirely lost. Also distinctive on the skyline is the wrought iron cage of the church's bell-tower at the centre of the village (Figure 63). For the rest, the 'villagescape' is now overwhelmingly red-tiled roofs and rendered limestone walls.

left: FIGURE 64. A narrow streetscape
(PHOTOGRAPH: ANTHONY LEWISON

right: FIGURE 65. The originally blank external façade of the houses along La Rue Sous le Barry
PHOTOGRAPH: DAVID AUSTIN

The first stage of the analysis was almost unconscious: walking around the village getting to know where the roads led and what lay along them. Even in such a small place this was confusing, because the streets are, for the most part, narrow and the buildings high with few opportunities to see between them (Figure 64). There are no long vistas, except from the inside, from the highest windows or those on the exterior face of the village, and even these, one quickly comes to realise, are very modern openings. From the south the originally blank external façade of the houses along La Rue Sous le Barry is evident (Figure 65). Even within La Place, which is much more open, all the streets and paths leading away from it vanish quickly behind buildings. The connection between places within the village, therefore, was and is a matter of familiarity engendered by movement and social relationship. Even from the outside, for all the surrounding hills and mountains, there is no vantage point from which the layout of the village and its streets can be seen as a whole. So, for all my years of visiting Cipières I went for the first time to Le Caire, which lies diametrically opposite to Anthony Lewison's house at the east end of La Rue du Coulet, only when I began the methodical mapping of the village terraces which I describe below. Prior to that I had no reason to go down some of the narrow blind alleys, where encounters would have been hard to explain.

At about the same time as our fieldwork Jean-Claude Poteur[43] conducted a morphological analysis of the village together with a narrative of the settlement's development as part of a village study for a regional inventory. Both the analysis and the narrative differ from ours in several marked respects. Most notably it is clear that Poteur's interpretation is driven by an *a priori* model derived from the accepted regional demographic history most coherently assembled by Baratier[44] and seemingly echoed in a very narrow selection of figures for Cipiéres taken from only three medieval and early modern documents. This general model and the analysis of the specific Cipiéres documents we profoundly dispute (see Siddle, Chapter 5). Poteur, on the basis of the Baratier model, suggests that the first medieval village of the 12th–13th centuries was tiny and sited on the platform next to the chateau, with a still-modest second medieval expansion of the 14th–15th centuries focussed around the present château and church. He then argues for three comparatively massive expansions, one in the early 16th century, one in the later 16th and the last at the end of the 16th and beginning of the 17th. It is our belief that Poteur's use of the morphological method is compromised by the subordination to the flawed demographic model and that his chronology has little regard for the general understanding of the trajectory of medieval settlement geography and archaeology. In particular the choice of the 14th–15th centuries for expansion seems to be contrary to what is happening elsewhere in Europe. This demographic model is also applied to his interpretation of how the agrarian landscape developed attributing most to the early modern period, and here again we disagree profoundly.

The cadastral map (Figure 66)

The primary artefact of the morphological analysis has been the first cadastral survey of 1842. This map retains the lines of triangulation and the vantage points

FIGURE 66. The cadastral map of the village, 1842

of the original survey stations, one on the *aire* (plot 154) at the east end of the village and one on the top of the church bell-tower. The survey is clearly highly accurate and measured in considerable detail as is true of this very organised and disciplined work.[45] However, all lines are straight and curves were reduced to curious angles, which vanish when encountered at street or field level. Redrawing, therefore, has meant some softening of the outlines in several places and since gentle curves can be so helpful in morphological analysis where they can indicate the alignment of elements now lost or severely foreshortened, they have been restored for the purposes of this study.

Almost the first thing that happens in morphological analysis is idle speculation about the possibilities for the shape of the earliest settlement and how roads and streets might once have connected. What one is dealing with are mental templates given by previous experience and typologies. Looking at the map of Cipières there is, for example, a strong distinction between the linear patterns of the east, west and southern parts of the village all pivoting about the church and the Rue du Portail. There is no single street line, which runs down the spine of the ridge from east to west, as one might expect from the topography alone. La Bourgade in the south also has a gently arcing alignment, which appears to have little relationship to the street pattern to the north.

The idea of the *village perché* also influences the mind: the form of the incastellamento with its narrow streets protected by outer walls or by the blind aspects of the outer façades of houses, all on a prominent location protected by the castle above. Here even today it is the eastern end of the village that most calls this to mind, while the western is more open and broken with little coherent outer wall. One street name, La Rue Sous le Barry ('the street below the rampart') also clearly hints at fortification and the incastellamento form.

FIGURE 67. A building in the 1960s before renovation
PHOTOGRAPH: ANTHONY LEWISON

Houses and buildings

There is then a need to examine buildings and see whether there are any clues to origin and development. This is nearly always a disappointment. Houses and buildings in a village are in a constant state of refurbishment, decay and reconstruction. Those in Cipières have nearly all gone through the horizon of radical redevelopment from the 1960s onwards as the village recovered from its near extinction following the agrarian crises of the first half of the 20th century. This has involved the conversion of nearly all the various types of agricultural building represented in the cadastral survey into modern dwellings with all the accoutrements of modern design and appliance. The redevelopment has thus transformed the buildings internally and only certain elements of the external façades have survived, such as doorways and a few windows. Floor levels have been arbitrarily changed and once blank walls opened

FIGURE 68. Elevations of buildings on the Rue Longue
DRAWING: DAVID AUSTIN

up with picture windows. Photographs taken by Anthony Lewison in the 1960s before the regeneration of the village fabric show how these buildings would once have offered important evidence for the vernacular architectural historian (Figures 64 & 67).

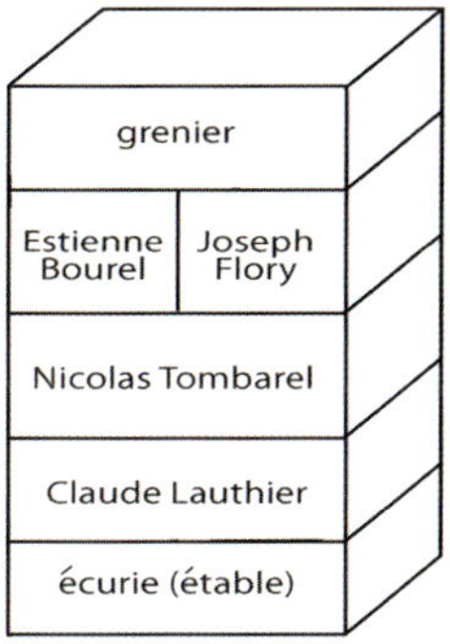

Schematic representation of a house in La Bourgade in multiple occupancy in 1727. (David Siddle)

Coupled with this is the complex development of the tenurial patterns in the village that, during the 17th and 18th centuries particularly, accelerated the sub-division of tenement so that one structure could be occupied, or owned and leased out, by many different people and families. It is hard to know who lived where, but what it did to the buildings was to drive them upwards and there are many signs of added storeys throughout the village of 1842 (Figures 68 & 69). The overall impression then is of immense structural complexity, over-ridden by the hand of modernity. However, there is one interesting and redeeming feature. Despite the complexity, for some social and/or legal reason the integrity of buildings has been largely maintained, so that the ground plan

FIGURE 69. Village building on the Rue Longue with evidence of raising
PHOTOGRAPH: DAVID AUSTIN

dimensions, the building plots, shown on the cadastral survey, appear to have had some long-term identity. If anything of the architecture is close to the point of origin, it seems to be these building plots.

Mapping the terrace structure

For financial, logistical and access reasons we eschewed excavation as a way of examining the physical structure and sequence of the village. Our collective experience is that small-scale interventions in places which are still densely inhabited give, at best, the story of a single building which might be idiosyncratic and exceptional. Even if it is not, then, without other extensive work, there is no way of knowing that it is! To understand the whole of a settlement's history a very high proportion must be excavated and even that will need to be bound together by morphological analysis.

However, a more direct relationship between the map and the physical structure of the village was thought to be essential in strengthening the quality of evidence to support our morphological interpretations. It was Andrew Fleming who suggested that the most direct relationship with the topography was the terrace platforms which had been dug into the ridge and the sides of the uvula, the stone from which might have been used to build parts of the early houses. This, I felt, would also relate directly to the house plots which seem to have retained their integrity, as I have already suggested. What I also came to realise in the process of mapping the terraces was that they assisted in identifying plan units or 'cells' and hinted at pre-existing terraces which linked through to those out in the agrarian landscape.

The mapping consisted of walking around with the 1842 map under a sheet of drawing film and noting all the breaks in slope and changes in level. Where it was polite and possible for me to do so, I peered into doorways and explored the basements of houses. For the native inhabitants it was clear evidence, once again, of '*la folie anglaise*', and for the English in-comers, a source of ethnic embarrassment. The older villagers were drawn to me like a magnet, however, and for the first time I saw collections of flints and other artefacts found throughout the commune. I sat on walls with my old map and strange cabbalistic squiggles all over it and pontificated about the deep and ancient past. I became a *magister scientiae*, at least for a day.

The base map (Figure 70)

The next step was to create a base map of our knowledge that effectively married the cadastral and terrace surveys. On this some of the sharp angles caused by 'straight-line' surveying in 1842 were smoothed and the relationships of alignment along streets, house plots and terraces were more closely observed and recorded. It is this map, which formed the basis of the morphological analysis which follows.

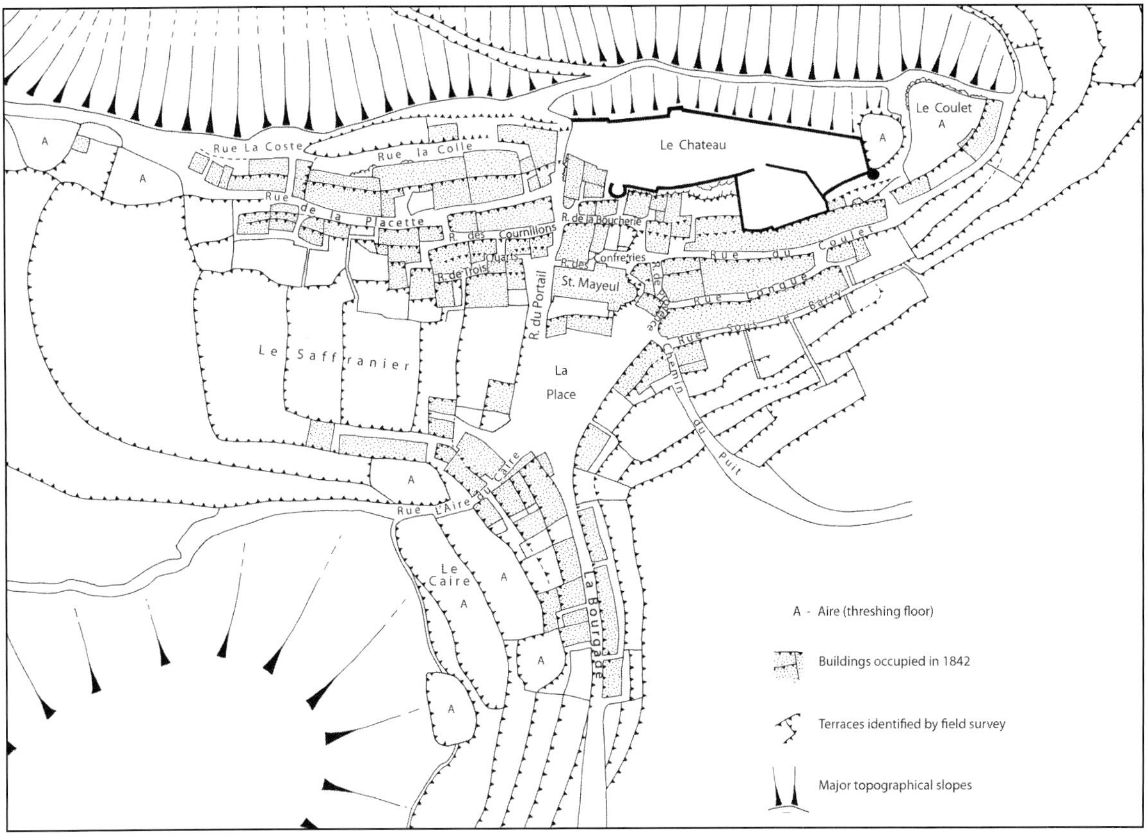

FIGURE 70. The base survey of the village
DRAWING: DAVID AUSTIN

The map also contains one other key part of the analysis. It was possible, I felt, to identify what may be called plan compartments or cells which, from their shape and from their relationships of abutment and misalignment with their neighbours and with the street lines, seemed to form coherent entities or units. The existence of the terraces also assisted in this process of cellular identification. The base map, therefore, depicts these elements within solid lines, rather than the hotch-potch of house plots shown on the cadastral survey, which tend to confuse the eye. The built areas were, however, identified by stippling. Nevertheless the intellectual process of reduction began here.

The retrogressive analysis: finding the primary elements (Figure 71)

After the creation of the base map it was important to begin the process of retrogressive analysis by attempting to identify those elements (shaded on Figure 71), especially the plan cells which seem most obviously to have intruded across what might be regarded as pre-existing and thus earlier alignments. Certain features then identified themselves very quickly.

On the peripheries of the village plan the construction of *aires*, open-air

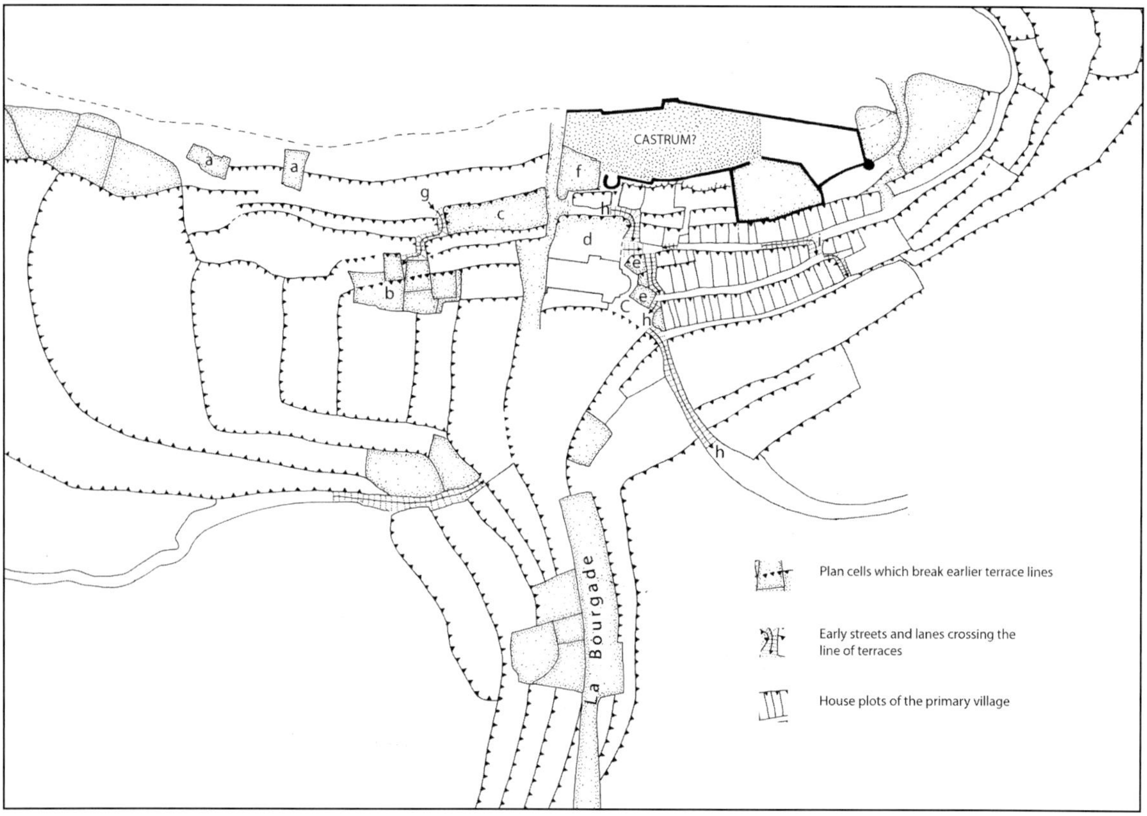

FIGURE 71. Identification of the primary elements
DRAWING: DAVID AUSTIN

threshing floors, especially the smaller ones, all broke across the alignments of terraces.

In the south, major components, including the line of La Bourgade also cut the terrace systems, which flowed out beyond the village at this point. Some of the Bourgade area, however, the north-western part in particular, did not cut the terraces and this suggests that it might have been developed earlier than the rest.

In the western part of the upper village, the terrace on the north side of La Rue de La Placette was disrupted at its western end by two small 'cells' (as on Figure 71), although this may not be significant. On the south it was possible to identify blocks of gardens and buildings which intruded across the terrace patterns (Figure 71, b). These were also, as we shall see, large bourgeois houses which belonged to a later stage of village life (see also Chapter 5). Also in this sector of the village was a terrace which, although built upon, again seemed to break the original terrace line and looked like the in-filling of an open space, which it was tempting to believe was the small square named in La Rue de la Placette (c).

In the eastern sector of the village, the area of La Rue du Portail and La Rue de la Boucherie, all seemed to break the original alignments. First is the large cell (d) to the north of the church which today is cut through by La Rue des Confrèries, in itself a suggestive name, related perhaps to an early guild or brotherhood. This cell emerged as I plotted the terraces, because not only did it cut the eastern alignments, but it also had clear traces of a north–south platform edge on both its western and eastern sides. Added to its misaligned northern terrace edge there was a clear platform which seems to have been part of a once greater church enclosure. My thinking then moved to the eastern end of the church where three small cells (e) seem to have been built into an awkward, but previously open space now below the more recent platform which carries the apse of the baroque building. I identified this also as a potential part of the church 'cell', especially remembering the discovery of burials in the area marked 'C' on the map during the 19th century.

The castle is a morphological mystery, because it has been so altered in the modern era. However, the enclosed area with stippled edges on the map seems to be an addition, largely because it overlaps the side of the crag on which the main part of the structure now stands. It is also possible to identify a roughly 'boat-shaped' area (fully stippled) which seems to define the highest ground and which may be the basic shape of the earlier castle and perhaps even its predecessor *castrum*. On this theme I have also tentatively suggested that the block of buildings in the south-western re-entrant angle of the Château was in-fill (f), perhaps where the main entrance once existed. A surviving round tower (if it is medieval and not a folly) might have once flanked this entrance as part of this block; in 1842 it was still owned by the Panise seigneur.

Another element plotted onto the base map was the places where the streets moved steeply downslope, most notably as they crossed or enabled access up and down the terraces. Three places particularly identified themselves. First, in the western village a lane dog-legs down the slope from La Rue de La Placette and La Rue des Cournillons, ending now in a garden above Le Saffranier (g). The terrace system persistently changes alignment there and seems to be a point in the morphology where there had always been some kind of access. This is unlike the nearby Rue du Trois Quarts which seems to be cut through the terrace system which is not discontinuous about this point and which, therefore, seems later. Next, a similar lane (h) at the heart of the upper village also dog-legs down from La Rue la Boucherie, through the junction of La Rue des Confreries and La Rue du Coulet, down La Rue de Provence and out of the village by way of the Chemin du Puit. Much of this today seems like part of the minor internal passages giving access to La Place, but must once have been a primary route from the vicinity of the Château gate to the demesne and other arable lands immediately to the south of the village and from there to the outside world. Finally, another dog-legging lane (i) comes down from La Rue du Coulet, through the east end of La Rue Longue, then down again to the east end of La Rue Sous le Barry and thence to the outside of the village. These three access routes seemed primary at this first stage of analysis.

As a last act at this stage, I added in the house plots from the cadastral survey for the three planning cells which were the most substantial and the most coherent in the whole village plan. They are strikingly different from any of the other cells which are all much smaller and less consistently divided (except perhaps for a central section of the north side of La Rue de la Placette). At this point I was already beginning to affirm my first impressions that the core of the early village may have lain at this eastern end: a single planned unit laid out below the Château and between it and the extensive demesne lands to the south. In my mind already was an argument for the village as a coerced settlement strongly under the dominium of the seigneur.

The first village (Figure 72)

The next stage was to map the form of the first village. The three main rows along La Rue du Coulet, La Rue Longue and La Rue Sous le Barry were straightforward, and needed only minor analysis in relation to the base map. One element of this was to see the rounded building at the west end of the southern row, at the junction of the Rue Longue and the Chemin du Puit, as a later addition (Figure 73). A quick inspection of it also suggested that it had been constructed abutting the rest of the row and did not lie on the building terrace itself, but rather on the sloping level of the street surface. With this removed from the plan, the 'central' street of the Rue de Provence ran straight

FIGURE 72. The first village
DRAWING:. DAVID AUSTIN

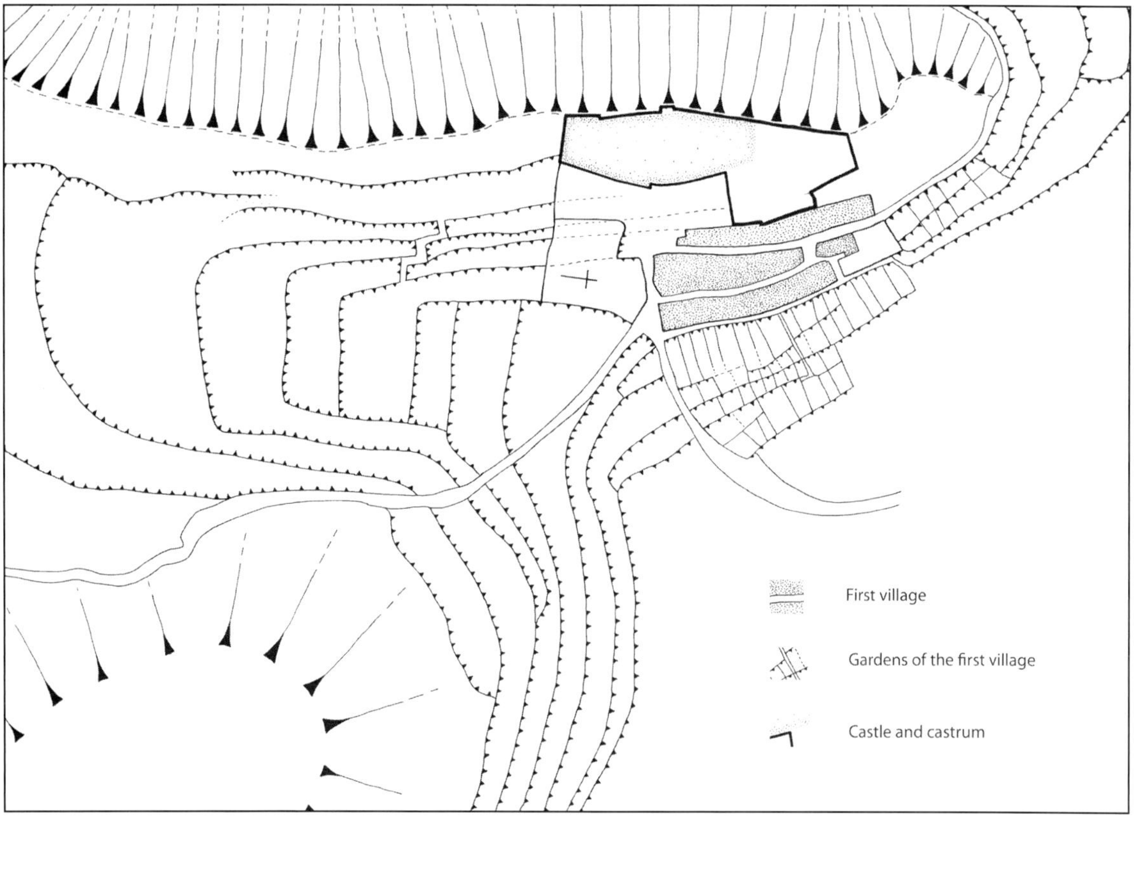

top: FIGURE 73. The rounded building at the end of Rue Longue

bottom: FIGURE 74. The gardens below the first village

PHOTOGRAPHS: DAVID AUSTIN

down the Chemin du Puit to the demesne lands at Le Puys and to what was perhaps the primary source of consistently running water signified by the place-name. This street morphologically can be seen as the pivot of the whole settlement.

To the west of this street lay the church enclosure with its cemetery, once bigger than it is today, including the present houses between Rue de Provence and the church which are morphological additions. In this primary phase the parish church of St Mayeul had been almost certainly Romanesque and smaller than the present building. We can only speculate that it lay more to the east rather than the west end of the enclosure. The limits of this enclosure seem to have been in part a terraced platform on the northern and north-eastern sides, in part a straight line down the slope, now La Rue du Portail, and in part the high terrace on the south side which still exists behind the buildings on the north side of La Place. This terrace was part of the terraced arc of the Le Saffranier uvula which could be plotted on the west side, under the later village.

The reconstruction of this terracing on the west side rests on the identification of how the second village was laid out. In essence this suggests that, south of La Rue de la Placette three large planning units were pushed southwards on terraces over the top of Le Saffranier. Once these were removed from the base map the lines of the earlier topography and terrace structure became visible, including the lane coming down from La Rue des Cournillons which could now be identified as an access down agricultural terraces to the floor of Le Saffranier. All of this suggests that the western end of the village at least had been laid down on a landscape already under cultivation, a realisation to which I shall have to return in a moment.

Returning to the village core, the position, if not the exact shape, of the early castle on the site can also be mapped, occupying a platform at the top of the ridge. This then left a space on the plan below the castle and it is proposed that this was originally an open space or Place, leaving clear ground for the castle defences as well as a location for communal action of all kinds. However, this does leave the rest of the present castle space unexplained, especially when one realises that its present western edge coincides so exactly with the western edge of the house terraces. This is accentuated by the additional observation that the gardens, still extant below La Rue Sous le Barry and mapped on the cadastral survey, also form a coherent unit with the house terraces above. It is possible with only slight adjustment of the 1842 alignments to speculate that these garden plots were also laid out on terraces and formed part of the first village (Figure 74).

All of this produces a hypothetical early village core which is broadly a rectangle enclosing seigneur, church and peasants. It and its gardens were south-facing with a strong suggestion, as already noted, from the name of La Rue Sous le Barry that the whole inhabited space was regarded as a compact and defensible unity. Its main entrance seems to have been on this south side in what is now the north-east corner of La Place. Importantly the old road, which descends from the Plateau du Calern to the west through the area now known as Le Caire, turns at the foot of the slope directly towards this entrance. Then at the east end La Rue du Coulet continues out of the village on another old road down the side of the Gorge towards the river itself and the crossing over to the Roman road.

An alternative first village and the castrum?

The resulting plan to be seen on Figure 72 left me, however, a little uneasy. There was the odd shape of the church enclosure and the impression that the alignments of the western terraces on the flanks of the ridge could be traced within the *incastellamento* village, especially across the church enclosure and the reconstructed early Place. Indeed the strange re-entrant angle on the east side of the church enclosure could be seen as part of an original terrace passing along the southern edge of La Rue du Coulet. This raises the possibility that the church enclosure was once smaller and that the core village may have existed at first only on either side of La Rue Longue, forming a smaller rectangle with the church enclosure. The space between this and the castle platform would then have been filled with old agricultural terraces and the whole unit would not have been so compact, perhaps with a partially isolated fortification. This all might suggest that the village was laid out in an already functioning agricultural landscape in a sheltered hollow below an isolated *castrum* with a church nearby.

An added spur to this thought is the strong clue in the layout of the gardens that this also has an early (upper) element and second (lower) one added to it: perhaps an analogue to the addition of the house terrace on the north side of La Rue du Coulet.

These speculations then raise the possibility that the morphological sequence should include a proto-village phase linked to a *castrum* or *mansus*.

Then the axis of the road through the early village caught my eye. It was potentially an old through-route not just within the commune from its highest lands on the plâteau to its lowest by the river, but also from Caussols to Grèolières. It is this road which links the core settlements of the lordship created in the later 12th century, under Barcellonan suzerainty, with Cipières as its caput and its physical centre. From the west it crossed the uvula where La Place now is, climbed one terrace to run along the Rue Longue and then climbed another at the point where even today there is access up to the Rue du Coulet.

Within the whole morphology, therefore, there is a powerful suggestion that Cipières began to be constructed at an already established centre of power, a *mansus* or *castrum* at a time when the structures of authority and resource exploitation were being fundamentally changed (see Chapter 5).

The second village (Figure 75)

The next stage of the village is essentially the addition of the western part along the spinal street, La Rue de la Placette. In this name also is the clue to where the central space of this redesigned village was. Another key aspect of the village in this format is that it breaches the principle of *incastellamento*, particularly on its new southern aspect where there appears to have been neither defensive wall nor unified blank façade. It also breaks the line of the western façade.

As far as the original village is concerned, there are clear signs that the eastern part, at least, of the old Place was in-filled. Here, as elsewhere in this developing

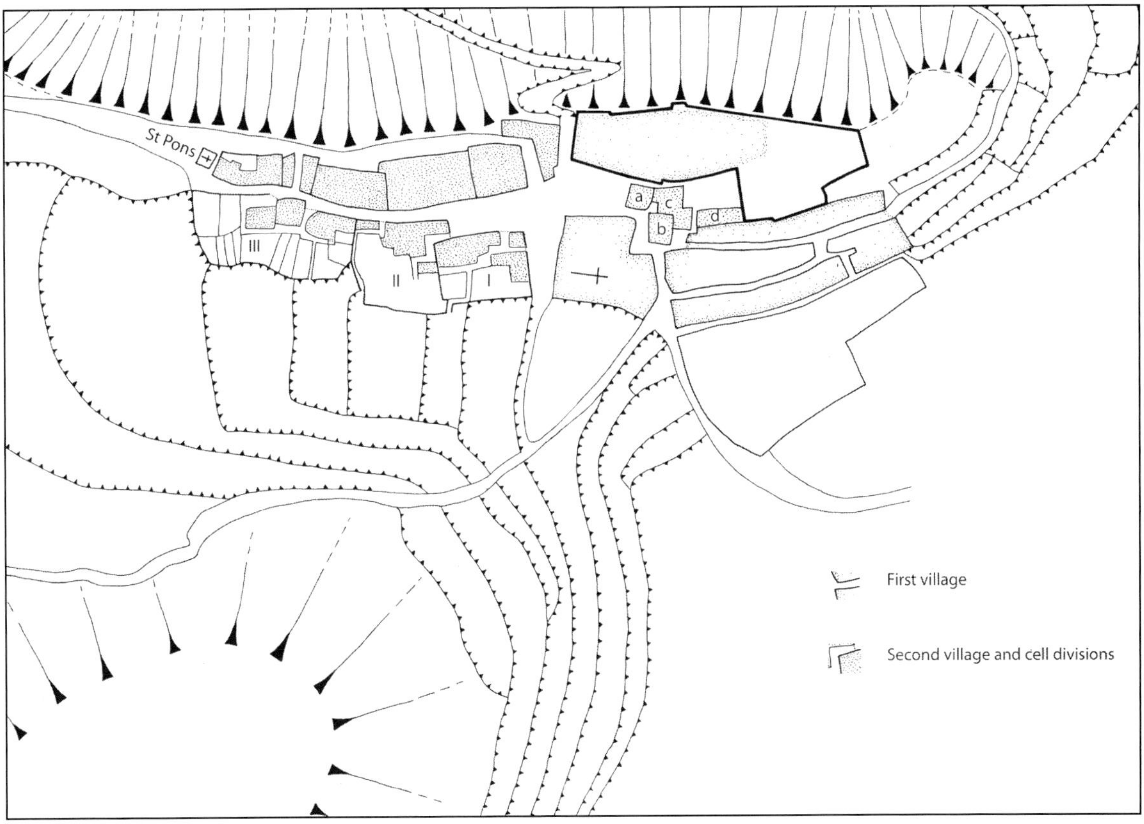

FIGURE 75. The second village
DRAWING: DAVID AUSTIN

village, the plan unit or cell had become not the long unified row, but smaller compact blocks which appear to abut and over-lap each other in ways which suggest accretion or gradual addition over a space of time. So in the old Place, as shown on Figure 75, there are two in-filling cells (a & b) to which seem to have been added a third (c), when access was also created through a passage to a small new row (d) built onto the back of the earlier houses on the north side of La Rue du Coulet.

The reduction in the size of the communal open space at the heart of the village seems to have been compensated by the Placette, an area definable morphologically on the base map as a rectangle between the Rue de la Placette and La Rue des Cournillons. What is left is an open space in front of the gate of the Château.

Leading from this space are La Rue des Cournillons, La Rue des Trois Quarts, both the northward and southward lines of La Rue du Portail and La Rue la Colle, as well as the old entrance street via La Rue de Provence. Hence the modified Place became a focus for all the streets in the village, and at the same time it opened a new through-route along La Rue du Portail, linking at the southern end to the old road to Caussols and at the north end to a track down the side of the Gorge, past another water source and eventually joining the original Grèolières road. By this means the whole north–south axis of the village was shifted westwards where it remains today.

The building cells in the western part of the village are clearly of two types. On the north are relatively large blocks which give a south-facing set of buildings along the north side of La Rue de la Placette and a north-facing set along La Rue la Colle. This interpretation is offered here and on Figure 75, but it has also to be allowed that the original plan for this north side was a single row of buildings, constructed against a very clear terrace cut into the bed-rock which is shown on the base map and marked as a pecked line on Figure 75. If this is the case, then the buildings on La Rue la Colle are later and at some time were made to breach the line of the original terrace. All of this is possible, although it then calls into question the access which leads from La Rue la Colle into La Placette, as well as the building cell on its east side, in front of the Château. What is worth noting, however, about the final plan of this north side is the presence of the Chapelle de St Pons marking the new western entrance to the village.

On the south side, there is a marked contrast. There is no single frontage line and no coherent rows and long terraces. Rather there appear to be three major units (I, II & III), each with its own internal lane giving access down the steep slope of the ridge to open areas demarcated by terraces which intrude onto the Le Saffranier uvula (Figure 76). In the two eastern units the original open areas were built over by later houses, which were readily identifiable in the very first stage of analysis (Figure 71). Once these are removed, as they are on Figure 75, they become visible again. Then comparison with the third, western unit, suggests that these open spaces were garden areas integral with the building unit

FIGURE 76. The western end of the village, the area of the cells with Le Château, the Notary's house and the Church
PHOTOGRAPH: DAVID AUSTIN

itself. This strongly suggests that these were of a different status or concept to the rest of the village whose gardens lay outside the framework of the settlement envelope. It is notable, in support of this thesis, that none of the internal lanes running down the slope leads from one of these units to another, although they could have been readily designed to do so. Also in support is the name of one these lanes, that in the easternmost unit, La Rue des Trois Quarts which, as can be seen from Figure 75, actually links three building cells within the larger unit.

When this was all created, and how, is a matter of even greater speculation. There may indeed have been little separation in time between any of these entities whether in the 'first' or in the 'second' village. What is clear is that these two halves of the village seem to have been constructed on two or even three different design principles. I have identified this first as a succession and interpreted it as a temporal succession and argued for related changes in routeway, access and public space. However, we must bring into play the other clear impression, based on this fundamental difference in design, that this relates also, perhaps primarily, to the dwelling spaces of different classes of peasant, their tenure and relationship to both lord and land. Later in Chapters 5 and 6 Rosamond Faith and David Siddle present a case for differences between early colonisers who came with the new feudal structure (*caslani*) and the incorporation of local peoples of a lower class (*maleservi*). Here it begins to be possible, as suggested by Rosamond Faith in her discussion on *caslani* in Chapter 5, to propose that the *caslani* may have had their extended family compounds in the large units in the western half of the village and the *maleservi* in the smaller and more uniform, more regimented units in the eastern. Indeed in this discussion by Rosamond Faith, their key role in village formation and management is emphasised and there is a strong clue here that the postulated social differentiation in the plan was something that ought to be found at the earliest stages of incastellamento. This would suggest that the two halves of the medieval village were created at very much the same time, but given that some elements of sequence can be found in the morphological analysis, we may be able to suggest that the process of drawing in the more subservient peasants on the eastern side was either a little earlier than the establishment of the *caslani* or conceived within a compound which held the *caslani* to be a little more externalised. The location of the *maleservi*, with their gardens, may be related also to the need to establish a workforce immediately adjacent to the demesne lands.

The third village (Figure 77)

After this there comes the part of the narrative which is almost certainly related to the modern era. In many ways it is a story of individual activity and bourgeois commercial life, but at the old core is still the agrarian peasant life and the seigneur.

The most obvious change is the addition of the modern Place on the uvula to the south of the church. This name appears first in the cadastre of 1531. This again shifts the focus of the community. New building happens on its east and

FIGURE 77. The third village
DRAWING: DAVID AUSTIN

left: FIGURE 78. The notaire's house
PHOTOGRAPH: ANTHONY LEWISON

right: FIGURE 79. The in-filled area at the castle gate
PHOTOGRAPH: DAVID AUSTIN

west sides, although not universally. There is, and remains, a large gap on the north-west side where there was the garden of perhaps the largest (a) of five big buildings (a–e) which were built into and across the old village plan. This was the property of the village *notaire* and in many ways symbolises the arrival of a professional and commercial middle class within the village, a phenomenon seen right across the region in the 16th and 17th centuries (Figures 76 & 78). Another of these houses (e), on La Rue de la Placette, uniquely among its neighbours, appears to have cleared away one or two previous house plots to create a shady enclosed and terraced garden in the Renaissance urban style which is still there.

The provision of the new open space also permitted the infilling of the old Placette (f) in front of the Château whose old gateway came, perhaps a little later, to be blocked by a cluster of buildings (g). This was matched by the infilling of the northern part of the old church enclosure (h), along La Rue la Boucherie, where there remained a small focus of shops and the common bread oven even as late as 1842 (Figure 79). The church enclosure was also further reduced by encroachment on the east side (i) by two small building cells and by the north-east corner of La Place which covers the old cemetery area (j). At this time, probably, burial began to be in the modern cemetery by the Chapelle de St Claude to the south-east of the historic village core (Figure 80).

FIGURE 80. Chapelle St Claude and its cemetery
PHOTOGRAPH: DAVID AUSTIN

La Place also acquired shops, notably the

oldest dated building in Cipières, (k; no. 203 on Figure 57), one of whose doors carries the legend 1573 and whose façade still has two large 'shop windows' (Figures 81 & 82). This may actually be the first building on this spot within the new village plan, and is consonant with the earliest reference to La Place in the documents that is in the cadastre for 1531.

Behind this building and the others on the east side of La Place, and integral to its planning, was a new block of gardens built on both new and old terraces (l). Perhaps, however, the most striking addition to the plan was La Bourgade and the area of *aires* known as Le Caire (Figure 83). La Bourgade itself was a completely new and narrow road which at its south-eastern end cut across the old terrace system and appears first in the cadastre of 1610. On the north-east side is what now appears to be a single row of buildings, constructed on a deeply-cut terrace, but which is probably two separate units, the larger to the north (m) and the smaller to the south (n) at the new entrance to the village. Both, however, had lanes giving back access to basements and to gardens, all built within the same design envelope.

top: FIGURE 81. Elevation of the shop front of 1573

above: FIGURE 82. The shop façade
PHOTOGRAPH: DAVID AUSTIN

On the south-west side of La Bourgade, the building cells are larger and have internalised access to back properties on terraces climbing up the hill behind. The southernmost of these units also contained an *aire* within its boundaries and this is also the only block of structures which significantly breaks the alignment of the old agrarian terrace system on this side of La Bourgade, suggesting it

FIGURE 83. La Bourgade and Le Caire
PHOTOGRAPH: DAVID AUSTIN

may be a slightly later addition, as on the other side of the street. The provision of *aires* within the village plan does seem to be a major part of this phase of development. On the western side of La Bourgade there are two very large *aires* on old terraces and three smaller ones, all of which look to be later and more individualistic units. This contrast in size and shape may suggest a difference in date or in class-constructed access (or both). It is entirely possible, in fact, that the two large terrace *aires*, which appear to carry the name 'Le Caire' in 1841, were the threshing floors of the medieval village before La Place and La Bourgade were added. In further support of this notion may be the appearance of four other of the smaller, more 'individualistic' *aires*, two each at the west

FIGURE 84. Detached house and *aire* at the west end of the village
PHOTOGRAPH: ANTHONY LEWISON

and east ends of the old village. Both sets are associated with further identifiable additions to the village plan, at the east end an extension to the row on the north side of La Rue du Coulet and at the west a small detached house (Figure 84).

This third village thus shows all the signs of extensive dynamic development in the modern era in response to the changes affecting the whole of the region within the broader European experience. There are signs of commercialisation in the shops and intensification of agrarian production in the massive addition of threshing capacity in the form of *aires*. With it comes a rural middle class in large houses and an expansion of population crowding into the compacted, extended and in-filled spaces and into a built environment of increasing elevation and sub-division. The zenith was the 18th century, albeit afflicted from time to time by the predations of transient armies and disease. Thereafter the long slow decline set in, which accelerated in the 20th century to leave it almost in terminal decline by the 1960s. Through the remarkable efforts of its communities, however, both new and old, this village has now revived and expanded well beyond its historic core and out into the surrounding countryside.

Conclusion

This narrative around three maps can, as I have stressed already, only be a framework within which the discussion of the village's social and economic complexity will be expressed. It is possible to interpret much of the narrative as one of organic and gradual growth or one of sudden and catastrophic change or a combination of both. Excavation might help, but the opportunity to dig on the scale needed is most unlikely and will reveal, I suspect, that too much has already been destroyed by the long-term processes of building production and social reproduction which still continue.

and what came before. First, however, we had to recognise that, within our limited resources, we could not hope to recover a total archaeology of the whole commune. Early on, we took the decision to focus on the upland topographies, most notably those of the Plateau de Calern. Here we felt the landscape features were at their most diverse, and we also knew from our extensive experience in British uplands that it was in these environments where we would find the most visible traces, the relics, of the ebb and flow of use and disuse which so characterise the archaeology of upland communities in Europe. Lower down, on the better land, the constant usage of the best land over a thousand years has obscured that process of change and is probably, as we see it now, largely an artefact of modernity, albeit with its morphological roots back in the Middle Ages. The memory of stone clearing and piling found in modern documents and ethnographic material in this region related almost entirely, in Cipières, only to the lowlands of the topography. Here the problems of identifying the past and of determining appropriate locations for our intervention are extreme, something which is also reflected in our experience of the optimal land on the valley floors in many parts of upland Britain.

Nevertheless, we hoped, even within this limitation, to attempt at least a landscape reconstruction of the large upland tract of the commune and to tie this to our documentary analysis to show how it all worked. Indeed, the early work of Anthony Lewison on maps and documents and those deceptively clear patterns on the air photographs suggested that this would be relatively straightforward. As we worked into the landscape, however, it was clear that simple transcription of the air photographs would not give us the results we needed to correlate the surviving remains with the historic maps and documents. It became clear early on, for example, that, although we could see the roads and dolines shown on the first cadastral map of 1842 (e.g. Figure 86), we could not trace with any ease the property-parcel or even, in some places, the *quartier* boundaries which gave the basic spatial units enabling us to connect our archaeological work to the written cadastres of the preceding centuries. We now, in hindsight, realise that this is because these boundaries were themselves not entirely stable and were potentially also likely to have been placed over the top of, and to have existed later than, a physical landscape which had been created under different ideas of use and access than those of modernity (See Chapters 7 and 8). Indeed we even believe that there was never any single and direct relationship between use and ownership for this vast area of the commune.

On the upland, therefore, we had to establish some basic critical understandings of what the various elements of the landscape might have meant and how they might have been created. What we also had to accept, and we have never been able to resolve this, is that the relic features we could see on the ground and in the photographs would be virtually impossible to date in absolute terms and would only reveal this through spatial relationships whether of pattern or of physical proximity. Even in our excavations, material useful

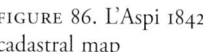

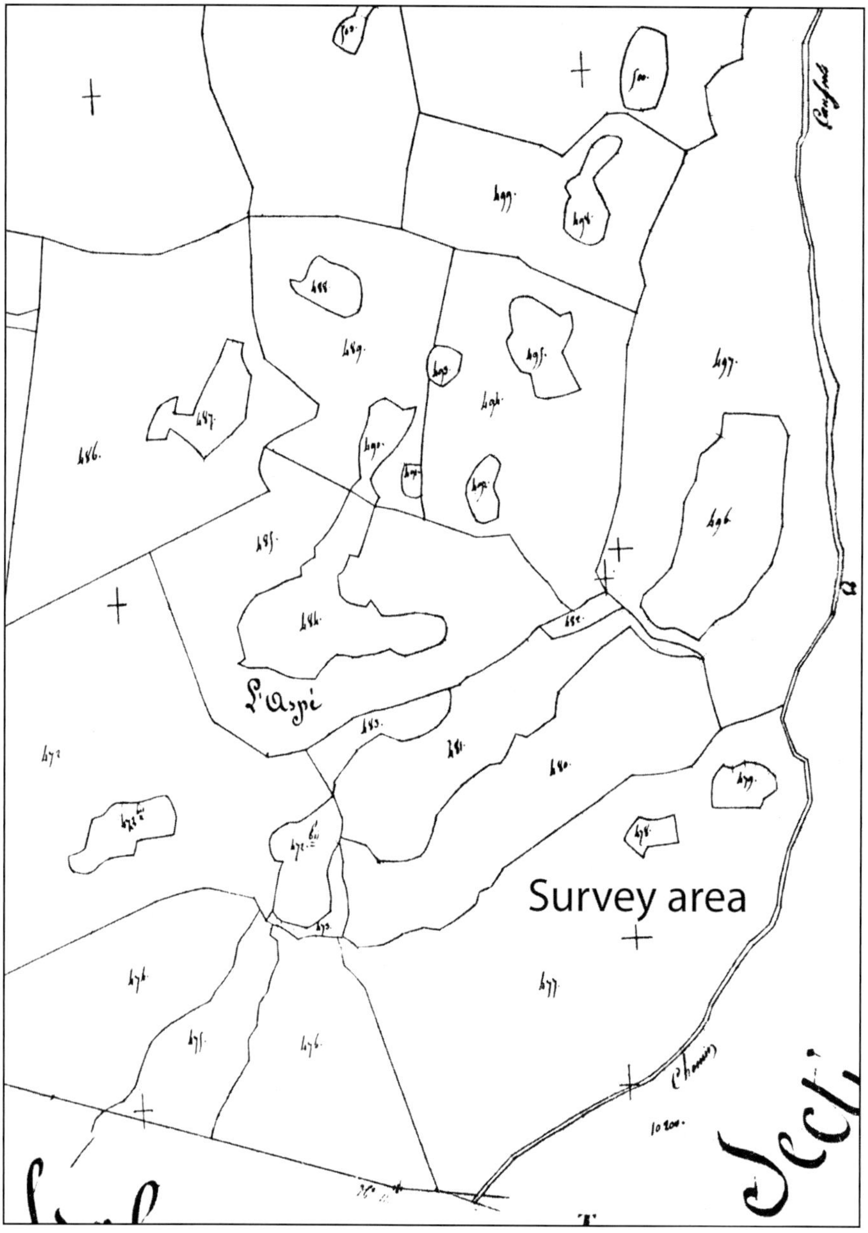

FIGURE 86. L'Aspi 1842 cadastral map

for radiocarbon dating was not collected because the shallow stratigraphies, the massive contamination by charcoal from the constant natural fires and the wide range of the standard deviations through the periods we were studying all meant that the results would have been deeply problematic and not worth the cost.

Our methodologies actually involved an intimate relationship with these individual elements of the landscape, so that we had to decide, for example, cairn by cairn, whether a pile of stones was really man-made or principally the result of weathering processes. Simply transcribing apparent cairns from the air photographs would have given a very false impression of land use: one more extensive than it actually was. This was more than simple 'ground-truthing' of air photographs. The air photographic images became underlays for us to navigate our way around these bewildering features and draw them onto surveys. Every other procedure, whether archaeological, botanical, pedological or documentary involved this kind of close relationship.

In specific terms we should define a little more closely what we intended and how we have set about doing it. First, there was the received understanding of the cultural forms we were seeing. It is difficult to begin any piece of work in a vacuum of objectivity and although little disciplined study and publication had taken place, it was received wisdom that most of what we saw was created by peasants of the *ancien regime* reacting to the population pressures of the 17th and 18th centuries and clearing ground to improve the quality of pastures and to undertake only small-scale grain and hay production in the more sheltered locations, especially the dolines. In other words the appearance of the cultural landscape could be explained by the dynamics of population, the economics of poverty and the archaeology of marginality. It also allowed little time-depth, although not everyone saw it this way, especially archaeologists like Jean Claude Poteur.[1] We came to feel that this view was based on a number of untested assumptions which seem to have been drawn, not from the totality of the landscape, but from economic history and studies of the architectural and spatial forms of settlement and occupation. What we have done is work from the very particular back into those wider pictures to re-examine some of the assumptions, Here our patterns of thinking began to find correspondence with the work of David Siddle and Rosamond Faith reported in Chapters 6 and 7.

Because we were building from the bottom up, stone by stone, person by person, we decided to be relatively selective and choose small areas that could be surveyed and examined in detail in single field seasons. This has had the advantage of completeness and also of allowing us to experiment with appropriate methodologies. It has had the disadvantage of not letting us see the whole picture, simply because we have not had the resource in the end to apply these methodologies systematically across the whole upland. Nevertheless we chose this path because we felt that any other way would have been too superficial and we have told ourselves that by the process of agglomeration the whole would emerge, at first as large speculative sketches of the frameworks of time and space, and then gradually, as we worked from place to place, the colours would be added and the forms given greater clarity and purpose.

Of course, we have been careful in selecting our survey areas to reflect the broad range of landscape types that we saw. In doing this we began by making selections within transect A picked by Anthony Lewison soon after he started to work in Cipières (see Preface). This was a kilometre wide and ran from north to south between the grid co-ordinates 968 and 969 shown on the IGN 1:25000 map 3642 Ouest and projected onto the IGN vertical air photograph (Figure

85). As such it ran at right-angles to the east–west grain of the topography and contained the majority of the western upland elements we have defined in Chapter 1. For those of us who came later to the project it had the added advantage of reconnaissance and research already done and a guide who knew his way around the terrain and the archive.

Within this transect, we selected two initial areas of study. The first (Figure 85, A) was land around two linked dolines on the relatively flat terrain of Les Poumeirès (zone III.6C) and near the southern edge of the commune, in the *quartier* called L'Aspi. The principal objective was to address the issue of how the agricultural features had been created and to begin thinking about the matter of date. The second (Figure 85, B) continued these basic objectives, but we chose a steep slope on the southern side (L'Hubac) of La Combe (zone III.2), partly because the visible features were at the other end of the spectrum of geomorphological and archaeological types to be found on the upland with large structures and one large area of good land on the valley floor, but also partly because we believed at the time, that this bottom land had once been held by the seigneurs of Cipières.

All of this work preceded our funding by the Regional Ministry of Culture which enabled us to start operating at a slightly larger scale and to undertake some excavation. For this reason we next chose two main field areas: the first (Figure 85, C) led principally by David Austin, a block of land within the Baoume de Brun *quartier* at the north end of Les Poumeirès (zone II.6C), focusing on a well-preserved *enclos* and *borie* (this chapter); and, the second (Figure 85, D, the area of Figure 223) led by Andrew Fleming, on an area in Les Baumes *quartier* at the east end of Le Plaine de Calern (zone III.6D) where one of the ancient long-distance roads to Caussols and its relationship to surrounding landscapes were examined (Chapters 4 & 10).

We should make it clear here that the archaeology was conducted in the context of a long-term, but episodic discussion with those who were working on the documents in the village archive as well as environmental scientists. In these discussions constant themes emerged which are relevant to the approach we took on the Plateau. First among these was the extent to which we could interpret the field remains as evidence of arable production or pasture. To this end the earliest work at L'Aspi was an attempt to see whether we could make the distinction. Once we were clear in our mind that arable was originally intended by most of the features we saw on the plateau top, (i.e there is little evidence of clearance for permanent pasture at the beginning) we then needed to discover how this conclusion would hold up in relation to better land at the base and edge of La Combe, a highly favoured and sheltered location on the upland which may have been a seigneurial possession. The issue then became: how was all this arable production managed at the same time as the undoubted use of the same terrain for pasture? (see Chapters 7 and 8 where it remains a thorny issue!)

Another important theme was chronology. The documents, of course, offered precision, but could we relate the sequences and social processes which were emerging in the analysis to the landscapes we were looking at? The answer is that we could not do so in any absolute sense, but soon we began to be able to record time depth and in La Combe, for the first time, we began to suspect that most of what we saw had their origins, if not also their termination, in a relatively early period, well before the readily accessible modern system of the 1842 map. This has been confirmed in Baoume de Brun and Les Baumes and indeed we became as convinced as we could be, using relative methodologies, that most of what we were recording belonged to the Middle Ages. This is also certainly supported by evidence presented in chapters using archival and historical evidence (Chapters 5–9)

Another theme that also emerged was the issue of property. As mentioned above, the archaeology of boundary was equivocal and apart from the major roads there was little ability to relate the lines on the 1842 map to the features on the ground. This, of course, confirmed our sense that much was far more ancient than the modern, but it then left us wondering what the land holdings of the early documents, especially those present in the 14th century, might have looked like and what was in them (Chapters 5–7). There were possible units of space to be found in the patterns of clearance and use we saw, but these could have been related to a variety of processes, most notably: swidden agriculture of small patches of ground undertaken by opportunistic individuals; sustained extensive episodes of planned expansion with many different families engaged in a collective enterprise; as well as systematic working and reworking within early defined property boundaries. Actually, as we have come to realise, none of these are mutually exclusive and we believe that we can see traces of all these.

Another issue is one of determinacy and indeterminacy. There is a temptation to discover simple or primal cause and effect in relation to the processes for which we are seeking evidence and explanation. We cannot necessarily agree on this, even as we write. Just as here I have stressed the volatility of boundaries and the overlay of processes at play, I found in the work on Baoume de Brun that much of what we were looking at was unrecorded human action which created physical patterns apparently unrelated to what the documents were telling us, let alone our interpretations, drawn from them, of cause and effect. For example, the notion of parcel and property so prominent in the official documents was not just largely invisible on the ground, but overwhelmed by the practicalities of work in a tough environment. So, the existence of a patch of cleared field, cut in two by a property division, was determined, not by social ownership, but by the exigencies of the micro-topography. It could have been created without reference to ownership and all its obligations which probably did not exist on the upland at this early time and then continued to be used as a partnership between neighbours. Some insights into the possible processes involved are presented later in the volume. On the other hand there was a clear sense in which the smaller, discrete dolines and some of the better fields, i.e. the very best land, lay at the centre of property units and were jealously preserved. There are clear indications of this in the relatively high tax values attributed to these areas in all the cadastral documents. So perhaps property in some senses was not a unitary concept, but was gradated out from the centre of a piece of land to its edges where it was more negotiable and volatile. As David Siddle shows there were also other aspects of volatility: the collective taxation values attached to particular *quartiers*, perhaps variable in size themselves, often changed dramatically from one cadastral date to another, especially on the plateau (Chapter 8). All of this rather suggests that we should be cautious about any sense of personal or even collective possession which modern usage of a word like 'property' might suggest. In a rural society such as Cipières it is perfectly possible for both understandings to exist alongside each other at the same time: one working with one's neighbours in the real world and the other in front of the seigneur or other tax officials whose perceptions were driven by top-down demands of render and obligation.

Similar thoughts could apply to the matter of status and class. As Rosamond Faith argues below (Chapter 5), the distinctions in the obligations of *maleservus* and *caslanus* are important. They had access to, and used, all the areas we studied in the field. In and around the village these distinctions may have meant something in terms of architecture, dress, custom, privilege and sentiment. They may have been physically visible, although little survives to help us for the Middle Ages. Out on the upland plateau, such distinctions were certainly not visible and may, there, have had less meaning than in the confines of the village. There is no evidence of class competition in the structures we were recording on the upland. Indeed, and again in the tough conditions, the pattern and practice of work, the 'workscape', was relatively uniform in similar micro-topographies. This is not to say that the plateau was a classless environment, but that in some aspects of people's lives the matter of class bore more heavily than in others. It was here that social mobility, ambition and opportunity jostled to improve the lot of the individual actor (or kin group/ostal) in the landscape. A good deal of this may have been associated with the hold of individual families and kin groups over sheep flocks as well as land. David Siddle argues (Chapter 8) that the hold of ostal groupings of kin which reflected itself in the holdings focussed in particular *quartiers* gradually broke down over the centuries within the dynamics of a growing land market, population change, inheritance and external politics. It is possible that earlier, once-discernible landscape characteristics, such as boundary markers, may have been blurred by increasing subdivision and individuation of land ownership and also by the developing dominance of pastoralism in the economy.

What were the types of features we thought we saw? Individually and in archaeological terms they could be reduced to some very simple categories, but when the variability of slope, soil and plants was added into the analysis this became complex. However, we have chosen, for the purposes of this narrative, to present the simple framework as a descriptive typology. We must, of course, issue the usual caveat that, at the edges of these taxonomic groups, one form shades into another and any one piece of landscape may have elements of them all. There are two criteria of typology: the individual visible structural features and the spaces between them filled with soil and plants which were created by the movement of stone. In the case of the former we have also adopted some flexible descriptive words which are about scale. We see these types and their descriptors, however, not primarily as reductionist tools, but essentially as elements of a usable vocabulary of things and a grammar of space deployed in the larger narrative of the community. We must also be clear that the typology correlates not with different systems of agriculture or crop production, but merely with terrain.

First are the individual **features**. The most obvious to the eye and the most abundant across the plateau are the **cairns**. As we use the term in this text, these are single, discrete piles of stones usually set on surface rock or a thin buried soil, ranging in size from **small** (Figures 15, foreground and Figure 108A), consisting of up to a few dozen boulders to **large** (Figure 173, left foreground), with many hundreds of stones of varying sizes and on up to **massive** heaps (Figure 8) which have had to be revetted to stop them spreading into the cleared areas. These latter are rare on the plateau, although there are some on Le Teil (zone II.4). They are much more frequently seen in the lowland areas of the commune particularly near the village. Cairns generally predominate in cairnfields and cleared fields, although they can also be found in association with all the other types of space. Some cairns also had spaces at the centre, suggesting that they had originally been built around the base of a shrub or tree which no longer existed.

A variation of this are the **linear cairns** (Figures 87 & 157) which have been laid out in relatively long lines and can be seen particularly in cairnfields on more steeply sloping topographies, following the direction of the jointing systems in the limestone. They were also used extensively to produce the proto-terraces. Rarely also they were markers of parcel boundaries, particularly where these ran downslope and across the line of terraces and proto-terraces, although this was usually only for short distances.

Stones from the clearance processes were also more formally consolidated into **revetment walls** (Figure 88), i.e. single-faced walls which retain the soil platforms of terraces and fields, and sometimes resolved also into being the edges of trackways (Figure 175). They can also be found holding back dumps of stone at the edges of dolines and uvulas to give the appearance of continuous walling when viewed from the floor of the doline itself. They are always dry-stone and can stand in some places over 3 metres high where the quality of building is as good as domestic architecture. Equally they can be as low as two courses of roughly stacked boulders.

Of similar dry-stone construction are the true **walls** (Figure 89) with two faces. These free-standing walls are very rare in the commune other than in the architecture of buildings and they are not a normal part of the cultural repertoire of agriculture in the region as a whole. This in itself has implications

87

88

89

90

91

92

93

FIGURE 87. Typology: linear cairns

FIGURE 88. Typology: revetment walls

FIGURE 89. Typology: walls

FIGURE 90. Typology: cairnfields

FIGURE 91. Typology: proto-terraces. Area of proto-terraces to the right inter-mixed with small terraces in the centre

FIGURE 92. Typology: dolines

FIGURE 93. Typology: doline cascades

PHOTOGRAPHS: DAVID AUSTIN

for the relationship between agricultural land and livestock. Animals must always have been closely tended in the enclosures (see below) or penned by temporary fencing.

These features, in a variety of combinations, delineated the **spaces** of land and land use which were the primary purpose of their existence. In the majority were the **cairnfields** (Figures 45, 90 & 101), areas where cairns are close together and the cleared ground lies between them. These can range from highly disciplined and regular arrangements of cairns to intermittent patches of clearance with cairns littered around in haphazard fashion. Perhaps the most striking examples of regularity are the long parallel lines on Le Calernet (II.6C) where the morphology strongly reflects the underlying beds of limestone (Figure 50). Some of these areas are very extensive and clearly stretched across many parcel (property) and even *quartier* (area) divisions without break or boundary. Others are much smaller and look like patches of ground broken by one family in one season of work.

Whereas the cairnfields look as if the cairns were cleared once and never moved again, the **field** areas seem to have their original clearance cairns moved to the edges of larger, open spaces uncluttered by these piles. Some of these areas are relatively **flat fields** (Figures 7, 8 & 44) fringed by cairns or revetment walls where the field is accommodating a gentle slope or is perched above a more severe drop in the terrain. There are more **sloped fields** (Figure 47) which have been cleared on the side of a slope, but one which is not steep enough to need terracing. They consist of relatively broad areas of soil which are retained by very low revetment walls. They are a common sight next to some of the dolines.

These sloped field forms shade off into **proto-terraces** (Figure 91) which are found on the steeper slopes where linear cairns have been used not just to liberate soil, but also to give some minimum protection against erosion. They are usually not very long, only up to five or six metres in length and have the visual effect of low benches. Subsequent solifluction has meant that their true size is often masked by soil and vegetation. Work in La Combe also shows that these were probably the antecedents of true **terraces** (Figure 42) with revetted dry-stone walls which are a common feature of lower slopes, gullies and valleys throughout the commune. As you move closer to the village from the plateau these become not just more frequent, but more massive, and more carefully designed and constructed. These have the appearance of large unitary terrace systems built on the grand scale by collective labour, but this may be deceptive, being rather constructed and reconstructed over very long periods of time to have the semblance of unity.

Although the terraces were important for cultivation, on the main plateau surfaces it was undoubtedly the discrete **dolines** (Figures 18, 92, 101 & 164) which provided the primary opportunity for arable production. These are depressions over collapsed karst features created by solution, some very deep and very large, others very modest. The floors of the dolines were usually flat, contained the best soils and richest vegetation, and after a storm there would be standing water for a

FIGURE 94. Typology: erosion surfaces
PHOTOGRAPH: DAVID AUSTIN

while. Revetment walls and large clearance cairns around their peripheries testify to how rigorously they were kept clear of stones. These also served to help keep animals penned into them while they dropped their precious manure. Closely related structurally to these discrete dolines are the larger areas of linked dolines, called **uvulas** (Figures 19 & 120), forming long valleys of very good land and here they shade off into the form of fields. These uvulas are never flat down their whole length and there are always differences in floor level which are marked and managed by revetment walls of varying heights. On the steeper slopes these have the characteristics of ornamental waterfalls or **doline cascades** (Figure 93) and at their steepest they can be simple terrace systems. All these forms showed extensive signs of constant reworking, probably over long periods of time.

Much of the activity we have just described is concerned with the attempt to create areas of soil in a rocky terrain and, having created it, then to keep it in one place. However, the processes of erosion by wind, frost and water were ferocious and it needed constant working to keep it under control. These same processes over the permable limestone also involved the constant leaching of organic nutrients out of the soil. This was always at its worst on steep slopes and where the stone used to create retaining walls was itself soft and friable, notably, on the plateau where the dolomite outcrops. These **erosion surfaces** (Figure 94) following cultivation left bare rock sometimes covered in scree, making it impossible for us to identify the former land use. Once all the types of cultural feature were recognised and recorded this left surprisingly few bare patches of **uncleared ground** (Figures 50 & 51) where nothing had happened to leave monuments behind. Even here, however, there must once have been clearance of vegetation, if not management of stone.

FIGURE 95. Typology: trackways: edging stones marking the course of the Chemin de Caussols between uncleared and cleared land in L'Aspi
PHOTOGRAPH: DAVID AUSTIN

FIGURE 96. Typology: *bergerie*
PHOTOGRAPH: DAVID AUSTIN

Lacing their way through all these traces of agriculture, there is an abundance of **trackways** (Figures 33, 37, 51, 95, 161, 162, 173, 175 & 176). These range from the well-constructed long-distance *chemins*, which are found on the earliest map of 1842 and can be identified easily from the air and on the ground, to more modest local paths which are to be found on the larger-scale *quartier* plans of the same date. There are also tracks which do not appear on the maps, some quite long-distance and structured and others just linking plots of ground together within the workscape. None of the tracks, of whatever kind, are consistently marked, especially over uncleared ground, but where they are it is in the form of lines of stone set on either side of a narrow worn track about the width of a mule with a rider on its back. Where these markers exist it is certain that there is some attempt being made to keep the beasts off growing crops.

Between all these traces of former agriculture are **buildings** of different sorts, most ruined, but with a few still functioning, notably the half dozen or so remnant ***bergeries*** associated with short-distance transhumance practices linked to larger units on the more lowland areas of the commune (see pp. 110–111 for discussion of dating and use). These structures on the plateau are referred to specifically in the documents from the 18th century onwards when we have clear reference to the economic significance of large capitalist flocks and the manure that could be collected from them when they were gathered together (Chapter 8). It is clear from the 1842 cadastral map that several were still in existence at that date, and from their plans and positions they are the structures which are readily identifiable as being the most recent buildings in the landscape (Figure 11). A few of them, indeed, are still being used. The most recent horizon of *bergeries* is constructed of mortared stone with pantiled roofs. A possibly earlier form, and these only exist now in a ruined state, had dry-stone walls and were not always certainly roofed with tiles. In plan on the upland landscapes, they are distinctive, usually with two adjacent rectangular buildings, one to house sheep and one to house the shepherd and his tackle, including oven and water cistern (Figure 96). The *bergeries* are often near and in association with unroofed enclosures, frequently ones which are, on architectural grounds, demonstrably earlier (Figure 97). Sometimes there was no covered building for the sheep, but only a shepherd's hut or ***cabane*** sited next to the open enclosure

FIGURE 97. Typology: *bergerie*
PHOTOGRAPH: ANDREW FLEMING

left: FIGURE 98. Typology: curvilinear enclosure
PHOTOGRAPH: ANDREW FLEMING

right: FIGURE 99. Typology: rectilinear enclosure
PHOTOGRAPH: DAVID AUSTIN

(Figure 89). Most are in, or very close to, dolines or uvulas and thus had access to the best grazing. The sheep could be provided with harvested water and stored fodder, and have shelter when needed. The *bergeries* also clearly, as they are today, related to the management of large flocks.

The **enclosures** are probably the direct predecessors of the *bergeries* in terms of function, although we must suppose some period of potential overlap. Architecturally many *bergeries* abut the earlier enclosures (Figure 97) and archaeologically there are a few cases of the decayed walls of enclosures being covered by later stone piles derived from continuing stone clearance. They are always of dry-stone construction and often, but not exclusively, they incorporate both corbelled and rough shelters. They seem never to have been roofed and some are built so that small cliffs form one or, exceptionally, two sides of the structure. In one or two places this has also involved a small rock shelter or cave entrance. In plan there are two distinct types, curvilinear (Figures 97 & 98) and rectangular (Figure 99), but there are enough hybrid examples to suggest that this may not be too meaningful, although the distribution might suggest an inner (i.e. closer to the village) group of early, broadly curvilinear forms and an outer group of rectilinear ones. Like the *bergeries* they are often found in close association with dolines, but not exclusively. Their high walls (up to 2 m high where they survive more or less intact) and fairly limited spaces suggest the management by peasant families of relatively small flocks of sheep and goats.

Archaeologically the remarkable **corbelled shelters** (*bories*) of the region have always drawn the most attention from scholars, and their ancient character the greatest speculation about their antiquity. Andrew Fleming discusses the dating and function of these structures at length in Chapter 10. They are circular in plan and dry-stone in structure with corbelled roofs high enough to permit a person to stand in the centre (Figure 100). The corbels are set to slope downwards and

FIGURE 100. Typology: *borie*
PHOTOGRAPH: ANDREW FLEMING

outwards which functionally makes rainwater flow off the buildings, so keeping the interiors dry. The walls themselves are usually not much more than a metre high and since the entrance is beneath a lintel set at wall top below the springing of the corbel, it means that anyone entering must stoop if not crawl. There are some variations in overall size of these shelters, but this offers little grounds for typological distinction. Some also have small internal shelves or niches built into the fabric of the walls, presumably to keep food out of the reach of rodents. A minority of these shelters still have intact roofs and there are signs in a few of them that they have continued to be maintained by modern shepherds needing protection from the violent storms and this surely must have been a function when flocks totalling over 20,000 animals were managed over the landscape (Chapter 8). Indeed having experienced the terrifying ferocity of one of these storms on the plateau, I can personally assert that their function as highly effective Faraday cages must have been their primary purpose. Some shelters stand alone in the landscape while others are incorporated into enclosures or the walls of dolines and large terraces. Their distribution is general, widespread and even, presumably, to provide relatively quick access to shelter from sudden storms for those working in these remote landscapes.

Apart from these formal and easily identified structures, there are many other instances where **rough shelters** have been made, often utilising rock features, such as deep clefts, small cliff faces, rock overhangs and cave entrances. It is not always possible in the field to distinguish between a chance placing of a large cairn and the collapse of a deliberately built wall for a shelter. However, once our eyes became attuned to the monuments we were seeing it did become possible to make the distinction with some degree of certainty in most cases. Their primitive nature and almost universal decay does suggest to us that they are a very ancient aspect of the landscape, but equally there were places where such things were built into doline walls and may have been maintained until relatively recently.

Perhaps the most fugitive of all the architectures we attempted to record were the bewildering array of suggestive circles and rectangles of piled stone which would appear in small clusters among otherwise ordinary cairnfields. Here it was not always easy to be convinced that we were looking at things with architectural meaning and Andrew Fleming and I did not agree that they were architectural. Some were probably, as indicated above, arrangements around former trees or bushes. In some places, however, these shapes seemed to be more than accidental heaps determined by underlying geology, geomorphology or even ecology. This impression was strengthened by their more frequent occurrence and more emphatic form in Andrew Fleming's work in Les Baumes (Chapter 4) and it may be that here, further out from the village these potentially earlier forms have survived later reshaping. They do not, however, feature in my typology.

There were also on the Plateau, as in the village and across the whole commune, several ***aires***, or threshing floors (Figure 98, to the left of the enclosure). Characteristically they were usually close to enclosures and using locations which would readily allow the wind to pick up the chaff and blow it away. They were both curvilinear and rectangular in form and about 15–20 m^2 in extent. Their floors were edged and paved with limestone cobbling which show signs of wear. Occasionally also they were slightly raised by the provision of revetment walling on the more steeply sloping sites to give relatively flat platforms.

We deployed these typologies in the surveys making field drawings on which we logged the occurrence of the different types. This, in fact, helped us to refine the typology itself which only finally emerged in the subsequent large survey at Baoume de Brun. In the first two surveys, we were a little over-elaborate and we failed really to distinguish between the features themselves and the spaces which resulted. We have, however, returned to these original surveys and applied the final criteria as outlined above for the sake of producing a coherent account.

3.2. The Linked Dolines in L'Aspi

The two linked dolines (Figure 101), numbered 163 (western) and 153 (eastern) in the recording, lie within the *quartier* called L'Aspi in 1842 and at the southern and upper end of the fault valley of Les Poumeirès (zone II.6C). We chose them and the size of the study area on four criteria: physically they were single discrete topographic units; we could readily identify the hydrological and solifluction catchment of the two dolines; they were at the core of a whole property parcel as it was documented on the 1842 cadastral map; and it was what we could complete in the two weeks of fieldwork we were able to undertake. Our methodology was the survey of man-made features, using air photographs as described above, and small-scale intervention to explore the sub-surface characteristics of the visible remains of agriculture, together with studies by Hepper and Crowther of the modern plant communities and the pedology.

The survey result shown in Figure 102 had several key characteristics which we used to identify our sample locations. At the heart of it were the two intensively worked dolines (surveyed in more detail in Figure 103) almost entirely enclosed by revetment walls up to 1.5 m high which retained large dumps of small stones. In the base of the dolines the vegetation today is predominantly a closed meadowland habitat with a rich growth of various grass species and some legumes such as vetches, clovers and sainfoin and occasional occurrence of lady's bedstraw and other plateau plants such as thyme,

FIGURE 101. L'Aspi: the linked dolines
PHOTOGRAPH: DAVID AUSTIN

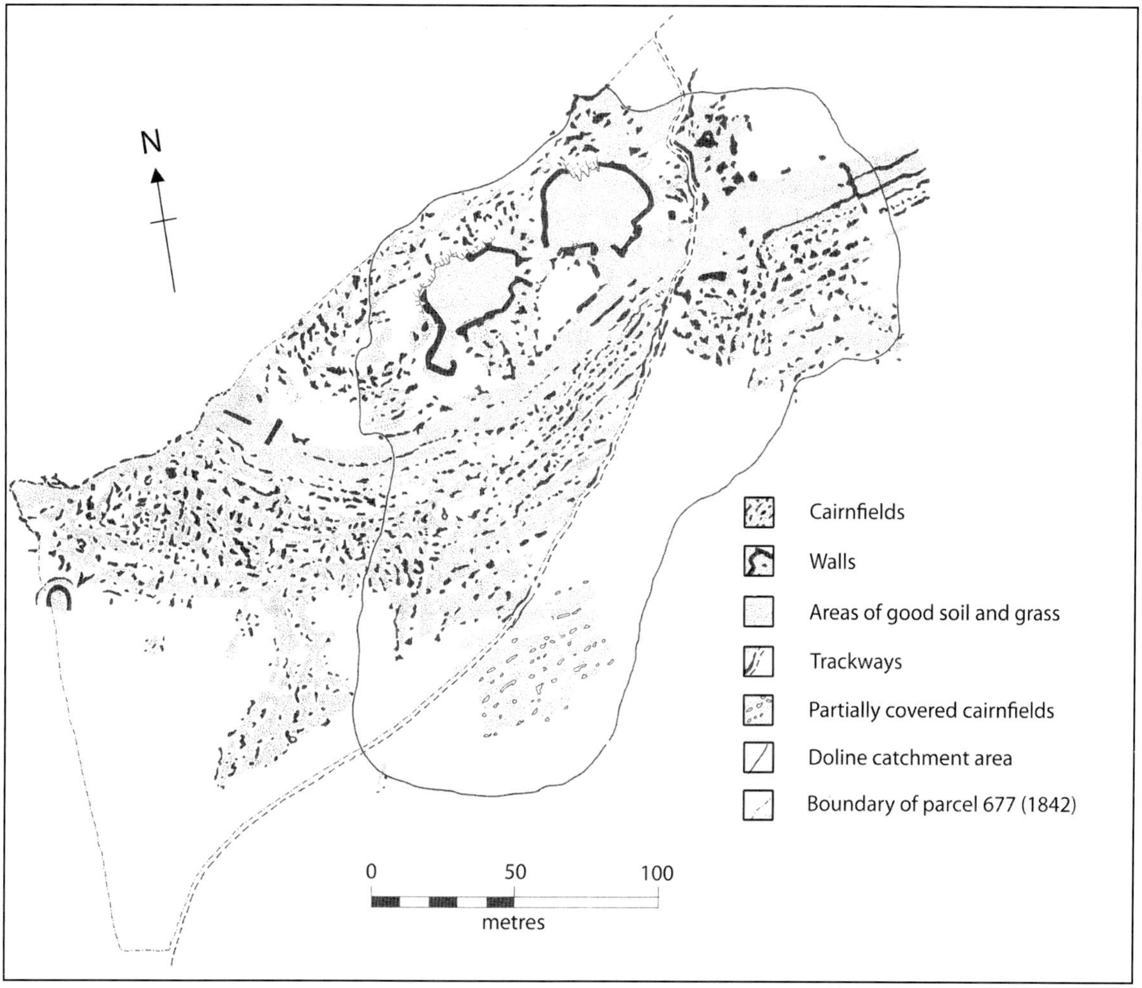

FIGURE 102. L'Aspi: survey
DRAWING: DAVID AUSTIN

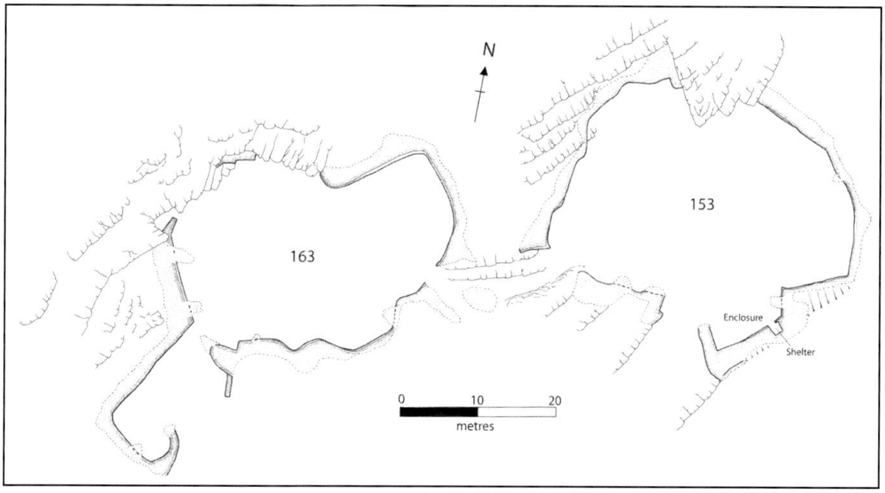

FIGURE 103. L'Aspi: survey of the two dolines
DRAWING: DAVID AUSTIN

St John's wort and small perennials.[2] It was clear, however, that whatever plant regimes through cultivation had existed in the past on the doline floor, they had left no botanical memory in the modern plant colonies. The sediments which support these plants are deep and represent a series of colluvial deposits laid down by steady water erosion as well as seasonal and episodic flooding of the doline floors through major storm events and spring thaw which brought soils down from the surrounding slopes. These highly valued floors were also easy to keep clear of stone after the erosion episodes, as the stone walls and piles of stone behind them would seem to attest. The sediments are particularly stone-free almost down to bedrock.[3] In the southern corner of the western doline, where the slope was the most gentle, the revetment wall deviated to produce the partial outline of what must have been an enclosure. It looked incomplete because its eastern side, the main access point, seems never to have been built. The reason for this we judged to be either that it was never finished or that the open side was originally closed by hurdles or moveable fence. The latter interpretation is reinforced by the existence of a similar open-sided rectangular enclosure in the other doline. This also incorporated a tiny roofless rough shelter, just big enough to crouch in under the protection of a cape.

The dolines lay at the northern foot of a dip slope which curved gently around them, and here the limestone bedded at about the same angle of incline as the slope itself. To the north of this was a narrow craggy scarp separating this area from the prominent uvula which formed the spine of the major fault of the Les Poumerés topography. Clearly the contortions of the surveyed area and the formation of the dolines themselves had resulted from this same fault zone. After clearance and the various farming regimes we were studying we could define seven microtopographical zones (Figure 104):

1. the dolines themselves;
2. the scarp top – heavy cairns on very broken ground of small crags and pavements with intermittent patches of good soil, sometimes perched;
3. the doline sides – medium-sized cairns in small cairnfields laid out in fairly regular patterns on the doline sides which were slightly steeper than the rest of the dip slope;
4. the bench – cleared fields with a predominance of linear cairns especially at the eastern end, while the rest, along the southern edge of the dolines, formed a narrower but longer field split by linear cairns which gave the impression of an unfinished cleared field just emerging from a previous cairnfield;
5. the dip slope cairnfields – these could be sub-divided into clearly defined blocks (a–i), some very regular, some irregular. The divisions between the blocks were marked by downslope linear cairns and clear strips of soil. These cairnfields were concentrated on the lower parts of the slope;
6. the ancient field – one regular group of heavily-overgrown cairns on the upper slope, forming a discrete patch;
7. the uncleared dip slope – the upper parts of the slope were substantially featureless apart from a significant but much overgrown patch of cairns which was cut by the long-distance track from Cipières to Caussols crossing the area;

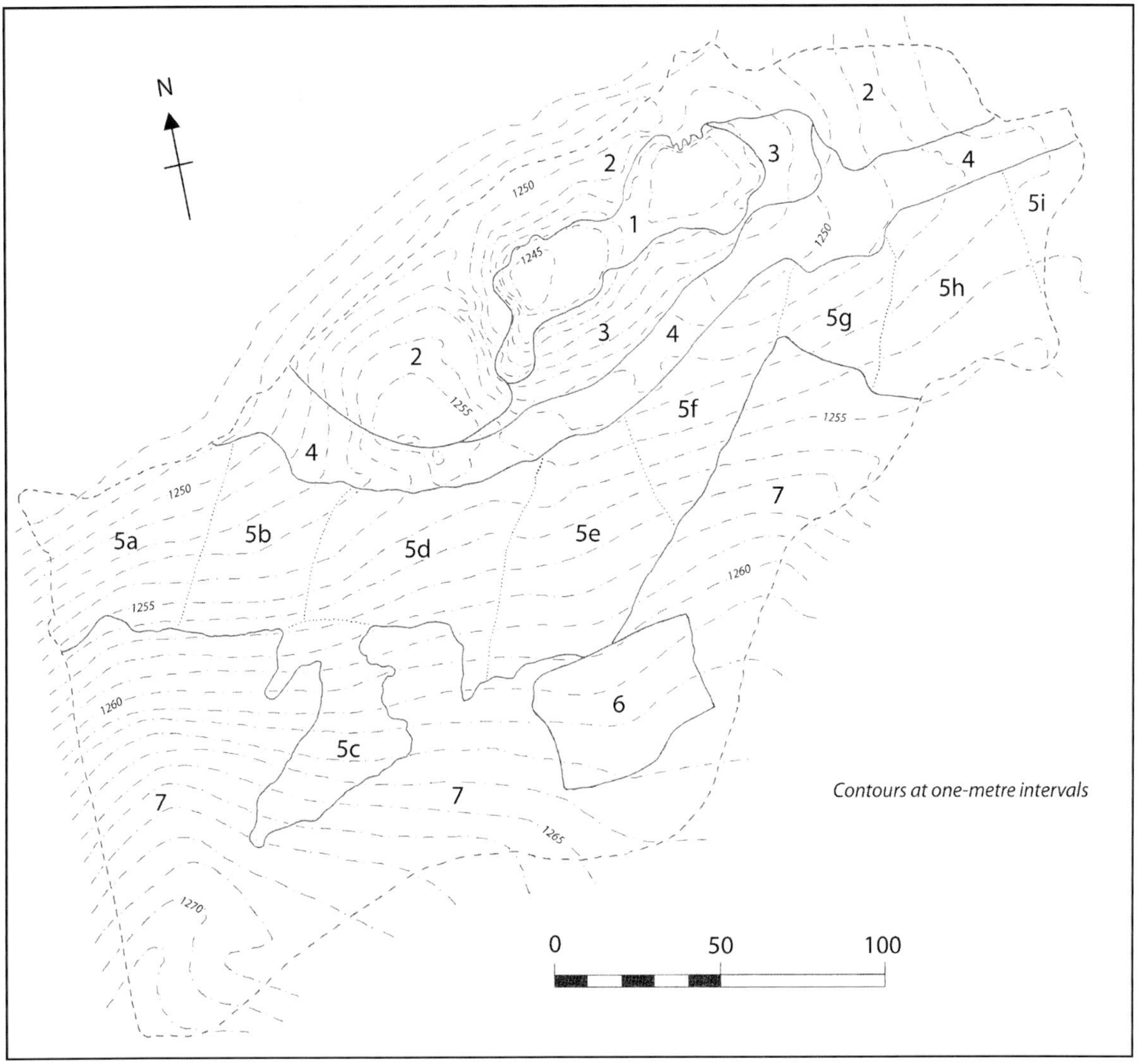

FIGURE 104. L'Aspi: topographic zones
DRAWING: DAVID AUSTIN

8. (Not shown on Figure 104) the Chemin de Caussols was clearly marked along its length by linear cairns and substantial hollowing. It appeared also to have stratigraphic relationships with the spaces defined above. For example, it clearly cut across the eastern part of the cleared field on a slight terrace, but it formed a boundary between a cairnfield and uncleared ground just to the south of this, where significantly the two areas were geomorphologically identical and provided the same opportunity for agriculture. Since the track was also the boundary of the parcel, this was a rare instance of the parcels being reflected in the underlying agrarian spaces. Just to the south of this again, the track palpably cut across the decayed cairnfield. The implications of this stratigraphy will be discussed later, but certainly as delineated in the landscape today, the road was a relatively recent feature. This conclusion, it should be noted, conflicts with the arguments made for the same road by Andrew Fleming in Chapter 4.

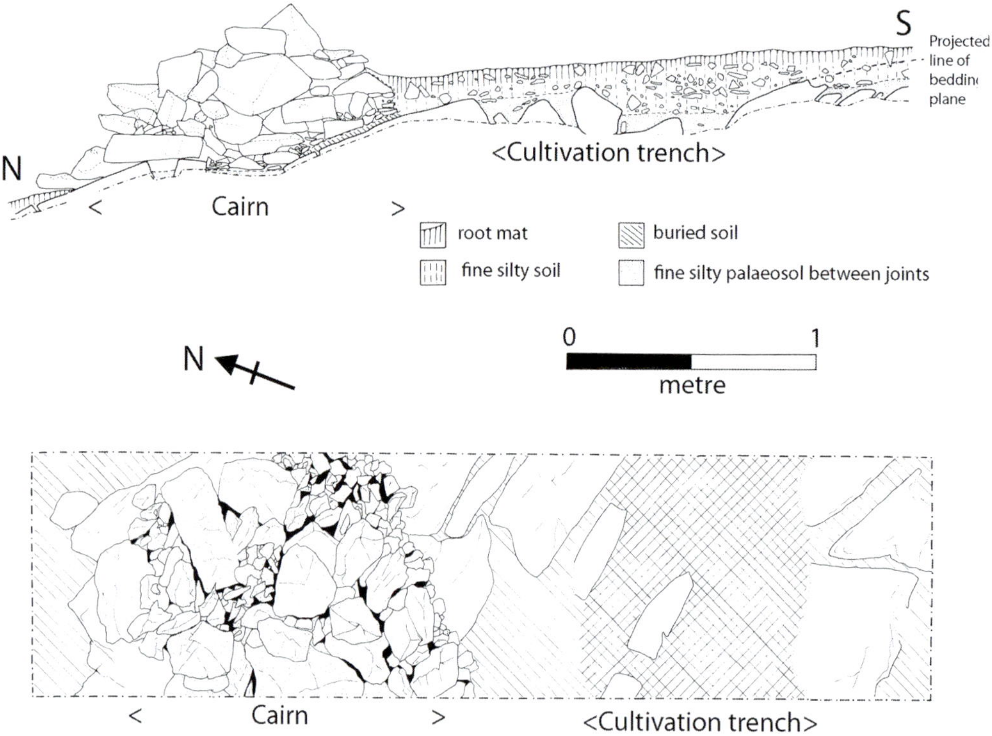

FIGURE 105. L'Aspi: trench 163D
DRAWING: DAVID AUSTIN

FIGURE 106. L'Aspi: Trench 163D (with cairn): A. With soil in cultivation trench L'Aspi B. L'Aspi: Trench 163D (with cairn). With soil removed from cultivation trench and showing section
PHOTOGRAPHS: DAVID AUSTIN

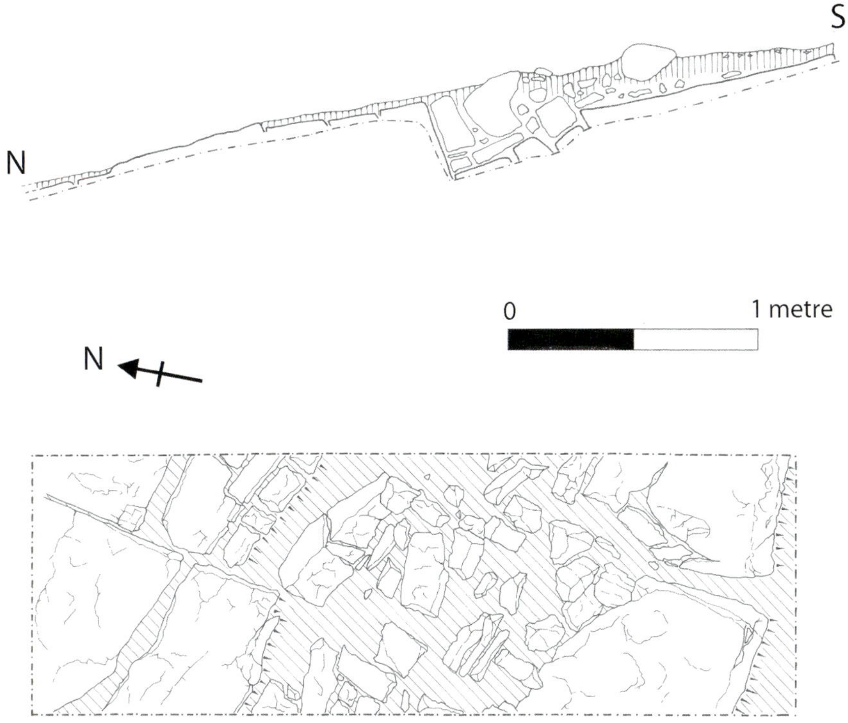

FIGURE 107. L'Aspi: trench 163C
DRAWING: DAVID AUSTIN

FIGURE 108. L'Aspi: Trench 163C (without cairn): A. Showing natural stone in bedding joint not removed; B. Showing natural stones removed by excavators to demonstrate the process of cultivation trench creation
PHOTOGRAPHS: DAVID AUSTIN

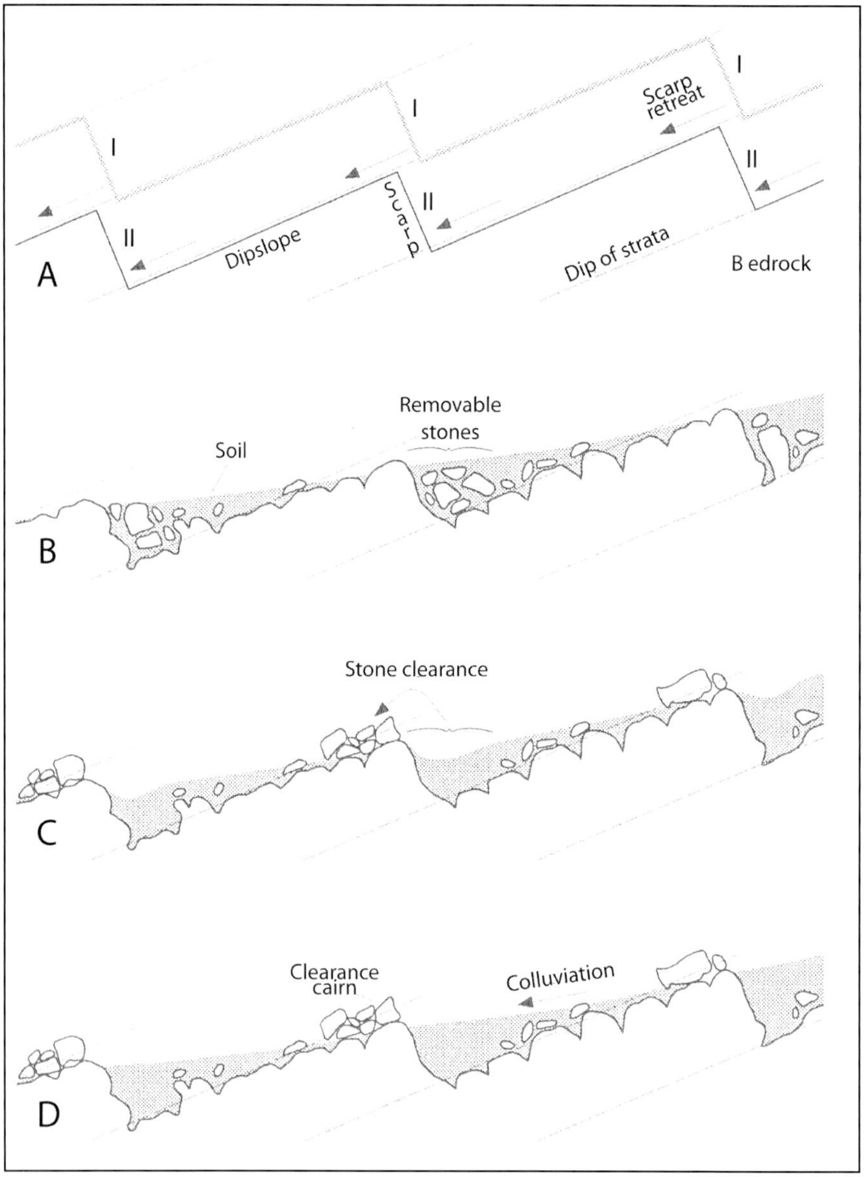

FIGURE 109. L'Aspi: geomorphological model of cultivation trench formation
DRAWING: JOHN CROWTHER

As discussed above, our first necessity was to establish how the extensive areas of cairns could be interpreted; especially of what processes were they the remains? We were also concerned to understand the physical characteristics of the very important dolines. In the case of the cairns we used the circumstance of the cairnfield on the dip slope (Figure 104, 5) where it was edged by the Chemin de Caussols (Figure 95). Here we could excavate, for comparative purposes, both a cairn with its associated space and an adjacent uncleared piece of ground (Figure 104, 7) which shared the same topographical and geomorphological characteristics. The trench within the cairnfield (163D) was designed to provide a section of the cairn and to cross the space upslope between it and the next cairn (Figures 105 & 106). The trench outside the cairnfield (163C) was selected to cross the same bedding joint as the excavated cairn lay on (Figures 107 & 108). In archaeological terms, the results were straightforward. In 163D the cairn of loose boulders surrounded by air pockets lay over a thin buried soil. Upslope there were two soil levels below the vegetation mat: the upper was full of small stones and was retained as a slight terrace behind the cairn; the lower was a dark soil in a shallow trench from which boulders, almost certainly those forming the cairn, had been prised out of a bedding joint in the limestone. This trench was clearly visible in plan and the top of it can be seen in Figure 108A, while Figure 108B shows the section with the cultivation soil removed. By contrast, in 163C there was no trench and the bedding joint was filled with boulders weathered from the parent rock on either side, as can be seen in Figure 108A. During the excavation we removed the natural stones to simulate the process of creating the cultivation trench and the result can be seen in Figure 108B. This evidence together with detailed soil analysis permitted John Crowther to create a formation model, expressed in the form of a diagram (Figure 109), for cairns and their related trenches, part caused by human action, part by natural process.[4]

From all the evidence accumulated in this programme of survey, excavation and sampling, it was possible to be convinced that a very extensive area had been cleared for cultivation as cairnfields which were the visible remains of strip trenches created, systematically and extensively, out of the natural limestone topography. Elsewhere there were broader fields where the ground was flatter and the cairns could be pushed further apart. At the centre there was the prized land of the dolines whose soils were deep but leached, highly compressed and almost totally cleared of stones by constant effort after the plough. How frequently they had been cultivated is hard to determine, but the answer could vary from very few in the case of the fields of smaller cairns and to almost every year in the case of the dolines (with their ready access to manuring).

3.3. La Combe

La Combe is a long uvula at the southern base of the Gros Pounch ridge and was a major east–west routeway through the Cipières upland as well as its richest piece of agricultural land (Figures 1, 110 & 111). Our work was on the south side (L'Hubac) where the techniques of survey and recording were much the same as in L'Aspi, but were made difficult by the dense growths of pine which were beginning to blanket the slopes in this area. This slowed down the process of survey and we decided to concentrate on the lower slope where the main features clustered (Figures 112 & 113). This meant that we were unable, in this instance, to examine a whole 1842 parcel. The selection, therefore, was primarily on topographical grounds, lying as it did between the floor of La Combe to the north, dry stream gullies on the east and west and the north-facing slope to the south (L'Adrech de la Combe). It allowed us this time, however, to examine the formation processes on steep slopes and what we imagined to be the soil reservoir of La Combe itself where we hoped for deep stratigraphy. In typological terms we looked at terraces, proto-terraces and cairnfields on the southern slope and a large cleared uvula, La Combe itself, at the base.

Thus, of the three microtopographical zones in this area, the south-facing north slope (l'hubac), the north-facing south slope (l'adrech) and the floor, we only surveyed two. Arguably there was also another zone, a slight bench at the base of the south slope, but this was so masked and altered by a recent vehicle track along it, that we could not be certain what was geomorphology and what was modern disruption. We were, however, just able to detect, at the western end, that the older, long-distance track from Cipières to Andon had run along this slight bench on exactly the same alignment as the more recent one. As far as we could tell this was fully integrated with the terracing system through which it passed.

In terms of features and spaces, the floor of La Combe was completely flat and almost entirely featureless apart from a low earthen bank which ran north–south from one edge of La Combe to the other. On the southern edge of the floor, just at the very base of the slope, were lines of cairns partially overgrown and with some recently eroding soil. These paled in size, however, alongside a massive heap of stones, again partially overgrown, at the bottom of the eastern stream gully. In part this was formed by storm surges of surface water bringing boulders down the eroding bed of the stream and choking a large sink-hole or cave. In part, however, it was clearly also the destination of countless baskets of stone gleaned from the surface of La Combe down the centuries.

On the slope there were three, possibly four, main zones of features and

left: FIGURE 110. La Combe: IGN vertical air photograph of context for survey area

AIR PHOTOGRAPH REPRODUCED BY KIND PERMISSION OF THE IGN; DRAWING: DAVID AUSTIN

above: FIGURE 111. The base of La Combe viewing north from the survey area

PHOTOGRAPH: DAVID AUSTIN

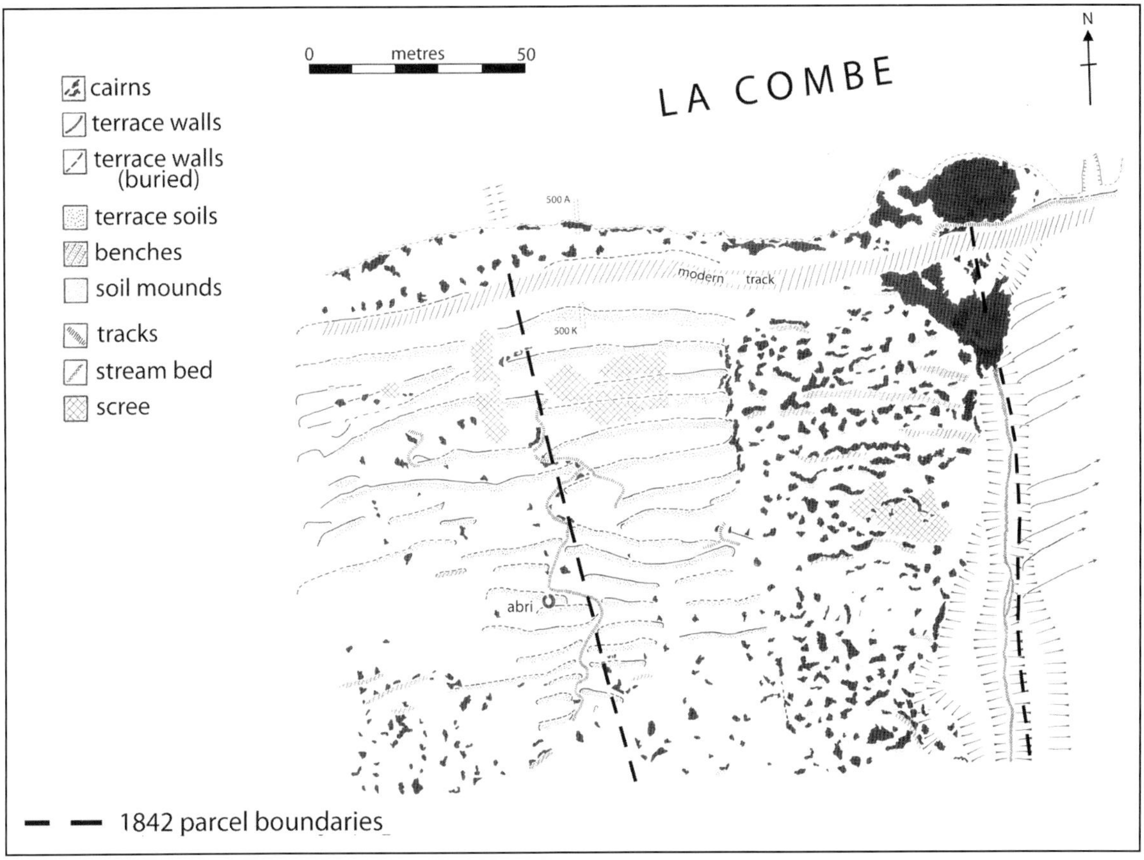

FIGURE 112. La Combe: survey B
DRAWING: DAVID AUSTIN

FIGURE 113. La Combe: IGN vertical air photograph of survey area
AIR PHOTOGRAPH REPRODUCED BY KIND PERMISSION OF THE IGN

spaces, all affected by eroding screes of varying extents. To the east there was an extensive cairnfield, incorporating proto-terraces, particularly towards the bottom of the slope. West of this, and the other side of a line of marker cairns, were much-decayed terraces retained by low revetment walls through which, and clearly integral with them, zig-zagged a narrow path up to and beyond a ruined corbelled shelter. West of this path the terraces seemed to be less abundant and well-structured with a tendency for them to be more like proto-terraces. Southwards, up the slope, the terraces petered out into a rather ragged cairnfield. Here in one relatively small piece of ground we could see all three methods of coping with the cultivation of fairly steep sloping ground.

We have interpreted the very sharp distinctions, first, as indicating three different work areas, probably parcels of some kind, where, in contrast to other parts of the plateau, we can see clear attempts at demarcation and sharp distinction between the effort of one 'owner' and another. This is important when we introduce our knowledge derived from documentation (see below). Secondly we have interpreted the distinctions we have seen, not as different approaches by different people at much the same time, but as the remnants of a sequence: the first efforts at clearance (cairnfields) to create short lengths of trench for cultivation; subsequent further clearance and creation of linear cairns as proto-terraces to retain the soil more effectively in long trenches; and finally the assembly of these cairns into revetted, true terraces. This sequence appears to be confirmed by the excavation of one of the terraces (see below: 500K) This interpretation suggests that those who worked these patches (or parcels) of ground had different strategies of effort over time, some not doing much after initial clearance, some attempting at least preliminary consolidation of the cairnfields, some investing a lot of labour to produce true terraces, and all not doing much toward the top of the slope where it was steeper and harder of access. What this might also suggest is that the initial episode of clearing to create cairnfields was a large, possibly collective, effort, ambitiously across the whole slope, after which the area was sub-divided into units where then individual action produced the ultimate differentiation we could show in the survey.

As before we then sampled and sectioned this area, focussing in particular on the formation processes of the terraces and the valley bottom. A deep trench through the floor of, and at right angles to, La Combe (500A) and across one of its peripheral cairns was cut by machine (Figure 114), and a little further upslope we hand-dug a trench through a terrace (500K; Figure 115).

The archaeological sequence of the floor is best seen in the section diagram for 500A (Figure 116) and in the soil analysis profile (Figure 117). Reading from top to bottom, we are suggesting that the surveyed cairn (8) was a relatively recent creation and was incorporated within the present cultivation horizon represented by the humic topsoil and turf (1). Below this was a layer of dark brown and highly compacted silty soils (2), no more than 200 mm deep at the top of the slope, but deepening steadily towards the centre of La Combe to just over 2 m at the northern limit of the excavation. Since this was only 5 m into

left: FIGURE 114. La Combe: Trench 500A cut by machine through the floor of La Combe
PHOTOGRAPH: DAVID AUSTIN

right: FIGURE 115. La Combe: Trench 500K cut through a terrace
PHOTOGRAPH: DAVID AUSTIN

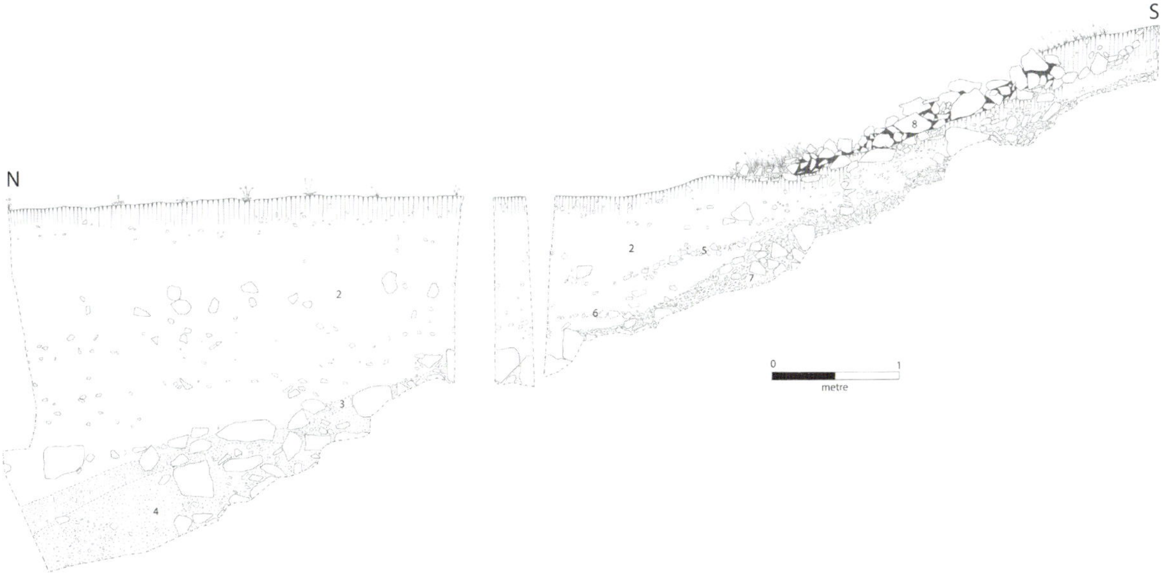

FIGURE 116. La Combe: section of trench 500A
DRAWING: DAVID AUSTIN

La Combe which was in turn about 30 m wide at this point, and since the rate of increase in the depth remained steady throughout the section, we should imagine that this deposit must be very substantial near the centre. Although archaeologically there was little visible differentiation in this deposit, two lines of stone (5 & 6) did indicate the faint presence of previous surface horizons where stone may have trickled into La Combe as part of erosion. Apart from its depth the other striking visual characteristic of this deposit was how stone-

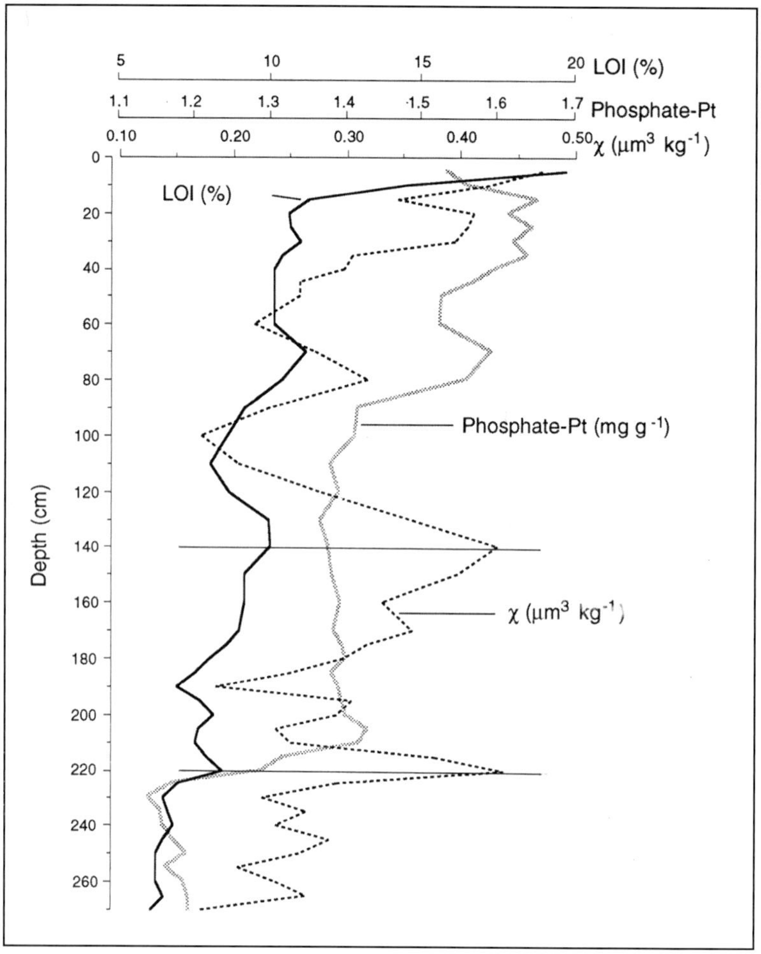

FIGURE 117. La Combe: interpretative soil diagram of 500A
DRAWING: JOHN CROWTHER

free it was, as in the case of the L'Aspi dolines, apart from a small area towards the top of the slope. Given that this deposit must have been largely due to soil in-wash from the slopes, we were forced to ask: where had all the stone gone?

Underlying all of this was a heavy red to yellowy–red clay with boulders (4) which was sealed by a horizon (3) transitional in colour and texture between the clay below and the silty soils above. Further up the slope this clay and its horizon contained a much higher proportion of small scree-like pebbles and stones. From its consistent angle of rest and its characteristics we took this to be the periglacial subsoils over which the primary climax vegetations would have formed with all deposits above falling in the periods of anthropogenic influence.[5]

It might have been easy to assume that this great depth of deposit in the floor of La Combe, as in L'Aspi, was created by anthropogenic intervention, but this is unlikely and the soil science does rather suggest that much had occurred before the Holocene with the historic periods of the last millennium represented only by the upper parts of the section. However, the lack of dating material can carry us little beyond this general observation.

Just as the deep deposits of La Combe paid handsome stratigraphic dividends, so also did the shallower section of the terrace (Figure 118). This can be interpreted as having four clear phases:

(I) At base there was a shallow trench (7) cut into a deposit of frost-shattered and eroded bedrock and running along the slope on the same alignment as the terrace.

(II) Almost completely sealing this were two layers of browny–red silty loams which looked like the A and B horizons of a buried soil and were associated with a pile of small boulders and stones (10) probably the remnants of a linear cairn.

(III) This was revetted and raised by the addition of a dry-stone wall (4), behind which deep deposits of brown silty soils had had been placed to form the main body of the terrace. The terrace wall also sealed a thin layer of soil (3) which might have been a former ground surface.

(IV) Above this was the turf and topsoil of the modern ground surface covered in one place by a shallow line of scree coming down this actively eroding slope.

In archaeological terms (I) might be interpreted as the first agricultural intrusion into the post-glacial terrain, perhaps in a cairnfield. This was followed by (II) the reorganisation into a proto-terrace of linear cairn and raised soils. Finally it was all made into a low-walled terrace. If this was the evolution of the currently visible features, it is also possible to speculate that the cairns and proto-terraces at the east end of the surveyed area were a patch of phase II ground not made into terraces.

From the documentary sources we can add one further element to the stratigraphy of the surveyed area. It is clear from our archaeological analysis that the last definable agricultural event was the creation of the terraces over the western two-thirds of the survey area. The eastern edge of this was clearly marked by a series of terminal cairns running from north to south up the slope and the whole work unit or parcel was defined by the terrace area itself. It is one of the clearest plot boundaries and 'property parcels' seen in our work on the plateau. Yet when we look at the cadastral map of 1842 where there is also a single boundary shown, it does not follow the cairn alignment, but cuts across the middle of the terrace area (Figure 112). If we pursue these parcels back in time the same basic division exists in 1792 and 1727, but all of it appears to have been just one holding in 1640. This suggests that at no time in the cadastral record was there a moment when the archaeologically detectable boundary could have served any purpose, nor could the parcel have existed in the form it does on the ground. We are forced to the conclusion that it must have been created before the 17th century and most likely at some point in the Middle Ages. This strongly suggests also that the two sequences observed in 500A and 500K are medieval and earlier. In particular the last phase of soil stability in La Combe must have been the result of terrace-building, probably in the Middle Ages. During most of modernity, therefore, there must have been gradual decay, erosion, soil creep and scree formation as we observed during the survey.

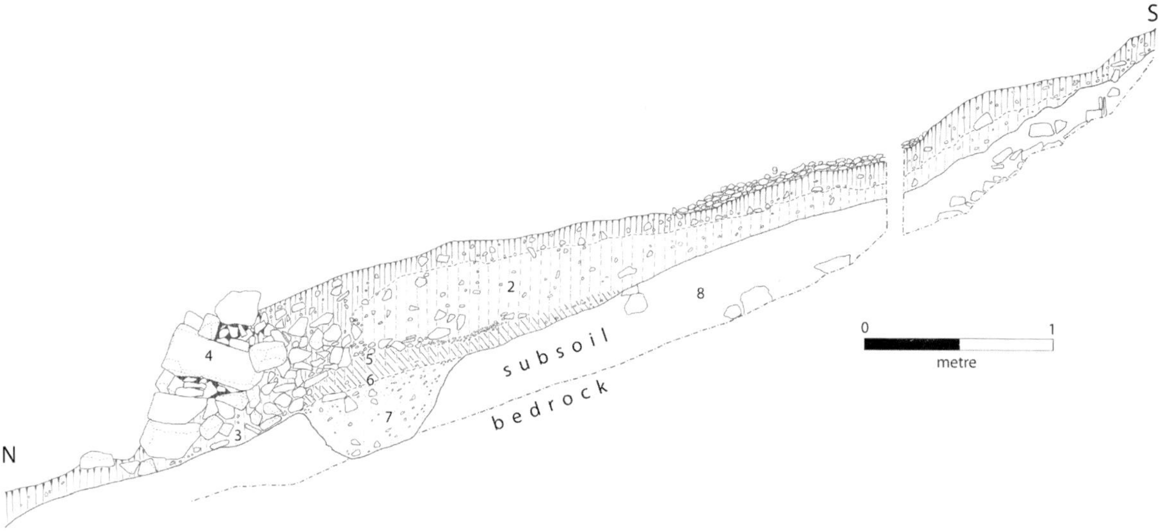

FIGURE 118. La Combe: section of trench 500K
DRAWING: DAVID AUSTIN

Once we had finished the work in La Combe, we were ready to move to a much more ambitious endeavour in Baoume de Brun and along the Caussols road. We were, by now, becoming more convinced that the relic landscape of the plateau was essentially later medieval in character. It was, in effect, one system which had been, in some places, constantly (whether continuously or episodically we cannot tell) worked and reworked to create a layering effect, and in some places had been cleared once and not used again in any significant way. In other words the archaeology of this upland margin was doing exactly what we hoped it would do: it was displaying depth of time, because the human effort was intermittent and highly variable at the extreme. We were also sure that, before the opening of the Middle Ages in the 8th–10th centuries, there was little, if anything, archaeological to signal that there had been a system of clearance, fields or terraces as its predecessor. The feeling was growing that the plateau at least had been *terre gaste*, at best rough grazing, before the processes of farm creation and *incastellamento* really got going in the 11th and 12th centuries (see Chapter 5)

3.4. Baoume de Brun

Introduction

In 1993 and 1994 we used the same techniques of survey we had devised in previous years, to map the stone piles, architecture and soils of a whole *quartier*, La Baoume de Brun, as it was shown on the cadastral map of 1842 (Figures 119 & 120) and on recent air photographs (Figure 121). Our intention was to capture on plan the exploitation and landscape of one complete unit of land, containing several parcels as it was known to the farmers of the 18th and 19th

opposite: FIGURE 119. Baoume de Brun: 1842 cadastral map

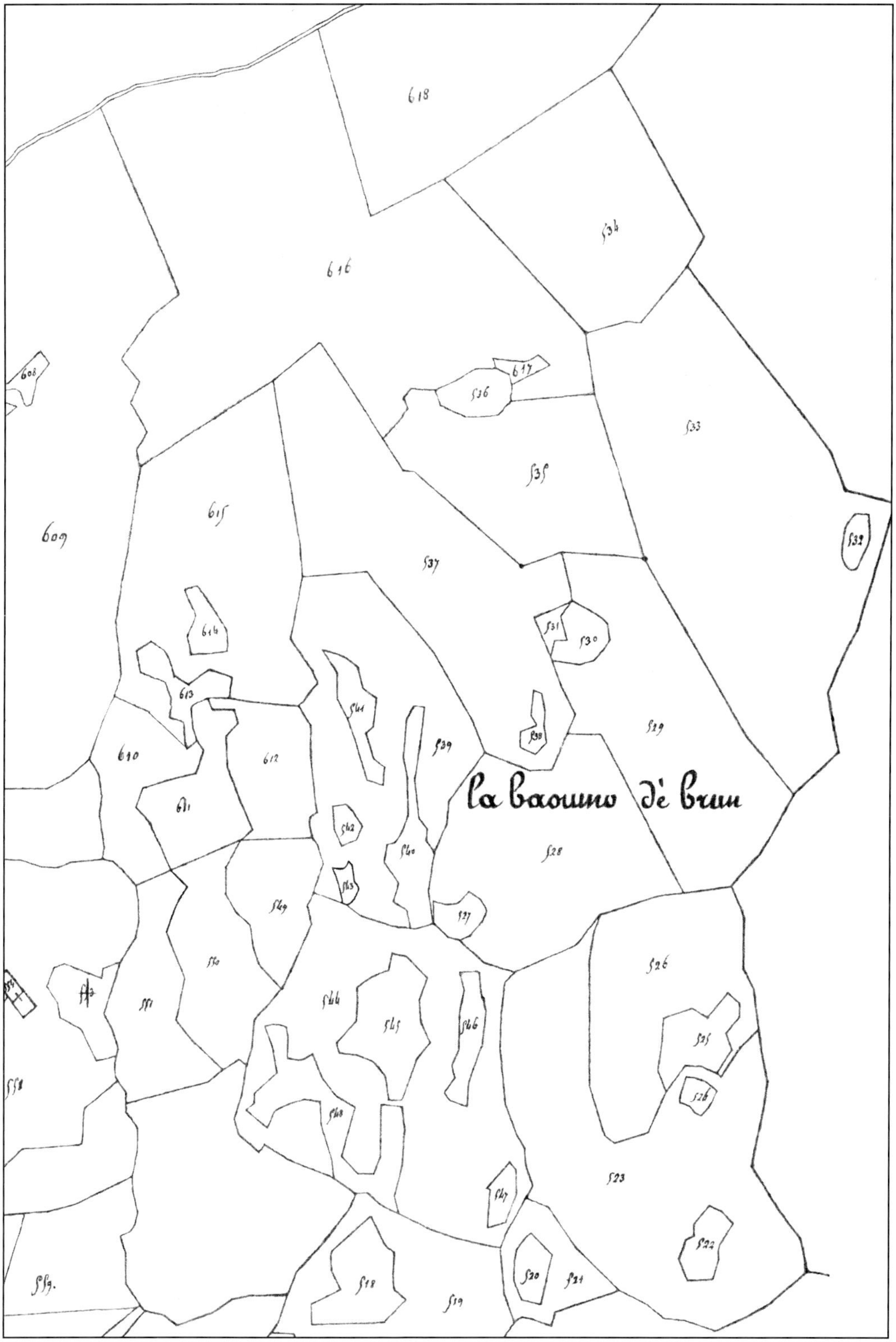
la baouno dè brun

FIGURE 120. Baoume de Brun: view of the survey area
PHOTOGRAPH: DAVID AUSTIN)

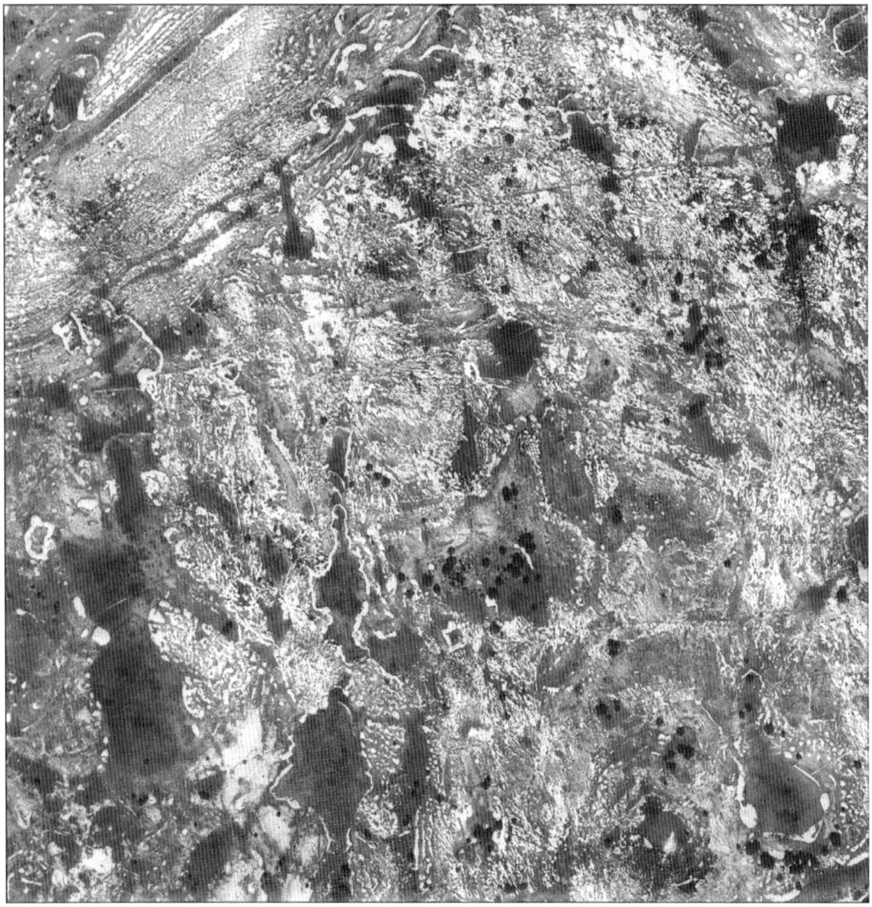

FIGURE 121. Baoume de Brun: vertical air photograph of the survey area
AIR PHOTOGRAPH REPRODUCED BY KIND PERMISSION OF THE IGN

FIGURE 122. Baoume de Brun: survey
DRAWING: QUENTIN DREW AND DAVID AUSTIN

centuries. This would give us the opportunity to explore the wider relationships between parcels and give us some clearer understanding of family strategies and time-scales. Unknown to us, however, the boundaries of the *quartier* were readjusted at some time between 1815 and 1842 in an area which seems in the 18th century and earlier to have been ambiguous in its identity. Between 1842 and the next cadastral map of 1936, however, which was then up-graded in 1981 for internal parcel ownership, the *quartier* remained stable. We only discovered this during the 1995 work on the archives, and so, although we surveyed the whole of the 1842 *quartier*, we failed to recover all of the earlier one, especially at its southern end, and we (under the direction of Quentin Drew) had to return in 1998 and 1999 to complete the task (Figure 122). Finally, we also excavated a prominent and well-preserved architectural complex consisting of a curvilinear enclosure, a *borie* and a rough shelter, with, nearby, a paved *aire* or threshing floor (Figure 142).

Microtopography

La Baoume de Brun, as depicted in 1842 and 1936, lies on the eastern edge of the Les Poumeirès fault (zone III.6C), on its boundary with Le Calernet (zone III.6A), and on its northern side there is a steep ridge which separates the plateau from the bench of Le Teil (zone III.4). In terms of the physical microtopography and soils we have characterised eight zones (Figure 123):

A. *The ridge of La Basse:* At this point the slope southwards is particularly severe and there was little sign of extensive land use in this north-western corner of the *quartier*. The cadastre of 1791 calls this La Basse and it is clear that it was then regarded as *terre gaste*. Towards the eastern end, the ridge loses its steepness and becomes a broadening of the next feature, the bench.

B. *The bench:* Just at the base of La Basse there is a broad bench which was once heavily cultivated as revetted linear fields, particularly at the eastern end, and it once also carried a major trackway. Soils from the western end of this area were excavated and sampled and were found to be relatively deep, with a stone-free topsoil. They seem to have been simply the product of slow build-up, behind the terrace wall, of colluvium from the adjacent relatively steep slope of La Basse.

C. *The doline cascades:* The land continues to slope southwards from the bench, albeit much more gently, down towards the plain of Le Calernet, but the terrain is broken by the lines of four deep valleys of varying dimensions which run north–south off the base of the ridge. Their deep silts are heavily revetted, so creating level fields. The final impression today is of a series of linked dolines set in terraced flights much in the fashion of cascades. The colluvial sediments which have accumulated on the floor of such closed depressions provide a record of erosional activity on the slopes within the catchment area, that is the ridge and the valley sides. These colluvial deposits appear to be transitional in character between that of the Aspi dolines, which reveals no evidence of a break in sediment accumulation, and La Combe, which shows indications of several phases of stability.

D. *Les Poumeirès doline:* Down the western side of our survey area there is a broad,

FIGURE 123. Baoume de Brun: topographic zones
DRAWING: DAVID AUSTIN

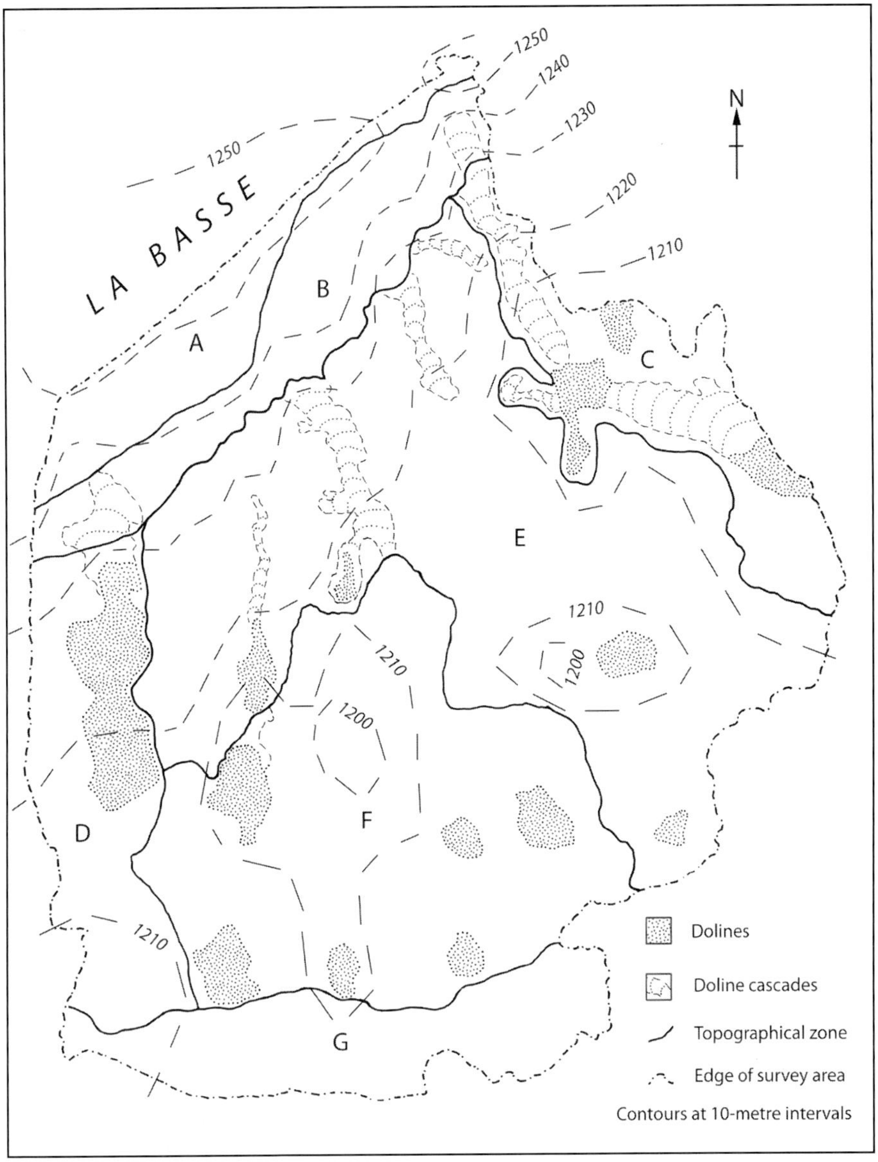

well-grassed doline or uvula which gives way westwards again to a smooth landscape of heavily cleared, although massively eroding, fields at the heart of which lay a still-active *bergerie* surrounded by grasslands made distinctively lush by recent manuring. This was part of the northern end of the distinctive and rich Poumeirès landscape.

E. *The pavements:* Over the northern part of the cascade area the ground between the valley features is very broken and eroded by solution and in several places the bare rock shows as limestone pavements, deeply fissured with grykes which dropped away occasionally into narrow cave (*aven*) openings. This zone was also marked by eroded outcrops which formed miniature and highly distinctive tor-like stacks of limestone strata. Within this sort of terrain isolated areas of cleared fields could be found on flatter ground which could be consolidated by linear cairns or small stretches of terrace. One such piece of land lay just to the south of the enclosure we excavated. As the largest of these cleared fields in this microtopography, it is characterised by two broad, sweeping, low terraces.

F. *Fields and dolines:* Further south, as the slope becomes even gentler, the cascades disappear and the landscape becomes one of broad, cleared fields and cairnfields, interspersed with deep dolines. The main central field has become highly eroded in a part where the plane of the dolomite beds is more or less horizontal to the present ground surface. Some of the cairnfields are somewhat intermittent where the terrain is more broken by pavement and eroded outcrops. The deep, discrete dolines have north–south axes and are clearly on the same system of limestone joints as the uvulas to the north. Characteristically, they have lightly terraced sloping fields on the south side and much more steep, also terraced, fields on the north with almost sheer edges to the east and west where they rise to the broken ground with cairnfields.

G. *The plain of Le Calernet:* On the extreme southern edge of the survey area appeared the more open and heavily cleared landscapes of Le Calernet. Here fields and heavy cairnfields predominate often in long strings along the regularly tilted bedding plains of the limestone as they do in l'Aspi.

The pattern of land: the workscape

The next stage of analysis was to separate out the various edges of human activity, by distinguishing patterns of different groups of monuments which appeared, to our eye, to have been once discrete areas of land (Figure 124). These are really frameworks of space in which work and other social activities once occurred. In calling these 'workscapes' we adapt, and partially misapply, a term ('taskscapes') coined by Tim Ingold,[6] but we seek to use it as a term to suggest how the human choices in the making of the 'cultural' landscape, although dependent on the opportunities given by the terrain itself, were not simply determined by what geology and geomorphology offered. The peasant worker never saw geology or morphology in the same way as we do, but merely what he or she could achieve with what God had given them, in terms of land, technology, energy, emotion and the expectations and obligations for the life to come. One major aspect of the cultural variability was the labour and obligations given by what Goody has called 'life cycle' the erratic and adventitious circumstances of childbirth, marriage and death,[7] all of which are addressed later by David Siddle.

For example the choice between making cairnfields and cleared fields must often have been a matter of such cultural decisions, since the terrains offered the opportunity for either, especially in zone F. We must also remember that the opportunity any one piece of ground represented was not necessarily a single event but an accumulation of what had gone before. So a cleared field may be the result of many separate or continuous acts of stone removal and piling, of which fields with small cairns may have been the earliest precursor. The temporal implications of this will be dealt with later, but it is possible to see in the map of work patterns degrees of intensity in the succession of labour. For example we can gain the impression from simple observation that the doline and uvula floors with their revetted stone piles and dry-stone walling have been kept clear for cultivation through many cycles of the community's existence. There are masses of stone piled up in the same sorts of proportions to be found in the landscapes closer to the village. By contrast the intermittent cairnfields have little patches of clearance, which probably represent single events and these possibly widely separated by time.

We have produced two interpretative maps in relation to this concept of workscapes, based on the detailed survey of Baoume de Brun. The first (Figure 124) identifies, by pecked lines, all the patches of ground classified by stone features and soil areas as reflected in the methods perfected in L'Aspi and La Combe and these are further identified as individual patches, the workscapes, by their internal coherence and consistency of practice and action. These workscapes occurred in different forms as reflected in our classification and are expressed by the colour regime shown on Figure 124.

This is further interpreted in Figure 125 as larger areas which show the intensity of land use and, indeed, non-use. This is where the early observation in this chapter about the upland displaying the flux of social action and economy is at its most apparent. Here, well out from the village, we are beginning to see land used at the limits of human capacity and need. Only the very best patches are used over long periods of time, whereas the rest is used only when need or aspiration pushes the capacity of the ground, but only infrequently. There are large areas where no or extremely little activity at all can be detected (white). Some where cairns have been created, but perhaps only once or twice (blue). There are others with fields where cairns are distributed around the edges or places which have large cairns where the ground has been worked several times, albeit perhaps intermittently (green). Finally there are a few places where effort over longer periods of time has been put in to create low or proto-terraces on moderate slopes and in the uvulas (orange) and there are the even fewer dolines where clearance was constant even into the relatively recent past (red).

Of course, as with all categorisation of this nature, the boundaries between the categories are ill-defined in the sense that any one piece of ground, one workscape or one level of intensity, isolated by this process may drift uneasily in the fieldworker's mind between one grade and another. The decisions depicted on the drawings remains thus a representation of personal judgements, albeit based on systematic, painstaking empirical observation.

What, however, these two drawings do show is, first, how much this terrain has been worked over time, despite the severe restrictions of nature and culture, and second, how much it is sub-divided into discrete blocks of management. The pattern of land and the workscapes they embody were fragmentary experiences, shattering the individual rhythm of life into a variety of practices, much at variance with the sense of monotony we gain from the general social histories of traditional peasant existence.

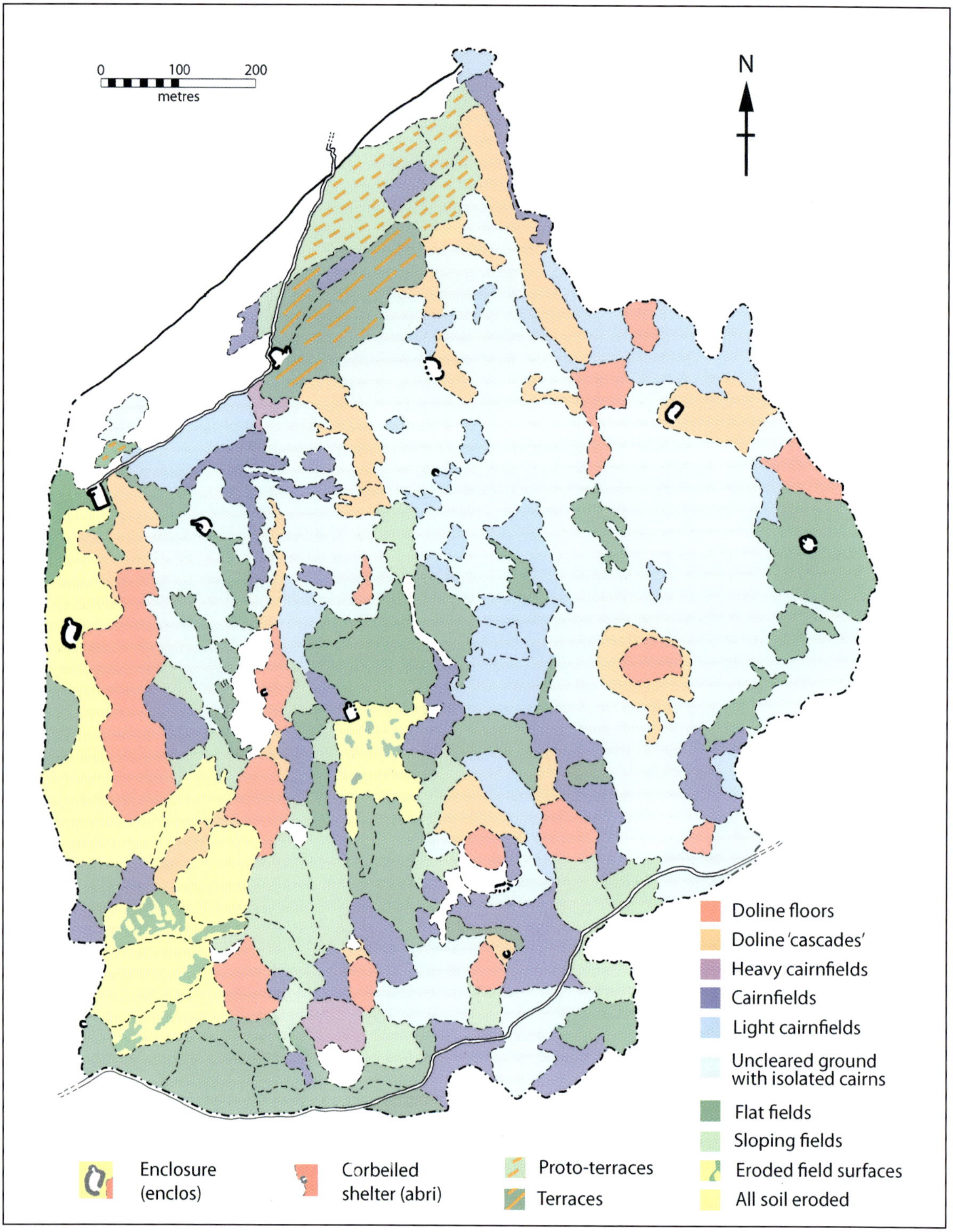

FIGURE 124. Baoume de Brun: workscapes

DRAWING: DAVID AUSTIN

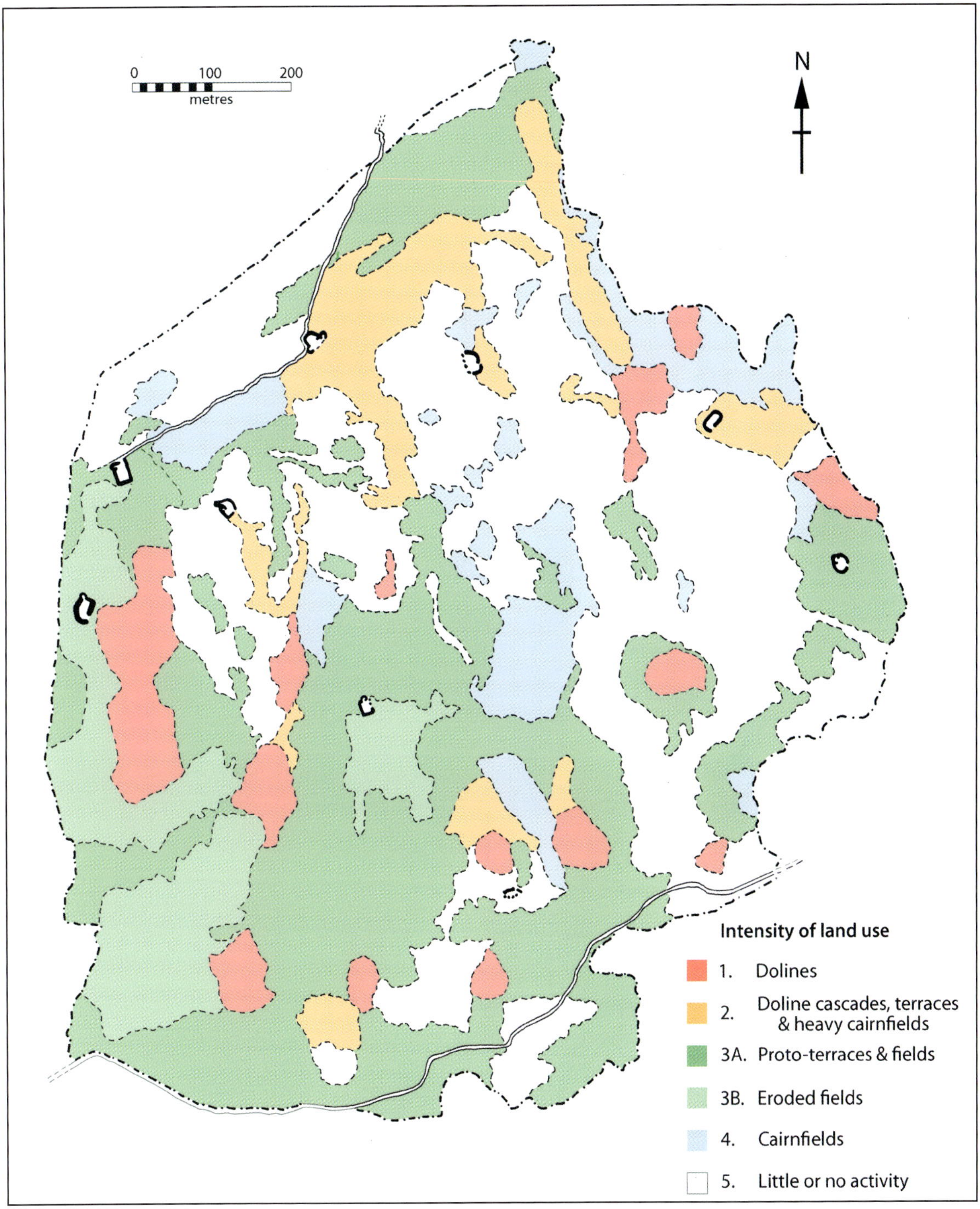

FIGURE 125. Baoume de Brun: land use intensity

DRAWING: DAVID AUSTIN

The structures

In terms of the architecture in the survey area, it is very obvious that the 1842 *quartier* of La Baoume de Brun had two different attitudes to space at work. In the northern half (zones B and E) there are nine roofless enclosures, four of which are curvilinear and five of which are rectilinear. *Bories* were attached to six of them, including a curvilinear one, which we excavated (see below). Notably these were all adjacent to the areas of doline cascades (C) or uvulas (D), i.e. the best land in those zones. In the southern half (F), however, where there was even better land, there are none, even near the substantial dolines, although isolated *bories* are still to be found in the same sort of quantities. In other words the *bories* were evenly spread across the whole area while the enclosures had a distinctive patterning. We should also note here that neither the *bories* nor the enclosures had discernible relationships with the pattern of land parcels, revealed by the documentary analysis which follows. They are probably then, as shelters for shepherds and sheep alike, much more likely to be related to patterns of pastoral management of which we know very little from documentary evidence.

We must also register the presence of two sets of structured trackway running across the area, neither of which is shown on the cadastral maps. The most impressive of these is the northernmost which crosses the ridge on the north-western edge and was a spur of the Chemin de Caussols to the north. It is narrow, no more than a metre across, worn into the surface of the bedrock and marked by lines of stones as it carefully picks its way through the cleared terraces and around the architecture of enclosures: in many cases it can be seen to post-date these agrarian features where its edging stones are placed on good soil. However, it is impossible to draw any absolute conclusions about dating from this alone. At one point it is clear that the track had at least two routes as it crossed the bare patch of La Basse on the slope of the ridge. The southern track was less clear, but was again marked by lines of stones and considerable wear.

The 19th and 18th centuries

The next stage of analysis was to understand the succession of properties within the *quartier* identified as La Baoume de Brun on the cadastral map and schedule of 1842, so that we could relate documented people and their families to the physical landscapes of the survey. The first task was to reduce the parcels as drawn and numbered on the maps (Figure 119) to their true property units, by amalgamating differently assessed units under the landholder (this process can be seen on Figure 129). Then the cadastres of 1791 and 1727 were each searched to find individual parcels of land which were ascribed to this *quartier* during the 18th century. This was not a simple task since all three cadastres used different systems of listing and numeration, and the earlier two had no maps. Despite this most of the properties were described by locational references to adjacent landholders or features such as roads or waste. These were done on the four cardinal compass points. Furthermore, both the 1727 and 1791 cadastres had textual emendations as superscripts or marginalia by which changes in the intervening period could be tracked. We also searched a range of other documents, especially the '*mutations*' or records of property exchange, which also covered the periods between these three dates.

The comparison of 1842 with 1791 seemed, at first, a straightforward exercise, since the 12 parcels of La Baoume de Brun in 1791 could be matched by 10 in 1842. The difference was likely to be explicable as the result of amalgamations by sale or inheritance. However, we immediately ran into the problem that it was impossible to connect by documented property transfers more than one or two of the parcels. All of this was then compounded by the fact that in the 1727 cadastres, where parcels were listed, not in numerical sequence as in 1791 and 1842, but under the names of individual landholders, there were only 6 identifiable properties in La Baoume de Brun with no evidence of these holdings being divided in the intervening period to create the larger numbers of the later date.

We only began to resolve this problem when we noticed that in the 18th century documents there was also a *quartier* of Clapiers de Brun which had disappeared by 1842. We made the assumption, correctly as it happened, that similarity of name may be a clue to proximity. For 1791 this gave us an extra three parcels with another two belonging ostensibly to Le Calernet, but whose numbers were intermingled with those of Clapiers. For 1727, there were also three Clapiers parcels. This of itself made matters worse, because now there were 17 parcels in 1791 which needed to be explained in terms of 10 in 1842 and nine in 1727. But the trick had been solved in that we no longer trusted to continuity in the boundaries of *quartiers*. For 1842 we then simply cast the net wider and recorded all the details of parcels in the adjoining *quartiers*. In addition, closer scrutiny of the 1727 cadastre, revealed that 20 folios were missing which might explain gaps particularly if the names of landholders involved were close to each other in alphabetical order which was how this volume was organised. Then the comparisons could be made and the properties tracked. All of this showed, however, that the making of the 1842 cadastre had in some instances involved the tidying of *quartiers* with loss of some, especially in ambiguous areas which may not have been worked for years. It also showed that at the time of the Revolution all the parcels were numbered in strict rotation around the landscape in a Rationalist mode disregarding the personalised recording of the previous centuries. This was in tune with the times, as was the moment of making maps in 1842 when the opportunity was taken to tidy up the ambiguities of administration implied in floating *quartiers* and to impose some rigour.

The end result of all this wrestling with names and maps was a reasonably secure sequence of parcel holdings which we could firmly draw (Figure 126). The first conclusion is that the major rearrangement of *quartiers* involved the creation of the 1842 *quartiers* of Baoume de Brun (BdB), Avenc et Baoume de

1727		*1791*		*1842*	*Site Code*
Clapiers 1 2300 cannes	→	Clapiers (C123) 2300 cannes	→	BdB7 3.515 ha	A
Calernet 1 ?	→	Calernet (C120) 1646 cannes	→	BdB5 1.34 ha	B
Clapiers 2 2956 cannes	→	Clapiers (C119) 2956 cannes	→	BdB3 1.603 ha	C
Calernet 2 ?	→	Calernet (C121) 2925 cannes	→	BdB6 1.574 ha	D
	⅔ →	Clapiers (C114) 2300 cannes	½ →	BdB8 2.172 ha	E1
Clapiers 3 3600 cannes			½ →	BdB4 1.856 ha	E2
	⅓ →	Baoume [sic], but was probably Clapiers (C122) 1300 cannes	→	BdB9 1.88 ha	E3
(Baoume 7) ?	→	Baoume (C177) 1350 cannes	+ → ↑	BdB1 2.596 ha	F
Baoume 1 3500 cannes	→	Baoume (C175) 3500 cannes	↑ ½ ½ ↓		G
(Baoume 8) ?	→	Baoume (C178) 2300 cannes	↓ + →	LC10 2.108 ha	H
Baoume 2 2440 cannes	→	Baoume (C176) 2440 cannes	→	A/B1 0.899 ha	I
Baoume 3 1300 cannes	→	Baoume (C182) 1125 cannes (but see App.1)	→	A/B3 0.891 ha	J
Baoume 4 1400 cannes (but see Appx 1)	→	Baoume (C173) 2550 cannes	→	LC11 0.419 ha.	K
Baoume 5 1125 cannes	→	Baoume (C174) 1125 cannes	→	GdP2 0.359 ha	L
Baoume 6 1100 cannes	→	Baoume (C179) 1100 cannes	→	BdB2 1.34 ha	M
(Baoume 9) ?	→	Baoume (C172) 2316 cannes	→	LC12 1.189 ha	N
(Baoume 10) ?	→	Baoume (C180) 1091 cannes	→	BdB10 2.864 ha	O
(Baoume 11) ?	→	Baoume (C181) 3525 cannes	→	GdP1 1.346 ha	P

FIGURE 126. Baoume de Brun: the sequence of parcel holdings
DRAWING: DAVID AUSTIN

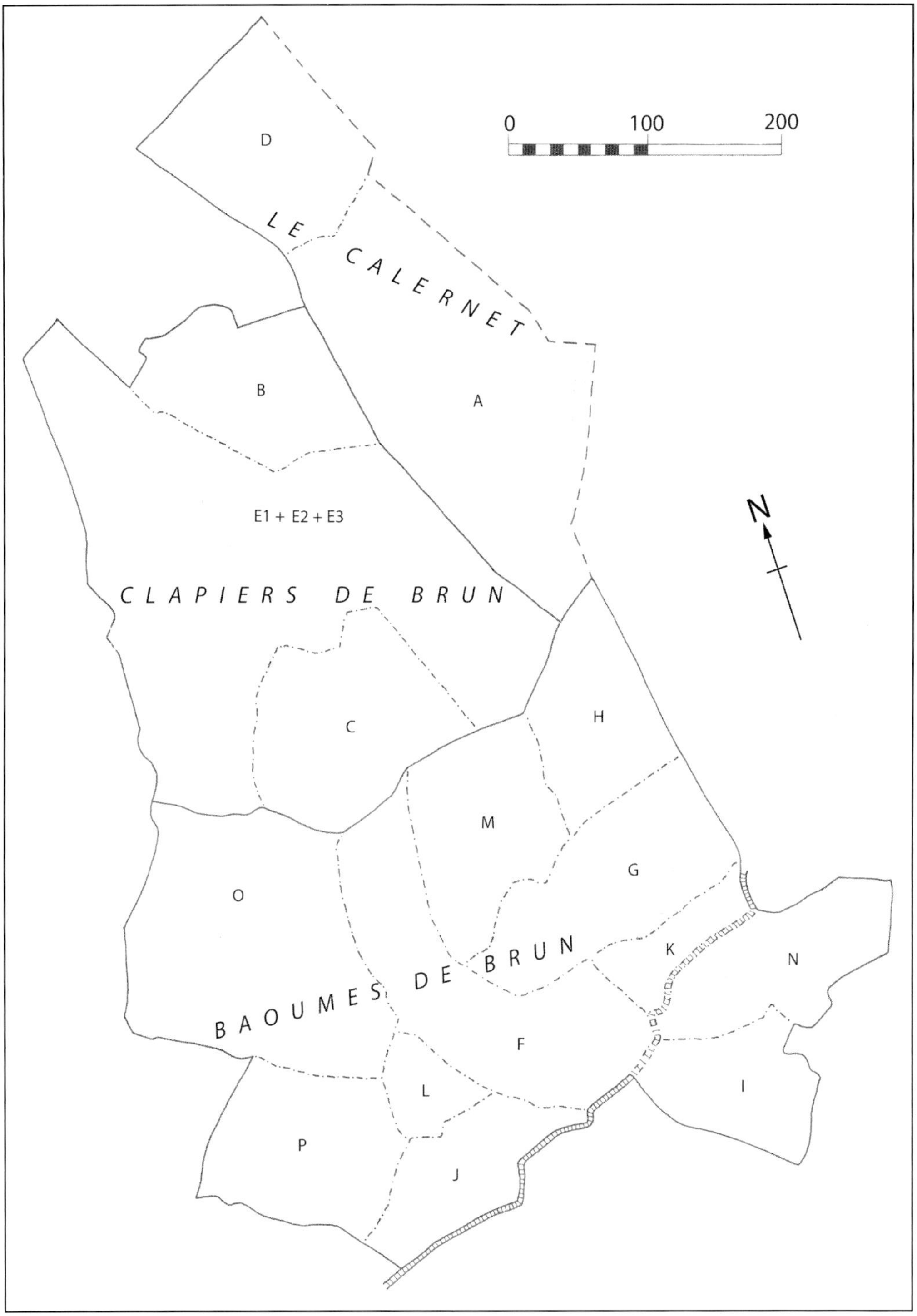

FIGURE 127. Baoume de Brun: 1727 property map
DRAWING: DAVID AUSTIN

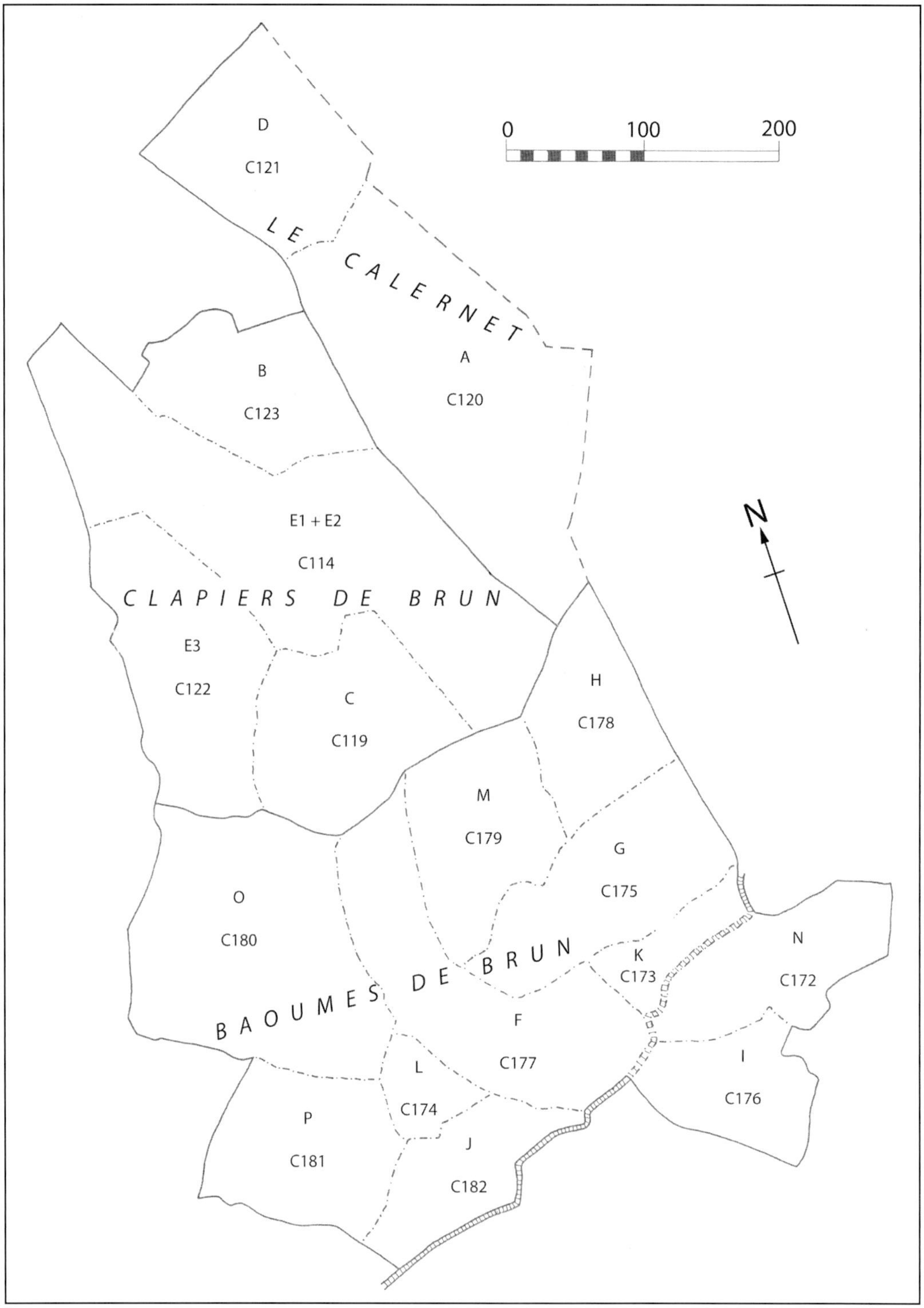

FIGURE 128. Baoume de Brun: 1791 property map

DRAWING: DAVID AUSTIN

Brun (A/B), Le Calernet (LC) and Graou de Palliers (GdP) out of the 18th century Clapiers de Brun, Calernet, and Baoume de Brun. The second is that other processes of exchange rearranged some of the parcel boundaries.

The table allows us to suggest immediately that the pattern and size of tenancies remained relatively stable through the whole period with only two splitting, one of them twice, and only one amalgamating. The pattern can also be illustrated by comparing the maps of parcels and their tenants for the three cadastres of 1727, 1791 and 1842 (Figures 127–9). Such stability seems to be a common feature of tenure in the eighteenth and nineteenth centuries on the plateau which rather suggests that, despite significant changes in population and the downturn in economic activity, the community was always careful to maintain the knowledge of asset, and to record the transmission of title. We can, however, see that the few alterations which are made have the major effect of fragmenting a large 1727 parcel (Clapiers 1), which seems to have involved about half the space then known as Clapiers de Brun.

The stability of the parcels is, however, in direct contrast to the volatility of the transfers which moved the land in and out of families, and, rarely, down the generations. Occasionally family strategies appear for a while and then disappear. The most noticeable is the purchase by Jean Baptiste Flory of five holdings in this area in the early Napoleonic period only for it to fragment on his death in 1829. To get a clearer view of this we would need to extend the analysis of land transfer over a wider area than has been possible in this small study (Figure 130).

Having understood each separate block of information available to us in its own disciplinary constraints, the next was to put it all together through the medium of maps, remembering that this is the procedure for putting the past community back into its spaces. The first thing to notice is the extent to which the 18th century *quartiers* broadly conform to the boundaries of the main topographic zones in the area. So, Baoume de Brun consisted largely of zone F which in agricultural terms is dominated by the discrete, heavily worked dolines, and Clapiers de Brun lay almost entirely within zone E, the broken ground of pavements and doline cascades. The new arrangements made at the time of the 1842 cadastre broke across all of this, and it is difficult to avoid the conclusion that the new spatial understandings are essentially bureaucratic and top-down. This further suggests to us that the intimate relationship the community had once had with this terrain had already been lost; it was ceasing to be familiar and was more remote to all but a few. So for Marie Girard or Jean Baptiste Joulian who still retained their strong hold on the legalities of ownership, the sense of working and being in recognisably distinct areas of the plateau would have disappeared. With this went loss of name. The cave, which gave its name to Baoume de Brun and which had once been central to the *quartier*, in 1842 became entirely peripheral, and Les Clapiers, so called for its bleak rockiness, lost its name entirely. Is this a real failure of the named owners to be intimate with their land or is it merely the bureaucrats riding rough-shod over the

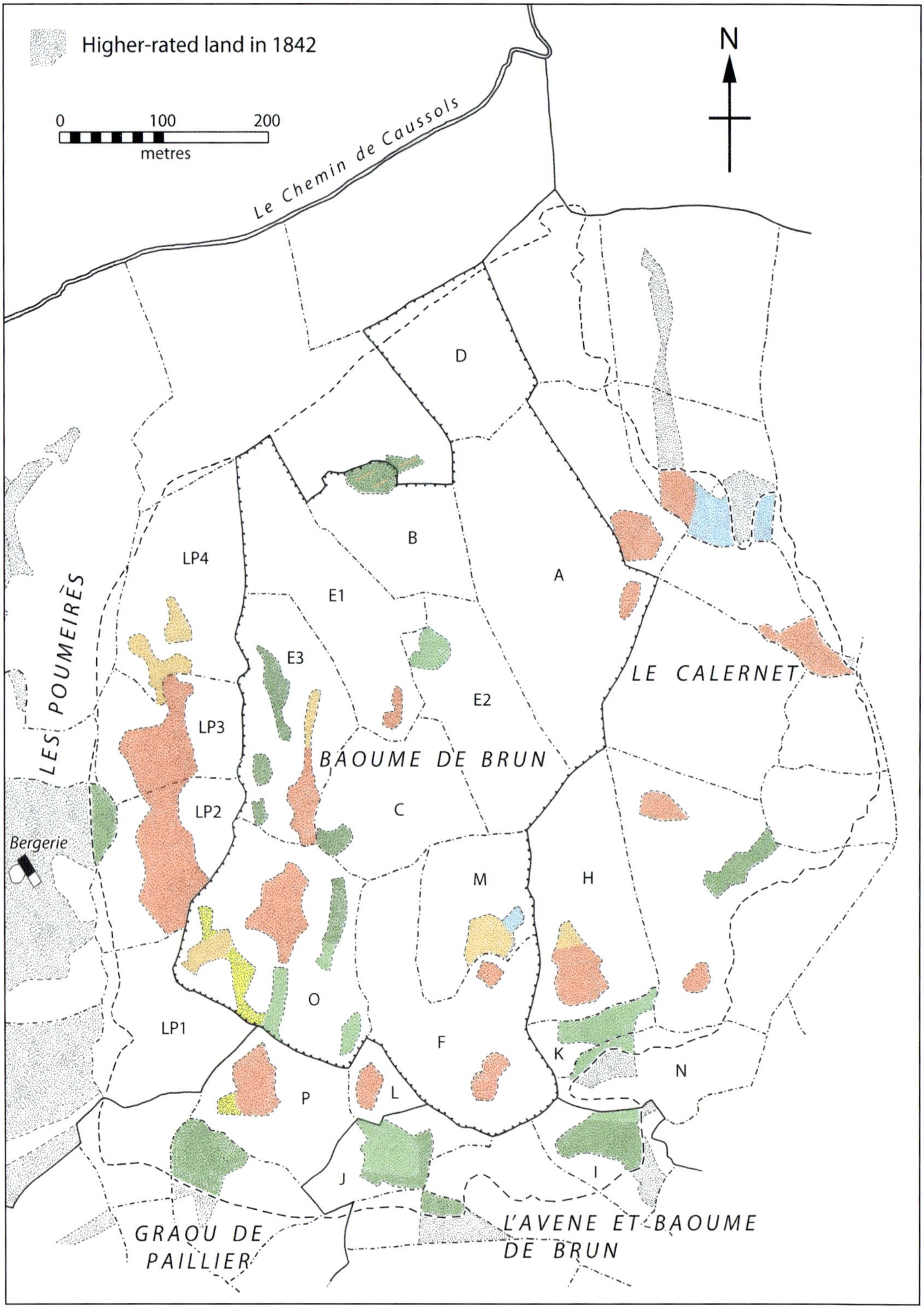

FIGURE 129. Baoume de Brun: 1842 property map and land use types

DRAWING: DAVID AUSTIN

1727	*1727 x 1791*	*1791*	*1791 x 1842*	*1842*	*Our Code*
Clapiers 1 Pierre **Isnard**		C120 Pierre **Suque**		BdB7 Claude **Guizol**	A
Calernet 1 ?		C123 Jean Antoine **Laugier**	Jean Baptiste **Flory** & Jean Joseph **Flory**	BdB5 Guillaume **Girard**, Husband of Stevecon **Flory**	B
Clapiers2 Heirs of Pierre **Mottet**	....**Maurel**	C119 Marie Honoriade **Girard**	Heirs of Jean Baptiste **Girard** d'Auban	BdB3 Marie Catherine **Aussel**, widow of **Girard**	C
Calernet 2 ?		C121 Bartolemy **Bourelly**		BdB6 Joseph **Aussel**, son of Adam	D
	2/3 Pierre **Camatte** (1758)	C114 Honoré Baptiste **Mallet**	1/2 Joseph **Crist** to Jean Joseph **Crist**	BdB8 Jean Joseph **Crist**	E1
Clapiers 3 Heirs of Joseph **Camatte**			1/2 Joseph **Crist** to Elizabeth **Crist**	BdB4 Elizabeth **Crist**	E2
	1/3 Jean Baptiste **Camatte** (1758) Joseph **Crist** (1782)	C122 Marie **Girard**, widow of Laugier		BdB9 Pierre **Girard**	E3
(Baoume 7) (Pierre **Laugier**)	Nicholas **Laugier** (1750 in 3 portions)	C177 Honoré **Tombarel**	Jean Baptiste **Flory**	BdB1 Marie **Flory**, widow of François **Pons**	F
Baoume 1 Guillaume **Lambert**		C175 Jean **Rous** of the house of Jean **Lambert**	Jean Baptiste **Flory** 1/2 to Marie **Flory** & 1/2 to Louis **Flory**		G
(Baoume 8) (Guillaume **Lambert**)		C178 Honoré **Tombarel**	Jean Baptiste **Flory**	LC10 Louis **Flory**	H
Baoume 2 Guillaume **Lambert**	Joseph **Lambert**	C176 Joseph **Lambert**	uncertain	A/BdB1 Pierre **Flory**	I
Baoume 3 Jean **Nicholas**	Bartellemy **Girard**	C182 Jean **Girard** dit Lourd	Guillaume **Bourelly**	A/BdB3 Guillaume **Bourelly**	J
Baoume 4 Estienne **Girard** dit Lourd	Claude **Girard**, son of Estienne (1750)	C173 Arnoux **Sauteron**, son-in-law of Claude **Girard**		LC11 Estienne **Sauteron**, son of Arnoux	K
Baoume 5 Estienne **Girard** dit Lourd	François **Girard**	C174 Arnoux **Sauteron**, son-in-law of Claude **Girard**		GdP2 Estienne **Sauteron**, son of Arnoux	L
Baoume 6 Pierre **Tombarel**	François **Pons**	C179 François **Pons**	Jacob **Carlavan** & (1830) Jean Joseph **Germinal**	BdB2 Joseph **Germinal** of Magagnosc	M
(Baoume 9) "**l'inconnu**"		C172 Honoré **Tombarel**	Jean Baptiste **Flory** to (1829) Pierre **Flory** to (1838) Pierre Jean **Joulian**	LC12 Pierre Jean **Joulian**	N
(Baoume 10) (Pierre **Laugier**)		C180 Jean Joseph **Joulian**	Estienne **Aussel**	BdB10 Estienne **Aussel**	O
(Baoume 11) (Louis **Seitre**)		C181 Guillaume **Girard**	François **Girard**	GdP1 Jean Baptiste **Joulian**	P

FIGURE 130. Baoume de Brun: the descent of parcel holders

DRAWING: DAVID AUSTIN)

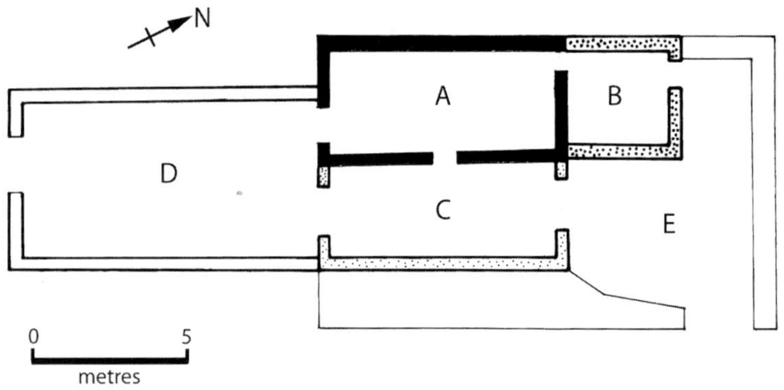

FIGURE 131. Baoume de Brun: *bergerie* of La Jassa de la Caus
AFTER ROC 1995; DRAWING: DAVID AUSTIN

traditional relationships with the countryside? We cannot be certain, but in the process of making the map of 1842[8] we do know how closely the cadastral surveyors worked with the village officials and we can be sure that while the edges of parcel ownership were strongly scrutinised, names and topographies had ceased to have real meaning and importance. If we can assume from this that there was a failure of intimacy and familiarity, can we also assume that despite the assessors' meticulous mapping of labour and pasture in 1842 for tax purposes, the real working of such ground for arable crops was at best intermittent and that most of the named owners rarely put in an appearance on their land, leaving it mostly to the shepherds? This is supported by the existence of the *bergeries* as the sole architecture of the plateau depicted and assessed in 1842.

opposite:
top: FIGURE 132. Pan-commune: *bergeries* in 1842 and before
DRAWING: DAVID AUSTIN

bottom: FIGURE 133. Two IGN vertical air photographs of *bergeries*
AIR PHOTOGRAPH REPRODUCED BY KIND PERMISSION OF THE IGN

One of these *bergeries*, La Bergerie des Poumeirès, still functioned just beyond the western edge of the survey area and sheep were moved in unified flocks over large areas of the Plateau de Calern. Sited inside a large doline the grasslands surrounding it were green and lush from the constant high phosphate and organic input to the soils from the sheep kept overnight on this rich grazing. Elsewhere on the upland only a few other *bergeries* still functioned, some more as overnight shelters within the circuit of the large flocks than as management focusses. These are linked today to other, larger *bergeries* on the lowland, one of which, La Jassa de la Caus in the *quartier* of La Graoux, was studied in 1994–5 by a young anthropologist from Nice for her MA.[9] Here the management was more complex and involved the over-wintering of stock. Here also the insemination of yews, lambing and shearing were handled before the animals were taken, between 2 June and 20 September (that year) onto the upland on a transhumance circuit which included the whole of Le Gros Pounch, La Combe and the higher parts of the Plateau de Calern in the west. The architecture of this lowland *bergerie*, a masonry, mortar-bonded and tile-roofed structure, showed relatively complex development from a single-storey, single-room building to a very large two-storey, four-celled operation with the latest addition in 1980 by the proprietor Pierre Martin (Figure 131). Roc's dating of the first appearance of

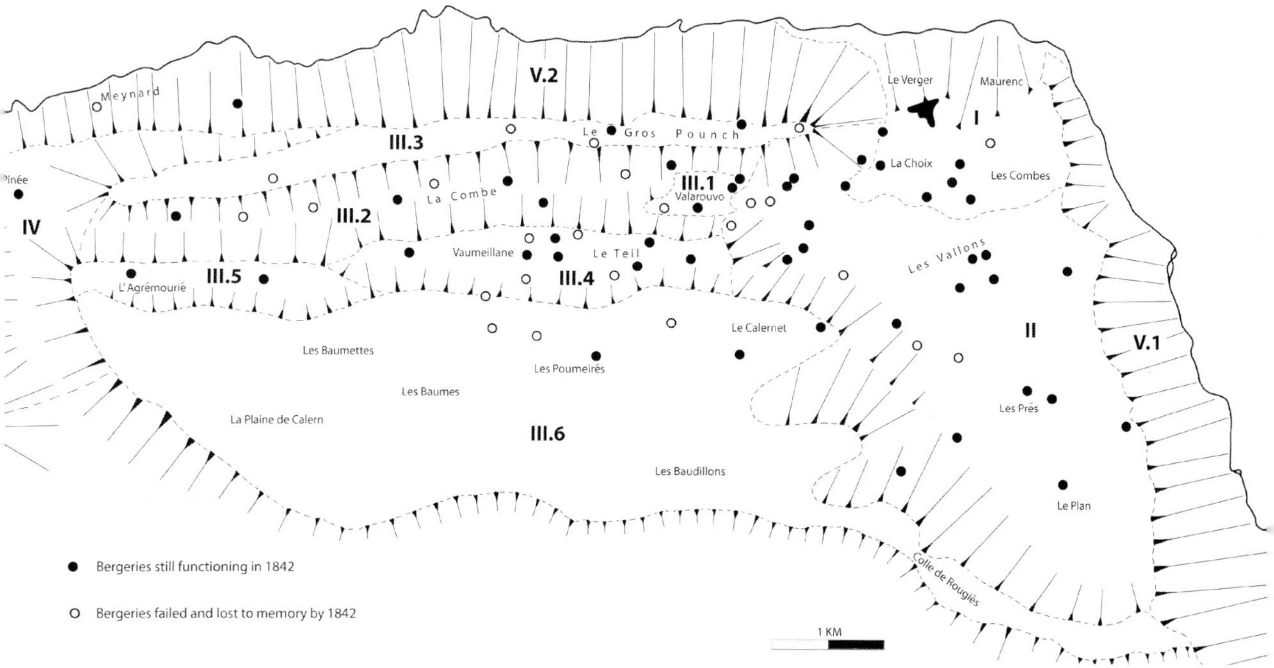

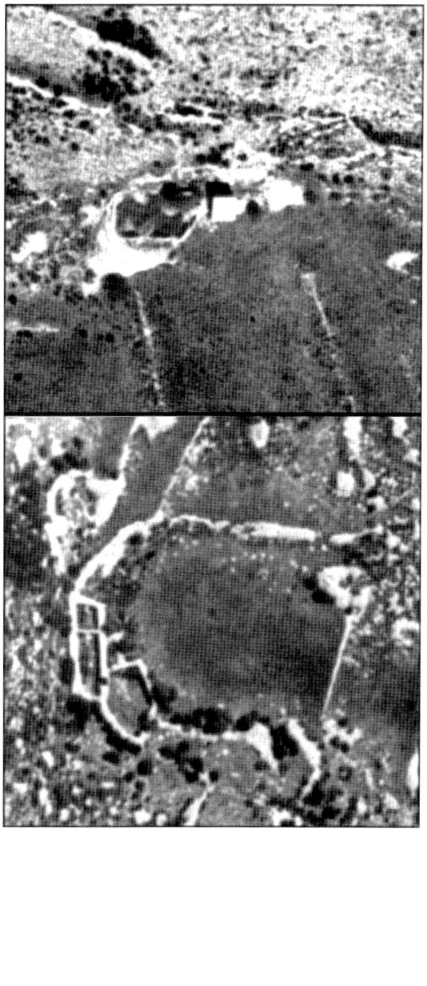

these buildings was 18th century based on a rather simplistic interpretation of the late 18th century regional maps of Cassini and Les Frontières de l'Est (1778).

If, however, the distribution of all the plateau's *bergeries* and *cabanes*, of all types detectable by archaeological fieldwork, is plotted in comparison with the 1842 map (Figure 132), it is clear that the pattern was already in sharp decline by the early 19th century, perhaps as part of a continuing consolidation of flocks into larger units and that the complete array of structures was likely to have been at its maximum use in the 17th and 18th centuries, if not a little earlier. This seems to be confirmed by the existence of field remains which appear to show rather more primitive forms of construction which had clearly vanished by 1842 if not long before. Also consistently in the archaeology we saw that *bergeries* and *cabanes* replaced the earlier enclosures, a few being built to abut them and utilise them as yards (Figure 133). The succession is clear. We should also note, from the distributions, that the *bergeries*, unlike the enclosures (see below) are also to be found on the lowland of the commune in almost as many numbers as the upland. This seems to suggest that they were managed in similar relationships to that recorded by Roc in 1994–5. Indeed if we look at a distribution of *bergeries* still functioning in the later 20th century, distinguishing at the same time those

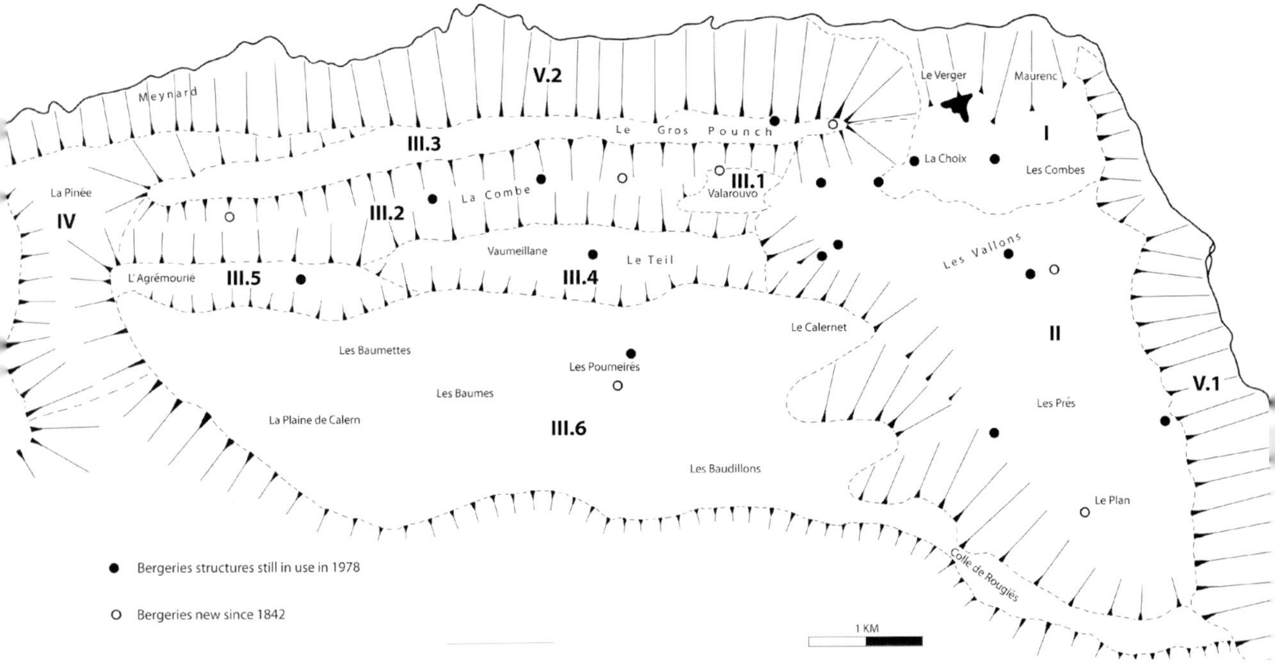

FIGURE 134. Pan-commune: distribution of modern *bergeries*
DRAWING: DAVID AUSTIN

present in 1842 and those created subsequently (Figure 134), we can see that the practice of managing flocks has remained in a constant state of adjustment and up-grading, albeit on a much-reduced basis in terms of flock sizes and those farmers still actively engaged. It is noticeable that there is a clear group of six lowland *bergeries* close to the village, all but one of which was also there in 1842 while the most change can be seen among the other 16 distributed on the more upland areas, suggesting that most volatility, as ever, was on the higher ground.

If the 19th century, as we are saying, was a story of increasing detachment from the workscapes of the plateau, what then of the 18th? The land itself was again assessed by fiscal officials and these calculations for taxation (in *cannes*) clearly made assumptions about the potential for arable and pastoral production on the plateau. The assumption was for a certain sustained level of arable production, but the reality must have been different. As we shall see, the 18th century was a time of great stress for the community of Cipières, with falling population and increasing migration both permanent and temporary from the village and its lands. We know from the sources also that the well-constructed masonry, roofed *bergeries*, were already in place and laid systematically across the upland and parts of the lowland where they came to acquire the names not of proprietors, but of *quartiers* in which they had become the principal functioning entities. These seem to fit the documented capitalist pastoralism of large flocks exploiting large areas of the upland landscapes and the rest of the commune (see Chapters 6–9).

Within this context, it is difficult to believe that arable production was anything other than intermittent and restricted to the good soils of the dolines and uvulas.

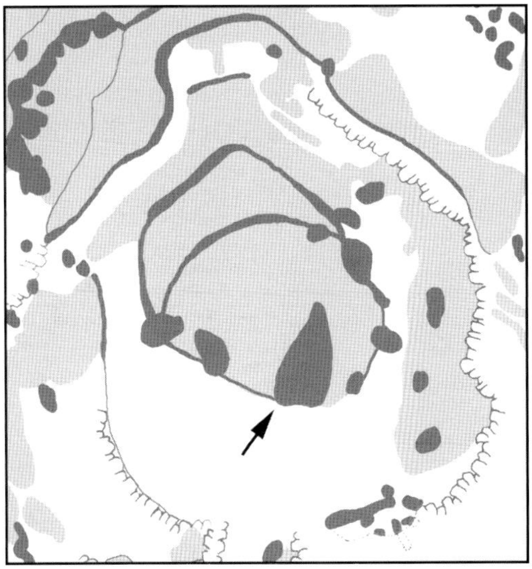

FIGURE 135. Stone pile in doline parcel 524
DRAWING: QUENTIN DREW AND DAVID AUSTIN

Indeed, the archaeology overwhelmingly demonstrated that it was only here that there was any trace of continuous attempt to keep the ground clear and to cultivate. The heaviest clearance was around the edges of uvula and doline floors and we can illustrate many places where the results of such stone clearance were systematically controlled. In one place even (1842 parcel 524) farmers had put a great heap of stone onto the floor of the doline greatly reducing the potential for arable production (Figure 135).

The work at Baoume de Brun again provided overwhelming, albeit circumstantial, evidence that the cleared landscape was early and that the regime on the plateau in the 18th century was, almost as much as the 19th, essentially pastoral in nature and likely to have been only infrequently used by its nominal owners. But could we get back further?

The 17th and 16th centuries

The gap in the documentary record between 1727 and 1610, the date of the previous cadastre, proved impossible to span in terms of the detailed succession of land and parcels. We had no useable *mutations* to show land transfers and there were no family linkages across the century. This confirmed the volatility of ownership. Could a link be made despite this? In both 1531 and 1610 there was a *quartier* called Baomo de Brun which contained five parcels of land. In 1531 there was also a *quartier* called Clapiers de Brun and this was probably the same as the Combo de Brun identified in 1610. At both dates again each of these *quartiers* also contained five parcels of land. These numbers are not easy to set against the 11 parcels in Baoume de Brun in both 1727 and 1791, nor indeed against the three in 1727 and four in 1791 in Clapiers de Brun. However, of the 11 18th century parcels in Baoume de Brun three were, in 1842, in Graou de Paillier, two in Le Calernet and two in Aven de Brun, which leaves four always in Baoume. Similarly in 1727 there are three holdings in Clapiers and two in Le Calernet which were, in 1842, in Baoume de Brun, which corresponds to the five of the previous centuries. All of this is suggestive, but not much more and we can only speculate about how the *quartiers* here were either adjusted or, more intriguingly, were simply misremembered at a time when few, apart from shepherds, would have known their way around this landscape.

When we compare 1531 and 1610, however, we are on firmer footing. The simple results of analysing the entries are shown below tabulated in Figure 136. The table shows that, for Baomo, there are some relatively secure connections between 1531 and 1610, both through the names of the owners and a simple equivalence of the assessment (value) figures. This seems to show both stable parcel size and stable ownership within families, as far as we can detect. For Clapiers this is not so easy. That Clapiers and Combo de Brun are the same *quartier* seems to be confirmed by the direct equivalence of the values. Apart from this we must be cautious. That 'Bense' is Pons and that the two Seytre holdings are the same as the two Girard ones can only be speculations. However, this seems also to be supported, albeit tenuously, by the equivalence of assessment values.

Building the bridge between 1610 (Figure 136) and 1727 (Figure 130), however, has proved impossible in any clear evidential way. We can only speculate again and here even more tendentiously. Apart from the names Girard and Seytre, there is no viable documented connection. These two names, however, appear to be in the wrong part of our area for the purposes of direct mapping. In terms of assessment, the parcel in which we shall be interested for the purposes of biography (E1) was in Clapiers de Brun in 1727 and was then the most highly valued in that *quartier*. This suggests that it was one of two parcels in 1610, one held by Anthony Pons and the other by Martin Flory. This has no direct connection we can yet establish with the Camatte inheritance nor, indeed, does the equivalent tenure of 1531 in the hands of Honorat Pons and Anthony Girard respectively. However speculatively, we still might tend to believe from all this that the volatility of land exchange we have already noted was something that was already occurring in the 16th century, but was accelerating in the 17th and 18th.

Nevertheless, in comparative terms, the key observation is that the parcel structure of the earlier 16th century appears relatively stable, when compared with the 18th and 19th centuries. The 16th and 17th centuries are a time when populations and the village were again growing and the holding of even the smallest and harshest of lands was becoming more important. The parcels within each *quartier* are scattered, however, among a wide variety of proprietors, and are thus the product of agrarian strategies which stress the individual (Chapter 8). They display, as far as we can determine, the same attitude to land and space as the centuries which follow. We must, therefore, begin to consider that the parcels were actually a product of modernity and created a relatively short time before 1531 or even as part of the very process of land regulation that brought the first cadastre into being

From all of this analysis we can begin to affirm that the parcels were a product of attempts to isolate the very best land on the plateau, and that they began as stable units transferred by inheritance and other social processes within families, but soon began to be exchanged increasingly frequently as their productive importance waned. The retreat from the plateau must have been

Quartier	*Date*	*Folio*	*Rate florins*	*Owner*	*Date*	*Folio*	*Rate cannes*	*Owner*
Baomo	**1531**	100	3	Lambert Pons	**1610**	33	?	Honoré Pons (Bertin)
		100A	3	Anthony Pons		14	15	Raibaud Girard (Magister)
		107	8	Peyre Borrel		92	42	Nicolas Borrel (Muraire)
		135	7	Guilhon Giraud		80	40	Raibaud Aubert
		148a	7	Jan Honorat de Cousegoulo		232	40	Jehan Honorat (Jolliam)
Clapiers/ Combo de Brun	**1531**	51	6	Honorat Pons de Gorge	**1610**	54	34	Anthoné Bense (?=Pons)
		80B	5	Louis Seytre		42	28	Fouquet Aubin
		80C	5	Jan Seytre		220	28	Michel Aubin (heirs of)
		121	6	Fouquet Girard		184	34	Martin Flori (Baumon)
		5	5	Anthony Girard		84	28	Girmantari Borrel

FIGURE 136. Baoume de Brun in 1610 and 1531

heavily influenced by the change to large commercial flocks and the system of *bergeries*. This retreat reached its final conclusion in the later 19th and 20th centuries when virtually nothing was deemed, even by the bureaucrats, to be worth ploughing.

The excavation of an enclosure

What has emerged is an increasingly clear view that the transition from the later Middle Ages to the early modern era was a crucial one and one type of archaeological structure seemed to offer a chance of understanding this a little more clearly: the small roofless enclosures and their related *bories* and shelters. As we have noted already their distribution within the study area of Baume de Brun was not uniform and, although they are abundant and had a clear relationship with the extensively worked landscapes (workscapes) revealed by the survey, they did not conform with any use that could be related consistently to the pattern of parcels in use during the modern era. This group of enclosures in the study area also demonstrates the typological distinction between curvilinear and rectilinear enclosures, although it should be noted that there are more than a few hybrid examples which hover morphologically between one and the other, although a decision was taken to classify these in one group or the other based on dominant form. Looked at more extensively across the whole commune the distribution might suggest an inner (i.e. closer to the village) group of early, broadly curvilinear forms and an outer group of rectilinear ones.

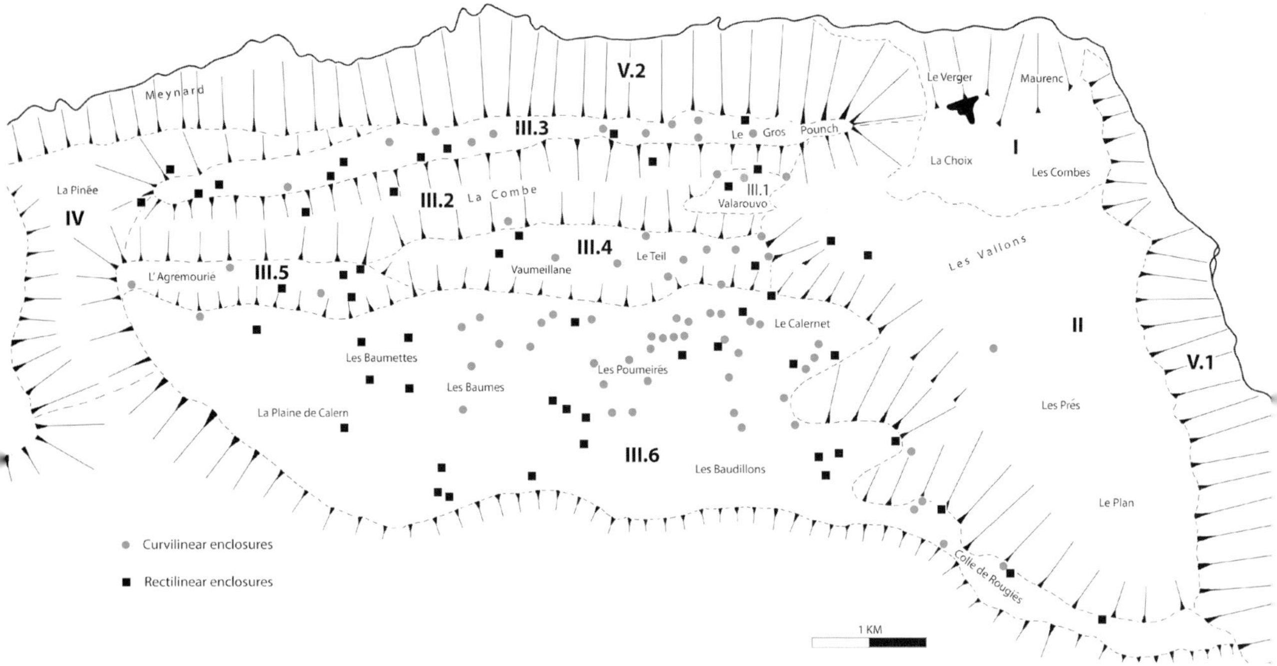

FIGURE 137. Pan-commune: distribution of enclosures

DRAWING: DAVID AUSTIN

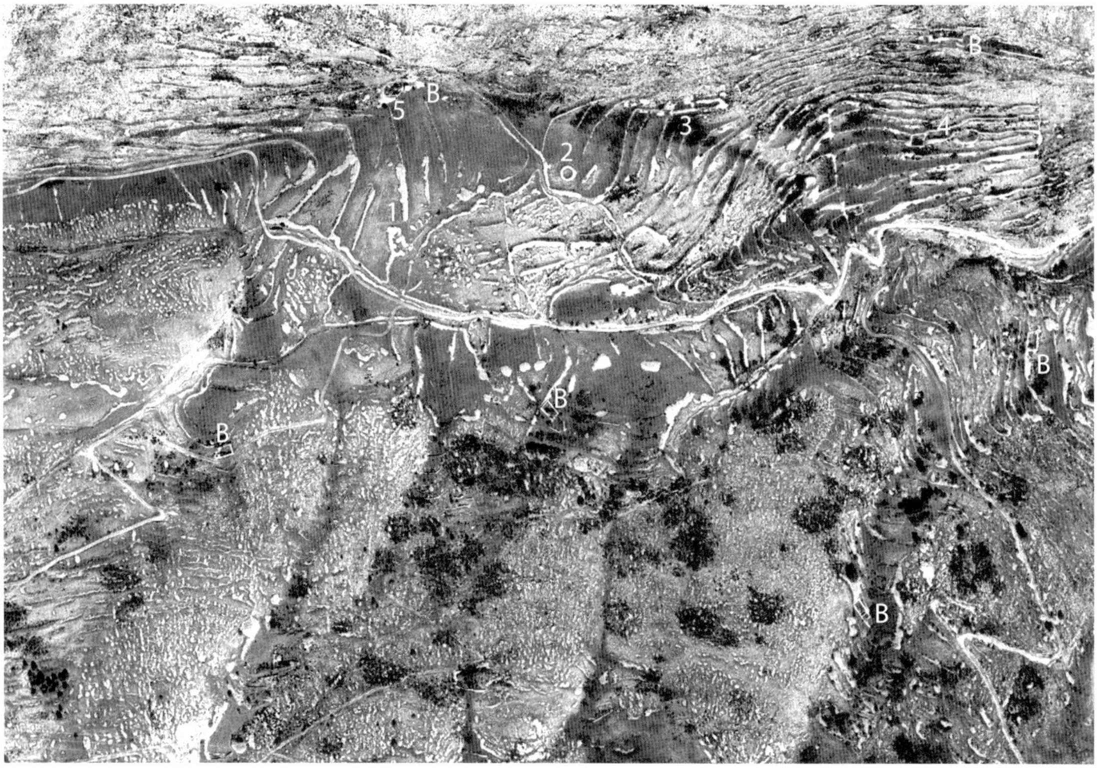

FIGURE 138. Valarouvo IGN vertical air photograph of enclosures

AIR PHOTOGRAPH REPRODUCED BY KIND PERMISSION OF THE IGN

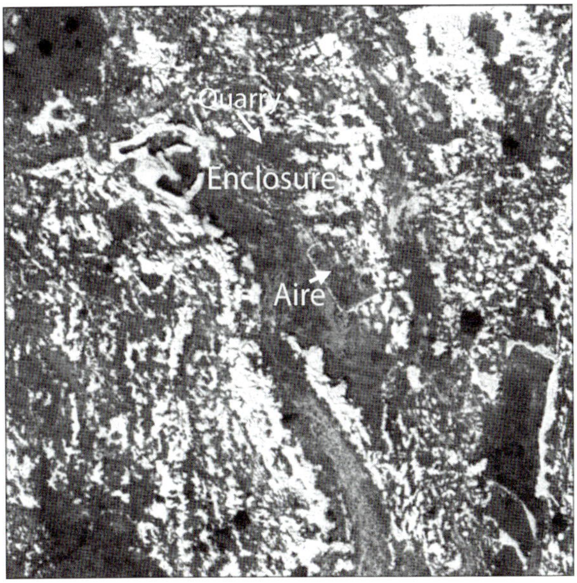

FIGURE 139. Baoume de Brun: vertical air photograph of excavated enclosure and environs
AIR PHOTOGRAPH REPRODUCED BY KIND PERMISSION OF THE IGN; DRAWING: DAVID AUSTIN

Their distribution across the commune does show, rather more clearly, however, that they are far more numerous than the *bergeries* and that they are almost exclusively limited to the upland parts of Cipières' territory (Figure 137). This wider distribution also confirms that their spread, as in the Baoume de Brun study area, was not uniform. Indeed they appear broadly to occur alongside patches of ground offering good pasture, usually but not exclusively dolines, and near the main long-distance trackways, including those, as we have seen in Baoume de Brun, which do not occur on the 19th century maps. One good example of this is the point at the eastern end of La Combe (Valarouvo) where the main access route from the village to the upland ceases for a moment its steep ascent and then forks four ways off to the Gros Pounch, along La Combe towards La Pinée, and then up onto the Plateau as the two long-distance roads, one towards Grasse and the other towards Caussols (Figure 138). The clear impression then is that these enclosures are pastoral structures linked to transhumance albeit of a short-distance kind from the Cipières lowland. We chose to excavate the most striking example of this kind of architecture that lay within the survey area (Figures 139 & 140) The intention was to provide some dating and to explore the development of the structures. We wanted also to see

FIGURE 140. Baoume de Brun: view of the excavated enclosure
PHOTOGRAPH: DAVID AUSTIN)

above left: FIGURE 141. Baoume de Brun: the excavated enclosure at the end of a long cleared field

PHOTOGRAPH: DAVID AUSTIN

above right: FIGURE 142. Baoume de Brun: view of the enclosure, quarry (to the right in the middle distance) and *aire* (foreground)

PHOTOGRAPH: DAVID AUSTIN

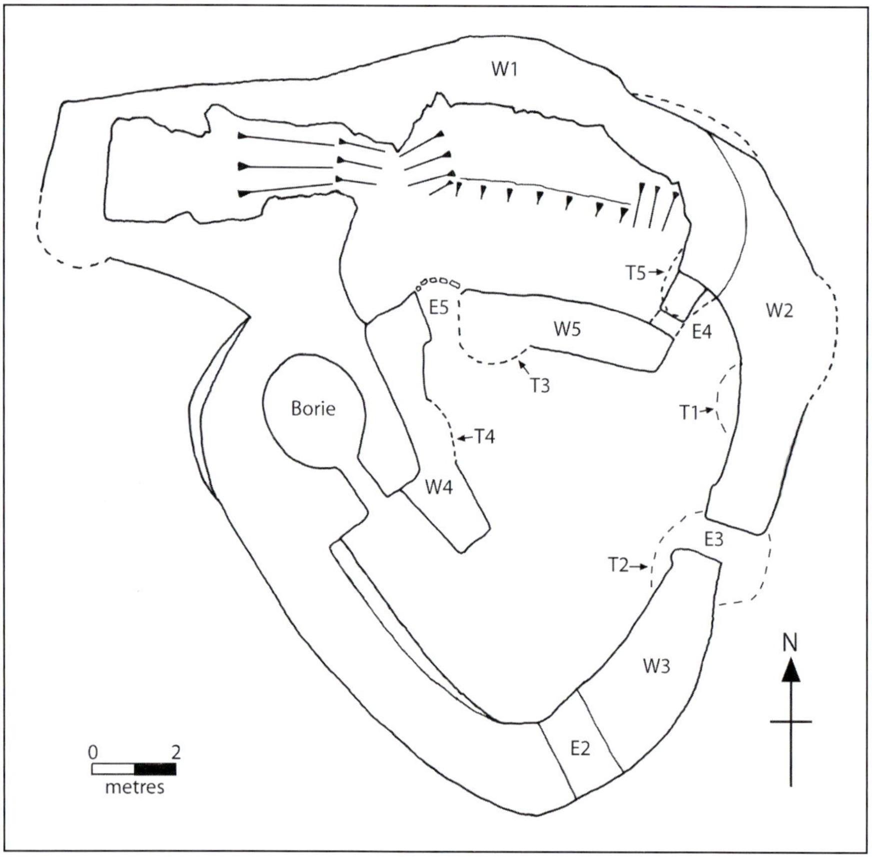

FIGURE 143. Baoume de Brun: survey of excavated enclosure

DRAWING: DAVID AUSTIN

whether we could develop some clarity about their function and relationship with the surrounding cultural landscape.

There was also, however, another motivation. We wanted to generate a descriptive picture of the way of life that this landscape represents, in other words to humanise the physical remains and to reflect the experience of the peasants who had at least a part of their life there. This would have to include narrating the pattern of human movement around the Baoume de Brun area and the journeying of people between there and the village or elsewhere. By this means we hoped to inject some sense of human agency into the account of social and economic structures. In this way the writing became a kind of biography: a life of people and, by metaphorical extension, a life of things. What connects these things is the human thread of action. We shall return to this biography later.

The partially collapsed enclosure we chose to excavate lay at the north (upper) end of a long curving cleared field area retained at its lower end by revetment (Figures 139 & 141). All the entrances to the enclosure faced this field area. To the east of it were the traces of a small, shallow quarry and an overgrown stone-floored *aire* or threshing floor (Figure 142). It incorporated a large corbelled *borie*, a small rectangular shelter and two internal courtyards (Figure 143). It was, however, its evidence of butt joins and blocked entrances which principally attracted us because this suggested a complexity of development and use not common to this form of architecture. In plan it was curvilinear and partially, on the north side, built against a small rock cliff. All its structural elements consisted of dry stone walls. Immediately to the east of the enclosure were the traces of stone quarrying and working areas which we believe can be directly associated with some phases of construction.

FIGURE 144. Baoume de Brun: excavation trench A in front of *borie* entrance
PHOTOGRAPH: DAVID AUSTIN

After clearing the dense vegetation we sited five small trenches at various locations inside and outside the walls to explore key stratigraphic relationships (e.g. Figure 144). At the same time we cleared tumbled stone from several additional places around the site to clarify the plans and sequences of walls. Out of all this we produced an interpretation with which we were reasonably satisfied, but we must also admit that it was possible to produce, on the same evidence, other sequences. However, most were broadly similar with only minor differences particularly in the later phases, and what we have produced here is the essential sequence. All of the detailed arguments are rehearsed in the full excavation report,[10] but only the conclusions and principal evidences are presented here (Figure 145). It should be noted, however, that the final conclusions on sequence which follow differ from those of the initial excavators, but are still based on the evidence of sequence and succession.

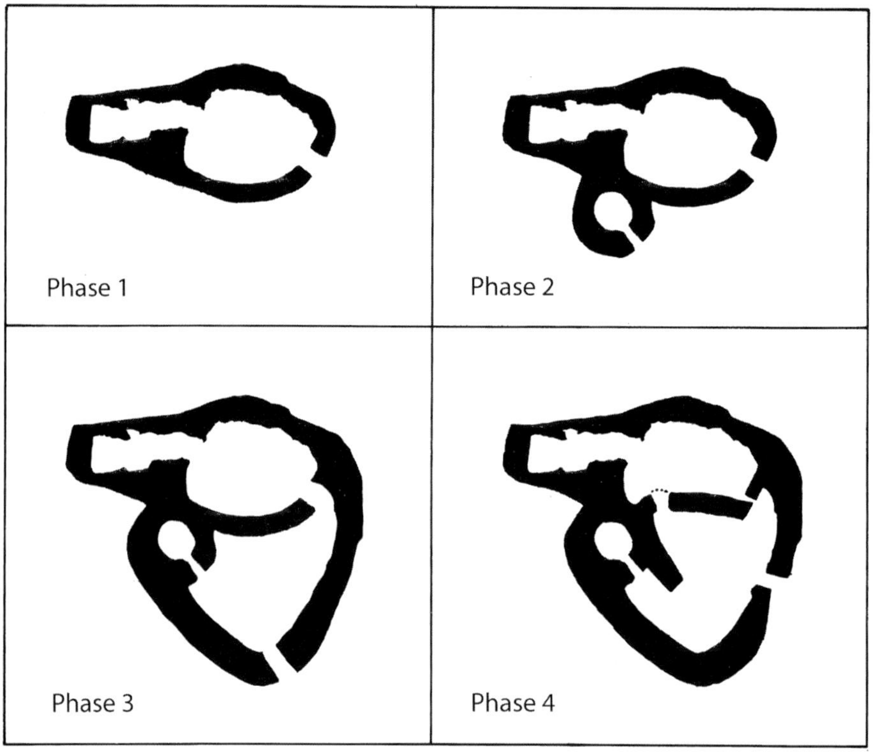

FIGURE 145. Baoume de Brun: excavated enclosure phase sequence
DRAWING: DAVID AUSTIN

Phase 1: The earliest elements appear to be the rough rectangular shelter and a small enclosure to the east, both of which utilise the rock-cliff as the north side. It is uncertain whether the south wall was on exactly the same alignment as the later dividing wall (W5), since no trace of this was found in the excavation, but it is likely that this does represent at least the approximate position. It is also unclear whether the entrance was at the east end as shown in the plan (E4), but the curving terminal at the north-east corner is certainly a primary feature and it was one side of an early opening. The curve of this early wall and the position of the opening do suggest that the phase-1 south wall lay a little further south than wall (W5) and this is how it is drawn in Figure 145.

Phase 2: The next detectable phase was the insertion of the *borie* into the early shelter, an action marked by a butt join on the new structure's north side. Phases 2 and 3 may, however, have been executed at more or less the same time, but the excavation and survey left us uncertain. In the two-phase interpretation it is possible to argue that the *borie* was added first, almost certainly in a slighter form than the one we surveyed in 1994, as there were certainly two distinct phases in the construction of its corbelled roof. However, this is not necessarily good evidence of even relative sequence: constant strengthening and refurbishing down to the modern day has masked any early relationships we might have been able to detect in the fabric of the walls. Because it was still a resource of the shepherds on the plateau until very recently we did not dismantle any part of

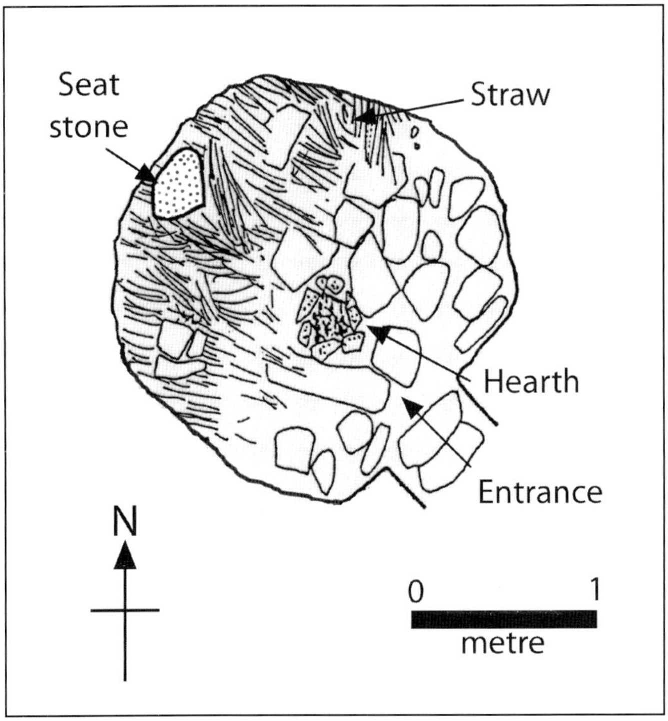

FIGURE 146. *Borie* interior
DRAWING: DAVID AUSTIN

it to examine its stratigraphy. Although archaeologically this was a problem, it had ethnographical benefits and we were able to record the internal remains of a night's stay which we had found on an earlier reconnaissance in a nearby *borie* (Figure 146). It is an indicator of the kind of arrangements we might have expected to see when the *borie* was first built. A large cube of limestone had been set up as a seat in front of a small central fire of pine-cones laid on rough flagging which formed the floor. Between the fire and the seat, straw had been scattered for bedding, strewn in such a manner that it was thickest in the parts furthest from the entrance which was diametrically opposite to the seat. On top of the straw to one side of the seat three stones had been laid perhaps as the base for a pillow, and in the wall behind the seat was a niche about a metre above the floor for the storage of food and other perishables. So the shepherd or farmer, sitting or lying, looked across the fire towards the sole source of light seeping in at low level onto the floor. The fire was a warm barrier against the cold night air as well as threatening animals, and the smoke rose high into the corbelled vault, filtering out through the layered stones.

Phase 3: At this point the enclosure was enlarged by the addition of a curving wall (W2) although it is uncertain whether the original south wall was retained. This may even have collapsed because the new wall had been built over a spread of loose stone tumble (T2). If this is so, then there was perhaps a period of abandonment and decay before the opening of phase 3. It should also be noted that both the tumble and the new wall also partially overlay soils which appeared to be the top end of the long field stretching away southwards. This suggested to us that the origins of this area of agriculture at least were earlier than the developed enclosure. The new entrance (E2) to the enlarged enclosure gave direct access also to the *borie*.

Phase 4 Preceding this next phase there seems to have been another period of decay and partial collapse which was tidied up by stacking fallen stone against the inner wall of the enclosure (T1). Following this the enclosure appears to have been sub-divided by a partition wall (W5), made of roughly dressed stone, at the same time as the eastern side of the *borie* was strengthened at the base by a metre high dry-stone wall (W4) with a flat top. This was also extended to make a short passage in front of the *borie* entrance. Other strengthening and re-roofing of the *borie* with better-dressed stones may have taken place at the same time. However the original direct access was lost when the original entrance (E2) to the enlarged enclosure was blocked and moved 3 m to the north (E3).

In phase 4, too, the walling on top of the natural cliff was added to heighten the inner enclosure. Indeed all of this back area of the enclosure seems to have been modified to permit the construction of a roof. The new partition wall, for example, curved parallel to the back cliff and the added walling on the cliff itself would have allowed a sloping pent roof to be anchored between the two. That the partition wall was intended to be load bearing is also indicated by the greater care taken in constructing it, using roughly-dressed and freshly-quarried stone, rather than the eroded fieldstone of the other walls. A shallow quarry next to the enclosure, directly to the east, was probably the source. As part of this careful building a niche had been incorporated into the north face of the partition wall, and this seemed to confirm that this had been intended as an interior surface.

Two gaps existed in the partition wall: one (E5) was clearly the main entrance and with its vertical jambs had almost certainly had a door at one time; the other (E4) at the east end was more enigmatic, being narrowed to half a man's width by a blocking wall built over tumble from the previous phase (T5). At this point the newly heightened back wall was slightly corbelled out as if partly to protect this entrance which itself was partially blocked by a very well constructed low wall.

Phase 5 This was a phase of decay when the enclosure was collapsing and tumble roughly stacked against the inner walls. The roof of the new structure at the back was lost and one of the jambs of its main door had fallen. In this collapse there were a few pieces of broken roof-tile, but not in sufficient quantities to suggest that this had ever formed the main roofing material which we must assume had been almost entirely organic. Only the *borie* was kept in a good state of repair and a few fragments of sandy-tempered, pottery accumulated in the entrance passage at this time. This was, in fact, the only useful dating material we found and does suggest that all but phase 5 had occurred before the 18th century when these types of ceramic were in circulation (Poteur, pers. comm.)

Providing absolute dates for each phase of the sequence is, however, ultimately impossible, partly because of the site's very shallow stratigraphies, but mainly because of the failure to find enough artefacts. The best we can do is to try fitting what we have into what we know of the wider sequences of the Cipières upland and the community. So we would like to suggest that phase 5, the period when the *borie* was in use but with a decayed enclosure, lies within the span of the last 300 years or so when the focus of animal husbandry seems to have shifted elsewhere, probably to the nearby Bergerie de Poumeirès which is still in use.

Prior to that, in phase 4, there was the enclosure with back barn and strengthened *borie*, an arrangement which suggests a small animal-management structure, but of a type which almost certainly precedes the larger, purpose-built masonry structures with tile roofs known to be in existence by the early part of the 18th century. It was clearly intended to handle a small flock of perhaps 25–30 animals at most and probably one restricted to the immediate vicinity. We would propose that this belongs to the early post-medieval era of the later 16th–early 18th centuries.

Before this, and separated from it by a period of partial collapse, was phase 3 when the larger enclosure had come into existence, being at least partially built over the soils of the adjacent field. This would have allowed stock husbandry on a similar scale to that of phase 4, but without provision for cover. All of this might suggest that this phase came at a time when the emphasis of agricultural activity on the plateau was beginning to shift towards pastoralism and away from crop production. We might very tentatively suggest that this was happening towards the end of the Middle Ages. Phase 3 or possibly phase 4 was also the time when the flagged stones of the *aire* (Figure 147) were laid out over the edge of the cleared field in front of it. These stones seem also to have been quarried and rough dressed rather than gathered from clearance. This might fit with a time when threshing grain away from the lord's facilities was becoming more possible, perhaps as the ties of lordship weakened when the middle ages turned towards modernity.

As said above it may be that the larger enclosure of phase 3 was created at the same time as the *borie* was added in phase 2, in other words they were not

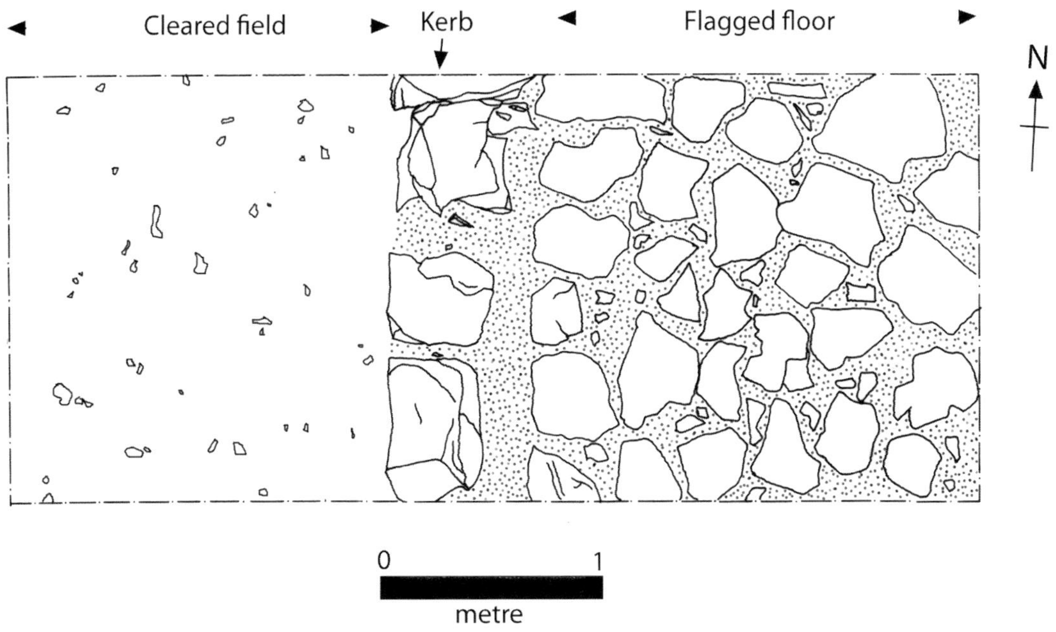

FIGURE 147. Baoume de Brun: plan of excavated *aire*
DRAWING: DAVID AUSTIN

so much distinctly different time periods, but simply stages in much the same process. For this reason we must be conservative and attribute phase 2 also to the end of the middle ages. This leaves phase 1 to be earlier medieval and to have been made when the cultural landscape, the workscape, of our surveyed area was being created, probably between the thirteenth and fourteenth centuries.

The Middle Ages

Our next step is to widen our account of the Middle Ages out into the whole survey area. For this period, however, we have no names for people we can directly associate with the patches of ground we are examining. We do, however, have a landscape and the biggest issue for us to address is the temporal relationship between, on the one hand, the pattern of landholding and fiscal demarcation we have tracked backwards from the first map of 1842 and, on the other, the pattern of land clearance and use, the 'workscape', which we have surveyed. We have asserted from the earliest work in L'Aspi and La Combe that there is a hiatus, a clear disjunction between the two, and, if we simply map one onto the other in Baoume de Brun, noting only the places where there is a direct relationship, the evidence seems indisputable (Figure 148).

The map shows us how infrequently the boundaries of the parcels and *quartiers*, whether new or old, have a relationship with the workscape, as, indeed, we had found in La Combe. In many cases the boundaries cross the workscape areas and where there is coincidence of property and physical boundary, it appears entirely adventitious. So, for example, on the south-western corner of Holding O (BdB10 in 1842), the boundary follows a low terrace retaining a single field divided between two adjacent parcels (Figure 149). At each end, however, the boundary then abandons the field edge to find its way across different terrains without visible marker. This again happens between E2 and C (Figure 150). Where the boundary lies between or across contiguous pieces of good land, essentially the dolines, the line travels briefly along a terrace wall only to abandon it once the contiguity disappears. The best example of this is where the three holdings O, E3 and C meet at the junction of three dolines (Figure 151).

Elsewhere there are rare incidents where property boundaries do appear to have been marked. These take three forms: 'cross walls', 'marker cairns' and tracks. The longest example of a cross wall lies between Les Poumeirès 2 and 3, where a low embankment incorporating stones has been laid across the flat surface of the large uvula which constitutes the best land in both parcels (Figure 152). It exists only on the uvula floor and is clearly the last event in that topographical feature's long stratigraphy. Nonetheless the boundary is for two parcels whose existence can be traced back to the 18th century at least. Elsewhere, as between holdings B & E, what can best be described as narrow linear cairns had been laid down slope over the top of, or abutting, other cairns, terraces and proto-terraces which lie along the contours in bands (Figure

FIGURE 148. Baoume de Brun: correlation of 1842 boundaires and workscape elements
DRAWING: DAVID AUSTIN

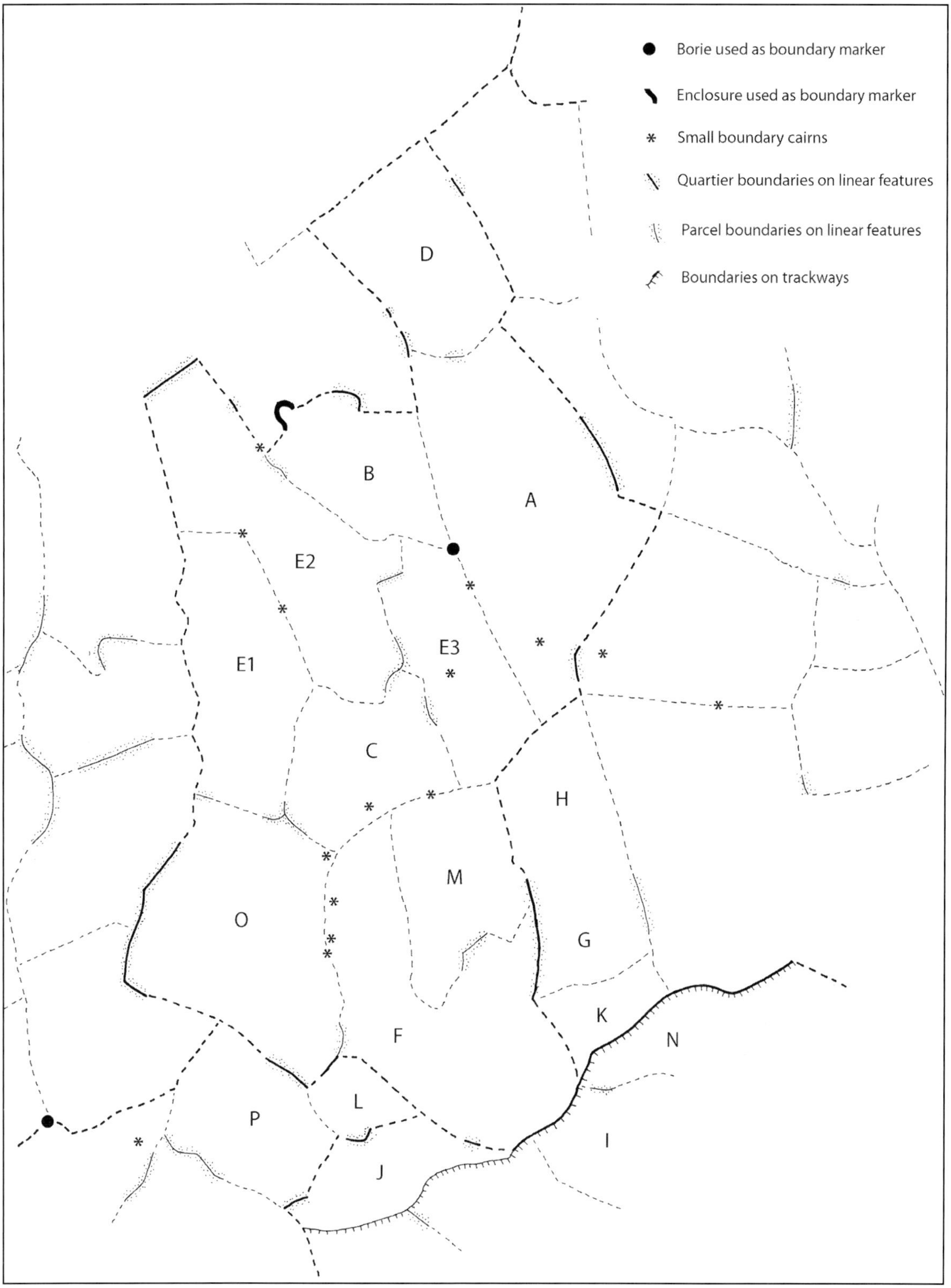
Borie used as boundary marker
Enclosure used as boundary marker
Small boundary cairns
Quartier boundaries on linear features
Parcel boundaries on linear features
Boundaries on trackways
D
B
A
E2
E1
E3
C
H
M
O
G
K
N
F
L
P
I
J

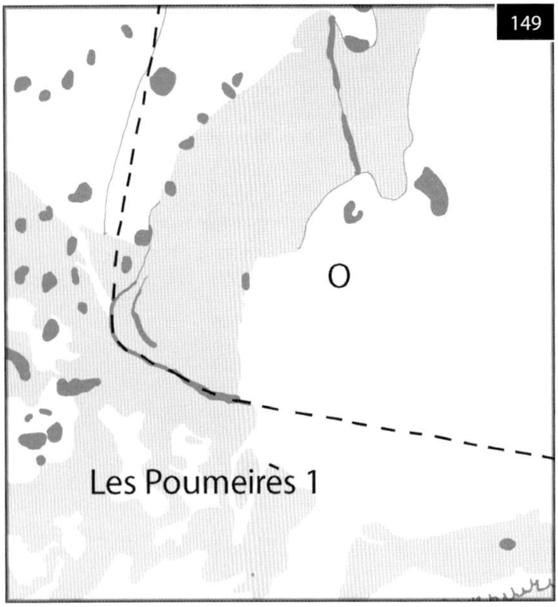

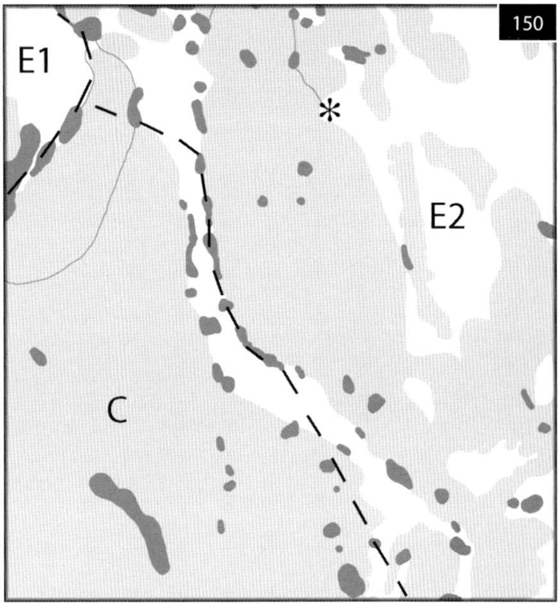

153). They are not continuous and appear to be indicators of where the property boundary falls in terrains where the cultural features lie completely at right-angles to the direction of landholding. Also in strict archaeological terms these are the last events in the sequence. Generally where the workscapes are respected it is in the case of doline or uvula terracing and parts of the edges of the larger cleared fields. Nevertheless this is not consistent and we formed the impression that at the time the parcel boundaries had been created, the only cleared land still functioning was the best of it.

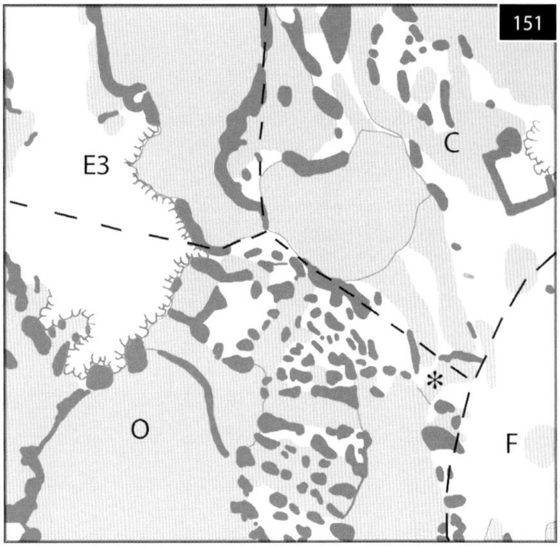

To reinforce this impression we would also note that when we were carrying out the fieldwork for the survey we would occasionally become aware of small piles of stones set in prominent positions on the top of rock outcrops, clearance cairns and proto-terraces. We recorded these as 'marker cairns' (asterisks on Figures 122, 143 & 153), but only where we were absolutely certain they existed and that they were deliberate acts, distinctly separate from the agricultural remains. When correlated with the property boundaries, there was only one instance (E1/E2) where more than one of these markers coincided exactly and another (D/F) where more than one lay approximately on the same alignment. Elsewhere two isolated cairns made exact fits and others made no fit at all. While our conservative criteria

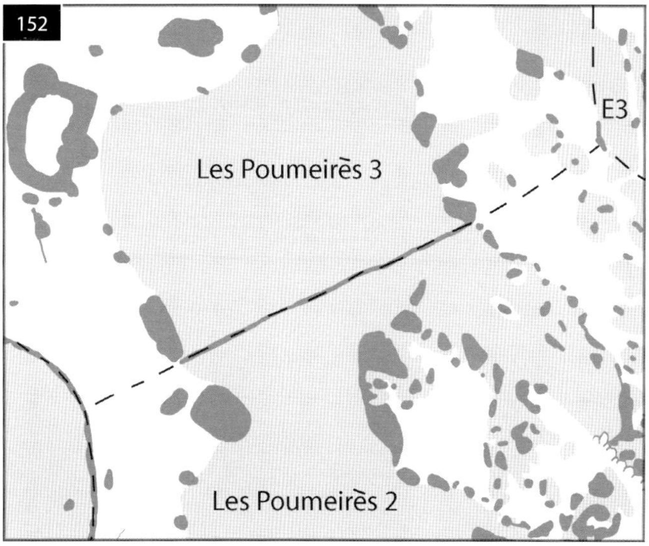

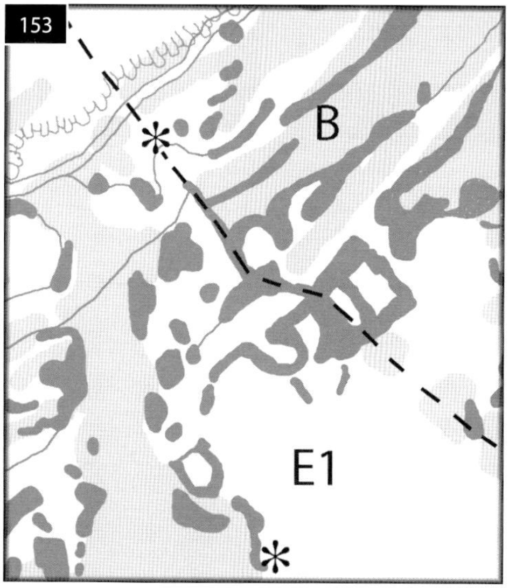

FIGURE 149. Baoume de Brun: boundary between holdings O and Poumeirès 1

FIGURE 150. Baoume de Brun: boundary between holdings C and E2

FIGURE 151. Baoume de Brun: boundary between holdings C, O and E3

FIGURE 152. Baoume de Brun: boundary between holdings Les Poumeirès 2 and 3

FIGURE 153. Baoume de Brun: boundary between holdings B and E1

DRAWING: QUENTIN DREW AND DAVID AUSTIN

of survey limited our recording of the occurrences of this phenomenon to a statistically unusable number, it is nonetheless worth noting that the only case of true coincidence of cairn with property (E1/E2) was where we know the boundary to have been made before 1758 when Pierre and Jean Baptiste Camatte were first recorded as holding the separated inheritance of Joseph Camatte. We cannot be certain that the cairns were erected then and much more fieldwork needs to be done to confirm all of this, perhaps by relaxing our criteria, but it is clear that marking the parcel was the latest and most selective act in the cultural landscape and was done on more than one occasion and probably for parcels we have now lost sight of because they were too early to be recorded. Couple this with the idea of fading intimacy and familiarity and the lack of daily contact and we may be seeing the addition of visible marks only when the knowledge of edges was fading.

If we now turn to trackways, there are, as we have described above, two structured tracks running through the surveyed area: the northern and southern. Neither of them appears on the cadastral maps of 1842, and only the southern is mentioned in the boundary clauses of the 1727 and 1791 cadastres, as '*le chemin voisinal*', i.e. a local track with no long-distance implications. However, it is this track which continuously serves as boundary for both parcels and *quartiers*. By 1842 the relationship with the *quartiers* and probably also knowledge of its existence had been lost, another example of fading familiarity. By then certainly it had lost its function, at least as far as the mapmakers were concerned. If we look closely at the line of the track, however, we can also see that its defining walls cut across the microtopographies of cleared fields and cairnfields. In other words there are the beginnings of a succession here (Figure 154). The clearances represented by the fields were followed by the track, which was in turn followed by the parcel boundaries using it as a marker. These should not, however, be seen simply as discrete blocks of time: the track almost certainly came into existence as the clearances of land were continuing and indeed the accumulation of stone along its length meant that the users were to keep clear of the ground around, probably because of growing crops. The track must also have been functioning when the parcels came into existence.

The northern track is even more time laden. This narrow path crosses Les Poumeirès from the west, runs along the bench (zone B) and then climbs onto the top of the ridge (zone A) before dropping rapidly down the steep slope to meet the main track from Caussols to Cipières. It is very clearly marked along its length by linear cairns and it edges around the side of terraces and enclosures. In places also the path is worn heavily into the surface of the rock. The overall impression is of a major routeway. However, its existence forms no part of the formal knowledge of the community, as represented by documents. Why? Could it be because, when the parcels were created and mutated, this track did not exist? This seems highly unlikely. If it was created in the 17th or 18th centuries after the parcels, it would almost certainly have been functioning into the 19th, given its obvious longevity of use. We are left then with the greater probability that it went out of use before the parcels were created, that it relates to a time before the 16th century. Since, however, it crosses and circum-navigates other features we must look for confirmation that these also may be as old as that.

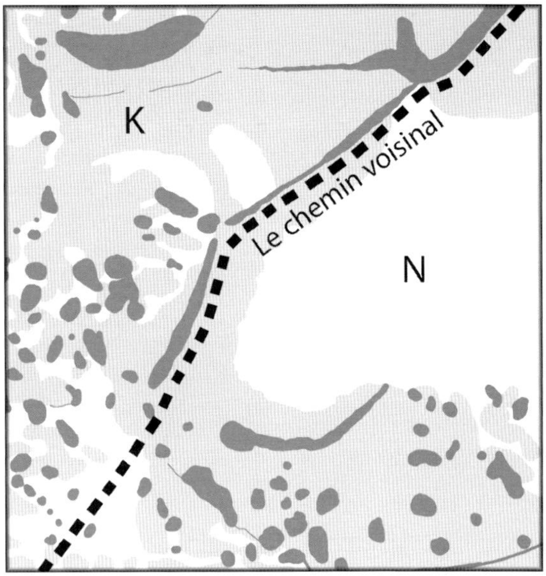

FIGURE 154. Baoume de Brun: line of le chemin voisinal

DRAWING: QUENTIN DREW AND DAVID AUSTIN

This brings us to a closer consideration of the nature and meaning of both the workscape and the parcel pattern themselves. We must again begin with the earliest cartography as our base point. Figure 129 maps the pattern of parcels indicating the land in each which was regarded by the cadastral officials as the most highly assessed. This is correlated with the survey results and land use classifications. Some simple conclusions are clear. As we have already seen, the majority of the boundaries of every parcel cut across areas of flat and sloping fields, all types of cairnfields, doline cascades and even, in the largest example, a large doline. The purpose seems obvious: the deliberate attempt, within the general limitations of the topography, to give each parcel a relatively even-handed access to a variety of land quality from the best to the worst, although this was not always possible. The dolines, with their relatively rich and sheltered soils into which water would flow regularly, albeit episodically, tended to lie physically at the centre of parcels with the rest of the land assessed as rough pasture. Thus the correlations show that all the dolines in the survey area were highly prized and were ranked as the best. All the other categories we identified in the field, however much intensity of effort they displayed, were only partially identified in this way. The rich and relatively well-watered doline cascades were largely ignored as were the areas of terraces, proto-terraces and heavy cairnfields in the northern part of the survey area, for example in parcel D (cf. Figure 124). When it comes to the areas of fields, whether sloping or flat, only parts of these were more highly rated. Of course, we must be extremely careful when using taxation assessments because these will not always correlate directly with other perceptions of land use and value whether to the peasant landholder or to the objective archaeologist and historian. However, the indications are consistent and abundant enough that both the stability of the pattern of landholding and the small number of changes we have seen going back in time demonstrate that this was a long-term principle of the parcel's space and its system of tenure.

We can be confident by now also that, at least in Baoume de Brun, this was not the principle by which the bulk of the workscape was formed and used, at least initially. The construction of parcels and their boundaries over-rides a previous landscape. This does not mean that the process of clearance and cultivation stopped entirely, but it does mean that the structural elements of the workscape were set and arranged well before the parcels we can detect from our retrogressive analysis came into existence. The mental approach of men and women to the spaces they moved amongst on the Cipières upland shifted, and the change must have been fundamental. From everything that has gone before, therefore, we can now be relatively sure that the physical relics of land use left on the surface of the Cipières upland is, in its structure and much of its detail, probably medieval in form and use with, only in some more favoured locations, later elaboration and effort.

Once we look back beyond the modern era, the quantity of documentation, however, rapidly decreases and we can only catch glimpses of the kind of detail we need for the types of analysis we have used so far. From the field evidence and the general conclusions we can draw from the documents, the workscape is related to a highly varying pattern of mixed arable and pasture, but can we express this in terms also of social structure? Our analysis to date has depended on the continuity of both property parcels and *quartiers* to identify the relationship with documented human beings. It is clear that these social structures are both fully functioning and already complex in 1531 (see Appendix 1). They are clearly, therefore, a legacy of something earlier, but how much earlier? For the area of Baoume de Brun we have no detailed medieval documentation and so the question is one for the historian working on the commune as a whole (see Rosamond Faith, Chapters 5 & 7).

What we can say from the archaeology, however, is that the patterns and arrangements of the 'workscape' have only a passing relationship to the *quartiers* and parcels as we have them in the modern era. They seem, therefore, to have been formed at a time when these structures were either absent or were still, in these upland areas, highly negotiable and fluid. In the medieval documentation, there is no reference to parcels, only to *terres* or plots of land held by individuals at least by the 14th century and there are no *quartiers* as such. Lands are simply said to be 'in' a named place, not all of which were still present in 1531 (see Appendix 1 and Figure 53). Whether these named places were administratively bounded spaces by this time or looser topographical indicators is not clear. If they did have administrative function, we have no evidence of what this was. The 'lands' (*terres*), on the other hand, we can presume to be bounded and known. However, from the records that survive we cannot tell whether it is the later parcels or the 'workscapes' which are intended. This may also differ across the face of the commune as a whole and from period to period. On the better and closer lands of the intensively worked lowland the 'lands' may have emerged early as strictly bounded and 'owned' parcels, while on the upland this might have been later and intermittent where the taking of land might have been more opportunistic and piecemeal in places and more sustained and focussed in others, notably the scattered dolines and uvulas of zone III.6. What we can be a little more sure about, as we have seen above in our excavation, is that the small roofless enclosures and the *bories* are most likely to have begun as part of the earlier workscapes than the later documented land uses.

We now come to some very difficult questions: how and when was the system of parcels and *quartiers* superimposed. Was it under the direct management of the seigneur, and was it all done as a single measure at one moment? Or was it the result of the slow decay of an older set of arrangements? Were the workscapes ever themselves property blocks, i.e. resulting from the strategies and efforts of individual nuclear families? This would seem to be highly unlikely because there is far too much differentiation in the potential productivity of the land. Adjacent neighbours would have had extravagantly different capacity to grow crops and pasture their animals. Was it then a pattern arising from collective action? If so, was it the coerced or voluntary collaboration of nuclear families or was it a practice located within larger social structures than the nuclear family, for example the *ostals* discussed later by Rosamond Faith and David Siddle? Here, in the *longue durée*, we need a solution which allows the creation of the workscapes, their operation and then the subsequent imposition of fixed boundaries when only restricted locations continued to be worked. This is the physical sequence we see.

It is certainly hard to avoid the impression that the workscapes were created when the territories were managed in much larger blocks. So could we be looking at exploitation by larger social units than the individual proprietor and their nuclear families, who cleared the ground area by area, rather than parcel by parcel? If so can we detect the boundaries of these? Is there any evidence of this in the 16th century apportionment of parcels, i.e. are there any vestigial indicators of these larger units? Can we find hints of such units of landholding mentioned in the medieval documents? We can only say at the moment that this solution would be neat and tidy, because it would mean that in the medieval life of the landscape the control of the non-seigneurial land would probably have been in the hands of a smaller number of social units. We are now beginning to see the possibility of the perception and manipulation of space in the village and its landscape undergoing radical change at the same time later in the middle ages and into the modern era. Many of the questions posed here cannot be directly answered from the fieldwork we were able to conduct nor from the narrow perspective of a spatially limited consideration of the documents. This must come in the following chapters and for some other time when our methodologies can be applied more universally and systematically across the whole commune and even beyond.

Biography of a parcel

To summarise what we have understood about the sequence of events in Baoume de Brun I want to present the biography of one piece of ground (E1). We have little notion of precisely when this piece of landscape was first cleared for cultivation, except to be sure that there are no signs of sustained occupation either here, or even elsewhere on the Cipières upland, before the 12th or early 13th centuries. What the *terre gaste* of that period consisted of is hard to tell, but it may have had a high incidence of trees as well as garrigue, given how frequently they appear in the naming of some of the topographies in this area (see Chapter 1). We are also unclear how precisely the landscape of this area functioned in the Middle Ages, before the parcels were imposed. The workscape involved perhaps several people from a large family or kin unit engaged in land clearance and cultivation. The main focus would have been on breaking ground on a relatively extensive basis, some of it quite difficult to cultivate, and in some cases the strategy must have been to clear and prepare just a few times at various intervals depending on the family life cycles and needs. Where the ground enabled, over time, more spacious fields to be cleared, then a more regular and systematic pattern of cultivation would have been possible, involving manuring by stock during fallow periods. This must have involved repeated acts of stone clearance.

The best land, in the dolines and uvulas, was slowly consolidated by cairns, then proto-terraces and finally terraces and low revetment walls and kept under intensive cultivation for long periods of time. In this area the stock was managed in relatively small flocks of sheep and maybe groups of other animals such as cattle within the enclosures. At first, this enclosure was relatively modest utilising a natural rock shelter beneath an outcrop of rock (phase 1), but over time as more land was cleared and the fertility improved, a better shelter was added to the complex (phase 2). These enclosures, in the general farming strategy, lay close to the earliest roads and tracks and their distribution shows that they spread out over the upland along the dendritic road system leading from the village. Thus the farming families built enclosures near the roads, but not elsewhere on their land as in the Baoume de Brun survey area where they were clustered up towards the northern track. This kind of response reinforces our sense of the upland being regarded as an extensive resource for colonisation, reaching out gradually from the village, a phase reaching its zenith in the fourteenth century at the time of Raibaude de Caussols, as Rosamond Faith describes later.

Perhaps it is after this that the area of Baoume de Brun then begins to change and develop into a landscape where pastoralism slowly gains the upper hand and the long retreat from cultivation starts. It is in this time that there seems to be first a hint of temporary disuse in the sequences of the excavated enclosure and then rebuilding over some of the previously cleared and cultivated ground to create a larger structure (phase 3). What then emerges is still mixed farming in the earlier way, but there is a much greater emphasis on caring for more stock in the larger enclosure. We must also envisage that the extensive clearing of ground decreased, perhaps dramatically, as the balance of the social unit switched away from the extended families towards the nuclear, individualised households. As this happened so then perhaps the parcels were laid out and places became *quartiers*.

By 1531, the populations were again beginning to grow, after the stresses of the later 14th century, but now in different patterns of social organisation. By this time the land was held in small, demarcated parcels, scattered through many different, nuclear families and created to give both good and bad land to the owner. Land use was focussed on smaller intensive areas of arable, but still this appears to have been a consistent activity despite climatic deterioration and those who issued the assessments in the cadastres and deliberations made an assumption that landowners were growing crops and did so for a few centuries to come. As time went on, however, this assumption became more and more detached from reality and the farmers burdened by expectations they could not achieve. Of the possible holders of the land in the early 16th and 17th centuries we can say that Honorat Pons and Anthony Girard in 1531 and Anthony Pons and Martin Flory in 1610 all belong to the older families of Cipières. They were living and working at the time when the *borie* and enclosure were at their largest (phase 4) and the relationship between the use of the land for grazing and arable production was still in some kind of equilibrium before the advent of big commercial flocks using the upland in an almost exclusive fashion. Already, however, the architecture of the enclosure with its roofed inner part was beginning to anticipate the arrival of the bigger, purpose-built *bergeries*. Despite this equilibrium, however, it is hard to believe, from what we have observed, that, when they were farming on the upland, they were doing much more than laying down crops in the very best of the fields and the doline and uvula floors. What grain they did produce, however, off this, the richest of the parcels in Clapiers de Brun, was threshed on their own *aire* next to the land rather than down in the village on the great *aires* constructed there in its big expansion during this era.

In 1727 the heirs of Joseph Camatte were in possession collectively while the inheritance was in dispute, but how they came to have it and precisely when Joseph himself had died we cannot tell from the records we have currently examined. We *do* know, however, that the parcel itself was created when this much larger holding was finally broken up, in or before 1758, when the two brothers, Jean Baptiste and Joseph Camatte, legally inherited it, along with others, from their father Joseph. The Camatte clan also could trace its associations with the village back to the early fourteenth century at least. The exceptional legal nature of this holding may also be indicated by the fact that it is unusually a single entry in the register which otherwise lists everything held by individuals under their own name. In 1727 this large tract of land, said to be in the *quartier* of Clapiers de Brun, was estimated at 3600 *cannes*, 2.5 *panaux* (baskets) of seed valued at 25 *livres*, 3 *panaux* for more impoverished land at 24 *livres*, 2.5 *panaux* of still more impoverished at 15 *livres* and 1600 *cannes* of infertile land at 15 *sols*, valued in all at 64 *livres* 15 *sols*. At first sight this seems to suggest a high degree of grain production, but we must remember that this was primarily an assessment for taxation purposes, a kind of rateable value. Indeed these assessments appear to have gone unchanged since the 16th/17th century at least which means that they could not have been reflecting any of the changes happening throughout that period.

Indeed the archaeology suggests that by 1727 the agriculture of this parcel was dominated by pastoralism and one controlled largely from a small number of major *bergeries*. Under these circumstances the early enclosure had fallen into disuse and only the corbelled *borie* continued to be kept in good order. The impression from the survey and documentary study is that only the dolines were actually in cultivation at this time and then very infrequently. This brings us to a critical question. To what extent did the individual tenant actually farm his or her land and what did they actually do at Baoume de Brun during the 18th century? The answer seems to be that for short periods of the year they took hay from their best land, mostly the dolines, and perhaps at key points in the cycle they supervised the manuring of the same land by sheep and goats. At all other times the shepherds took care to lead the collectivised flocks around the open landscape, letting them graze on the rough unworked pastures between the best land, but keeping them away from the hay fields themselves at critical points in the growing season, largely between May and June. There must also have been an element of maintenance, especially on the best land, where terrace revetments and small shelters needed to be kept in good order. Where such land was ploughed, as it probably was from time to time, and re-seeded, the work would also have involved continuous stone clearance since frost action as well as cultivation frequently brought them to the surface. As we have seen, it is only here that the cairns continued to accumulate. Both the Camattes and Joseph Crist, who seems to have held the parcel briefly before 1782, probably actively farmed their own parcels, but there is plenty of evidence for the 18th century that many tenants sub-let their land to others, especially if they were absent from the village for long periods of time.

At some time between 1782 and 1791, Marie Girard, the widow of Jean Joseph Laugier acquired the parcel from Joseph Crist and through her it passed to Pierre Girard whose head of family was Jean Francis Girard known as La Pesso and who owned it in 1842. In 1842 the parcel was assessed for 0.123 ha of grade 5 'labour', i.e. the lowest quality of ground which, in the estimation of the cadastral assessor, could be used for crop production. This is not to say, however, that it *was* used in this way. Indeed it is much more likely at this time that it yielded only a good crop of hay with perhaps some patches of legumes or hardy grain. In 1842 this parcel was held by Pierre Girard, whose head of family was Jean Francis Girard known as La Pesso. Pierre's main occupation was farming and he held other parcels in the commune. As such he was a modest farmer and he belonged to one of the oldest clans in the village. By now the long retreat from what had been won in the Middle Ages was almost over.

3.5. Summary

Topographies

In the overview it is worth reiterating the marked distinction between the lowland and the upland of the community. The lowland consists of the lands around the village and down to the river (I), the gently rising and intersected landscapes to the south up to and including Le Plan (II), the isolated col of La Pinée (IV) and pockets of flatter ground along the otherwise steep gorge to north and east (V), such as Meynard. The upland has two major components, the better, more sheltered land along Valorouvo (III.1) and La Combe (III.2) and on the benches above it to the south, Le Teil (III.4) and L'Agrémourié (III.5); and the more exposed and less consistent and poorer land on the Plateau de Calern (III.6) and along the ridge of the Gros Pounch (III.3).

The agrarian sequence in the field remains

I would characterise three, maybe four, very broad bands of cultivation remains and their related structures from the work described in this chapter. What is proposed is an evolutionary model of expansion from a settled core out towards an increasingly difficult periphery:

1. *'Constant' intensive cultivation fields and terraces.* These are the well-constructed and consistently maintained and enhanced structures of large revetted cairns and terrace systems. These would have begun as relatively modest clearance structures which were then enhanced over constant use and long periods of time: from observations 11th or early 12th centuries, although we cannot rule out a slightly earlier date. These 'constant' lands are most obviously topographic zone I where they are likely to have been part of cultivation practices continuing without interruption into the late 19th and early 20th centuries. Of course as one moves further away from the village, especially into zone II, these might probably begin slightly later and perhaps fall into disuse rather earlier from the later 18th

century onwards. In such circumstances of constant refurbishment and enhancement, what we can detect from fieldwork is really only the last phase of use.

2. *Less intensive use, but still long-term sustained and consistent effort of maintenance.* This is clearest on the relatively flat areas of the upland, Le Gros Pounch, La Combe, Le Teil, Vaumeillanes, L'Agrémourié and some parts of the Plateau notably in Le Calernet, Les Baumes and Les Poumeirés. These are areas of heavy cairnfields, fields of all kinds, dolines, terraces and proto-terraces. On the heavier slopes within these topographic zones these traces of cultivation vanish. The work in La Combe also showed the processes and stages through which land was cleared into cairns and then worked into terraces and proto-terraces at the bottom of the steeper slopes. This was because, within these topographic zones, the margins showed the episodic nature of agricultural effort where the input produced fewer good results. Within the peasant economy, these were probably where work happened only when labour was available within the family cycle and the need greatest. For reasons discussed above it is possible to argue that the clearances here began perhaps as the village expanded at the end of the 12th or the 13th centuries. This then gathered momentum again later in the Middle Ages and into the modern era when the enclosures were added to the repertoire for managing small flocks. As the modern era developed in the 16th and 17th centuries so the management of pasture came to dominate with the introduction of the *bergerie* system.
3. *More intermittent and opportunistic land use with pockets of more sustained activity.* On the higher lands, such as Baoume de Brun, and increasingly, as we look towards the southern and western limits of the Plateau, some areas of land were worked only on a few occasions (cairnfields) and never returned to, while some were worked into proto-terraces and some into full terraces and maintained over long periods of time. Away from major lower slope areas (soil rich with solifluction), there were also fields where cairns were cleared into larger piles with some more coherent structure to them, but which were not very large and probably only represent episodes of clearance and cultivation. Much of this clearance we see as medieval, perhaps seen where the land was not returned to; the lesser and decayed cairnfields for example. However, the later Middle Ages may have seen a return and consolidation of the better pockets of ground. By the time the larger flocks came into existence, however, little more work was done, except perhaps within the dolines.
4. *Single use or very infrequent clearance and use.* The model here is the landscape at L'Aspi. I see these areas, furthest from the village, being cleared in small patches, planted and cropped until the fertility drops (2 or 3 years at most). The cultivators then moved on to the next patch (i.e. similar to a swidden system), leaving behind a 'quilt-like' pattern

of cairnfields. Perhaps later there was a return to some of the cleared patches with some, but modest enhancement. In such areas the dolines, however, were constantly cultivated or at least had a lot of attention. Such clearances are likely, for the most part, to have been medieval, perhaps 13th and 14th centuries with relatively little activity beyond that. This represents the 'high tide' mark of land use strewn with the debris of many different circumstances of motivation and activity.

Before the Middle Ages: I see Cipières as a territory largely of *terre gaste* until about the 11th or, perhaps at the earliest, the 10th century. There are no early (Iron Age) occupation sites within the commune of the types identified by Bretaudeau[11] and Gazenbeek[12] except on the extreme heights of Colle de Rougiés and debatably Le Gros Pounch. There are also no Roman or early medieval sites in the Commune identified in our (or others') work. I suggest that Cipières was largely seen as a rocky upland (hence perhaps its place-name) with perhaps a little, as yet unidentified activity in zone I. If it was anything it was probably a rather scrubby and perhaps wooded area used intermittently by the scattered and dispersed communities in neighbouring territories. Caussols (on lower and more hospitable land) and Greolières (on the main regional Roman through-road) may have used it for pasture and woodland resources. I would argue that not all the medieval villages of the region would necessarily have had the same origins or early history. Simply because they looked very similar later does not mean they necessarily shared the same early histories.

Pre-village (11th and earlier 12th centuries): The village site seems to have been the locus of a *castrum*, a church and perhaps some pre-village farming settlement. The land close to the village, including the terrace system now under it, was the best and first to be cleared and settled. This is probably in a more dispersed pattern, the ghosts of which may be the Bastides mapped from the 1842 cadastre (Figure 155) as well, perhaps, as the *mansus* of the Lérins grant. This will be discussed later by Rosamond Faith. There are five *bastide* farms in 1842, as well as perhaps another one surviving only as the name of a small *quartier* (Bastide du Matheron). This might suggest a network of dispersed farms, some of which may have been substantial, around the village itself and on some of the better land. Figure 155 also shows structural complexity in I, and peripherally in zone II.1, reflecting all the primary activities of a medieval settlement core: i.e. reliable and constant surface running water, relatively good arable, meadow (Les Près to the south and the River Loup meadows to the north), rough summer pastures (Le Plan and the Plateau), habitable places, milling, storage (*masure*), easy communications, and, maybe, defensive capacity.

Later 12th and 13th centuries (and early 14th?): This is the phase of major village creation and the huge extension of the cultivated areas. There would have been

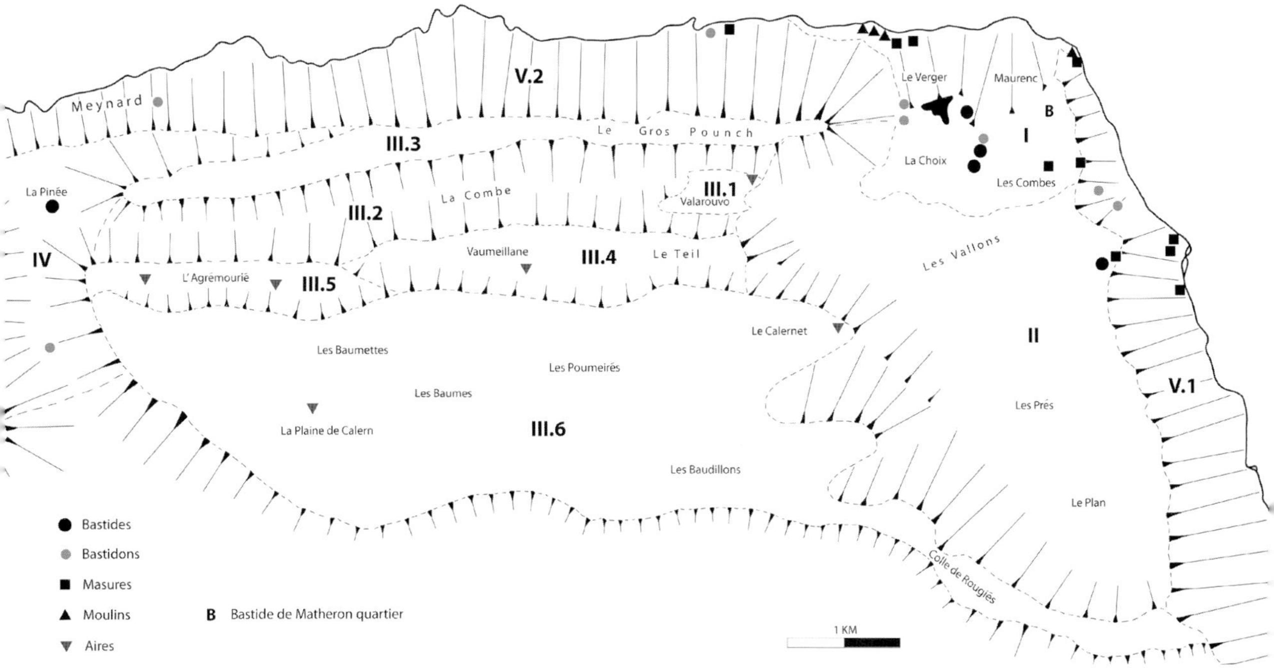

FIGURE 155. Pan-commune: distribution of other buildings in 1842

DRAWING: QUENTIN DREW AND DAVID AUSTIN

intensification of the old core lands and extensification into zone II and up onto the better areas of the 'upland' zone III with more opportunistic forays on to the plateau itself (categories 2 and 3 above).

Later Middle Ages (14th and 15th): For the most part I see the system outlined above continuing, but almost certainly falling away from its greatest extent. I would envisage the lowland core lands being preserved and developed in more or less of a continuum, although the phases of post-medieval use here will have wiped out any evidence of a hiatus if it existed. The 'upland' areas, however, I see as falling away whether temporarily on the better land or permanently on much of the Plateau and Le Gros Pounch. This is when the small enclosures come into the landscape.

Late 15th and 16th centuries: This is a period when the village is expanding and as the one in which the process of conversion to a largely pastoral economy was accelerating and the move towards the *bergerie* system began. More of the former cultivated grounds fall into decay on the 'upland' zone III and, I suspect, on some of the outer areas of the lowland, particularly the southern sub-zones of zone II (Les Prés and Le Plan). The arable focus now is on the old core and on some of the massive terrace systems of, for example, Les Pesses (the valley up to La Combe).

Late 16th and early 17th centuries: Here I see the further consolidation of the core and the completion of the switch to the *bergerie* landscape on the upland. However, we must note that many *bergeries* came also to be established in zones I and II at this time, including the present structure at La Bastide du Puys very close to the village itself.[13]

17th and early 18th century: I would argue for the beginnings of a gradual retreat from arable at the core. If anything happens on the 'upland' outside of the dolines it is more incidental and related to the strategies of family or individual subsistence. The tax goes on being assessed as if it had arable potential, though. It is certainly noticeable that there were six *aires*, well spaced out, on the upland until 1842, although all but one (out on the southern boundary of the commune) were attached to *bergeries* and probably reflected some arable production in the home, well-manured *pâtures* in the immediate vicinity of the buildings. The existence, archaeologically, of other *aires* (not documented in 1842) which I see as being relatively late in the sequence (later 15th onwards), given the excavation at Baoume de Brun, may reflect more the breakdown of the centralised control of threshing and milling, especially out on the periphery (with the one vestigial example of this being recorded out on the far edge of the commune in 1842). The lowland *aires*, without exception in 1842, were attached to the *bastides* exclusively.

Later 18th and early 19th centuries: This is probably when the decay begins to accelerate and other arable areas begin to fall out of production, although the Napoleonic period may have seen some impetus to bring land back into use at least for the duration, while the markets were inflated and supply disrupted. I take it as symptomatic of the decay that in this period there were major adjustments of the *quartier* boundaries, most notably on the Plateau and in Le Plan. This does rather suggest that it was possible here, rather than at the core, because there was much less vested interest in locking in the old pattern of territorial organisation, due to effective abandonment.

19th and 20th centuries: Continued decline leading to a major collapse of the agrarian system by the mid-20th century. Regeneration of the core from the 1960s onwards is based not on agriculture, but driven by a growth in regional population and a diversification of the economy towards tourism and the servicing of major conurbations on the coast.

CHAPTER FOUR

The Les Baumes Landscape Survey: dating the basic agrarian landscape of the Plateau de Calern

Andrew Fleming

An initial survey of part of the Cipières–Caussols road suggested that its construction was largely integral (that is, contemporary) with the cleared parcels of land through which it ran; other roads demonstrate comparable relationships with the agrarian landscape. It is argued that most of this 'primary clearance landscape' contains a recognisable range of characteristic features, and was closely linked with the dendritic pattern of roads originating from Cipières village; this landscape dates from the later Middle Ages. It is argued that with plenty of labour available at this time of high population and large extended families, each zone of cleared land was cleared quickly; the names of the quartiers *on the plateau probably date mostly from this era. On the basis of a landscape survey carried out on the Plateau de Calern, in an area* c. *1 × 1 km, which covers most of the* quartier *of Les Baumes, it has been possible to delineate the features of this primary clearance landscape in more detail – notably the hierarchy of zones of land use, ranging from the richer soils of the dolines, uvulas and stream terraces to less favoured stony areas dotted with clearance cairns. This chapter also discusses quarry zones, doline entrances, pollards, and the nature of parcel boundaries, which were frequently discontinuous as archaeological features. Probably dating from this period is a series of primitive enclosures and the footings of small ovoid or rectangular cabins and of longer rectangular buildings, some more convincing than others. The arguments are illustrated in detail, case studies dealing with a section of the Cipières–Caussols road, a group of 'primitive structures' along the Les Baumes road, and descriptions of parts of the agrarian landscape studied during the Les Baumes survey.*

4.1. Introduction

The archaeological landscape of the Plateau de Calern looks extraordinarily rich and complex – whether one encounters it on the ground or contemplates its representation on large-scale aerial photographs. In the early years of our research it seemed likely that it would prove impenetrable by the methodologies of landscape archaeology, and the successful 'reading' of the history and development of this landscape is a major achievement of the Cipières Project. Furthermore, our attribution of the 'primary clearance landscape' of the Plateau de Calern to the later Middle Ages, rather than to the early modern period, represents a clear departure from the interpretation put forward in current archaeological literature. Poteur's model for the development of the village at Cipières envisages the bulk of this growth as post-medieval, with an expansion from 35 farms in 1471 to 110 houses in 1540 and *c*. 200 in the early 17th century.[1] Poteur's model for the physical development of the village and his perception of the demographic situation are however disputed elsewhere in this volume (Chapters 2, 3 & 6). Poteur also apparently implies that a good deal of the archaeological landscape of the commune, including that of the Plateau de Calern, dates from the end of the 17th century to the middle of the 20th.[2]

I would dispute, as has David Austin above in Chapter 3, the reading of Calern's archaeological landscape as mostly or essentially post-medieval in origin. The keys to understanding for me were provided in my own work, which was carried out mostly in the *quartier* of Les Baumes (as depicted on the 1842 cadastral map). After initial work on the eastern edge of this *quartier* (and to some extent elsewhere) on the relationship between archaeologically-visible roads and adjacent archaeological features, ground survey was carried out over a larger area, covering most of the western two-thirds of the *quartier*. To fit in with the organisation of this book, the results of this survey have been divided between this chapter – which covers basic analytical principles before discussing (mostly) the late medieval landscape – and Chapter 10 which covers the post-medieval period. Inevitably, there is some degree of overlap between the contents of these two chapters.

4.2. Methodologies

The enlarged air photographs obtained from the IGN by Anthony Lewison in the early years of the project have formed an invaluable resource, facilitating both an overall appraisal of the archaeology of the plateau and immediate inspection of detail in any given zone. Many features can be plotted from air photographs, either directly onto a drawing film overlay (if small-scale areal distortion is regarded as unimportant in this context), or after the application of correction factors. As with most such archaeological applications of air photography, ground checking is essential. From air photographs alone it is often not possible to tell the difference between a medium-sized cairn and a collapsed shelter, or between a collapsed corbelled shelter with a hole in the roof and a cairn with a bush or a clump of vegetation at its centre. Vegetation-covered terraces, both in uvula zones and on hillsides, may be largely or completely invisible on air photographs not taken at times when the sun was casting long shadows. Features which cross limestone pavements – such as low walls – are invisible, lost against the white dazzle of the rock. So are more subtle or less immediately obvious features, such as the edging of stones demarcating a threshing floor, the wear on rock surfaces resulting from persistent use of a route or road by flocks of sheep, evidence for quarrying in the form of sharp-edged rock faces or scatters of working debris, and the scatter of broken tiles within a ruined structure. Clearance – particularly linear clearance – almost always follows the roughly parallel lines created by beds of limestone reaching the surface, and it is not always deducible from an air photograph whether one is dealing with weakly developed clearance piles or weathering of exposed rock. (It may not always be possible to make such a hard and fast distinction from the ground either, but it is much easier). Most wall-faces or revetments cannot be seen on the air photographs, especially since many of them are now in an advanced state of collapse.

An initial 'reading' of the landscape was achieved by taking the Caussols to Cipières road, a fairly prominent feature on the air photographs, as a starting-point. This road, still a public right of way, is defined for much of its length by side-walls displaying varying degrees of preservation; its width is also variable. Chronological relationships were inferred between the road and archaeological features linked with it, directly or indirectly, on the assumption that the creation of the constructed road itself must have been completed within a short and well-defined chronological horizon. The stretch of road which was studied formed the boundary between the 1842 *quartiers* of Les Poumeirès and Les Baumes, and further south ran through L'Aspi before crossing the southern edge of the Plateau and descending towards Caussols. The road could be shown to be contemporary with a range of representative constructed features of the archaeological landscape, and a fairly comprehensive picture of what may be called 'the primary clearance horizon' (or 'the primary clearance landscape') was obtained at an early stage. Support for this understanding of the archaeological landscape was later obtained from a study of the Les Baumes road, which branches off the Cipières–Caussols road in a south-west direction, gives access to a number of cleared areas in the Les Baumes *quartier*, and then, after becoming essentially a footpath, peters out near a sink-hole.

A later stage of the investigation involved the study of a zone approximately 1 × 1 km, corresponding to the area covered by one of the large IGN air photographs. This zone lies somewhat further west, almost entirely in the *quartier* of Les Baumes. The objective was to work at a scale which would demonstrate how a representative range of geomorphological features was approached and treated by those who cleared land, grew crops and pastured livestock on the plateau. It was necessary to make an appraisal of an area large enough to permit the observation of recurring patterns in the archaeological landscape. Working at this scale, building on the insights provided by the road study, proved highly successful. Instead of studying and recording cairns, clearance piles and terrace walls one by one, these features were 'read' as normal components of 'fields' or zones of clearance whose size, edges and relationship to dolines, uvulas and doline cascades were regarded as of critical significance in reading the agrarian landscape. Scale is of the essence here; interpretation is a matter of pattern recognition, observing recurrent relationships, making distinctions between background noise and key relationships, and building models for past processes which utilise convergent observations and arguments.

4.3. The archaeological landscape

Most of the archaeological features on the plateau relate to *clearance* (fields of cairns, and linear cairns which conform to the angles of dip of the underlying limestone); to *soil retention* (the terrace revetment walls, some more intact and impressive than others, both in suites on uniform slopes and in 'doline cascades'); or to *enclosure* (walls around the edges of doline floors, walls defining or sub-dividing 'fields'). There are also enclosures and buildings for sheltering livestock and those who tended them – the large, relatively modern *bergeries* with their tiled roofs, the enclosures with largely upstanding walls, often integrated with small tiled or corbelled shelters, and also some corbelled shelters (*bories*) which are free-standing. The roads and tracks depicted on the 1842 and 1936 cadastral maps are also archaeologically visible for the most part. There are a few neatly paved and edged threshing floors (*aires*), and also areas of bare rock defined by lines of stones which may once have served the same purpose. Less prominent, especially at first sight, are features which may be termed 'primitive structures'; they are usually defined not by faced walls, like the *bories, enclos* and *bergeries*, but rather by much cruder linear piles of stones. Some of these may once have been faced walls; others may always have looked much as they do

FIGURE 156. These 'primitive enclosures' in the Les Baumes *quartier* may belong to the primary clearance phase on the Plateau de Calern
PHOTOGRAPHS: ANDREW FLEMING

FIGURE 157. Les Baumes: larger 'primitive structures', probably the remains of roughly rectangular buildings
PHOTOGRAPHS: ANDREW FLEMING

FIGURE 158. Les Baumes: smaller 'primitive structures'
PHOTOGRAPHS: ANDREW FLEMING

today. Both may once have been completed by organic components – wood, thatch, or even turf. They include small irregular enclosures defined by collapsed walls (Figure 156); collapsed shelters, including some once corbelled (some of these are hard or impossible to distinguish from well-revetted clearance cairns); the low, collapsed walls of 'primitive' buildings and shelters *without* corbelled roofs, including a few apparently long or relatively large buildings (Figure 157), and more small ones, which are mostly square or rectilinear (Figures 158 & 159); quarries (some forming the rear or side walls of stock enclosures); and zones of

FIGURE 159. Les Baumes: smaller 'primitive structures'
PHOTOGRAPHS: ANDREW FLEMING

FIGURE 160. Les Baumes: stone-getting zones of unknown date
PHOTOGRAPHS: ANDREW FLEMING

quarrying, with frequent small clusters and piles of stone which indicate casual stone-getting rather than systematic clearance (Figure 160).

A point always to be borne in mind is that in all periods livestock would often have been penned in dolines, in order to capture their manure, so that archaeologically distinctive 'stock enclosures' would normally have represented no more than a proportion of livestock-handling options available at any one time.

4.4. The Cipières–Caussols road

The key to the understanding of this landscape and the assignment of a dating bracket to what may be termed the primary clearance phase (in terms of what is archaeologically visible, at least) lies in the relationship between the Cipières–Caussols road (Figure 161) and the archaeological landscape through which it passes, especially where we studied it, mostly along the Les Poumeirès/Les Baumes boundary. In theory, in terms of horizontal stratigraphy, the road might be relatively 'early' – in which case there would be a number of walls or other structures approaching it or recognising its prior existence. It might be relatively 'late', and would therefore *cut through* or at least 'respect' various pre-existing features. In fact, the third scenario – that the road and the archaeological landscape through which it passes form an integral horizon of construction – is the one which *generally* obtains here. It is important to stress the word 'generally', since there are places where a field wall runs up to a (probably pre-existing) side-wall of the road, and also places where it is clear that the road was built through a zone which had already been cleared or had pre-existing boundaries. The important point is that, in general, the road has not been made *substantially* later than the 'fields' (if it had, it would cut through

FIGURE 161. The Cipières–Caussols road descending towards the Bench on the way to the village. This is a fairly representative image of a medieval road; note that it is terraced into the hillside
PHOTOGRAPH: ANDREW FLEMING)

them much more comprehensively) or substantially earlier (otherwise far more boundaries would 'approach' it).

The Cipières–Caussols road has not been 'designed' in the sense that it has a uniform width and standardised system of construction; on the contrary, it is heterogeneous, manifesting itself variously as: a broad, walled road which might be called a drove-way or *draille* (though not a particularly wide one); a narrow, not always well-defined, path along which mules or humans would often have had to pass in single file; a path running between enclosed land and a stretch of open ground (and thus defined along one edge only); and a path running across open ground, especially through L'Aspi where it approaches the edge of the Plateau. Noticeably, the road has been 'allowed for' in the creation and demarcation of cleared zones, and constructed to fit into the local particularities of the occupied land which it traverses. In other words, it threads its way through the 'fields'. In general, the greater the local evidence for agrarian activity, the better defined the edges of the road. It also has designed *practical* relationships with the 'fields' and enclosures amongst which it passes, in the sense that it is possible to observe gateways into such fields, and triangular funnel-shaped areas which would facilitate the transfer of small numbers of animals into the road or adjacent enclosed land. It is clear, then, that the *route* connecting Cipières and Caussols must already have existed when the land through which it ran was cleared and in part enclosed, when it became necessary to accommodate it as a constructed road. These relationships are described in detail below.

4.5. The primary clearance horizon

This horizon of integral construction, this relationship of accommodation between roads and 'fields', as we might term it, is to be found across the Plateau de Calern in general, as far as we can tell from fieldwork on the ground and perusal of aerial photographs. The argument is strengthened by *similarities* between different roads in terms of their appearance as field monuments – and they are almost all components of a dendritic network of communication ultimately emanating from the nucleated village of Cipières. These roads – known as *chemins, carraires*, or *sentiers* on the cadastral maps – enabled villagers both to reach their lands on the plateau and to travel to destinations further afield, such as Grasse or Andon (see Figure 27). The main stem of the road system led up from the village to the mouth of La Combe. From here, a major routeway, the road to Andon, ran along the edge of this dry valley. Branching off this road were through-routes to Caussols and to Canaux, as well as a route to the eastern part of the plateau which was, in part, an alternative route to Caussols. There were also access roads to different parts of the plateau including, for instance, the Les Baumes road, a short branch running west from the Les Baumes road, a road running up to the Baoume de Brun from the Cipières-Caussols road (all three of which have been studied by the Project) and the one which ended at La Clapoua (see Figures 29 and 31).

Striking similarities characterise the patterns of clearance visible in the enclosed and 'occupied' land through which the roads pass. After a few days' fieldwork along these roads and the land beside them, surprises are rare; roads and cleared zones exhibit a variable but ultimately limited and repetitive range of characteristics. The cleared zones represent responses to local geology, whilst the priorities and purposes of the road makers remain within rather limited parameters. The *character* of roads and 'fields', as well as the *relationships* between them, make it clear that not only must the dendritic road pattern on the Plateau de Calern relate to the period of occupancy of the nucleated village of Cipières; the same must also be true of the primary clearance zones through which the roads pass. We have thus defined an archaeological horizon in the landscape.

The chronological depth of the *creation* of this basic horizon is likely to have been relatively short. This is argued not simply on the basis of the limited range of morphological variation of both roads and 'fields'. A 'field' – especially an arable field in harsh terrain, like the one studied at 153/163 which consisted of specially prepared linear cultivation trenches between long linear cairns (see Chapter 3) – is unlikely to have been cleared piecemeal over the centuries; such a field is useless unless at least a substantial proportion of it is cleared and brought into cultivation more or less as soon as it is required. This requirement for rapid installation holds even more true for a 'cascade' of terraces whose retained soils are dependent upon the supply of nutrients and irrigation supplied by short-term rushes of water occasioned by melting snows or torrential showers of rain. Such benefits should be exploited to maximum effect, and not allowed to run to waste. Much the same, in a somewhat different sense, is true of a road, which virtually by definition is required and used in its totality (though obviously the 'ends' of roads which served distinct areas of land, rather than leading to distant, off-plateau settlements, may have been *extended* further 'into the wilderness' in late construction phases). We may also define the identified 'primary clearance horizon' as occurring at a time when people were hungry, perhaps even desperate, for agricultural land (and maybe cleared pasture too); the cleared areas with which the roads are integrated (notably the ones studied along the Les Baumes/Les Poumeirès boundary) are frequently of low value. We may safely assume that when this clearance took place most of the dolines and uvulas, as well as the zones of deep-soiled terraces on slopes and cascades, had already been claimed. The analysis which Lewison carried out for his thesis[3] showed that approximately 88% of Transect A (by area) was cleared land of one sort or another. The roads and the contemporaneously cleared agrarian lands beside them must date from the time of full occupancy of the plateau, a situation which must surely correspond to a population peak in the nucleated village of Cipières.

The archaeologically-driven idea that the primary clearance of the Plateau de Calern took the form of a relatively rapid series of events is supported by the model of social process and structure in the early *incastellamento* village, outlined elsewhere in this volume. The demographically dynamic, expansive, labour-rich nature of the extended families of the *ostals*, and the practice of keeping a large supply of labour on the farm imply a recursive, mutually reinforcing relationship between an eagerness to colonise new land and a copious supply of mouths to feed and hands to work. The process would be ratcheted up by the massively increased levels of social interaction generated by patterns of life in a nucleated village. This situation would help to create *both* a more competitive context for new clearance ventures *and* opportunities for assembling ever larger labour forces by mobilising obligations of kinship and affinity. The more successful and prosperous 'houses' would be able to attract more labour in various anthropologically well-understood ways – in-marriage, fictive kinship, the services of more farm servants, and so on. Partible inheritance may also have played a significant role in this scenario.

As we show below, in demographic terms there are two main potential time horizons for the primary clearance. The first might have been during the late Middle Ages, sometime between the 11th and the mid-14th centuries, when the population of this nucleated village, like those of many other European communities, was burgeoning; Siddle has argued in this volume (Chapter 6) that the population of Cipières may have been around 1400 by the late 13th/mid-14th centuries. The other might have been the 16th and 17th centuries, the period after the *temps de malheur*. Siddle argues (Chapters 6 & 9) that the population recovered from *c.* 1050 in 1471 to *c.* 1350 by 1531, staying at a level of *c.* 1300 until at least 1698; by the time of the 1806 census, however, it had declined to 941.

Poteur[4] has suggested that this was the period when many of the structures of the agrarian landscape were created. But this idea becomes much less attractive when one realises how many of the Cipièrois were earning their living elsewhere during this period, and how important large flocks of sheep had become in the village economy (see Chapters 7 & 8); it seems unlikely that this was a time for major episodes of land clearance or making significant investments in agrarian land. But in any case there are persuasive arguments for preferring the later Middle Ages as the time horizon of the primary clearance on the Plateau. According to Poteur,[5] Cipières and Caussols were under the same ownership from at least the mid-12th century until the Revolution; both their churches were in existence by 1158. In the late Middle Ages, Cipières and Caussols lay on the road between Gréolières and Grasse – the regional urban centre – and people would have regularly taken this route on manorial, social and economic business. Although the deeper snows must have regularly created delays and difficulties for travellers in winter, this would have been a route taken in 'pre-feudal' times by lords journeying between their strongholds living off the country[6] and later by many people with duties to perform within the political and social landscapes of feudalism. A *publica via qua itur caussolis* is mentioned in 1336.[7] Unfortunately we cannot be entirely sure that this refers to the one we have studied, since there is also a road which goes to Le Calernet and then branches into two routes which cross the southern edge of the Plateau; each is labelled as leading to Caussols on 19th and 20th century maps. The *maleservi* based at Caussols sometimes had to transport goods to Cipières and Gréolières under their corvée obligations; good links between these places were clearly essential. By the fourteenth century, when the manors of Gréolières-Hautes, Cipières and Caussols had been brought under the control and ownership of one person, Raibaude de Caussols, there must have been much traffic on the 'public roads' mentioned in mid-14th century documents.[8] Furthermore, the documented fact that, by the 14th century, individual small land-holders such as the *maleservus* Pierre Leverii had widely scattered parcels (see Chapter 7) implies that, if they were regularly working these parcels, roads would have been needed simply to manage the volume of inter-*quartier* movement, and control it in these times of intensive and competitive land use.

Some parts of this road were not just fitted into a field pattern; they were actually *engineered*; that is to say, digging as well as wall-building was involved. As the road climbed the long slope out of Caussols and onto the southern edge of the plateau, and further north, as it descended the northern edge of the highest part of the plateau, along the boundary between Les Poumeirès and Vaumeillane, the road was cut into the hillside, so that it runs along a narrow, revetted terrace walled on the downslope side – what may be called a 'cut and wall' technique (Figure 161). It is not known whether the roads were constructed by *maleservi*, as an extension of their duty of *corvée*, or by the community; it is tempting to suggest that *maleservi* would have been employed in stretches of rough terrain which were largely unclaimed in an agrarian sense (and thus without 'local' farmers who would have a direct interest in supplying their labour). For the construction of the Cipières roads in zones of difficult terrain, a context of feudal obligation seems more appropriate than the more 'liberal', diversified 16th century, when the Cipièrois had more opportunities for working away from the commune, and took them (Chapter 9). In the 16th century *corvée* for making and maintaining roads was a public work.[9] Insofar as the fields and cleared zones with which the roads were integrated were intended for use as cereal-growing areas, rather than simply representing cleared pasture, the 13th century would surely be a more apposite time zone for primary clearance on the plateau than the 16th, the time of an apparently greater emphasis on pastoralism, a more diversified, extra-Cipières economy, and the beginnings of a trend from large extended families towards nuclear family structures (see Chapters 6 & 9). The reverse sequence – an *extensive* use of the Plateau de Calern in the late Middle Ages, followed by an *intensive* use in the 16th century, is much harder to envisage against the known social and economic history of Cipières as it us understood from the documentary record as described by Rosamond Faith and David Siddle in the chapters which follow.

4.6. The short chronology

At this point it is worth explaining why I am not entertaining a long chronology, involving some parts of the visible agrarian landscape on the plateau going back to Gallo-Roman times or late prehistory. Some of the reasons for taking this view will already be apparent. But we may also add arguments based on the degree of preservation exhibited by the archaeological features and standing structures on the plateau. An obvious distinction may be drawn between the state of decay and general appearance of the three enclosures on the southern edge of the plateau,[10] which are generally accepted as probably Iron Age in origin, and the condition of the well-preserved walled structures known or inferred to be of recent age, like the *bergeries*. The structures which we assign to the primary clearance phase occupy an intermediate position between these two states of degeneration. For example, relatively short stretches of the walls which flank the Cipières–Caussols road, in the section where it looks most like a droveway (Figure 162), display a fairly comprehensive range of weathering stages within a sequence of degeneration – good preservation, collapse into piles of rubble, degradation to small angular stone chips, and partial or complete burial beneath a cover of soil and vegetation. Thus the weathering state of our features establishes their relative chronological age and provides an argument which is essentially independent of those already deployed.

FIGURE 162. The Cipières–Caussols road approaching the junction the Les Baumes road from the south. This section looks like a broa droveway. Note the differing states of preservation/weathering of th side-walls

PHOTOGRAPH: ANDREW FLEMING

FIGURE 163. Cairnfields in Les Baumes, to illustrate the point that cairns in a given field often bear close similarities to one another

PHOTOGRAPHS: ANDREW FLEMING

Patterns of weathering and degeneration also support another argument made above – that in any given area, clearance was achieved quite rapidly, and was not the outcome of piecemeal clearance over long expanses of time. Although the state of preservation of clearance heaps varies considerably across the plateau in general, cairns within a local group are often strikingly similar to one another – whether they are now represented by small heaps of limestone chips or large piles of chunky blocks (Figure 163). This must be the result of people in a given area clearing stones with a characteristic local geological provenance, into heaps of much the same size and shape – and then of the cairns being affected by freeze–thaw conditions which would be more or less uniform in any given locality. In general, this suggests that much of the clearance was the work of gangs with agreed working methods, clearing particular pieces of land systematically over quite short time horizons, rather than sporadic acts of clearance spanning long periods of time. It looks much more likely that land clearance resulted from sustained action following a decision to upgrade the quality of a whole tract of land, rather than from casual, piecemeal actions. If this is correct (and see the arguments deployed earlier) the diversity of degradation states among cairns and clearance piles probably results more from variations in the character of the local limestone and local exposure conditions than from the simple passage of elapsed time over the time-frame of 500 to 1000 years already postulated (see above).

4.7. The later archaeological landscape

Before describing the primary clearance landscape, and the light which it sheds on later medieval agrarian practice, I should mention those features of the archaeological landscape which are to be excluded from detailed consideration and analysis in this chapter, because they were constructed more recently, mostly in the post-medieval period. Fairly self-evidently, this includes enclosures (*enclos*) with walls standing often to a height of over 1 m, along with the intact or almost-intact *bories* incorporated or associated with them. Such stock enclosures may alternatively be accompanied by roughly square buildings with low-pitched tiled single-slope roofs, though the roofs have often collapsed and the tiles have sometimes been removed. The eventual availability of tiles may well have seemed like an improvement on corbelled roofing; tiles were presumably rather less subject to freeze–thaw processes and would have facilitated the gathering of rainwater into gutters and then into troughs or cisterns. I also assign the free-standing *bories* to the post-medieval period. Incentives to build these structures, or to repair them, would have been much lower once the cost of purchasing tiles and transporting them had become manageable (but that of course would have depended on who was making the investment). In general, these free-standing *bories* are scattered across the plateau surface (see below) in a fashion which implies no systematic relationship with the zones of cairns and terraces.

4.8. The context of early clearance and agrarian practice

We have no direct evidence for the nature of the vegetation cover on the Plateau de Calern in the period immediately preceding the late medieval clearance episodes. It is, however, possible to make quite a strong case for a mixture of garrigue and woodland. This scenario seems intrinsically likely in any case, given that the evidence for settlement in the region in the immediate post-Roman centuries suggests scattered farms and hamlets – a pattern which is unlikely to have generated the persistent high-intensity grazing which would be necessary to create and preserve more open conditions on the plateau.

The names of the *quartiers* are significant in this context. We have evidence (Appendix 1) that some of them can be traced back into the early 16th century, and a few to the later Middle Ages. It is debatable, however, how far medieval and later *quartiers* represented the same concept, and how far their boundaries were fixed and stable over the centuries. Among the locative names relating to the plateau which are recognisable in mid-14th century documentary references are La Faye (*La Faya*), Les Baumettes (*Las Balmetas*), La Juillée (*Al Jully, La Jullyer)*, La Clapoua (*La Claposa*), L'Agrémourié (*Agramenc* or *Lagremeliar*), Vaumeillane (*Veil Meyana*), Le Calern (*Calern*), and probably L'Adrech de San Meya (*Lardreth de salm)* as well as Les Pesses (*Les Pesses*).[11] These references, which include mentions of vegetation (see below), cairns (La Claposa), public roads, and a well-distributed set of plateau locations, indicate that a mature version of the plateau clearance scenario being sketched here was in being by the mid-14th century. With reference to our study area, it is worth mentioning that in 1531 there is also evidence for L'Aspi (*Aspe*), Le Rouré (*Roure)* and Le Teil (*Teil*), Baume de Brun (*Faissos de Bruni*) and Les Baumes (*Baumo*).[12] Les Poumeirès (*Poumaris*), is also mentioned, though this might refer to a *quartier* of this name near the village rather than the one on the Plateau.

There is some evidence that the pattern of *quartiers* was not entirely stable over the centuries, and scope for debate about the fixity of their boundaries over time, as noted by David Austin above in Chapter 3. However, it is clear that when they were mapped, in the 19th century, *quartier* boundaries quite frequently followed roads which, we have argued above, are medieval in origin; so change probably had to be enacted within this basic, old-established framework. It seems that the medieval village *parlement* met intermittently and for particular purposes,[13] but the significance and public prominence of the agreements reached at such meetings would have strengthened claims to land. By around *c.* 1530 the assembly was meeting regularly.[14] The fact that *quartier* names were known to have entered the documentary record, and thus taken on legal and fiscal status, would have supplied a further incentive for not making radical changes – except perhaps in areas which had been abandoned for several generations. It would be virtually impossible to change them thereafter, especially since members of the village council would also know that they were entering the documentary record. We may assume that many of them went back to the late Middle Ages – and it would obviously be necessary to name any substantial area taken into cultivation and occupancy during the primary clearance phase.

It is interesting that several of the *quartier* names refer to trees and bushes. As reference to Appendix 1 makes clear, the name La Fage (La Faya in 1333) (*Fagus,* beech) is recorded from the 14th century, and La Pinée (*Pinus,* pine) (at the western end of the plateau), Le Fraï or Le Fraissinet (*Fraxinus,* ash), Le Teil (*Tilia,* lime) Les Poumières (*Malus* spp., crab-apple) Le Rouré (*Quercus robur,* oak) are in place by 1531. Off the plateau proper, L'Eouvé (*Quercus ilex*, the evergreen oak) is also recorded in 1531. In terms of smaller trees and shrubs, to the 14th century record of L'Agrémourié (*Ribes uva-crispa*, wild gooseberry) we may add, for 1531, L'Aspi (*Populus tremula*, the aspen) the off-plateau *quartiers* of La Font de la Sine and La Sine (*Crataegus*, hawthorn) and La Juillée (*Rosa* spp., the wild rose). One or more of the names Le Bausset, Pas de Bouis, and Embouisset must surely relate to the box (*Buxus sempervirens*), though only Le Bausset seems to go back to 1531.

What are the implications of these vegetational names? One might ask whether at Le Fraï, for example, the name derived from the fact that the area once had significant numbers of ash trees, or whether it refers to one distinctive ash tree which remained after clearance. In the case of *Les Poumières,* the name is in the plural. As for *La Faye,* one would expect beech to have been the 'natural' climax vegetation at this high altitude; it is an intolerant tree, shading out competitors, and there would presumably have been at least some beech *woods* at higher altitudes. In the case of *l'Agrémourié* and *La Juillée,* one wild gooseberry or rose bush would hardly stand out; indeed wild roses and gooseberry bushes grow almost everywhere in the commune. In contrast, the aspen may have been a rather rare and perhaps vulnerable shrub on the plateau.

In fact, the initial naming of the *quartiers* may to some extent have been comparable to choosing a category of names for the roads on a new housing development (Oak Drive, Ash Crescent, etc.); in other words, there may have been some conscious nominalism. This suggestion is supported by the fact that there is little duplication of *quartier* names. In chronological terms this would imply that there was a relatively brief 'naming horizon', on the plateau at least, an idea which would accord with the model of a plateau claimed and cleared quite rapidly in competitive circumstances. On Calern in general, there was evidently a strong preference for names which refer to natural features; the use of personal names to label *quartiers* may have been generally discouraged. In other words, people preferred a more objective, 'natural' naming system rather than one based on property claims. This may imply that although the people who cleared and named the plateau may have been locked into a competitive situation, they also operated in a context where land tenure was known to be fluid, complex and changeable, and agreed on uncontroversial names which could stand the tests of time and change. In other words, perhaps this is an indication that land could be rotated between different users, or re-assigned by the community.

If many of the 'tree and shrub' *quartier* names do go back to the primary clearance phase (and the ones cited do not look like more recently interpolated sub-divisions) they provide quite good evidence for a pattern of garrigue and woodland (including deciduous trees) over a significant proportion of the plateau surface at the time of primary clearance. This vegetation cover may not have been universal. The name of the plateau itself, Calern, is apparently of pre-Indo-European origin[15] but the differentiation represented by the names of the *quartiers* of Le Calernet and La Baisse de Calern, which today include some of the best land on the plateau, located in a lower 'basin' on its eastern side, might be held to reflect the location of an early 'bridgehead' of plateau occupation. When the higher, less easily accessible zones of the plateau were cleared, Le Calernet, and perhaps the other likely bridgehead, La Combe, may already have been substantially opened up.

The archaeological features visible in today's landscape give the impression that primary clearance must have been all about moving stone around; but this must have been largely undertaken as a secondary stage of the overall clearance programme. The deeper-soiled, fertile, relatively protected runs of uvulas, which we would expect to have been targeted for clearance at quite an early stage, are likely to have contained substantial trees and undergrowth. We cannot demonstrate this directly now. But outside these deep-soiled areas, it is occasionally possible to find clearance cairns which are C-shaped or even S-shaped in plan; it is tempting to interpret these as stones cleared round one tree or a pair of trees respectively, and the same may be true for some of the 'doughnut' or O-shaped cairns. It is very likely that those who cleared the plateau would have deliberately left some standing trees, to provide shade and shelter for humans and livestock. Such trees would presumably have been lopped or pollarded. A documentary source from 1357[16] refers to these practices; pollarded and lopped oaks are still to be found in the commune, with one or two near the village and considerably more of them on Le Plan (see Figure 26). Lopped branches would have been available to roof shelters (including the small rectangular ones to be discussed below, which must have had organic roofs) and to repair tools, make sticks, and so on; leaves might have supplemented the diet of livestock. Presumably there would once have been considerable numbers of such trees, or pollards, which did *not* have stone-piles around them. In this kind of environment, it is tempting to suggest, corbelled shelters would have been unnecessary, until lightning strikes had eliminated the last of the isolated standing trees.

Probably shrub vegetation, notably including box and other thorny species, was also allowed to flourish, or even deliberately maintained, especially in areas with thin soils, and zones damaged by the extraction of stone for walls and terraces. Box, which still occurs in distinctive clusters on the plateau today, would be useful as material for the roofs and walls of temporary structures, and thorns could be used to make temporary sheep enclosures. There are sites on the plateau where discontinuous stretches of low, linear stone piles (either collapsed walls or linear clearance) invite the suggestion that they were supplemented by, or cleared along, dead hedges (though unfinished walls or boundary lines are always a possibility here). Arguably, high goat densities would pose a threat to these areas of scrub, unless they were closely herded.

4.9. Lewison's model of land use

Anthony Lewison[17] divided land on the Plateau de Calern into five categories – doline, field, terrace, cairnfield and waste. In his sample area, Transect A, he found that on the main part of the plateau – the area under discussion here – dolines covered 4%, 'fields' (mostly uvulas) 45%, terraces 8%, cairnfields 31% and 'waste' 12%. He assumed that the first three categories had been arable land – which if confirmed would mean that, within one of the better areas of the plateau, some 58% of the surface area would have been potentially in cultivation. He also pointed out that in 1842 only 20% of the land was classed as arable, and suggested that quite a high percentage of the 'fields' and 'terraces' had become pasture land, the soil having degenerated since the heyday of the occupation of the plateau. Lewison also noted the critical importance of sheep to the arable economy ('an arable parcel was always wedded to a parcel of pasture'). His account makes clear the importance of the dolines as arable land, where the '*terra rossa* base of a compact and clayey nature' helps to retain moisture, the soil is deep, and nutrients are replenished by colluviation and solifluction. The dolines were already sun-traps and presumably radiation thrown back off the doline walls (the 'walled garden effect') would also have helped crops to ripen quickly. In any agrarian system imaginable, the most reliable crop-growing areas would have been the uvulas and dolines. Anyone able to grow crops in several dolines, located in different parts of the plateau, would have been able to spread the risk of harvest failure. Post-medieval crop mixes were often of wheat and rye (maslin), but lentils were also commonly grown, and fallow years were evidently inserted into a rotation cycle (see Chapter 8); it seems that even though two crops per year were being taken, much arable land would have lain fallow at any given time. Sheep could have been penned in dolines which were lying fallow, and thus manured them; after the crops had been harvested, they could have been driven into all or any of the dolines. In theory, the plateau itself would have been out of use between November and May for climatic reasons. But insofar as this principle is contradicted by some documentary evidence it may be worth noting that stock could be moved onto or off the plateau in a few hours. If circumstances warranted, it might well have been possible to take advantage of a weather window, or covered stores of fodder, etc and make use of parts of the plateau off-season. In farming practice, the taking of calculated risks is hardly unknown.

4.10. Principles of landscape interpretation; zones of exploitation

This land-use model is a sketch, a basic account partly determined by the ecology of the plateau and partly derived from Lewison's account of past practice in Cipières. But it provides the basic framework for field interpretation of the plateau's archaeological landscape.

The most extensive areas of valuable land occupied the uvulas – relatively large, low-lying basins with relatively deep soil. These were generally subdivided by low terrace walls, which in some areas are well preserved and have probably been well maintained up to fairly recent times, given the value of the land. Next in importance came the dolines, and also the 'doline cascades' – flights of step-like terraces which occupy narrow declivities which are dry in summer but probably carry short-lived rivulets and streams, winterbournes fed by flash floods and melting snow in winter.

FIGURE 164. Les Baumes: a relatively shallow doline with collapsed revetment wall. The entrance passage is on the far side

PHOTOGRAPH: ANDREW FLEMING

The floor of a doline was generally surrounded by a revetment wall – often, probably, running round almost the full perimeter, as in an amphitheatre (Figure 164). Like other features of the primary plateau landscape, such walls may have quite fresh-looking faces in places but elsewhere may be represented by piles of stone or are apparently buried beneath grassy slopes. In some places, matters are complicated by piles of stones evidently cleared to the edges of the doline floor. Material for the revetment walls was often quarried piecemeal from the doline's sides, which often look somewhat disturbed, a phenomenon which should be distinguished from the intentional creation of terraces in such locations. Minimal clearance of doline sides is most noticeable where dolines are very small and/or unusually deep (and hence of low value); there are some quite good examples near the OCA observatory.

In most dolines, it is possible to pick out the entrance for livestock (which was created initially, in all probability, as a clear exit route for tree trunks removed when the doline floor was cleared) (Figure 165). This may be a zone on the doline side which corresponds to a natural break in the geology – for

FIGURE 165. Les Baumes: cleared doline entrances. Left: note the possible 'primitive structures' flanking the entrance. Right: an apparent double entrance-way; note the collapsed *bori* 'guarding' it

PHOTOGRAPHS: ANDREW FLEMING

FIGURE 166. Les Baumes: field edges. Left: linear clearance cairns approach from the distance, and stop along an intermittent 'wall' or line of cairns running from left to right. Right: a cairnfield on the right stops along a 'headland' running from bottom right to top left. Note the probable 'primitive structure' in the foreground
PHOTOGRAPHS: ANDREW FLEMING

example, where geologically-based 'steps' are not present. But the entrance is also quite likely to be represented by a walled or partly walled funnel, perhaps 5–10 m in width, flanked by walls or 'linear clearance' turning inwards down the side of the doline. Sometimes there is more than one entrance, a provision which is quite understandable particularly if there is a neighbouring doline into which sheep might be driven after the first has been adequately grazed and/or manured.

At a doline, it may also be possible to note structures which date from a later phase than the primary clearance – a *borie*, perhaps, or an enclosure with walls often still standing a metre or more in height, made of blocks obviously quarried from nearby beds of limestone, and still mostly sharp-edged; severe frost-shattering will not be much in evidence, and the roof of a *borie* is quite likely to be almost intact. However, there are many dolines which do not possess 'late' structures, or where 'late' activity seems to have been restricted to partial refurbishment of the basal revetment wall.

Some dolines form the nuclei of 'fields' – zones of cairns, circular and/or linear, which extend out onto the surrounding land, and whose outer edges are usually marked by a more or less clear transition to uncleared ground. Sometimes a doline – often a small and/or very deep one – may lie within a zone of uncleared ground – that is, a zone of thin soil, often marked by a continuous scatter of frost-fractured stone chips among a fairly characteristic suite of vegetation, and displaying few signs of clearance. Such a doline may contain signs of rather perfunctory human activity – it may, in fact, simply have seen occasional use as a sheep-pen. But other dolines in areas of bare ground may be associated with small well-defined fields of cairns. This sort of cairnfield will usually not surround the doline completely; it is likely to be attached to about one-third of its circumference.

Some dolines or doline groups have much larger 'fields' attached to them, whose outer edges, the zones where they meet undisturbed ground, can be

FIGURE 167. Les Baumes: field edges. Left: a near-continuous wall (the cairned land is to the right). Right: a more intermittent but still fairly continuous field-edge (the 'field', with numerous semi-natural terraces, is on the left)
PHOTOGRAPH: ANDREW FLEMING

located without much difficulty. In Les Baumes, for example, there are long spurs of uncleared ground leading down from the hill summits, interspersed with more concave, dolinic ground with deeper soils; the latter have been cleared, with cairns and terraces (many following the geology quite closely). Usually the edge of such a field is not difficult to define; the cairns will stop along an identifiable line (Figure 166), there may be a collapsed wall or linear clearance cairn (preservation conditions are quite likely to make it impossible to tell the difference) or there may be a longer, more continuous faced wall (Figure 167). In some places the long axes of stones placed along a line on the ground surface may indicate the field edge. On a slope, the line along which the edges of terraces stop will be clearly distinguishable from the undisturbed ground beside them. At times there will be a scatter of one or two small cairns on the bare ground, beyond what otherwise appears to be the edge of the field; it is to be expected that sometimes families may have rather perfunctorily attempted to make their fields slightly larger.

One feature which may help to define fields, and demonstrate that they were often relatively large, is the long terrace. Many terraces are quite short and overgrown, and it is not always possible to tell how far they are geological, or at least based on geological features. However, there are also long-running terraces; some of these are quite useful for demonstrating the width, or the minimum width, of a particular field. Occasionally one long terrace may run from one edge to the middle of a field, and another one, just below it, may start near the point where the first one finished and continue to the other edge of the field. One may thus use two adjacent terraces to confirm the width of the field.

Next in importance to the uvulas and the dolines come the flights of small terraces which occupy narrow declivities which are dry in summer but probably carry short-lived streams in winter. These have been termed doline cascades (Figure 93). Sometimes these narrow linear 'staircases' of stream terraces are very long, and some of the zones which flank them may be taken up with terraces and clearance piles. Elsewhere, they may be flanked by extensive quarried zones from which stone destined mostly for the terrace walls of the 'staircases' has been extracted piecemeal, to the detriment of local grazing quality. On the ground, such zones are not marked by true clearance cairns but rather by frequent small casual piles or scatters of stones, evidently the debris from episodes of stone-breaking probably enacted by individuals (Figure 160). It is usually in such zones that patches of bare rock have been exposed, presumably by sheet erosion following the fragmentation of a continuous cover of surface vegetation. Presumably in these quarried zones wind-thrown trees, once rooted in the deeper limestone fissures, produced cavities which could be enlarged and explored by those looking for sources of stone. The quarried zones are quite extensive, and they are a reminder that the people who cleared the plateau would have found the cumulative area of the small terraces incorporated in a doline cascade to be the equivalent of that of a doline, and perhaps in some ways more valuable for being slightly better irrigated, better supplied with down-washed nutrients, and possibly more efficient 'sun-traps' for ripening grain. In these circumstances they would not have hesitated to damage the grazing potential of neighbouring thin-soiled areas by treating them as stone-winning zones.

It may seem surprising that the builders of the revetment walls of these flights of (mostly) small or tiny terraces did not create discrete, identifiable quarries within which their stone-getting was concentrated. Such small and medium-sized quarries do exist, but they are not common, and they evidently relate to activities which post-date the creation of the primary plateau landscape – most obviously the construction of *bories*.

4.11. Boundaries

The plateau contains, then, sub-divided uvulas, managed dolines, sets of stream terraces, and 'fields' indicated by terraces and clearance cairns (round or linear) – as well as zones of thin-soiled, uncleared pasture and areas damaged by extensive piecemeal quarrying. I have used the term 'field' in quotation marks to refer to areas displaying fairly uniform patterns of clearance and exploitation, often with an identifiable relationship to the landscape (e.g. cairns clustering round a doline, or a set of linear clearance piles and terrace walls which conform to geological stratigraphy). However, these are not 'fields' in the sense that they are surrounded by continuous or near-continuous boundary-walls, as medieval fields would be in the British uplands. In our fieldwork in the Les Baumes research area, we spent a good deal of time trying to define 'parcels' of cleared land by attempting to invest them with continuous boundaries. In general, the passage quoted by Faith (see Chapter 7) for a 1321 boundary at Caussols running

FIGURE 168. Les Baumes: a low, straggling 'boundary wall' running through the middle of a cleared parcel of land
PHOTOGRAPHS: ANDREW FLEMING

FIGURE 169. Les Baumes: unfinished walls. Left: note the importance of facing stones. Right: this wall also began with carefully-placed facing-stones (foreground) but there were also some 'throughs' (middle distance)
PHOTOGRAPHS: ANDREW FLEMING

'from cairn to cairn' has resonance for the Plateau de Calern. Certainly 'field edges' can be identified quite frequently, in that zones of cairns tend to stop along a distinguishable line where uncleared land takes over; this may be marked by a wall (usually not very long or continuous), or stretches of linear clearance, or lines of placed stones – or the transition between disturbed and undisturbed ground may be coherent and obvious to the eye. The edges of zones which have been quarried to make terraces and deep-soiled trenches are not hard to pick out. Usually it is obvious which area adjacent to a doline has been cleared or quarried. Usually the boundaries of cairnfields are very obvious. Geological edges and transitions in the stratigraphy quite frequently dictate where the boundaries of 'fields' will occur; for example, the 'strike' of the limestone will suddenly change direction and the axes of linear clearance cairns will respond to the change. Occasionally there is a fairly persistent line of contiguous stones which runs through the middle of a cleared zone rather than following its edges, a low rather unconvincing 'wall', which must be regarded as a boundary of some sort (Figure 168). Here it is worth noting that although many walls now look like untidy straggles of frost-fractured stones, observations on what appear to be unfinished walls show that they were built with some care (Figure 169). Finally, there are upright, deliberately placed single stones (Figure 170) usually less than a metre in height, which seem to represent boundary marks of some sort, though in one case they probably indicate the line of a through route. Some are in lines, although the distance intervals between individual stones may vary considerably. Doubtless concentrated fieldwork along these lines would recover further marker stones, upright or fallen, probable and possible. It must be a matter of conjecture how far these presumed boundary marks date from the time of the primary landscape and to what extent they represent later sub-divisions.

FIGURE 170. Les Baumes: boundary stone
PHOTOGRAPH: ANDREW FLEMING

This said, one must emphasise that even though one may learn to 'read' each area of the plateau – to see how humans responded to each uvula, doline, convex or concave slope, and so on – it is much harder to identify 'fields' in the normal sense of the word – that is, parcels of land or 'fields' with closed, completely definable perimeters. If it was important to fully define boundaries of 'properties' at this early period, they must have included, as well as the archaeologically obvious barriers or edges, such as walls (continuous, hyphenated, or tokenistic lines of stones), cairns or sets of terraces stopping along a clear line; natural features, such as abrupt changes of geology, or distinctive trees; and imaginary lines joining various features, perhaps including small standing stones set up for this purpose. Clearly, poles or sticks jammed into grykes or wedged into the tops of cairns could also have supplemented stone boundary marks; and in a well-populated landscape, the menace of a raised fist, or an admonitory shout, might also have served as reminders of where boundaries were supposed to lie. But in all probability many boundaries would in any case have been seasonal and temporary, with sheep kept well away from cropped areas in the earlier part of the summer and encouraged to graze freely after the harvest. *If* we regard the people of the Middle Ages as conceptualising the occupation of the land in terms of the creation of well-defined, closed *parcels,* we must conceptualise the nature of medieval boundary-marking as involving a continuum of boundary features, ranging from fairly long stretches of continuous walling at one end of the spectrum, to an imaginary line joining two archaeologically or geologically indicated points at the other. As we shall see below, this *was* the situation in 1841, where the matching of parcels marked on the cadastral map in the *quartier* of Les Baumes with features visible on the ground (or not) shows just this range of boundary forms. Of course this is not to say that the parcels and boundaries of 1841 necessarily perpetuated those of the later Middle Ages; the match between the two was rather obviously selective and partial.

There is another possibility. If *large kin groups* were the significant occupiers of the land in the late Middle Ages, they may have held relatively large units of land, perhaps the size of *quartiers* as later known to us, with just a few major boundaries separating them from comparable neighbouring units. Probably the roads would have played an important role in the system, as immovable boundaries and 'neutral' corridors of no man's land which commanded easy and universal recognition. In this model, there would have been flexible arrangements within these holdings, and we might envisage a more relaxed role for the 'edges' visible within the primary cleared landscape. In other words, the 'fields' should not be seen as 'parcels' in a legalistic sense, but rather as ecologically coherent zones of land exploitation (which in any case they are). By 'ecologically coherent' zones I mean a doline and its fringes, or a doline cascade and its immediate catchment and adjacent quarrying zone, or a block of 'horizontal' geological strata turned partially into a set of low terraces. These were unitary zones in the sense that particular clearance, construction and maintenance strategies were demanded and invited by their geology. In this scenario one would interpret 'edge features' such as walls or short stretches of walling – leaving aside roadside walls, of course – as casual recognitions of the edges of topographically defined zones of activity and exploitation, rather than 'closes' or parcels.

Unfortunately there seems no way of determining archaeologically which of these alternative scenarios applied in the later Middle Ages. Were these 'legal parcels' with poorly marked boundaries, or 'exploitation zones' with unimportant linear edge features? A further complication arises if we envisage the 'exploitation zones' as appropriate for the late medieval context of *ostals* and large clans and extended families (Chapter 5) and suggest that with later social fragmentation came a greater emphasis on smaller families and correspondingly smaller holdings. If this were the case, one might expect many of the linear boundaries on the plateau – walls, stretches of walling, lines of half-piled stones – to date from perhaps the early 16th century, a time when population levels returned almost to those of the later Middle Ages. However, there seems no pressing archaeological reason to take this view – no sense, for example, in which these stretches of walling appear later than nearby clearance cairns, or over-ride earlier features.

4.12. Structures

There is evidence for more primitive structures or cabanes, many of which do seem to be associated with the primary landscape. On air photographs, these 'primitive structures' reveal themselves as anomalies in the local clearance pattern of cairns/walls – L-shapes, rectangles, 'square brackets', square 'cut-outs' in broad tumbled walls, or short walls which run at right-angles to linear clearance heaps which follow the strike of the geology. Often several of these anomalous features occur together, in one particular area within a field of cairns. On the ground, an area with structures may be picked up because the cairns and clearance heaps within it look unusual, and may be a little taller than the local average.

Inspection of such areas reveals a variety of distinctive archaeological features. The most obviously identifiable ones are rectangular areas defined by low tumbled walls. A few are somewhat reminiscent of the 'long-houses' found in the British uplands (Figure 157), but others are like smaller, rectangular or near-circular *cabanes* (Figures 158 & 159). They are of varying sizes and their apparent entrances also vary in size and location. There may be what look like small 'yards' or small enclosures, or small structures of stone enclosing ovoid or near-circular areas. Sometimes the plan of a 'primitive structure' does not conform to a rectangular, ovoid or circular shape, yet it is still looks as if it has been created intentionally. Caution is necessary here, because for every feature which may be described as 'probably' a built structure, there are two or three which would be more honestly categorised as 'possible'. However, the possibles and probables do tend to occur together, in groups confined to fairly well-defined areas – though there are also a few apparently isolated examples. Presumably some at least of these structures represent cabins which had roofs made of organic materials (box, juniper?) attached to timber frameworks. There are also small rectangular stone-free areas, each with one open side, set into heavily degraded terrace revetment walls or linear clearance heaps. This raises the possibility that some structures may have been made entirely of organic materials, with stones cleared and piled around them. These groups of rectangular structures, small yards or small enclosures and possible circular or ovoid structures are not particularly uniform in their appearance, but they are not uncommon. For the archaeologist, they raise a practical issue; at what point along the continuum running from probable to possible should a structure be before one decides to record it? But they are much less problematic in conceptual terms. The primary phase occupation probably involved intakes by substantial numbers of people at around the same time horizon; everyone who worked on the plateau in the summer would have needed shelter from the midday heat. If the *bories* are accepted as post-medieval, the 'primitive structures' are the only structures available to fit into the medieval time-bracket.

Christine Rendu, working on the Montagne d'Enveig, in Cerdagne in the eastern Pyrenees (some 500 km west of Cipières) has identified stone-footed structures which compare in size and character with the smaller examples from the plateau de Calern; some of them abutted against large rocks.[18] Some are prehistoric, others date from the early or high Middle Ages; others originated in prehistory but were re-occupied in the medieval period. At Enveig the earliest corbelled structures were built in the early 15th century and represent a distinct 'horizon' associated with milking sheep and making cheese. The small roughly rectangular *cabanes* which preceded them were defined by low walls and made of perishable materials; their long axes measured no more than 3 or 4 m internally. Some charcoal fragments on the floors of these *cabanes* have been interpreted as deriving from roof coverings.[19] Pollen evidence showed a major burst of

FIGURE 171. Les Baumes: possible primitive threshing-floors. The lower one has a line of placed stones along the 'front'

PHOTOGRAPHS: ANDREW FLEMING

woodland clearance in the 9th–10th centuries, followed by an unprecedented rise in 'agro-pastoral activities' in the 11th–13th centuries.[20]

Also probably to be associated with the primary phase of clearance on the plateau de Calern are small, primitive enclosures, with low, 'tumbled' walls (Figure 156); they are usually well away from the dolines, and tend to be unaccompanied by identifiable structures. They are often roughly ovoid or irregular in plan. It is tempting to suggest that the capacity of these enclosures would be appropriate for small flocks, perhaps *trentaines*; many are smaller than the enclosures of the later period. The medieval *cabanes* at Enveig are generally unaccompanied by enclosures, though Rendu points out that timber enclosures are mentioned in contemporary records.[21] It is possible that we have also observed threshing floors of comparable scale and simplicity which date from this 'early' phase, though such identifications can only be tentative. The relatively recent threshing-floors on the plateau are obvious; they are rectangular in plan, paved neatly, and edged with small upright stones. Beneath certain obvious quarry-faces, however, there are fairly level quarry-floors, largely clear of stones, which would have served as relatively primitive threshing-floors. At least one has a line of possible edging-stones (Figure 171). Such *aires* would not necessarily have benefited from the wind exposure which is a design feature of the best later examples. However, threshing was one of the medieval *banalités* and it may well have been advantageous to thresh some grain covertly on a floor which, to anyone making enquiries, could be represented as simply the base of a quarry or an area of stone-clearance.

4.13. Roads

The intimate relationship between roads and the cleared zones through which they passed has already been alluded to, and I have also made the obvious point that 'routes' must have preceded constructed or visible roads, at least where they led to distant, off-plateau destinations. Perhaps they were marked in ways which have not survived into the archaeological record. We have also mentioned that roads sometimes ran across or beside 'uncleared' zones of bare ground. Sometimes such zones are tiny. At one point along the Les Baumes road, a road which normally takes the form of a walled corridor suddenly stops, and one has to walk across a small triangle of bare, uncleared ground, which lies at a meeting-point of three 'fields', before resuming one's progress along a walled corridor. There is archaeological evidence that the concept of the road as a walled corridor, rather than a casual passage left between the fields, developed and was taken more seriously over time. For example, at the point where the Cipières–Caussols road, going south, leaves the fields to cross the large bare ground zone at the southern edge of the plateau, there is evidence that a broad funnel has been converted into a narrower corridor. In two places on the Les Baumes road people have started to build the road as a corridor across pre-existing 'bare ground triangles' (as described above), and there is also evidence on the Les Baumes road that a field has probably been extended slightly to convert a road which went through a narrow passage into one which consisted of a much narrower, more walled corridor – again, an apparently 'grudging' acceptance of the right of passage through local fields. There are three widely-separated sectors within the study zone of the Cipières–Causssols road where rather tentative attempts to replace a relatively wide 'droveway' with a narrow corridor have been made (see below). The succession from a wider roadway, more like a droveway *(draille)*, to a narrower corridor, whether walled or represented by a hollow way developed along one edge of the droveway, may suggest that over the *longue durée* the roads were most commonly used by pack animals.

Rendu has drawn attention to the *munyidores* of the Enveig – the sheep-milking corridors which apparently date mostly to the 15th and 16th centuries. These were like short stretches of narrow lane, some 70 m long;[22] they come in two widths, 1.5–1.7 m and 2–3 m.[23] It must be a possibility that individual stretches of the roads at Cipières could have been used for corralling flocks of sheep and milking them one by one – and that the *narrowing* of these roads in places might also represent their conversion to this purpose.

The Les Baumes road has one section where the side-walls were partly refurbished with blocks taken from a nearby quarry zone, though the incompleteness of the wallside roads here and the character of the quarry zone suggests that this project was unfinished. Finally it may be worth speculating that the dendritic road pattern may have been locally supplemented on the plateau by 'natural' droveways. The strike of the bedrock in some areas has created east–west corridors, some of them quite broad, which would have provided easy passage through parts of the terrain after clearance of surface vegetation. Some of these are used by sheep today. There is little direct archaeological evidence that these 'natural droveways' were used in the Middle Ages, although in one or two locations the placing of a thin wall or line of stones across them does suggest that they were sometimes 'blocked', with shepherds evidently being visibly dissuaded from using them.

The general appearance of these modifications suggests that they mostly took place during the 'primary' phase of the archaeological landscape – that they were elaborations of concepts developed during this phase, and not developments which occurred significantly later. Broadly, the behaviour of the roads, as we might expect, provides evidence for some familiar tensions and dialogues between the interests of the community and those of its constituent social groups.

4.14. Detail: roads and the primary clearance phase

The above text constitutes a general essay on the primary clearance phase, written on the basis of conclusions drawn from numerous field observations. The sections which follow are designed to illustrate these conclusions in more detail.

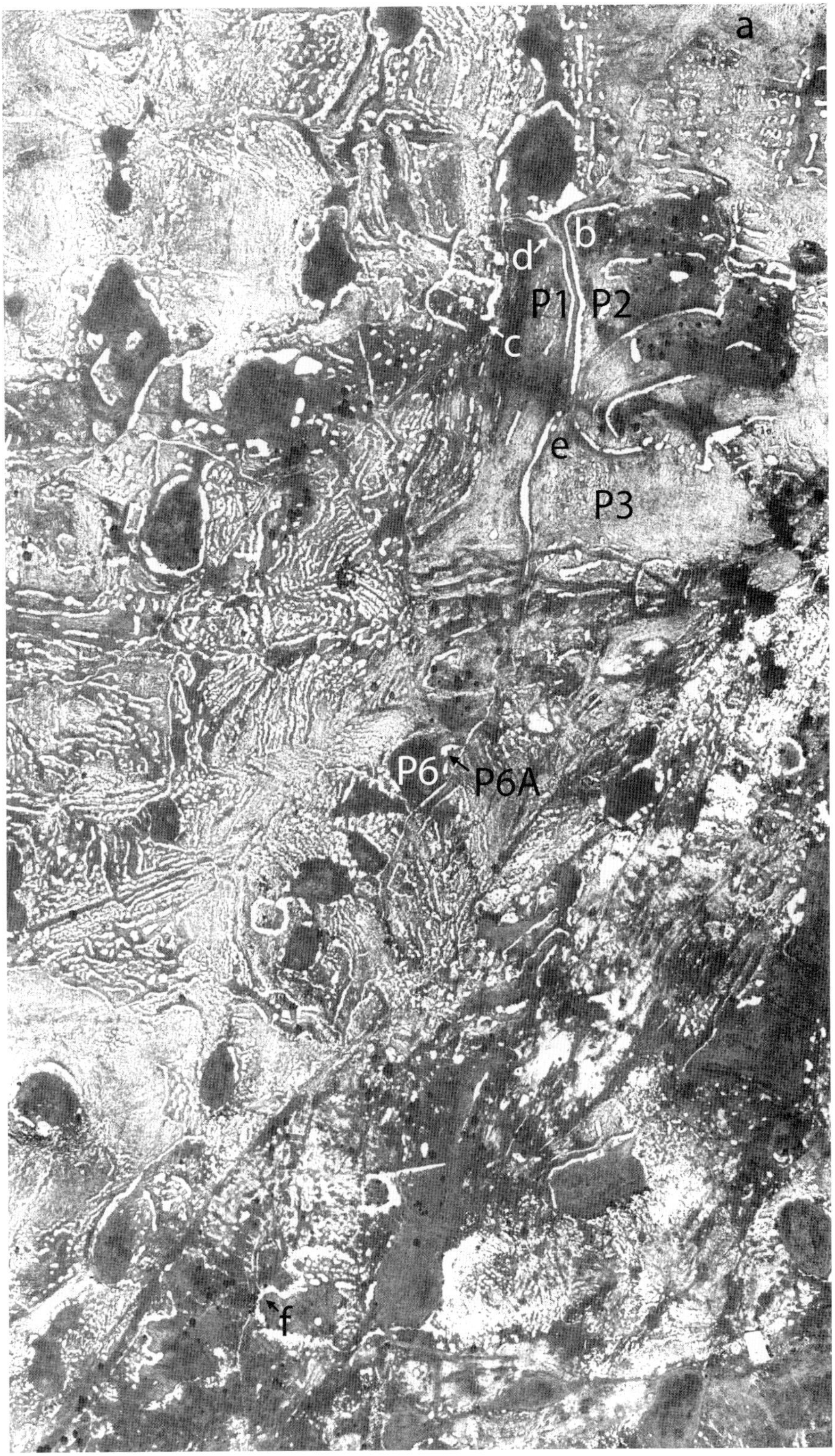

FIGURE 172. Air photograph of the eastern part of the Les Baumes *quartier*, to illustrate aspects of the primary clearance zone. The letters are referred to in the text

AIR PHOTOGRAPH REPRODUCED BY KIND PERMISSION OF THE IGN

As already noted, it is the relationship between roads and the features with which they have contact which is the source of the narrative developed for the *quartier* of Les Baumes. It is best to start with an air photograph (Figure 172). The Cipières–Caussols road, having climbed the slope (Figure 161) to reach the high part of the plateau enters the picture from the north-east (a on Figure 172), where its line is only intermittently marked by short stretches of walling. It becomes much clearer at the triangular space (b) which marks the junction (Figure 173) with the Les Baumes road, which runs west from the junction before turning south and then south-west (at point c). It is possible that livestock were sometimes penned and handled in this carefully-designed triangular space, in the south-west wall of which is an apparent gateway (d, and Figure 174) leading into the neighbouring field (P1). South of the junction it runs through a broad uvula, with relatively clear 'fields' to east (P2) and west (P1), bounded partly by constructed walls and partly by geologically-determined edges. Here the road becomes a broad, walled corridor, flanked by a broad, thick wall with well-preserved faces to the east, and a less impressive, more tumbled wall to the west (Figure 175). It is hard to avoid the inference that the deep-soiled parcel P2 was claimed first and provided with a solid west wall; the inner (east) face of the west wall of P2, and that of the western portion of its north wall, have been rebuilt. Clearly it was just parcel P2 which was the concern of the refurbishers, and not the road as an entity; the *outer* wall-faces were left untouched. As one follows it south, the *west* wall of the road varies considerably. It starts off as quite a well-preserved blocky wall with both faces fairly detectable, before becoming a bank totally covered in vegetation (though facing-stones can still be picked out) and then a broad, spreading bank of sharp-edged stone chippings, with encroaching vegetation at its lower edges (Figure 176). There is no evidence that sporadic late refurbishment has been responsible for this state of affairs; what we are observing here is the variable pace of weathering and vegetation growth, which has not been 'completed' during the time which has elapsed since these walls were constructed.

A little further, south at the point (e) where the south wall of P2 curves away to the east, the configuration of the junction of the road's east wall with the south-west corner of P2 suggests that there may have been an intention to put a gateway into P3 here. Now the road changes its course and begins to traverse the western edge of an area of thinner soil, containing a few small cairns. Its eastern edge is now defined first by a wall, then by a slight break of slope, then by the edge of a shallow hollow way, and then by no surface trace at all. Evidently it was not important for this thin-soiled parcel P3 to be protected from passing livestock by an effective, continuous barrier. It is a characteristic feature of this road that the strength of its side-walls, and indeed the presence or absence, tends to correspond to the differential value of the lands through which it passes. Much further south, as it approaches the southern edge of the plateau and the descent to Caussols, there is an extensive tract of thin-soiled land showing no trace of the road whatsoever.

FIGURE 173. Junction of the Cipières–Caussols and the Les Baumes roads, viewed from the west looking east along the Les Baumes road

FIGURE 174. Possible gateway leading from the junction of the Cipières–Caussols road with the Les Baumes road into a nearby field

FIGURE 175. The Cipières–Caussols road immediately south of its junction with the Les Baumes road

FIGURE 176. The Cipières–Caussols road looking north towards its junction with the Les Baumes road. Note the varying states of preservation of the wall along its western edge (represented by the pile of chippings in the foreground)

PHOTOGRAPHS: ANDREW FLEMING

As one proceeds south, just beyond the south-east corner of parcel P1 is parcel P6, a small doline which has had small rounded stones cleared off its surface and onto the (abandoned) western road-side wall. Parcel P6A is a small enclosure attached to this wall. From here, the course of the road is best followed on Figure 177. At this point the road resumes its character as a walled corridor whose width can vary markedly over short distances, depending on

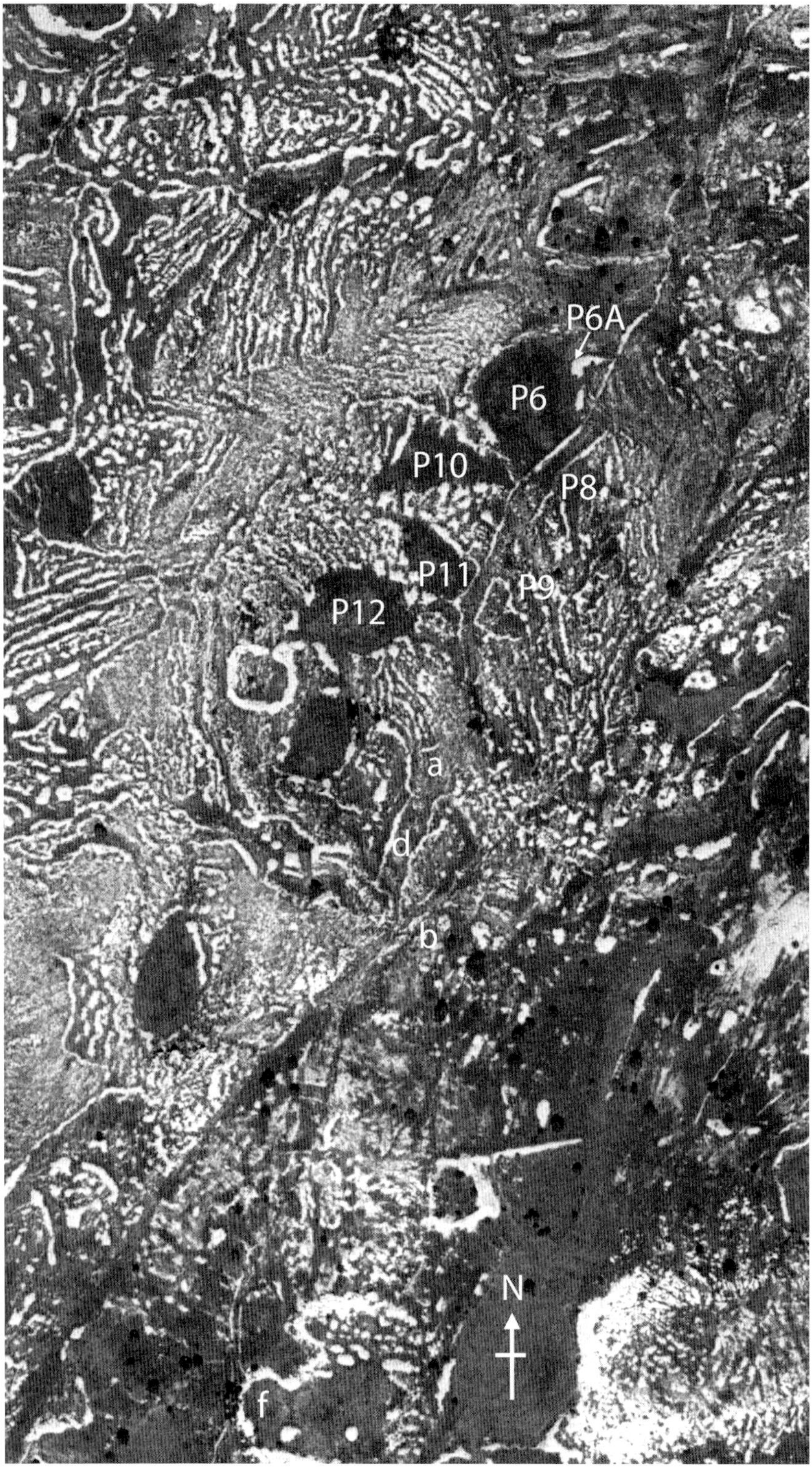

FIGURE 177. Part of the Cipières–Caussols road from the air. The letters are referred to in the text

AIR PHOTOGRAPH REPRODUCED BY KIND PERMISSION OF THE IGN

FIGURE 178. The 'primitive' boot-shaped enclosure (P9 on Figure 177) beside the Cipières–Caussols road, viewed from the south. The enclosure is on the right of the picture in the middle ground, with the road, here quite wide, to its left
PHOTOGRAPH: ANDREW FLEMING

the character of the land parcels which flank it. It threads its way through a 'busy' landscape, running past a series of small, shallow dolines to the west; the small zones which border them (and the road) carry clearance cairns. On the left (east) is land of lesser value, sporadically cleared. But there is also the small, 'primitive' enclosure P9, boot-shaped in plan, whose straight west wall seems to have been built to respect the course of the road; it contrasts strongly with the irregular, curvilinear wall which demarcates the rest of this enclosure (Figure 178). On the west side of the road, there are no fully enclosed 'fields', but it does seem that the presence of different parcels of cleared land is signalled by short walls which are integrated with the western wall of the road. Opposite P6 it is possible to suggest that there was a parcel P8, its west wall flanking the road and then turning through an acute angle to head roughly south as a 'hyphenated' boundary composed of stretches of wall/linear clearance cairns. To the west of the road, heavy cairns have been placed on a triangle of ground between parcels P10 and P11 (both dolines) and a suggestion of a linear boundary between parcels P11 and P12 (another doline) curves to form the flanking wall of the road. The road is evidently threading its way between occupied land parcels. A little further south the road widens (a on Figure 177) to form what looks almost like a narrow 'green', with the walling configured to form a gateway at its north-west corner. Starting to the north of the wider area 'a', and continuing through it, is a well-defined hollow track. South of 'a' the road narrows (b) and for a short while follows a geologically-conditioned channel. The character of the road in this zone is well illustrated by Figure 179. From here the road climbs slightly onto a clear, grassy ridge. Its sides are well-defined, mostly by collapsed walls and stone piling. A low wall boundary joins it from the west. The road takes care to incorporate the western edge of a small semi-circular walled structure (f) on a rocky boss. Then it starts to run

left: FIGURE 179. A section of the Cipières–Caussols road,looking north, threading its way through stony ground
PHOTOGRAPH: ANDREW FLEMING

above: FIGURE 180. The Cipières–Caussols road, looking north, running along the contour
PHOTOGRAPHS: ANDREW FLEMING

along a geologically-created terrace which runs along the side of a large doline to the west, and climbs onto the terrace immediately above the first one. Near the point where this swerve occurs, the parcel boundary which approaches the road from the east is apparently continued to the west by a line along which the clearance cairns to the south stop. It looks as if the behaviour of the road may have been influenced by the presence of a pre-existing boundary here (not illustrated). The road continues along the contour (Figure 180), running above and beside a major doline. A section of the road further south is illustrated in Figure 102.

4.15. Detail: along the Les Baumes road (1)

Further insight into the nature of the primary clearance landscape may be obtained by considering the landscape further west, in the vicinity of the Les Baumes road whose junction with the Cipières–Caussols road was noted in the previous section. Unlike the Cipières–Caussols road, the Les Baumes road is not a through route. It is a 'field lane', one of three such in the western part of the plateau (see Figure 29) which are designed to take landholders into zones of agrarian activity. To reach their parcels of land, individuals would often have had to diverge from the Les Baumes road, taking paths which have presumably left no trace in today's landscape. The road eventually becomes difficult to follow, and dies out near a small swallow-hole. Its 'behaviour', however, is very similar to that of the Cipières–Caussols road. That is to say, it varies in width and in the character and strength of its side-walls; in some stretches, only one side-wall is present. It also gives the impression that it is integrated into the pattern of the 'fields' through which it runs; its side-walls may turn away to continue as the boundaries of what are evidently fairly well-defined parcels of land. Conversely, it does not take the traveller to any of the high-walled or tile-roofed *bergeries*; indeed one gets the impression that this part of the plateau was not highly valued in recent centuries. The quite comprehensive dendritic pattern of roads on the plateau must surely, then, relate to a time of maximum pressure on resources, when access to different areas had to be carefully managed.

After passing point 'c' on Figure 172, the Les Baumes road runs up a gentle slope on an incline, passes over a broad ridge, and then turns south-south-west to run through a most interesting zone (Figure 181). The road enters the picture from the north-east (top right) corner (a). Eventually it enters a small triangular 'green' (b). From here a stretch of road heads west, its southern side-wall fairly continuous, its north side-wall less so. This road is not indicated on the 1842 cadastral map, and it does not continue beyond the western edge of Figure 181. In this area the focus of attention is the doline (A). In relatively recent times a *borie* (B) and a *bergerie* (C) have been built here. The doline is surrounded by a near-continuous revetment wall; its entrance ramp is clearly visible to the north, leading onto a saddle separating the doline from its neighbour. Three parcels of land (D, E, F) surround the north side of the doline, taking up about two-thirds of its circumference. Their edges are defined by near-continuous boundaries – walls and linear clearance piles. D and F are occupied quite densely by clearance

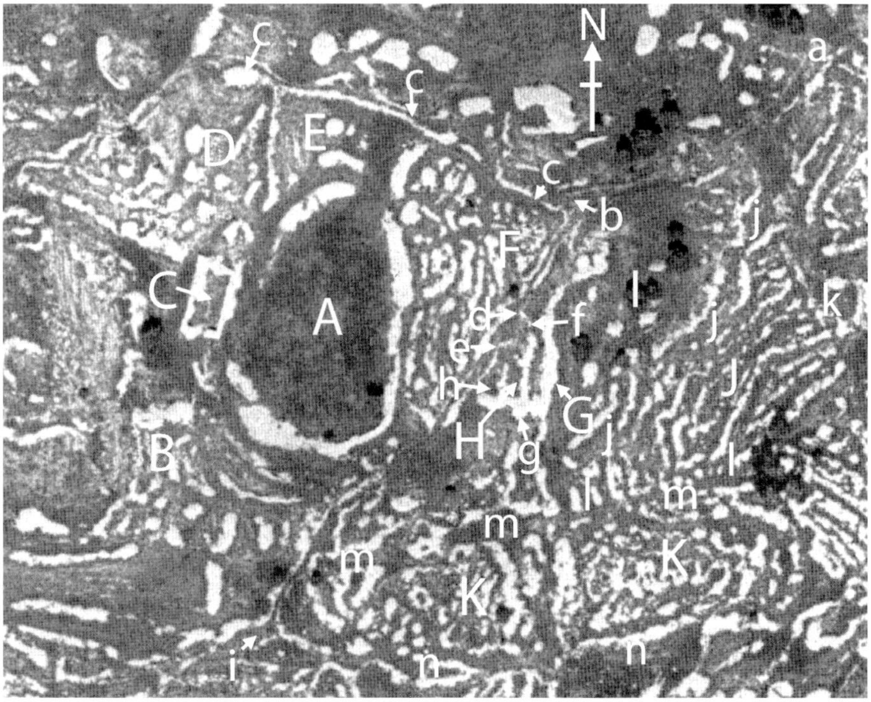

FIGURE 181. Les Baumes; a doline with several phases of occupation. Note the Les Baumes road, entering at top right and leaving near bottom left. The letters are referred to in the text

cairns. Figure 182 shows a view of parcel F from just above the *bergerie* C, looking east across the doline.

Parcels D, E and F are linked by the fact that their boundaries include the side-walls of roads which are evidently part of the network of communications. The eastern side of the triangular field F is bounded by the side-walls of the Les Baumes road, whilst its northern edge is bounded by the south side-wall (c) of a road coming off the Les Baumes road – a side-wall which continues as the boundary of parcels E and then of parcel D. Parcel D shares a boundary with parcel E; parcel E marches with parcel F. Whatever the niceties of ownership and usufruct, the coeval use and occupation of doline A, parcels D, E and F and the roads which form their boundaries to north and east is clearly demonstrated here.

Halfway along the stretch of the Les Baumes road which runs past parcel F is an opening formed by two short stretches of wall coming off the eastern side-wall of the road (d, e on Figure 181). The opening forms a small forecourt for the long building G, whose west wall is joined by the curving wall (e). Wall (d), which contains a gateway (f) about halfway along its length, joins the north-west corner of building G. Building G was evidently quite a massive structure (Figure 183). On the air photograph, its east and west walls may look like linear clearance piles, with further clearance to the south creating the coincidental impression of a long structure. However, faces are clearly visible along both the east and west sides of its east and west walls, and the distinction between the south-east corner of the building and the terrace wall which joins it from the south is clear. The floor of the building is clear of stones and quite level. It is not clear why the east wall is so much thicker than the west; it is possible that the wall was constructed on an underlying rib of rock with a clearance pile placed along it. Another building, H, is attached to the southern part of the west wall of Building G. Its entrance, like that of Building G, faces north. Buildings G and H are linked by the fact that they share a slightly sinuous south (end) wall, whose south face is clearly visible for most of its length. This wall has been slighted by a clearance cairn (g) which has been

top: FIGURE 182.
Les Baumes; doline A and adjacent parcel F (see Figure 181) looking across the doline from *bergerie* C. Note the thick wall of the 'primitive' long building in the background

bottom: FIGURE 183.
Les Baumes: Building G, seen from the north

PHOTOGRAPHS: ANDREW FLEMING

piled onto it. One has the impression that Building H, which was evidently reached from a small 'yard' (h) to the west, may have been an animal shed of some kind; access to the forecourt of Building G seems to have been impeded by the curving wall (e). This site is most important to the interpretation of the Plateau de Calern as a whole, in that it is hard to doubt the mutual relationships between the road, the 'forecourt' indicated by walls (d) and (e), the gateway (f) and Buildings G and H, along with the triangular cairned parcel F just across the road. If most other rectangular buildings like G and H were free-standing, and have been exposed to several centuries of physical and chemical weathering, it is not perhaps surprising that their remains are regarded with scepticism by the field archaeologist.

The Les Baumes road continues in a south-west direction, running past the south-east corner of doline A and then climbing to point (i) on Figure 181, where its side-walls diverge, suggesting that they were integrated with the boundaries of contemporary parcels of land. Figure 184 looks north-east, back across the area of Buildings G and H, with the road running past them from the foreground of the photograph. To the east of building G is an open, grassy zone I, containing four or five cairns; it is separated from the roughly trapezoidal parcel J by stretches of long clearance cairns (j). Parcel J is bounded to the north-east by an intermittent line of clearance (k) at right-angles to the grain of the geology as displayed within J; along its southern edge is a string of further circular or ovoid clearance cairns (l) which lie along a natural passage or 'lane' (m) running roughly east–west which leads towards the Les Baumes road. On the hillside above (m) is the ovoid area K, which is bounded by the Les Baumes road to its west, the 'lane' (m) to its north, and perhaps by clearance features (n) which may extend the boundary suggested by the wall running east from the Les Baumes road at (i). Two long clearance cairns running north–south

FIGURE 184. The Les Baumes road (marked by ranging-poles) running past Buildings G and H (the massive-looking structures in the mid distance)
PHOTOGRAPH: ANDREW FLEMING

through K, with a potential passageway between them, suggest the possibility that K might be regarded as two parcels rather than one. Parcels J and K are both much easier to see on the air photograph than they are on the ground. This should cause no surprise. This landscape is now shorn of many of the features which would have made it recognisable (and readable) to the people to whom it was once familiar as a workscape. None of the contemporary roofed buildings and shelters survive, there are no pollarded trees, marker posts, areas of crops, recognisable flocks of animals, or people in their own settings – locales made familiar with many a story or anecdote.

4.16 Along the Les Baumes road (2)

The final area to be visited here lies further along the Les Baumes road (Figure 185). The road enters the picture from the north-east (a), passing a doline to the south. On the other side of the road is a zone of surface stone-quarrying, with blocks of limestone lying around on the ground or perched precariously on other blocks at various angles of repose. The stone blocks look so fresh that it seems almost as if the stone-getters have just walked off the site. Indeed we may not be looking at medieval quarrying here (although post-medieval structures are not obvious in this locality). Like comparable sites elsewhere in the Les Baumes *quartier*, this quarrying zone is a reminder that, despite the abundance of stone in this landscape, those who had to build walls here did not necessarily get it from just anywhere; where possible, they tried to obtain 'blocky' limestone.

The Les Baumes road then turns south. A funnel entrance (b) leads into a narrow walled corridor which crosses the sill between two dolines. On the other side of the dolines, the side-walls diverge to form another triangular zone (c), the eastern wall curving east to form a long boundary-wall which runs for a considerable distance further east (d). Straight ahead are two conjoined *gouffres* or swallow-holes, probably the features that have given this *quartier* its name. There is also a *borie* here (e). It is well-placed; from this location it is possible to see most of the *quartier* of Les Baumes. The area round the swallow-holes looks very like a potential stock-gathering zone, with another roughly square animal management area (f) at the mouth of the road as it continues further south-west. To the right is a triangular enclosure (g) which gives access to the doline further west (A). This enclosure seems to be *both* of integral build with the northern side-wall of the road (at the south-west corner) *and* later than the road, whose side-wall it appears to transgress at the north-east corner. It looks too as if the north side-wall of the road has been fairly comprehensively demolished within the area of the enclosure. Here the conclusion must be, both from these relationships and from the uniform state of degradation of the walls in this zone, that road and enclosure are approximately coeval.

The road continues. Its right-hand side-wall becomes sporadic and then non-existent, but on the left the wall is continuous, evidently keeping road

FIGURE 185. The Les Baumes road near its south-west end

AIR PHOTOGRAPH REPRODUCED BY KIND PERMISSION OF THE IGN

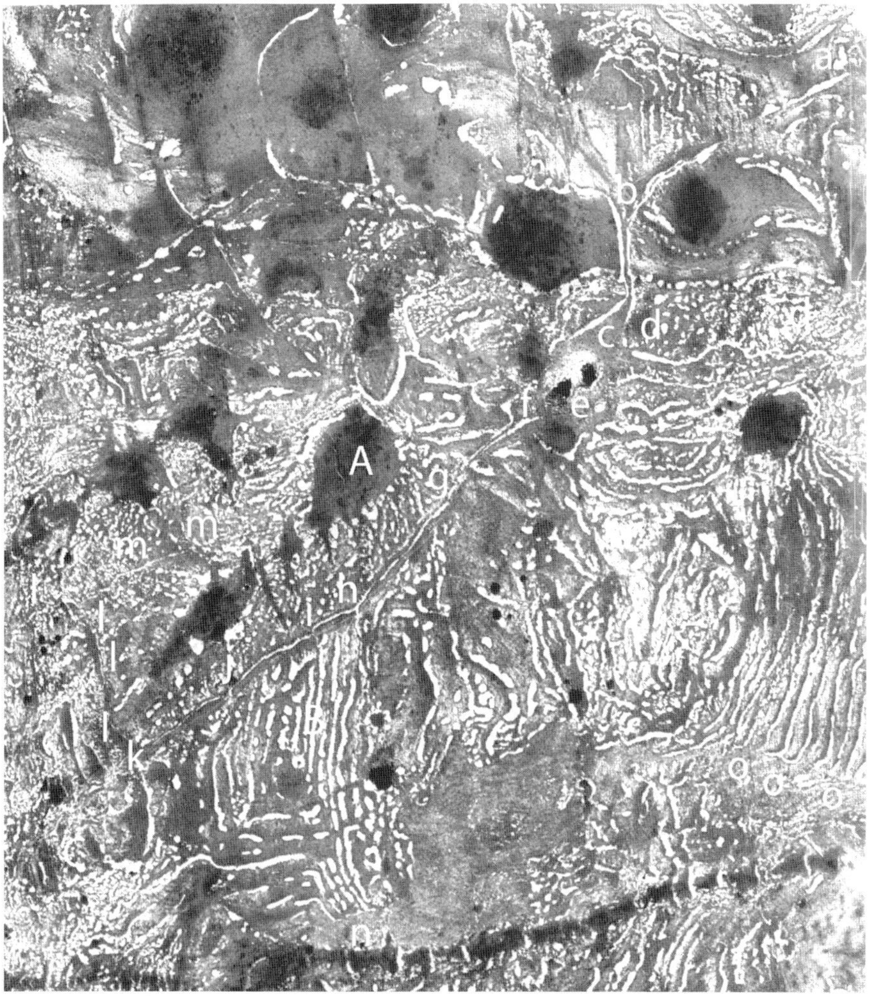

traffic off the substantial 'field' (parcel B) to the south. Three apparent 'internal boundaries' of this field connect with the road's southern side-wall (at h, i, j). This side-wall actually comprises the slightly 'scalloped' edge of the field which has been created by the presence of these sub-divisions; in other words, those who constructed the south wall of the road were primarily concerned with the field-edge, and not with any notion that the road corridor should possess a straight edge.

The right-hand (northern) edge of the road, by contrast, is less clearly marked, at first undefined, then indicated by a low but continuous break of slope. The clearance cairns of the 'field' on this side of the road have a rather uniform appearance, which is visible on the air photograph, and differs comprehensively from the pattern visible on the other side of the road in parcel B, with its long clearance piles respecting the prevailing geology. At (k) the road opens out a little and its north wall sweeps north to form a continuous terrace (l), evidently a parcel boundary which eventually curves to run west. This boundary is joined, incidentally, by a thin, straggling wall (m) apparently cutting through the middle of a cleared zone; this wall is illustrated elsewhere (Figure 168). On the south side of (k) the road is joined by a boundary-terrace approaching from the south, evidently the eastern boundary of a parcel at C. The road now becomes a 'cut and pile' affair which is much less obvious to the eye; that is to say, a minimal effort has been made to clear a narrow 'footpath' which continues south-west for a short distance, then turns south and is untraceable beyond a small swallow-hole (beyond the edge of Figure 185). Although there is clearance in this zone, the road has now entered a thin-soiled terrain without very much to recommend it. The change from a proper road, with each edge well-marked or at least well-respected by adjacent zones of clearance, to a meandering footpath, corresponds to the transition from a zone of uvulas, substantial dolines and relatively deep-soiled terraces, to a zone of thinner soil and bare rock. In general in this zone, the relationship between the road and the primary cleared landscape, and between clearance styles and local geological circumstances, could not be clearer.

Other classic features of this carefully-exploited landscape are visible on Figure 185. A very long doline cascade is visible running from east to west along the lower edge of the picture. Usually only a proportion of the short terrace walls built along these cascades is visible from the air. At the southern end of the longest of the clearance piles in parcel B, a near-continuous straggling wall (n) forms a kind of parcel boundary, separating the 'parcel' from a large thin-soiled zone to the north of the doline cascade. Further east, the linear clearance piles of another distinctively cleared zone curve west at the edge of the 'field' (o), and the boundary between cairned areas and the thin-soiled zone is often marked by stretches of straggling, intermittent walling, or zones where the cairning ceases along an apparently agreed line.

4.17 Conclusion

Of necessity, the account presented above represents simply an introduction to the immense variety of the cultural landscape of Les Baumes. Limitations of time and resources have precluded the recording and descriptive analysis of entire parcels of cairned land, which might have followed the 'reading' of the landscape at the scale undertaken here. It is also the case that numerous 'primitive structures' are apparently to be found within the *quartier*. I have refrained from discussing these on a site by site basis, because, as already noted, they are individual, self-contained 'sites', and their assignment to the categories 'probable' or 'possible' are matters of judgement and opinion. Often their only real 'associations' are with each other, in the sense that where one occurs, others are often not far away. These primitive structures do not, however, apparently form very recognisable patterns – a characteristic which may perhaps be seized upon by those who are sceptical about their validity as archaeological features.

On the other hand, we do not know how far their locations were determined by features such as the presence of trees; it is also possible that the form of tenure by which parcels of land were held forbade or discouraged the erection of permanent structures.

An immense amount of work has gone into the creation of this cultural landscape. Those who built these walls and cleared the land have responded in remarkable and intelligent ways to the highly variable heritage of the Plateau de Calern. Evidently they were unaware of the evils of geographical determinism! Here, I have mostly been concerned to show the *patterning* of their responses, and the *connections* between different features of the cultural landscape – sometimes expressed as the regular recurrence of recognisable features, sometimes as physical connections, as when the wall at the side of a road changes direction and becomes simply the boundary wall of a cleared parcel of land. In the final analysis, one has to recognise that this is surely one of the finest upland 'medieval landscapes' in the region; it will be for others to develop its potential.

CHAPTER FIVE

Settlement, Social Structure and Politics from the 5th to the 14th Century

Rosamond Faith

The end of the Roman imperial system and the great villa estate was followed in our area by a period of comparative independence for the peasantry and very much less intense exploitation of land and people. The predominant settlement pattern was one of dispersed farmsteads and hamlets, served by small chapels. On the analogy of similar areas elsewhere in Provence it is argued that the effective unit of social organisation is likely to have been the large family clan – although small nuclear households also existed. Authority over such a society could only be exercised by the owners of great estates in the form of the exaction of surplus produce in the form of food renders and the centres of castra *territories are likely to have resembled fortified houses with storage depots rather than residential castles. In the 11th century local lords became increasingly powerful at first in the absence of any centralising authority and subsequently as agents of the 'state' in the form of the Catalonian–Barcelonian counts. Settlement began to be nucleated around true castles, a process which enabled a section of the peasantry, the* caslani, *to secure a dominant social position, and superior housing, within the emerging village of Cipières. At Caussols, by contrast, the principal demesne (*reserve*) of the then owner of the three villages of Cipières, Caussols and Gréolières, was worked by a servile class – unusual in Provence. With the development of the village at Cipières a more communal way of life developed as did 'social capital' and the political community of the village, although dominated by the heads of clans or* ostals, *was capable of collective action and organisation.*

5.1. Introduction

We observe Cipières and its territory over a long trajectory, from the 5th century to the 20th. And we see it sometimes in close-up, sometimes from a distance imposed by the paucity of the information available to us, sometimes from the written record, sometimes from the material. Enormous changes to place and people took place in this period, which later chapters describe. By the end of the early modern period, described by David Siddle, the physical character of the village as we know it today was firmly established, although development continued outside this narrow framework in the shape of dispersed dwellings and small farms. However, before the establishment of the village some important changes in settlement pattern and social organisation had taken place, the village itself being only the last, and the longest lasting.

There is scanty evidence for the earliest inhabitants of our region but investigation of one category of site, the hilltop *enceinte*, shows that some Iron Age sites were occupied, or re-occupied, only into the 3rd century AD with a very rare exception such as the inland promontory of Baou de S Jean at Gréolières, where occupation was revived in the 4th–5th centuries (and which was to be of importance again in the 11th, as we shall see).[1] Fragments of quernstones and suggestions of fields and stock enclosures on some of these sites suggest very small-scale mixed farming, probably much as in the Esteron valley, 9 km north of Cipières where the native Ligurian farmers worked out of similarly dispersed sites.[2]

The experience of other parts of the late Empire under pressure from barbarian incursions might suggest that a fragile peasantry might have come under the sway of the villa-owning class, but although a major Roman road passes Cipières to the north on its way from Vence, the nearest Roman town, we know little about the extent of Romanisation in the region and there is no apparent evidence for any major villa or for any significant Roman influence on rural settlement or landscape. As the Roman administrative system decayed, the church to some extent preserved its structure and some of the Roman towns of the region, such as Vence, Antibes and Frejus, continued as seats of bishops and small trading communities. But out in the countryside the end of the Roman social order, the collapse of the villa system of antiquity, the slackening of the demands of the state for taxation and the unsettled and often violent conditions which succeeded Roman provincial government allowed if not the enrichment of the peasantry, at least their comparative independence. The desertion of the *enceinte* farms itself implies that a better living could be found elsewhere. In fact it is possible to see the period of the 5th to the 11th century as a relatively favourable one for the peasantry, one in which they may have managed to retain more of their surplus produce, albeit a surplus very hardly won, than before or after. The economic world of antiquity had decayed, a world in which slavery was widespread and the state, and rural landowners as its agents, exacted peasant surplus as tax. The economic system of the feudal world was not yet in place, when landlords would be able to extract surplus directly in cash, kind and labour from a peasantry who had become to a greater or lesser degree, their subordinates and tenants. This is not to say there were no powerful individuals who dominated the countryside: there were, but their relationship to the rural population was no longer what it had been in the heyday of the Roman landowning class nor what it was to become in the heyday of the feudal landowner. The *villae rusticae*, the territories which had supported a central high status establishment, underwent a gradual transformation. While the villa as a domestic building was abandoned the term *villa* remained in use to describe a territory containing a range of farms and settlements.[3] Centres of power and control appeared in new forms. The testament of Abbo, *patricius* of Provence of 739 shows that he kept five of his properties as his *cortes* or headquarters, worked on a bi-partite manorial system and heavily dependent on slave labour, while the freedmen-farmers on the rest of his vast property were tied to him only by the payment of dues owed since antiquity from their dispersed farms. Similarly, on the lands of Count Leibulf in the region of Arles in the 9th century, 'there is ... neither demesne nor tenures, but land which is the master's and houses where he stays when he wishes'.[4] As an adherent of Charles Martel and representative of the Carolingian royal house Abbo wielded considerable political power over a large area and Leibulf represented the highest order of Carolingian lay society. Such higher orders of authority may have had little direct influence on the ground in areas like the Arrières Pays: here power and power centres are likely to have been expressed in forms which depended less on the direct exploitation of a servile population on an incipient demesne, rather on a looser control over the surrounding countryside in which an important role was played by providing a protected space and the storage and distribution of surplus.

The church was becoming important in the countryside, attracting donations from the new Visigothic and Burgundian aristocracy. A major power in Provence was the 5th century foundation of S Victor de Marseille. Four of its properties lay in the Var within 20 km of our area, and are here taken as a useful source of relevant information for rural social structure in a period when our own area of study is devoid of documentation. In view of the analysis of family structure put forward by David Siddle, the farming families of S Victor's lands could prove to be particularly significant. The monastery's properties – corresponding loosely to present day communes – were described early in the 9th century as *villa(e)* or *ager(agri)*: these contained individual farms, *colonica(e).* Two studies which have located these farms on the ground have shown that they were both dispersed and of considerable size; in the case of one villa the area of the present-day territory contained only eight farms, scattered over the entire area. Elsewhere there were farms which were grouped in small hamlets.[5] Mixed farming was the rule, although in the more mountainous regions there were *bercariae*, specialised pasture farms or sheep runs. The families working these lands were very varied. The majority were nuclear, with two or three unmarried workers, possibly relative. Some were run by two or three women alone. However, while the nuclear family predominated there were some households, particularly on the sheep-farms, which contained large extended families or work-groups consisting of the farmer couple and their children, married and unmarried, and large numbers of unmarried men and women, resident farm workers of the type known in England as 'servants in husbandry'. Evidently there was a wide group, mostly but not exclusively kin, who had strong claims to be supported in return for their labour. Many hands imply many mouths and a farm could not support an indefinite number of people. In response to this there seems to have been an accepted code which both ensured the rights of family members and set the limit to those rights: two priorities recognised in many peasant societies. While the farm might support a large family, it was one in which the capacity to reproduce was limited: only one son was permitted to marry, the rest could remain on the farm, working in return for their keep, if they remained unmarried. The daughters could marry and often seem to have brought their husbands onto the farm. The married son would take on the titular headship of the farm and no doubt of the family too – in the language of our document he 'ruled' the farm. David Siddle's ratio of one *chef* to 30 persons would not have looked out of place on some of the S Victor farms.[6]

One advantage of these large families, besides ensuring a living for the members by 'the farm inheriting the people' rather than 'the people inheriting the farm' was the very large workforce they had to deploy: unlike the nuclear family they would not be handicapped by supporting numbers of children not yet old enough to work. They were ideally adapted to seasonal transhumance which took young adults up the mountain with flocks and herd from spring to autumn, while leaving enough competent adults to work the arable near the farmstead and gather the essential winter fodder for animals and people alike.[7] It is generally on the farms specified as sheep farms that we find them on the S Victor lands. While we lack any direct evidence of farming and family systems at Cipières before the early modern period – and such evidence is rare for Europe as a whole – David Siddle has demonstrated that the 'veritable clan or *gens*, headed by a *chef du foyer*' was still in vigorous life then. To suggest that it had its roots in a past which was probably not so very different from that of the S Victor families is simply to suggest a credible chronological depth for those roots. Siddle demonstrates the advantages such a large unit, based on the *ostal* and its land, could have in the late medieval and early modern period. The huge labour inputs necessary for the initial clearance of the plateau and the creation of the 'primary landscape' proposed by Andrew Fleming and David Austin, the scatter of the lands of a single holding over a wide area and between several *quartiers* revealed in the fourteenth century records, the labour intensive mixed farming of small plots and terraces, the supervision of flocks grazing among worked parcels of land, the perpetual stone clearing, all these demanded labour which the large *ostal* family could more easily supply. We need to ask ourselves when, and under what circumstances, these kin groups could have come into being as an effective (though not the only) social grouping. Siddle suggests that they were 'a normal response to a colonising situation', and it is interesting to remember that such family forms have been seen elsewhere in just this light: by Pierre Toubert as artificial creations formed to take advantage of the new opportunities offered by *incastellamento*, by Le Roy Ladurie as the product of particular conditions in late-medieval Languedoc.[8] In order to do that we need to address the question of the settlement pattern in our area, and we find that it is inextricably intertwined with its political history.

5.2. *Mansus* and *castra*: 10th–13th centuries

From the point of view of the relationship between the people of the countryside and the powerful, a crucial period was that between the barbarian invasions and the bringing of Provence under the rule of the centralised quasi-royal counts of Barcelona. This was the context for the emergence of local powers based on defended places which functioned essentially as war-bases and headquarters.[9] Southern Provence had been preserved from the Burgundian influx in the 6th century by Visigothic intervention and subsequently became an appanage of the Franks. In 879 it became part of the Lower Burgundian kingdom under Boso although Burgundian influence and formal control were resisted in eastern Haute-Provence by local lords, many of whom owed their position to the Carolingians. A cultural mix resulted: a self-conscious identification with Rome gave Latinate names to members of some Provençal families, both peasant and noble, while others were Germanic and we meet a Boso, which had been the family name of the Burgundians, as a lord in the Grasse area in the 12th century.[10] The counts of Provence became independent magnates in the Burgundian kingdom. It was Count William 'the Liberator' who has the reputation of having driven out the Saracens, the crucial battle often supposed to be at La Garde Freinet, their final stronghold, in 972. This led to the widespread redistribution of land along the coastal strip, greatly profiting the counts, but also allowing the lords of the Arrière-Pays to become more powerful. The era of powerful counts ended with the death of Roubaud II in 1008 and in the political vacuum that resulted local power bases were established, both unofficially by lords such as those of Castellane and officially in the devolution of justice to the level of the *vicomtes,* such as that of Marseille.

An important, though distant, shaping force on the landscape were the monasteries. Some like Lérins and S Victor had been founded in the 5th and 6th centuries, but the concept of these places as spiritual and ideological foci in the landscape was given a powerful impetus in the later 8th and 9th centuries when they were founded or developed as instruments and symbols of centralising authority both papal and imperial. Although Carolingian dominance faded in this region, these institutions remained and developed strong ties with the rural communities of their hinterlands. Pious local nobility were attracted to them as sites of the most intense Christian cult, as places where burial accompanied by the gift of an endowment would ensure continuing intercessionary prayer. They were to the fore in donating property, a process which often overturned the wishes of their family. The monks of the abbey of La Daurade, Vence early in the 1th century, 'cutting down an enormous forest', restored two of its chapels and secured their exemption from all demands from Lambert and Raimbaud, the major barons (*proceres*) of the area.[11] Several donations to Lérins were of entire properties: Bertrand de Coursegoules giving 'all his land' in Coursegoules, Bouyon, Bezaudun and La Gaude in 1155.[12] Others were gifts of revenues in kind, or single farms, such as the *mansum qui in territorio Sartophili opidis adjacet,* 'the mansus which lies in the territory of the *oppidum* of Sartoux' given in 1030.[13] The term *castrum* begins to appear and the lords of *castra* evidently had the power to exact renders in kind from the neighbouring farms. The gift to Lérins of Boso *miles* of Grasse was a *mansus* in the castrum of Mougins 'from which he used to receive yearly four shillings Melgorensis, three modios of barley and thirty loaves of the best bread' which was now to go to the monks and Laugiers de Gréolières took bread, barley, *garbage, civada* and *espalla* from his Nice properties in the 12th century.[14] In northern Europe the *mansus* was a peasant tenancy, but in southern France the term implies greater independence. Here the *mansus* was an allod with a single named owner. It could be of very varied size and social status, from a single farm to a sizeable property with a central courtyard house.[15] The term came in as away of denoting the properties of the kind and size which the church was dealing in: a religious house could no longer sustain its authority over an entire *villa.* It is with the gift of a *mansus* to Lérins in the 11th century that Cipières enters the historical record. An otherwise undated memorandum in the cartulary of the monastery records the bequest by Eldeiardis of 'a *mansus* in Cipières which her husband Raimbald used to have', her sons Petrus and Ainricus being witnesses. Eldeiard had entered the convent at Lérins, and was soon to die there, and this gift was her 'dowry'. The witness of her sons was presumably intended to secure the gift, but the property does not appear to have remained in Lérins' possession. Her husband had been equally devout, if he can be identified with the local noble (*procer*) involved in the restoration of the abbey of La Daurade, and if he can be identified with Raimbaud d'Orange, he was of high Burgundian family, 'founder of a line claiming descent from a paladin of Charlemagne.' and stemming from the southernmost part of the Burgundian kingdom.[16] However, the painstaking genealogies given by Cais de Pierlais do not seem to bear out this identification with the count of Orange.[17]

The lords of *castra* evidently had the power to receive receipts in kind from the neighbouring *mansus.* That Lérins was active in the property market and receiving donations and that a transferable surplus could be obtained from the countryside suggest a quickening of the economy. One sign of this was that Grasse, although its gardens, mills and vineyards must have given it a quasi-rural aspect with its two churches, was well on the way to becoming a significant town, whose more prominent people were looking to the countryside as a place to establish seats of authority and profitability: the presence of Grasse people, and Grasse investment, in Caussols is a recurrent theme in its history.[18] By the 12th century many villa territories had become identified as *castra* and by the 13th this usage, which can be detected as early as the 8th century, was widespread and continued into the 14th century. It was used as a term for a territory, presumably always one with a castle of some sort as its centre. This is how the benefactors of the monastery at Lérins located the gifts they made to it: Escuvia, the lady of the *castrum* of Magagnosc, 'sold land near the R. Siagne to Lérins in the 12th century'. Boso *miles* of Grasse gave a *mansum* in the *castrum* of Mougins.[19] These early castral territories may well have had ancient roots – it has been suggested that some may have been vestiges of hillfort or *oppidum* territories, with natural boundaries.[20] The term need not have implied the organised subjection of the territory: the *castrum* at the centre of the territories of these local lords is likely to have been at first little more than a defended hilltop or fortified residence and the most likely context for their evolution was an increased need for security.[21] But a secondary function, as well as providing a 'modest *maison forte*' for the owner, could well have been as collecting points at which agricultural surplus was stored against the visits of the proprietor: grain silos have been found on such sites in the region of Pélissanne.[22] This may be the archaeological counterpart of the fact that it was perhaps as receivers of peasant surplus, rather than as direct exploiters of the countryside, that the lords of the *castra* initially made their mark.

The landscape in which these *castra* were established and from which the castral lords were evidently able to draw off a certain amount of agricultural surplus was not necessarily centred on the sites which later became true castles with castle-villages at their feet. When in 1047 three brothers, Stephen, Guilemus and Ingilrannus, gave to S Victor the church of Ste Marie with a small vineyard and two *sparani* 'in the *villa* of Gréolières in the *castellum* which which is called Majone' but there is seemingly nothing at the present-day site of Gréolières which would justify calling the area a *castrum*.[23] Its central place was elsewhere. The *castellum* of Majone has been identified with Baou S. Jean, an ancient promontory site some kilometres away from, and at a higher altitude than the present village of S. Pons, which is thought to have replaced it.[24] We encountered Baou S. Jean earlier as a prehistoric *enceinte*, occupied into the 6th century, but whether or not it was deserted after that, it had evidently become an important place by the 11th or 12th century, for it has the remains of a Romanesque chapel, traces of fortification, and some kind of tower. The church of Ste Marie, also part of the brothers' gift, has been identified with the still standing church of Notre Dame de Verdelaye, on the outskirts of the present village of Basses Gréolières, which local people continued to cherish as a centre of cult into the 17th century. It is thought to have served as a baptismal church, on the lines of the Italian *pieve* churches, for a wide area.[25]

Nor does there seem to have been anything which would have earned Cipières the title of *castrum* when, sometime in the 12th century, Lérins received a property there. Here too there was a chapel on the outskirts of the village, just as was Ste Marie at Gréolières. If this was S Pons, on the road from Cipières which climbs over the plateau to Caussols, its site is now marked only by a cross, but 50 years ago the remains of walls, an altar, doorway and arch were enough to identify it as Romanesque. These outlying chapels – S Laurent at Gourdon is another local example – which have been dated on stylistic grounds to the twelfth century are common in the locality generally and several maintained a strong hold on the loyalties of people in the neighbourhood.[26] They have been identified as links in a 'pre-parochial network of pastoral care', and with a 'pre-castral' form of settlement serving – and this is what is most significant for our purposes – a rural population whose houses and farms were dispersed over the landscape in scattered farms or small hamlets. Marie-Helene Froeschle-Chopard has used the location of chapels to distinguish two distinct forms of settlement in the late 11th century. There were centres of power such as Bau S Jean, which had a fortified building and its own chapel, perhaps serving a small group connected with the centre, or a small fortified village. Apart from these, settlement was largely dispersed and served by rural chapels, now 'mute witness to disappeared generations'.[27] These chapels provide some of the best evidence we have of groupings of people before nucleation: David Siddle, in Chapters 6 and 8, provides a historical and geographical context for them.

All this was to change when as part of a European response to the Gregorian reforms of the 11th century a parish system was put in place and brought under the authority of bishops in the resurgent urban centres. A new kind of church took the place of the rural chapels, with baptismal and burial rights and a resident priest to ensure that the new demands on parishioners could be met by a more regular attendance at mass. A church was in place in Gréolières by 1079 when a 'church of the castle' is mentioned, at Cipières and Caussols by 1158.[28] The new parish church implied a much more articulated sense of what the parish was: its boundaries and the identity of its parishioners. There was a strong association between the new parish churches and centres of landlord power, but this is not to imply that the parish church was necessarily the same as a castle chapel, as S Jean seems to have been, nor that the priest was in the landlord's pocket. (David Austin discusses the church in the village in Chapter 2).

If there was still a largely dispersed settlement pattern into the 12th century this may in itself have been a brake on the development of the focussed seigneurialism of the later medieval period. Arguably we should perhaps look to the 10–11th century as an interim period where lordship still rested on the comparatively weak exploitation of an essentially allodial peasantry. Poly has described the 10th century as a favourable time for the Provençal peasantry, when lords 'neither have a monopoly of the land nor a firm control over people' and for Baratier exactions from the peasantry at this period 'seem less oppressive ... than a century later after the organisation of the rural seigneurie into firmer structures'.[29] In Poly's view, it was their rights over people rather than their ability to exploit the rural economy, which most characterises the strength of the powerful in this period. The public rights to hospitality and justice-giving became increasingly privatised and considered part of the comital patrimony. When parts of this were alienated, these rights came into the hands of the powerful, unattached to any public office. The allodial peasantry suffered in the process: appearing in court, and losing, as individuals unprotected by the solidarity of a community.[30] Nevertheless they appear not to have lost control over their lands and lives. Even fiefs – the landholdings which in much of Europe were so influential in giving rise to a class of landed lesser nobles – could in Provence be granted to peasants.[31]

5.3. From *castra* to *incastellamento*

Local lords with their *castra* appear at first sight to have much in common with the stratum of lordship frequently suggested as the context for a significant change in the landscape: that of the phenomenon of *incastellamento* – the creation of new settlements around, and dependent on, castles. While it is the fusion of these two processes – castle building and the nucleation of settlement – which is the essence of *incastellamento*, it may be helpful here to consider them separately. From the now extensive body of work on the subject we can separate out several distinct strands. Classically in Duby's *Mâconnais* the morcellation of seigneurial structures, the emergence of a lesser landlord class and the concentration of this lesser *seigneurie* on the direct exploitation of their land and tenants have been seen as the context for a more focussed exploitation of the peasantry, through *banal* lordship – the exaction of peasant surplus through new 'customs' and seigneurial justice. In Fossier's model of *encellulement,* it was the establishment of the seigneur as a physical presence in a small locality which he controlled for the benefit of his family which shaped the settlement pattern of western Europe. For Bisson and others it was not so much the physical environment as the rise of unbridled seigneurial violence that marked a 'feudal revolution' in the countryside. Toubert characterised as *incastellamento* the nucleation of settlement around seigneurial castles in Latium, but Wickham's work on central Italy shows that, while castles can indeed be found there, they did not play the same dominant role as they did in northern Europe. Work on the Vaunage region north of Nîmes similarly plays down the effect, and extent, of *incastellamento* there. A radical change in peasant tenancies and the terms under which they held their land has been suggested for England after the Norman conquest. An overall trajectory of profound change has been adopted by Poly, both in *La Provence et la société feodale* and in the synthesis which he created with Bournazel: but he is careful to single out the individual characteristics of the Midi which gave these processes, all of which can be found there, an individual character.[32] It was not only lords who brought about the nucleation of settlement around the foot of a castle: peasant families 'with no visible links to the comital aristocracy' achieved this in south-west Aquitaine and in northern Italy. In short, we would do well to separate out the physical changes in the landscape and the built environment, the nature of the seigneurie and the status of the peasantry before we try to relate them to a model which will be appropriate to our own area, and while doing this we should keep in mind the particular characteristics of the Midi. We cannot afford to ignore the fact that we are here in *le pays du droit écrit.* As British historians more familiar with the enserfment experienced by the peasantry in much of northern Europe, we cannot but be struck by the extent to which the peasantry of the Midi retained, despite considerable pressures and exploitation, their personal freedom and powers of communal organisation. We will see that in the population crisis of the late 14th century, when the seigneurs in the region were anxious to get or retain tenants, they were prepared bargain with them and draw up legal documents which formalised the arrangements.

There is another factor to be taken into account: the strength of the Provençal state. All over western Europe locally powerful lords were coming to be the effective source of authority at the expense of weakened central powers. But while in many areas it was the small castellans who became the ultimate beneficiaries of the leaching away of authority from central powers, in Provence under the Catalonian-Barcelonan counts and Charles d'Anjou comital authority was preserved and disseminated through the hands of connections of the comital house. The specific regional motor of change was the shift of authority, following a disputed succession to the county of Provence, to Raymond-Berenger of the house of Barcelona between 1112 and 1125.[33] This brought local lords into a tighter dependence on the count and, in 1112, 89 Provençal castellans swore oaths of fealty to him.[34] Following the joining of the counties of Provence and Catalonia under Raymond Berenger V a new administrative structure of baillies and vigueries was imposed after 1166. Under the rule of Charles d'Anjou from 1246 to 1285 the Barcelonan system of administrative and judicial control was extended and centralised. Charles abolished the quasi-communal authority of the consulates and replaced it by direct rule. He was largely an absentee ruler, whose main interests were in the Holy Land and his south Italian realm, and enormous power devolved to the vicomtes, whose offices became hereditary, and other families who wielded administrative power in the localities as well as being large landowners there. Towns, not remote castles, were the true centres of power. In the twelfth to fourteenth centuries the four places in our area were shuffled between members of the important houses of Grasse – which became the seat of comital administration in the area – and Nice, with the count intervening only to secure his rights. Below the vicomtes the *baillies*, who came from much humbler backgrounds, did the real administrative work, and held the lower courts on the count's lands. A minor nobility, the *domicelli*, represented in our area by the Robion family at Cipières and Gréolières-Hautes, seem often to have been not far in social status from the upper ranks of the peasantry. We find a *domicellus*, acting as steward (*seneschallus*) at Cipières.[35]

The immediate spur to castle building in our area was likely to have been the campaigns of the counts to control the local nobility particularly the Castellanes by military force, a process which had begun under the Barcelonan counts but was asserted with new energy by Charles d' Anjou, whose local 'enforcer', Romée de Villeneuve, played an important role in the history of our area. The count operated by implanting de Villeneuve and his family in strategic positions while making sure that comital authority was gathered back into his own hands. The physical presence of this process in our region generally is the clustering of settlement around a castle, typically on a hilltop. But the four different places in our small area, although all of them experienced the heavy influence of the count to whom they were pressured into ceding their interests, had different experiences.[36] The two fees of Basses and Hautes Gréolières gave rise to two medieval villages 500 m from each other, each with its own castle, church and lands.

5.4. Gréolières-Basses

When the three brothers, Stephen, Guilemus and Ingilrannus, gave to S Victor the church of Ste Marie with a small vineyard and two *sparani* in the *villa* which is called Gréolières in 1047 it was 'with the consent of their *seniores* or lords Amicus and Rostagnus and their wives'. The *villa* was evidently part of a great estate, comprising most of the diocese of Vence, which had come to Rostang from his mother. Rostang's descendants may have included Bertrand d'Aiguines and his brother Truand who by 1235 had inherited lands in Cipières. Between 1220 and 1235 the brothers ceded to the count the *castrum* of Gréolières and all the rights which they had in the vicinity. He granted it to Romée de Villeneuve in whose family it remained, as Gréolières-Basses.

5.5. Gréolières-Hautes

The distinction between Gréolières Hautes and Basses was first made in 1235 and it may be that it was about at this time that a second castle was built, on higher ground, possibly by Romée de Villeneuve or the count as part of a string of fortifications to defend the road and the Loup valley. This would have been an essential line of defence against the Castellane family up the valley, who were both leaders of the resistance to comital authority and reivers like the lawless barons of the Scottish–English Border, preying on the flocks going up to and coming down from the mountains.[37] In the 14th century Gréolières-Hautes was in the hands of Raibaude de Caussols who also had Cipières and Caussols and it was through the marriage of her granddaughter to Gerard de Villeneuve, who obtained Gréolières-Basses, that the two fiefs were united.

5.6. Caussols

There were eponymous seigneurs in place in Caussols and Cipières by the mid-12th century known to us simply as 'N de Caussols' and 'Pons de Cipières' and 'Galfridus de Cipières'. It is argued that they were in fact members of important local families, who come into view more clearly in the records of the 13th century. Then the *castrum* of Caussols – this was possibly the deserted site with a small keep on the Caussols–Cipières road known as Villeveille – was in the hands of one of the chief families of Grasse. Bertrand de Grasse in 1216 obtained Caussols from his brother Targe in exchange for the *castrum* of Cabris. In 1224 he acquired La Malle as well. The consuls of Grasse laid down stringent conditions, forbidding the inhabitants of their town to move to either Caussols or Cabris, and the inhabitants of either to move to Grasse. In 1224 the count granted Targe the greater part of his rights in Caussols reserving his rights to fealty and jurisdiction.[38]

5.7. Cipières

By 1235 hereditary property in the *castrum* of Cipières was in the hands of two brothers, Bertrand d'Aiguines and Truand, who in that year who ceded 'all they possessed there' to the count of Provence. He in turn granted it to Romée de Villeneuve and Bertrand's daughter married Romée's son. This property may have become the Robion fee in Cipières, at Boyet on the Loup. Actual lordship of the *castrum* granted by the count in 1224 was in the hands of Targe de Grasse who by then was already lord of Caussols as well. By 1297 both places had descended to Raibaude de Caussols, a descendant of Targe, and her husband, Reforciat d'Agout. The count's property in Cipières may have gone to the Robion family, co-seigneurs there and holding from him in 1297.[39]

These divergent histories are a warning against assuming that building a castle always led to profound change in local society and settlement. Caussols, although referred to as a *castrum* in the 12th century, differed in its social structure and seemingly dispersed settlement pattern, probably also its husbandry, from Cipières, where a new nucleated settlement was created around the castle and profoundly shaped by it. Both Gréolières villages were in the hands of Romée de Villeneuve by *c.* 1235 when the upper castle was built. The castle at Hautes-Gréolières looks like an alien intrusion into the landscape, its village the result of an enforced division of the old *castrum* territory to create a separate domain for strategic purposes. But while Basse-Gréolières, although hard hit by the plagues, remained a substantial and enduring village throughout the Middle Ages, Hautes-Gréolières, although there was a seigneurial house and a prospering community of weavers there in the mid-14th century, failed to survive the severe crises on the later part of the century and by the late 15th century had only 15 heads of households to 440 in the lower village.[40]

5.8. Power and rights in the countryside

Power at the top of this society was complex. As feudal lord, the count demanded an oath of fealty from his castellans, but as ruler of Provence he has been described as 'a sovereign, some of whose subjects hold fiefs, rather than a 'feudal prince'.[41] He had both those rights which, as was common in post-Carolingian Europe, were a vestige of public powers in a privatised form, and others which were what any powerful figure could claim from his freemen. It is through the systematic recording of these rights in 1252 that we first learn anything about the status of the peasantry, as different demands were made on different categories of people.[42] This differentiation of obligation must in its turn have accentuated and perpetuated such distinctions.

Cavalcata, the obligation to supply an armed, sometimes mounted, man, and *alberga,* the obligation to supply hospitality, were obligations of a kind which originated in a period where there was a close personal association between the powerful and those who fought and hunted in their company, and who could be expected to entertain them on their itinerations. Although highly resented, open to exploitation and burdensome, all over western Europe they marked out the free man. In our area of Provence by 1252 they had been commuted for cash payments, the *alberga* being reckoned on the hearth. In 1224 Bertrand and Targe de Grasse gained exemption from *auberge* and *cavalcade* for their lordships of Cabris, La Malle, Cipières and Caussols, but by 1252, when the count had successfully established his hold on the region, they were evidently exacted. *Quista* was a money payment, the equivalent of northern European tallage. Baratier has identified the people who owed it with the *homines de casamento* and *maleservi* encountered in seigneurial records. As *caslani* were also liable to *quista* it seems that what marked out *maleservi* as an inferior class, insofar as comital demands were concerned, was possibly that they owed this one at a fixed rate: they are identified as *homines de quista al mercedem* in the comital documents; *milites* were exempt.

These were all dues owed to the count in his 'public' capacity: other dues were essentially feudal, owed to the seigneur: in our documents we find them paid by members of the village community. 'Aids' were payable on the marriage of the seigneur's daughter, the knighting of his son, his passage overseas, his ransom or his purchase of property worth more than 50 *livres.*[43] Also seigneurial were the rights to justice. Although the count had rights to *justicias* from all four places – the right to try important cases – Raibaude de Caussols or her agents held courts for day-to-day business in her *fortalicium.* A notary recorded the proceedings. This was both a seigneurial court which could impose penalties but it was also a public forum, on occasion a *parlement.* Although Raibaude's court was seigneurial, both in its setting in her hall and in the heavily feudal overtones of the homage and oaths of fealty performed there, it was also the forum for much village business. As well as being the locus for sometimes savage seigneurial discipline and the enforcement of the restrictions of banal lordship, it was also an important resource for the inhabitants where family arrangements, succession, dowry arrangements, land sales, leases and exchanges and livestock contracts were duly witnessed and recorded by the notary. In these multiple roles, the court resembled the manorial courts of medieval England. Two notarial registers from the time when Raibaude de Cassols was lady of the seigneurie of Caussols, Cipières and Hautes-Gréolières give a glimpse into the middle years of the 14th century. We are fortunate to have been able to draw on the admirable work on these registers of Colette Samaran, pupil of Georges Duby, which focusses on many of the aspects of French rural society which have remained central for the nearly 50 years since she wrote.[44]

The notarial registers show, although possibly not completely, what was owed to the lady as landowner as opposed to what was owed to the count as overlord. The principal categories of people who appear in the fourteenth century sources for our area are *maleservi* and *caslani*. They were distinct not only in legal status, family structure, economic status and relationship to the seigneur, but also in their physical setting: their houses and farms. So investigating these differences may contribute to our picture of how the area may have developed on the ground and in the street.

5.9. *Caslani*

Their name, in Provençal *cayanalo*, which derives from *castellani*, links these people to the castle: they are people whose way of life is determined by their relationship to a new and distinctive kind of space and their status derives from their position in a new and distinctive structure of lordship. There are only a few scattered references to them in the Cipières documents, and the term was probably going out of use in the 14th century, but there are parallels for them elsewhere in Provence. They were people of free status, who needed the protection of the powerful in return for the promise of personal loyalty. In the 11th century they are found giving oaths of allegiance to the bishops of Nice and to the abbey of Lérins. At La Garde Freinet, where they are interpreted as *vassaux roturiers*, close to the seigneur, they were in charge of the castle in his absence. In the Vésubie valley they seem to have had minor judicial authority, receiving a portion of the revenues of minor justice. In Catalonia Bonnassie sees similar close association with the seigneur: members of castle garrisons were co-opted from the richest stratum of the allod-holding peasantry as 'armed auxiliaries of the *seigneurs banaux*' and 'village allodialists' became *milites castri*. Even where *caslani* were associated with much more 'knightly'-sounding people, such as the lesser lords and knights (*seigneurs-chevaliers, personnes chevaleresques*) of the upper Var, who had 'men' of their own and served in person in battle, albeit on foot, they were farmers as well.[45] While in much of Europe the legal and social status of peasants was being eroded, their comparative freedom in the Midi comes through strongly in descriptions of this class. This is not to say that they enjoyed the comparative autonomy that their 10th and 11th century counterparts had enjoyed, Peoples of all levels of society were coming to be defined in terms of their relationship with lords of all kinds and the *caslani* were no exception. 'Peasant fiefs' are a characteristic of the freer peasant status in the south, and the sons of Cipières tenants went to do homage to the lady when they came of age, just as feudal vassals did.[46] The permeability of the noble class and the possibility of falling out of it, made for a fluid social situation. Among the class of minor nobles, *domicelli,* there may have been people who were not much above the *caslani* in social status and may have been below them in wealth. The *caslanus* we meet in the 14th century records was certainly subject to constraints which emphasised his personal subordination to the seigneur and her interest in the land he farmed. He did homage on succeeding to or acquiring land. This process was reinforced by the imposition of restraints on and fees for its alienation, penalties for letting it deteriorate. Land transactions must take place in the seigneurial court. Permission was needed for a *caslanus* to marry someone from the servile *maleservi.*[47] But apart from the 'public' obligations of alberga and the 'feudal' obligations to her – homage, aid and tallage – there is not much sign of the land which was the essential part of these being tenancies held for *rent,* either in cash, kind or work.[48] And many of the restraints on his personal liberty which we might expect in a northern European context – seigneurial control of marriage and dowry, the demand for labour rent – were absent.

The Cipières records show traces of the survival of three important elements in independent peasant societies. An upper stratum of peasants, the *boni homines, probi homines, prud'hommes, meliores, seniores* who are prominent decision-makers, representatives of the community, respected elders, is recognised in most descriptions of medieval society. The *boni homines,* who we can probably identify with the heads of *ostal* families, were unquestionably important at Cipières. Fifty-six men described as 'holders of *hospicia* and the *maior et senior pars*' were summoned to a *parlement,* representatives acted as 'arbitrators and jurors of the said castle' and one as a town crier. Pons Argentin, Hugh Flores senior and Feraud Berenger negotiated as elected representatives on behalf of the community over the purchase of a meadow in 1336, two others over pasture rights in 1336 and in an important episode in 1368 it is 'certain men of the *castrum* of Cipières' who make the journey to Nice to petition the seigneur for permission to take over the lands of Caussols. All these transactions must have been preceded by some kind of election, however informal, and in the case of the Caussols business, the collection of a common fund. Other transactions, such as the enfranchisement of a *maleservus* at Caussols in 1345, needed the consent of the whole community there.[49] Evidently in the 14th century the assent of the inhabitants, either as a body or through their chosen representatives, was essential to sanction important village transactions. Had this been true in an earlier era? Might the peopling of the early castle-village have been on terms collectively negotiated with the seigneur? It is unknowable, but not impossible. Another important idea in peasant mentality is that of 'founding fathers' – that is of families that were thought of as the aboriginal inhabitants of the village, and who alone had rights in its common resources.[50] Perhaps the fact that *caslani* families retained their distinct identities for so long reflects some such idea. This can only be speculation but some such division may have been part of the way in which medieval Cipièrois thought about the past. We know that only certain properties there owed *cens.* This was not a simple rent but a 'recognition' payment, in other words one by which the tenant recognised the seigneur's personal authority. Others were 'free of render and service'.[51] A similar distinction was made by the inhabitants of S Tropez in the 13th century, who claimed that only the houses in being when the *cens* was first imposed owed it: later houses built by the inhabitants themselves were exempt. The protest was a communal and determined one which the community won: it seems to reflect memory, real or imagined of some earlier episode in which rent had been demanded for a particular category of houses: it is just possible that this was when the village was first established.[52] Possibly *cens* payers at

Cipières had newly built houses which were part of the fabric of the early village and which their predecessors had taken on in return for a payment which recognised the seigneur's authority. David Austin detects distinct stages in the construction of the village in Chapter 2. This may well be evidence of just such a process: the earliest settlers most tightly associated with the castle, the more independent *cens*-paying *caslani* occupying the earliest quarter, the rent-paying and much more servile tenants, including perhaps the *maleservi* (although these are not well evidenced at Cipières) the smaller properties built at subsequent stages.

5.10. *Maleservi*

The *caslani* at Cipières coexisted with an inferior class, the *maleservi*, who are only very occasionally mentioned in the records. At Caussols it seems as if all the tenants – 33 households in the mid-14th century – were *maleservi*. They were significantly tied and dependent people. Their obligation to pay a fixed *quista*, instead of a negotiated sum, is very reminiscent of the servile obligations of northern Europe. The *maleservus* was granted a composite holding called a *casamentum,* comprising a house, land, garden vines and meadow, and the service they owed derived from this grant. This links their servile status – unusual in Provence – to their complete economic dependence on the seigneur: '*L'acquisition d'un casement determine la condition du tenancier.*' The granting of a dwelling can often be found as a determinant of servile status.[53] The *casamentum* was a small-scale enterprise, generally run with no oxen or only one ox. As this land unit was considered to be part of her demesne and paid its rent in kind and essential labour the seigneur made sure it remained intact: no alienation was allowed. In the sense that the *maleservus* owed rent in barley, wheat and wine, it was a kind of sharecropping arrangement.[54] The other *maleservi* obligations drew not so much on the peasants' skills and labour-power, as did the labour rent owed by the serfs of northern Europe, but on a resource that European landlords were rapidly learning to exploit more effectively: peasant capital in the form of time and livestock. The *corvée* due from a *maleservus* family, with one beast and no other driver, consisted of five trips to Gréolières-Hautes to carry necessities to and from the *hospicium* there and one trip from the *hospicium* at Cipières, staying overnight if necessary, at harvest time carrying corn from the Lady's threshing floor there. This was presumably to market as his beast is obliged to make a further journey, staying for another day if needed, to Grasse or other places around Cipières.[55] The value of these services is shown by the facts that they were still in force in 1609, and that *corvée* was eventually transferred to the service of the state and remained a prime grievance until the end of the Ancien Régime.

Maleservi families are more likely to have been small and nuclear than those of the *caslani*. They did not produce the wide kin group which could retain within its ranks a permanent hold on the tenancy, as the holding of a *maleservus* who died without a male heir would revert to the lord. *Maleservi* holdings were inalienable and had to be kept intact, But with growing population, even small holdings like this could seem an attractive proposition, and people applied for them or married *maleservae* women to get one.[56] In contrast with the successful long-lasting lineages of the *ostal* families of Cipières they gave very limited opportunities for providing a living for joint heirs. This raises the possibility that, long after the distinction between *caslani* and *maleservi* had disappeared, the social difference between them would still have been recognised in the physical difference in their housing. The *maleservi* families are likely to have had apartments or cottages much smaller than the larger kin-groups of the *caslani.*

Maleservi evidently played an important part in Raibaude de Caussols' management of her estate. She integrated her three villages by using *maleservi* labour and livestock to transport produce between them and to markets at Grasse and elsewhere, but they were distinctive in their social structure and the existence of a demesne must be important in the distinction. Caussols seems to have been the main production centre and was better endowed for this as we see in 1368 when it is depopulated but still had a seigneurial home farm. Size and structure were perhaps involved in all this. There was ox pasture at Caussols so probably fairly large fields there, and land in the broad open valley of the commune may have been under the plough.

There may have been people of even lower status. The transport service owed by the *maleservi* represented only a small part of the work of the agricultural year with the main manual work being the cultivation of the demesne – ploughing, sowing, weeding, harvesting and threshing. Feraud Robion, co-seigneur, demanded manual work on his demesne at Cipières. These basic jobs, Samaran suggests, must have been done by paid farm servants, *valets* or 'servants in husbandry' living around the *curia.* Were these people, seemingly not owning land and therefore invisible in our documents, have been housed in the castle precinct itself, as living-in 'servants in husbandry'? Did many work as farm servants for other villagers, like the two Cipières men who were hired to plough and sow two fields for the Argentin brothers for 4 *livres* 10 *sous*? The *journaliers* of the seventeenth and eighteenth centuries were the successors of these day-labourers.[57]

Elsewhere in Europe we find a very strong association between the inferior status of some peasants, whose obligations were increasing towards a lord, and their exemption from the demands of a higher, more 'public' authority – the king or the count – which, while onerous, were nevertheless a mark of free status and were owed by the upper ranks of the peasantry.[58] However, in our area even the *maleservi,* in other ways of such low status, owing both rent in kind and labour rent in the form of carrying service also owed duties to the count which were normally associated with freedom, or at least honourable dependence. They did homage and paid aids, which have a very feudo/vassalic tinge, they owed *alberga* and service on cavalcades. They had a notable ability to act legally and collectively, as when they negotiated grazing arrangements and assented to the emancipation of one of their number and they evidently retained common rights.[59] In both Caussols and Cipières the farmers as a group – or rather the heads of families – had considerable and formally recognised authority.[60] For all these reasons we might perhaps see the 14th century *maleservi* as previously independent peasants whose economic and social status had been reduced – perhaps fairly recently – as a result of the increased (or entirely new) emphasis on demesne husbandry, encouraged no doubt by the growth of the market locally, in the context of the establishment of the small triple lordship of Caussols, Cipières and Gréolières-Hautes. If there was growing pressure on land from a rising population they may well have included families who had been glad to get a holding on any terms.

The fact that the *caslani* are so different from the *maleservi* suggests that, from the point of view of the local peasantry, the experience of nucleation connected with *incastellamento* might have been very different from that connected with the establishment and exploitation of a seigneurial demesne alone as at Caussols. This extends far beyond the difference in their housing. *Incastellamento* at Cipières had evidently brought into being an upper peasant class, the *caslani,* who, while subject to considerable formal restrictions, were nonetheless free and independent. The descendants of the *cens*-payers may well have benefited from the new social relationships of the castle-village. Evidently to become a *caslanus* at Cipières didn't mean losing free status in the way that becoming a *maleservus* at Caussols did. By contrast with Cipières, Caussols seems to all intents and purposes to have been a village of tied serfs, akin to the 'inlands' or demesne centres of Northern Europe.[61] Presumably the existence of a labouring class, the *maleservi*, preserved the *caslani* from exploitation to a certain extent. Did these distinctions lead to strong differences between Caussols and Cipières in terms of their social structure as well as their physical being, and perhaps contribute to the greater viability of Cipières as a settlement? It may be that the strong social identity of the village of Cipières owed much to the existence of the *caslani* class.

5.11. Banal lordship and the creation of social capital

The creation of banal lordship – the exploitation of the peasantry through the establishment of seigneurial monopolies and jurisdiction– plays an important part in most accounts of the intensification of lordship. Two principal strands are involved: the establishment and exploitation of seigneurial monopolies of capital equipment and new controls over peasant family arrangements, particularly those involving property. To compel tenants to use the seigneur's capital investments made such investment financially worthwhile. It also made it possible for the seigneur to profit from the processing end of peasant household production, as well as simply taking a cut in the form of rents and renders. Resentment of *malos usos*, 'bad customs' (*maleservitudines* at Cipières), a wide term to describe these new seigneurial controls over peasant lives, was felt all over much of western Europe. And while Caussols produced a saleable surplus, both there and at the other villages banal rights may have been as important as demesne production. Raibaude could profit from her tenants' land by controlling the point at which value was added – processing by threshing, fulling and baking. Threshing was done by leading horses or mules over sheaves laid on the floor or ground. Raibaude had her own threshing floor at her *hospicium* at Cipières. Her tenants were forbidden to borrow a neighbour's animals if they did not have enough themselves, but had to use – and feed – those from the demesne: for this a payment was owed and from which no doubt a profit was made.[62] However, we know from the work of our archaeological colleagues that there were small threshing-floors on the Plateau de Calern, so there were evidently ways of getting round this prohibition (Chapters 3 & 4). Raibaude had a fulling-mill (*paratorium)* on the Loup and her tenants were obliged to use this. Jacob and Raymunda, weavers mentioned at Gréolières-Hautes in the mid-14th century, may alone have been engaged in cloth production on a sufficiently large scale to make this investment worthwhile, but perhaps cloth was woven for household use by many other families too and the lessee of the mill had to make cloth for the seigneurial household.[63] As bread was so essential to the peasant diet the seigneurial monopoly of a village oven was one of the most widespread, and most resented, of *banalités*. However, it could provide a profitable opportunity for a village entrepreneur. The seigneurial oven in the public square at Cipières in 1357 was leased out to a tenant who paid rent of 20 *livres* a year and baked bread for the lady and her household and the rest of the village. The profits of the seigneurial corn mill were also leased. Raibaude also had mill and oven rights at Caussols so presumably until then had a mill and oven there too.[64]

Banalités affected everyone: there was resistance at Cipières when someone was exempted from payment of multure.[65] They were undoubtedly exploitative, but there may be another side to this. Just as the creation of the castle-village had brought people together in new, much more cheek-by-jowl arrangements of living-space, so too the compulsory use of seigneurial installations of oven, threshing floor and fulling-mill may have brought them together in new relationships and conflicts. However resented, *banalités* may also have been an important factor in creating new and more communal spaces, and new and more associative ways of behaving. The common oven in a small square acted as a meeting place: the earliest surviving minutes of the council refer to the appointment of a baker and the bakery is still an important focus of village life.

CHAPTER SIX

Population, Economy and Society 1050–1531

David Siddle

In this chapter the evolution of the Cipières community and its landscape is examined in terms of responses to the major phases of advance and retreat in population which affected not only Cipières but all societies in the broad region in the country and indeed in Western Europe as a whole.[1] *These trends reflected periods of change in climate and phases of quite rapid expansion or collapse in economies. The case is made for the occupation of this landscape by large extended family groups (*ostals*) in the centuries before the Black Death. The chapter also traces the subsequent developments through the period of population recovery and economic expansion in the 15th and early 16th centuries.*

6.1. Introduction

If there is some evidence that people were occupying the Cipières landscape from the early Bronze Age, as Andrew Fleming suggests in Chapter 2, improving techniques of measuring climate change[2] indicate that the serious ameliorations occurred in the Roman period and then again between the 9th and the 14th centuries[3] opened up a new range of possibilities. Rosamond Faith (Chapter 5) argues that this was a relatively good time for the local peasantry, who were moving out of defended settlements and occupying a wider range of environments. The second period of climate change coincided with the Saracen incursions and there was good reason to move away from the coastal zone. Perhaps it was at this time that they began to settle the inland valleys like the Loup? Even though the archaeological evidence for such developments is either limited or unexplored (see Chapters 2, 3 & 4) we can speculate that this conjunction of population pressure and climatic amelioration could have led to a further opening up (or re-opening up) first of the lower slopes of the Loup and then of the uplands for both pasturing flocks and for crops. With sequences of good harvests and warmer winters we can carry the assumption that this would eventually lead to the development of a fairly settled indigenous population in the area below the Cipières plateau in the period before the development of nucleated settlement as described by David Austin in Chapter 2 and Rosamond Faith in Chapter 5. The question we leave hanging in the air is this: was it in this period that the first elements of the 'workscape' described by Austin in Chapter 3 emerged or did these changes accompany the process of village formation?

If this phase of population expansion did, in fact, begin with the scattered homesteads of the large kin groups of the late 9th century AD our much firmer historical evidence suggests that it came to a peak in the late 13th century. This is the period between the *incastellamento* of the 12th century and the onset of poorer harvests in the early 14th century which culminated in the Black Death in 1348. There is also no doubt about the subsequent period of declining population leading to a general recovery in the mid-16th century.

6.2 The 'field full of folk' 1050–1348

Although archaeological evidence is inconclusive we have suggested in the introduction to this chapter that the earliest early medieval settler groups in the Cipières landscape may well have occupied the lowlands by the river Loup, some lower slopes and areas close to the bench below the plateau (topographic zones I & II and see Chapter 5). It is here where they first grazed their animals and gradually cleared the woodland for potential arable land. Perhaps it was in this period that the massive stone clearance piles which characterise the bench began to be formed? Rosamond Faith argues that this picture of a settled pattern of large kin groups in linked homesteads before *incastallemento* may look familiar to those who study similar environments elsewhere even if the evidence is vestigial. Were these the families that were served by the chapels and *enceintes* which provided the religious and defensive foci for these kin groups in the centuries before village formation?

But whatever happened in the earlier Middle Ages there are powerful arguments for the view that the first real period of population expansion occurred in the 300 years after the 1st millennium for this was the well documented period of village making which affected the whole of Western Europe.[4] We also know that this expansion took place in a period of relatively settled political and economic circumstances dominated by Latin Christendom with its changing attitudes to the winning and control or taming of 'wildscapes' or *terre gaste*.[5] There is also the strong evidence for an ameliorating climate. It is over 30 years since Le Roy Ladurie used harvest dates to point to the significance of climatic change in creating opportunities for this expansion into the uplands during this time.[6] More modern scientific research based on magnetic and tree ring evidence gives us a much clearer view of these ameliorations[7] (Figure 186). There are also some indications that there were changes in agricultural

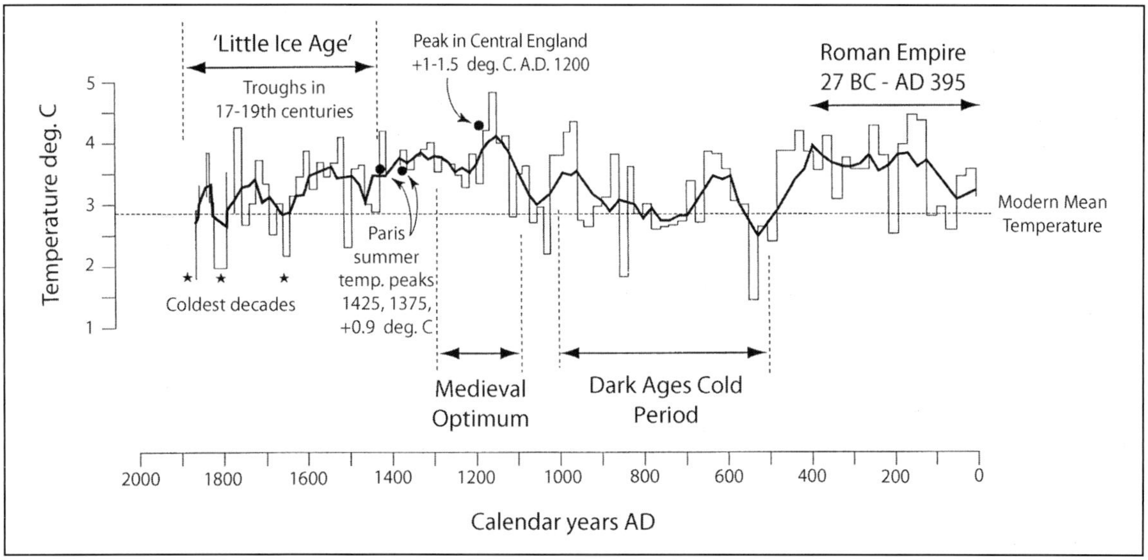

FIGURE 186. Graph of climatic changes in the medieval period

techniques in this period leading to improved yields.[8] Better diet and good harvests improved life expectancy. Add to this the commercial expansion which occurred in a period of political stability, and it is un-surprising that populations mushroomed everywhere, especially between the mid-11th and mid-14th centuries[9] Braudel gives a figure of 0.4% per annum spread over this period.[10] Indeed rural population densities at this time may have built to levels which were only possibly replicated in the last years of the 18th century when the issue was blurred by migration to towns.

In the relatively settled political and economic circumstances of a fully Christianised Western Europe, there were also changing attitudes to the control and management of upland areas. These were reflected in an impetus towards the clearing of *terre gaste* and expansion into remoter areas,[11] what Bloch has called 'the great age of clearing in France'.[12] It was also a direct response to the land hunger in the lowlands and valleys produced by population growth. It was partly a product of this expansion that mountain areas such as the Pré-alpes were drawn into this much more definitive early colonisation. Here too Cistercian and Benedictine monastic houses encouraged the clearing and improvement of upper surfaces,[13] making a virtue of necessity. In this period the opportunities for trade, industry and commerce were growing rapidly and towns were expanding. In our region it was especially the trade in wool products and hides which provided a leading sector.[14] But in many ways this major phase of colonisation was also driven by feudal enterprise. As the market for grain and wool expanded, lords could combine spiritual credit with commercial gain. This was the case in Cipières, where *castrum* was followed by *incastallamento* (see Chapters 2 and 5). Indeed, it was a period in which the rural settlement pattern of much of western Europe, with its patterns of defendable villages and small market towns, was finally confirmed.[15]

So the impetus to expand frontiers into areas previously marginal to use, may have been seen at first as mainly religious and ethical, but it combined conveniently with the urge to extract surplus and tribute (see Chapter 5). It also forced people to consider opening lands to the plough which were close to the limits of even the improved medieval farming technology and many such upland landscapes were cultivated for the first time. Rosamond Faith quotes notarial documents evidencing settlement of the further reaches of the plateau at this time (Chapter 5). Milder winters also led to the development of quite complicated rotation systems which allowed for the cropping of land in a cycle incorporating some spring and some winter sowing (see Chapter 7).

Within the tight limits of an agricultural economy still constrained by low yields, despite improvements in rotation, these forces soon led rapidly to overpopulation throughout the region. Further to the north in the Pré-alpes of Savoy, Binz and Duparc estimated that this expansion reached a dangerous maximum in the decades before the Black Death in 1348–50. Using *compte subsides de chatellan* (1334–1347) Du Parc[16] shows that there was in fact a doubling of the number of households in the Isère valley in the period between 1296 and 1347. Similarly, Binz deploys local taxation records to suggest that in 1335, the population in Faucigny had reached a density of 35 per km^2 and the size of 'household' or *feu* averaged 7.4. Even accepting the limitations of such a calculation this is a third higher than later 16th century estimates of maximum households size. He estimates a further 31% rise (an average of 2% per annum) between 1333 and 1347. Binz also used the evidence from clerical pastoral visits to propose that the population of Genevois reached between 250,000 and 300,000 with the population of Savoy as a whole as high as 400,000.[17] This is almost half the present population of the province, a truly remarkable figure in the age before significant urbanisation. With the number of households doubling between 1297 and 1347 this region was a veritable '*pays surpeuplé*'.[18]

Conditions could scarcely have been very different further south in Dauphiné and Provence. Baratier was perhaps using less reliable sources than those available to Binz, but he too recognises a 'spectacular' rise in population especially in the half century before the Black Death.[19] Indeed he suggests that an increase in the number of counts of heads of *foyers* after about 1250 gives an indication of the need by princes and lords to find a new basis developing taxation. Here too population expansion seems to have reached some kind of dangerous early maximum in this period.[20] It must be remembered that, despite the growth of towns and commerce, most of this expansion occurred within a still largely subsistent economy and in an environment largely cleared of protective cover of woodland (Chapters 3 & 4). It was also a region naturally prone to localised droughts, floods and storms. This made the increasingly numerous new colonisers ever more susceptible to food shortages, poor diet and eventually to epidemics.[21] When one considers that all but a small fraction of this population depended directly on the product of the soil it is easy to imagine the pressure on resources.

General estimations of this kind, however crude, can form a background in setting the parameters for our more detailed study of Cipières, but it leaves us to unpack the character of these estimates as they apply to our particular pre-Alpine environment. It is here that we meet a serious problem of interpretation. Namely, all our estimates of population for the periods before the 19th century censuses draw either on listings of household heads (or those who turned up to a village assembly) in the earliest period and on '*propriétaires*' with land in the parish and houses and stables in the village in the 16th century and after. Baratier[22] tackles the 'always thorny' problem of deriving a satisfactory coefficient based on the mean number of persons per hearth (*feu*). His earliest estimations seem to have been that in the medieval countryside one might expect households of slightly over 5 persons per hearth.[23] For Provence Baratier uses the work of Bautier which yielded an average of 5.1 per hearth, but he was working from lists compiled in the town of Carpentras near Avignon which was the only complete surviving census and this dates from the mid-15th century. Indeed he may be on more secure ground in estimating urban populations than he is for rural areas for his evidence for the countryside is entirely absent. Estimates for rural Provence rely on a census of Expilly, not in the medieval period but in the mid-18th century,[24] 400 years after the medieval population maximum! It is from this very slender basis that he postulates a figure of 4.5 persons per household (*foyer*) as a working mean to carry forward to his calculations of total populations in Provence, using the village *affouagements, alberges, assemblées* of the earliest assessments. These were usually lists of heads of *foyers* which were of indeterminate size (Figure 187). They may or may not have been complete and may not have included the poorer elements of the population. This index is barely satisfactory even for all the later periods when proprietors and households were identified separately and Baratier himself recognises this deficiency in his later work.[25] It certainly presents us with a very different, but perhaps only marginally more accurate, coefficient than that derived by du Parc[26] for this period. We therefore decided to approach the whole question of estimating the population of our community using different parameters

FIGURE 187. The participants in the General Assembly of the Community of Cipières, 6 November 1334

Pascal, Petrus, Raymundus fil. Petri **ALBERTI**
Bartholomeus filius Albini Fulconis, Johannes ALBINI
Bartholomeus Johannes senior Petrus Rostagnus AMEDI
Guillelmus, Poncius, Raymundus frater Guillelmi ARGENTINI
Hugo AUDIBERTI
Raymundus BARRECA
Feraudus frater Hugonis Guillelmus frater Hugonis, Guillelmus frater Raymundi, Hugo, Raymundus **BERENGARII**
Raymundus **BERAUDI**
Guillelmus BONOFOS
Fulconis **BORRELLI**
Raymundus BROTINI
Johannes, Guillelmus **BRUNI** fratres
Bertrandus CALVINI
Petrus CIGALONI
Bertrandus, Johannes, Guillelmus alias Senequius, Guillelmus alias De Porta **CHAMATI**
Johannes FER
Hugo Senior, Hugo Junior, Petrus, Raymundus alias Reboll, Veranus **FLORI**
Albinus, Jacobus FULCONIS
Petrus **GIRARDI**
Gaufridus GIRAUDI
Raymundus ISNARDI
Petrus, Guillelmus JULHE fratres
Raymundus HELSIARII
Guillelemus senior, Guillelemus junior, Hugo, Petrus LATILI
Fulconis, Guillelmus LAUGERII
Bartholomeus, Guillelmus, Hugo LAYETI
Guillelmus LENOERII
Jacobus MUTONIS
Bartholomeus, Guillelmus, Raymundus NIRELLI
Hugo, Petrus PAUTERII fratres
Bonifacius PORCELLI
Raymundus REMUSATI
Guillelmus, Pontius SCOFFERII fratres
Guillelmus **SEYTRE**
Jacobus, Raymundus VESIANI

Bold: Surnames of Chefs de Foyer in 1471 (Source: ABdR B200, f. 392 et seq.)

6.3. Kin and continuity in Cipières before 1531

The basis for our earliest estimates of the population of Cipières/Caussols in this period derive from two or three *assemblées* in the late 13th, early 14th and late 15th centuries.[27] It is our serious contention that, at least for our community, attempts by Baratier and after him, Durbec to calculate populations from such assessments by using a multiplier based on assumed *household* sizes which were derived from later surveys provide us with serious under-estimates of total population. Much of our argument for this contention is based on what we know of the surge of population in the 12th and 13th centuries and also the human ecology of the processes of settlement: the demands made on social and economic systems of labour generation in a society largely reliant on compliant if not willing participation. It is also based on what is known of the social and economic structures of family organisation in such regions in this period.

We believe that there is sufficient evidence both archaeological and historical to support the view that the key to understanding Cipèrois social and economic formations lay in the period *before* the 1st millennium, that is before nucleation *(incastallamento)*. Both David Austin (Chapter 3) and Andrew Fleming (Chapter 4) make strong cases for the view that these thin-soiled limestone soils throughout much of the lands of Cipières demanded a large investment in hand labour: grubbing out stones to create cultivation trenches and piling them to make mounds; flattening slope areas for terraces; then building those terraces and stone piles. Austin's and Fleming's identification of the earliest workscapes on the plateau surfaces may have been prepared for farming in this way from an early date. Fleming's subtle exposure of the Cipières to Caussols trackway and the lands abutting onto it has shown how the plateau could have been exploited both for farming and for pasturing flocks during this period of early population expansion (Chapter 4). This argument is pursued in Chapter 8. The flocks were likely to have been proportionate to the quite large assarting domestic groups. Perhaps this was the origin of the *trentenier* as a measure which characterised 'partible' flock sizes according to the proportionate family sizes? The measure persisted throughout the period and into early modern times (Chapters 7 & 8). There is also evidence of the use of burning to clear land for pasture at least as late as the 14th century[28] and it was the most obvious method to choose in earlier periods. Rosamond Faith provides evidence (Chapter 5) that the population surge of the 13th century took farming onto the far reaches of the plateau even if it had not been there before. This was the context in which we can argue for the deployment of the labour force generated by the extended families that characterised the early expansion of population through the period of nucleation, just as it may also have been a feature of the late 15th and early 16th century population revival.

To understand the nature of this phenomenon it is necessary to look back to this period before *incastallemento*: to those continuities of social and economic practice that evolved in the early medieval period, if not before and which had initially provided subsistence security. These mechanisms catered for the difficult conditions of an assarting group of kinsfolk who were opening up (or perhaps re-opening in the case of resettlement after the Plague) the upland margins of a farming system. It was almost certainly a system which favoured collaborative decision making and action and the development of kin-based mutual support which operated through marriage, inheritance, god-parentage and collective skill development. That these social and economic structures seem to have survived, as we will argue below, until the time of nucleation and well beyond reflects the continuities of behaviour of the original assarting groups: families coming together to win or to re-win, the land previously considered by those who lived in the lowlands as 'wilderness' or 'waste' (*gaste).*

What is clear is that a domestic economy involving large tracts of newly managed landscape, the caring of flocks of animals and catering for vicissitudes of harvests on marginal land, would encourage cooperation rather than open competition for resources. Moreover, people who worked together tended either to live together, or close to each other, whether in villages or in hamlets. This could create collectivities of people linked by blood and marriage. In the earliest stages of settlement, and irrespective of existing systems of overlordship, it is most likely that these assarting groups of kinsmen lived in small dispersed hamlets: often perhaps a string of related families, who built their houses in proximity and reasonably close to a source of water. As far as possible in a rugged landscape, the lands which were farmed surrounded the houses of their kinship group – perhaps collected in the five or six simple (wooden) dwelling units which made up each hamlet focussed on a water supply (wells, solution hollows, *baumes*, rainwater cisterns, springs), remembering that it was always possible to move water from place to place in animal skins. All the evidence we have from other areas in the broad region[29] suggests that these groups of kin almost certainly operated together as economic and social units, differing in size and composition according to local practices and the opportunities and restrictions of winning land and gaining a subsistence. They probably comprised between fifteen and thirty related individuals, sometimes more sometimes less, under the headship of a senior *'peyre'* or '*capitou'*. This form of organisation was particularly prevalent in, if not exclusive to, upland areas. When they were at their most developed, they represented veritable small clans of people sharing the same surname and location. These were somewhat similar to the *zadruga* in the Balkans,[30] which have provided family historians with a classic case.[31] Whatever their varied purpose, they appear in one form or another in a number of cultures, most often in upland areas of southern Europe and they certainly seem to have also characterised upland areas over large areas of southern France.[32] These collectivities varied in name and character. They were called *consorties* or *'sociétés de consorts* in the Auvergne[33] or *communautés taisible* in Nivernais where they survived into the seventeenth century.[34] In the southern Massif Central and Languedoc they were sanctified by legal agreements between kin (*affrèrements*). They were first noticed in the earliest surviving documents of 1350s and 'much in vogue in the following century' during the recovery period after *le grand malheur* of the Black Death in 1348. Indeed, Le Roy Ladurie remarks that large groupings were a *sine qua non* of working land in mountainous regions and has produced interesting analysis based on the *affrèrements* of Languedoc.[35] He points to the development of such 'patrilineal, lineal or fraternal institutions' in the fourteenth century in the area near Montpellier and then elsewhere in the Cevennes. He concludes that 'recourse to the *frérèches (*these groupings of married kinsmen*)* 'sprouted like mushrooms in regions where land was unrewarding and difficult to work'.[36] According to Cheveneau, it was also an early feature of alpine pastoral management where large family groups gathered their flocks in enclosures:

> *'En regle des enclos ont entoure des villages abritent une famille au sens large (40–50 personnes) avec ses troupeaux suffisant protégée par ses murs des incursions des animaux musable: loups, renards, felins et visites undesirables specialement a la nuit avant les chiens était en laches.'*[37]

There is also strong evidence for this early form of settlement in Haute Savoie, where the term *gens* survived into the 18th century to describe the clan type associations between people of the same family who had lived together in adjacent houses over the generations.[38] In fact this term was in use throughout the mountains of the south and we find some similarities with the formations in Basque regions first identified by le Play[39] and later explored by French demographers for other adjacent areas of the Pyrenees.[40] The characteristic strength of these groups lay in their ability to hold together as a system of social and economic support under what is called in Provence a *cap de oustal,* a senior male. It is he who would organise the considerable labour involved in this environment in clearing rocks and the deployment of human resources for collecting, herding and foraging as well as the tasks of arable farming. In these circumstances, we would argue, it was natural for them to identify senior family heads to speak for them and represent them to outside authorities of church and state. This explanation of the meaning of listings of this kind finds further validation in the attempt to limit taxes which were imposed 'by *foyer*' in the first instance. Groupings of this kind may also have been 'avoiding some form of *mortmain*' the regulation by which land reverted to the lord of the manor if the head of house died without leaving a male successor.[41]

In Aveyron and nearby areas these kinship groupings, where they were called *ostals,* survived into the 19th century.[42] In Basse Provence there are references to *oustals* in Rougiers (in the Var). In Cipières we meet the word only in the period when it was becoming a relict feature of social and economic organisation, in the first property taxation document (cadastre) of 1531, where it appears in entries apparently as an alternative term for *maison* ('*masson*'). It appears for the last time in the 1610 cadastre. It is because of this that is the term is used here and it is useful to quote Rodgers' definition of an *oustal* in Aveyron as:

> 'a fusion of a family line ... structured to outlive any individual or household ... characterised by impartible inheritance and stem forms of household formation in which sons shared dwellings and work with fathers, brothers with brothers. Non-inheriting siblings, aunts and uncles may be part of the prime household for as long as they remain single. The classic ostal, therefore, includes an older couple, their eldest son and his wife and children, unmarried siblings and perhaps some adult aunties (*tatas*) and uncles (*tontons*).'[43]

These more complicated arrangements do not mean that everyone had to be embraced within these very large units and as Rosamond Faith has shown, there is evidence from elsewhere in the region that different forms existed alongside each other. This almost certainly reflected the case in feudal Cipières where *maleservi* families had a different tenant status and rights (see Chapter 5).

Given the circumstances of settlement and the culture of the region, outlined above, it is perhaps no surprise to find the term '*ostal*' surviving in the earliest cadastres of Cipières. But we speculate that these social and economic mores were woven into the feudal structure before the period of *incastellamento* and surviving into the development of village society. There is certainly evidence of these collectivities (some akin to Ladurie's *freiresques*) in the earliest surviving documents of the village society of Cipières. The village assembly in 1334 may represent a fairly late stage in this development and certainly provides evidence of a wider variety of family forms which seem already to be apparent at that time, ranging from the larger '*ostal*' collectivities to somewhat smaller units (Figure 187). Such variety makes the task of deriving a co-efficient to calculate total population quite difficult. But it seems entirely reasonable to assume that in the psychological upheavals involved in adapting to new ways of village life, as many features of the old *ostal* farming and living arrangements as possible would be incorporated. How were ways found to cope with the ramifying kinship structure within the built environment of the village even as the population expanded? We might expect it to lead to some interesting conjunctions of living spaces and apartments. The reconstruction represented here, with dwelling and storage units on four levels, is based on what we know of house forms in deserted villages (e.g. Grèolieres and Rougiers) as well as buildings we know to have survived from sixteenth century Cipières (Figure 81). So we argue here that these kinship formations provided the basic social and physical building blocks of settlement before, during and after the process of *incastellamento*. We also contend that Baratier's calculations of household size, and therefore of population, which were based on enumerations taken at a much later date, may have very little value for the earliest period of population increase and colonisation. What we suggest is that the early records indicate that settlement by affinal or consanguinial *confreries* of kin persisted, at least in some form, throughout the medieval period and led towards the continuities of surname which we find in the list of inhabitants until the present time (Figure 188). In these circumstances we can only agree with Le Roy Ladurie that this phenomenon of larger kinship association is reflected in the level of

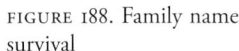

FIGURE 188. Family name survival

patronym survival (or disappearance) in the environments where such practices were common. Elsewhere, studies of patronym survival (or the lack of it) in the lowlands suggest a much more fluid relationship between families and land and community.

We also might envisage the settlement of the village community as taking place within the social mores of such kinship groupings and that the fabric of the village house, with its three/four floors was adapted to this basal social formation. Certainly such houses were well adapted to cope with the needs of a large stem family, of a potential size outlined above. Although we must wait until the eighteenth century for evidence of apartment dwelling in Cipières there is parallel evidence of multiple occupation of large houses with several floors both in Rougiers and in Gréolières. Indeed, the form of house is common in the region as we know from inventories of building plans.

For the moment, our task is to explain the implications of this approach for the calculation of total community populations of Cipières at the time of each male head count. Our argument here can be simply stated. We suggest that our estimates for the population of Cipières, if based on a simple deployment of the Baratier household multiplier of 4.5 per named person in the listings, would produce a considerable underestimate of actual population in years both before and after the Black Death.[44] Indeed, each listing that we have in our possession for Cipières lends support to this view. Our first estimate derives from Durbec[45] in a taxation listing for Cipières of 1252, which gives us 29 *feu*. A simple application of the Baratier multiplier of 4.5 per household would yield a population of only 145. This would give Cipières a population of little more than a hamlet at a time when we know population was expanding rapidly throughout the region. If, on the other hand, one considers each named individual in the assessment as a representative (*a cap d'oustal*) of a collectivity of kinsmen, a unit with up to perhaps 30 individual members, as in examples quoted above, then the population would have been closer to 1000, even without taking any account of the *maleservi* who may not have been part of any listing at this time. By the same logic, the 42 names (*caps des oustals*?) identified by Durbec in an *alberga* for 1297[46] would lead us to a maximal population of around 1260. These figures accord much more closely with the requirements of a community of settlers and also with what one might call the 'spirit of the age' as identified above. Here it is possible to compare with the very different social and economic situation in the open plain of Caussols, settled as a series of dispersed tenements by much smaller nuclear family units, generally as *maleservi* casements. Thiery[47] uses archaeological evidence to identify 33 places of dispersed habitation of this kind. Here, too, the population increase was very dramatic. Thiery uses the same sources as we have for Cipières to identify family names in Caussol, which increased from 15 in 1235 to 68 in 1334. Here, without the securities of the larger kinship group and more open to the effects of the Plague, the collapse during the 14th century *temps de malheur* was dramatic. Only three family names from the early 14th century document appear in the *albergement* of 1471. The situation in Cipières was very different. Here family name survival extended throughout the historical period. Durbec also draws attention to the numbers of Cipièrois who were 'in Grasse' at any one time, finding their names in the Grasse cadastres of 1250–1252; 1342 and 1433, and who, on the evidence of later Cipières cadastres, were certainly members of long-term Cipières families with commercial links throughout the region.[48]

Further support for the veracity of these adjusted estimates is provided by the fact that the 1297 *albergement* indicated that the 42 *ostals* each had 99 sheep and goats, i.e. 4148 animals.[49] This is a figure much closer to the *etats de betails* of later periods. If this was so, then assuming that each *cap d'oustal* represented as many as six or seven families (each with about 15 sheep and goats) the total population of the community, increased by non-tax-paying families of the hierarchy, was probably closer to 1400.

Coming closer to the middle years of the 14th century we have a listing of 71 participants in a 'general assembly' of the community of the inhabitants of Cipières'.[50] The listing is characteristically in the form of 15 linear entries (Figure 187).[51] Following the approach outlined above we have recognised a total of 36 potential *caps d'ostal.* A simple application of a multiplier of 'around 30' would yield a population of just over 1000. But some are, by my reading, quite clearly very large collectivities of kin, more of the scale identified by Cheveneau. The Berangarii for example, have nine named individuals who were potential husbands and fathers within the *ostal* a potential group of around 50 individuals. Some entries seem, however, to be representing smaller units, (*frèreches*, either extended families or perhaps even the nuclear families of *maleservi*). Nor can we assume that attendance at such a general assembly was obligatory. We mentioned above the potential absentees in Grasse and there were possibly others elsewhere. Even so an estimation of something closer to population of over 1000 fits more closely the general model, presented above, of a 14th century 'maximum' population 'which may never again have been exceeded'. We argue this against the evidence of the 1531 cadastre which by this time registered individual 'proprietors' of land and property and we can assume that in this period of more open land exchange and increasing individuation, that they represented smaller kinship units. Here in these different economic and social circumstances, a Baratier co-efficient of 'around five' per proprietor/household is more applicable and in this case 270 proprietors represents a population of around 1350. Within the admittedly broad limits of estimation implied by these calculations an early population peak of something close to the same number, which may or may not take account of a *maleservi* population, certainly provides us with a more plausible measure to set against the population maxima identified in other similar Alpine environments quoted above.

Whatever its origins in previous patterns of use, if our population estimates are to be believed, this period between about AD 1100 and 1330 seems to have been the period of major expansion for both pastoralism and agriculture and this is a conclusion which our archaeology colleagues reached independently. The implications for Cipières of such a high early peak of population both in terms of labour force for clearance and wall construction on the one hand and pressure on resources on the other, are clear.

We would expect that such an expansion, over a dramatically short period, would be evidenced in the landscape: that whatever happened in the long period before *incastellamento* and beyond, it was in this phase of population expansion that the first great work of piling and walling and terracing (continuing in some form throughout the historical period) was at its maximum. Whichever way we calculate this early population peak, it yields us a population which fills the fields with a labour force well capable of sustaining the back breaking tasks of clearance and landscape control/management in what David Austin calls the early 'workscape' (Chapter 3). We will return to the nature of this labour force and the development of clan hierarchies in the village later in this chapter.

6.4. The '*temps de malheur*' 1348–1450

If the climatic amelioration, accompanied by the economic and commercial boom of the previous two centuries, had taken people up to the economic and ecological limits of expansion, assarting high into the marginal uplands of the *garrigue*, this halcyon period came to an abrupt end in the first decades of the 14th century. The collapse away from this first peak of population expansion took place during a period of climate change. It was signalled by a period of storms, floods and bad harvests that caused localised famines in 1323 and 1329. It began a long, if intermittent, phase of climatic deterioration which has been called The Little Ice Age[52] (see Figure 186). These events were the precursors of worse times to come both politically and socially. Indeed, for the southern half of France, the late Middle Ages coincided with a time of economic recession and of plagues, famines and wars which made the century from 1340–1440, truly a *temps de malheur*.[53]

Between 1340 and 1450, it was the persistent turmoil of famine, plague and war as much or more than climate change which ravaged the country. For France as a whole, this period was considered as the most violent in its history[54] with a full battery of Malthusian forces at work. Wars and food shortages and consequent anarchy produced widespread village abandonments. Indeed, there is a general consensus that the re-occurrences of bubonic plague added to the intermittent phases of the Hundred Years War and that the changing climate produced a catastrophic and general economic downturn. It meant that the whole of France endured a massive downward plunge in population.[55] This was particularly true of Provence where the impact of the Great Bubonic Plague of 1347–48 was fierce. Here the crisis of 1348 was repeated at roughly 10 year intervals throughout the following century and population was reduced by between a third and a half with many villages abandoned.[56] During this period the southern regional population as a whole fell by between 50 and 75%.[57]

During this period, new economic and social contexts emerged in the region. Family and kin relationships in upland areas were played out in very different economic and social circumstances from phases of earlier settlement, and social parameters were altered. In many areas, older kin continuities were shattered.[58] The circumstances in Cipières appear to have been somewhat different. Although the tenant settlement of Caussols was decimated,[59] Cipières itself seems to have suffered rather less. Here kin continuity rather than discontinuity characterised the evolving social formations at least until the 16th century. If, in other areas of the region, sheep filled the spaces previously occupied by peasants and their crops, in Cipières there was at first a better integration of pastoral activity and arable husbandry (Chapter 7). Indeed, even at the time of the next peak of population in the mid-16th century the arable and pastoral economies still seem, to some extent at least, to have worked in parallel (Chapter 8). In the 16th century, however, urban market expansion created a new set of commercial relations which increasingly privileged sheep and commercial profit over arable farming and subsistence (Chapter 9).

One measure of the impact of this decline in population was the disappearance, from the listings, of household heads in subsequent inquiries of whole families, as in the case of Caussols quoted above. Le Roy Ladurie points to evidence of an almost total fracturing of this bedrock feature of southern societies in this period. In many Languedocian communities, 70–80% of patronyms disappeared over this period. In St Guillen le Desert, for example, out of 132 tax-paying family heads in 1398 the family names of only 54 remained in 1442. A further half disappeared in the next 40 years, a reduction over the whole period of 80%.[60] What is perhaps equally significant is that, as Le Roy Ladurie indicates, there was a reassertion of large family groups (these he calls *families taisible* or *consorties*) for a brief period of recovery of the *gaste* in the 16th century. It was as though rural society reverted to an earlier structure to accommodate the need for clearing and assarting. Ladurie argues that this period was followed subsequently by the development of smaller proto-nuclear families through a system of primogeniture, though some family *consorties* survived in Nivernais until the 17th century. We will examine echoes of these later developments in Cipières even though the impact of population decline was not so dramatic here as elsewhere.

What is clear is that a family with multiple sub-sets was more likely to survive through the generations. In other words, the development of economically bonded lineages was a natural concomitant of large family groupings under a single head of household. A sign of this kind of society was the long survival of family names. By the same token systems characterised by nuclear households were demographically fragile, being totally dependent for their survival on the creation of a single male heir.

6.5 The long recovery 1450–1550

The late 15th and early 16th centuries, at the end of the Hundred Years War and in a briefly ameliorating climate before the real onset of the next phase of the Little Ice Age, led to improving economies and a recovery of population. This seems to have been common to western Europe as a whole. As Braudel maintains, this period represents a time when there were often 'as many people in the countryside as there had been two centuries earlier',[61] quoting Brantome's reference to France being as 'full as an egg'. Elsewhere, in southern Germany for example, people were regarded as so numerous they seemed to 'grow on trees'. The graph of Cipières population changes (Figure 189), based on the methods of estimation outlined above, certainly reflects these movements, with a surge of population peaking in the mid-16th century. This development took place in very different socio-economic and political circumstances to those of the earlier peak of population. Feudal power structures had given way to a more open market for land and produce. Family inheritance systems were evolving towards primogeniture and stem family forms.

This trend is reflected in the first Cipières cadastre of 1531,[62] with its 271 'proprietors' listed for the first time as individual property tax payers (with tax paid on land and dwelling buildings for both humans and animals). Indeed, as implied above, the rapidly changing circumstances may even have stimulated the inquiry. But we still need to find some thread which takes us through the period of distress, which may have ended by the 1460s in Cipières and the expansion which followed. With no intervening records for this period (1471–1531) for our community we are left again with Baratier who tells us that in eastern Provence, where population was reduced to between a third and quarter of that in the 1330s, villages were restocked by immigrants from Liguria, representing a 'veritable re-colonisation' in some cases.[63] This phenomenon is evident in Cipières only through the appearance of the 15 new patronyms in the 1531 record, whether from Liguria or not (Figure 6.3). Fortunately, however, the 1471 *larem foventes* assessment [64] is close enough (two generations) to the first cadastral survey of 1531 to make some comparisons. Even allowing for a very rapid expansion through the 60 years following the 1471 listing, the relationship between the 35 '*foyers*' of 1471 and the 270 'proprietors' of 1531 suggests that each *foyer (ostal?)* in the period of the earlier inquests represented a median of between six and seven families, or around 30 individuals. Further support for this hypothesis is the apparent increase in numbers within the main family name 'clans'. The Bourellys, for example, had one named individual in the 1334 *assemblée* (Fulconis), four named individuals in the 1471 listing, and 37 'proprietors' in 1531. A similar picture emerges for the Florys, the Girards and the Pons name sets. It is not difficult to see how *sobriquets* made their appearance in the later cadastral records. If each '*foyer*' (*ostal*) had a population of around 30, it is possible to envisage a village with a total population of just over 1000 inhabitants once more, or a figure close to the number of inhabitants before the Black Death. If we follow this logic then the period of population decline seems to have ended, as one might have expected, by the mid–late 15th century, coinciding with the dawn of a 'long 16th century' of great discoveries and commercial expansion (Figure 189).

So in the light of an unusual level of survival of family names in Cipières it is not so surprising that, despite a dip in population during the *temps de malheur* (and the temporary abandonment of Caussols), significant continuities of lineage were maintained. Of the 36 patronyms appearing in the first extant, but probably incomplete, list for the 1334 assembly (Figure 186) as many as

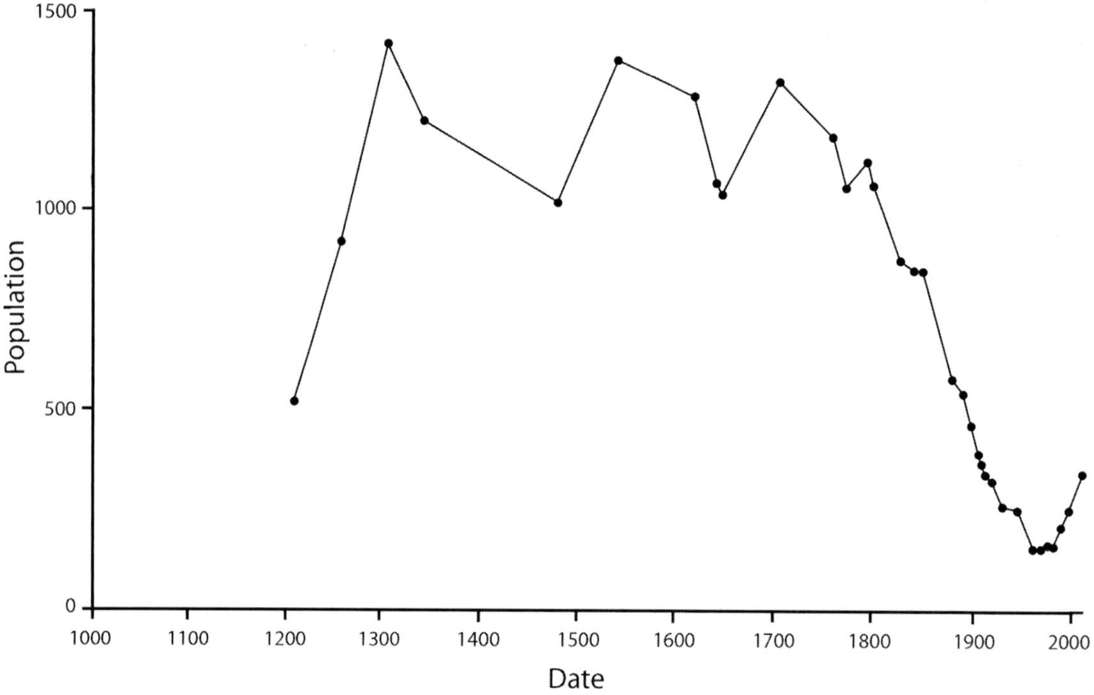

FIGURE 189. Cipières population graph

31% survived the vicissitudes not only of the next hundred years, but also of the following six centuries (Figure 188). Moreover, of the 56 patronyms which survived more than three generations after the re-population phase of the 15th and early 16th centuries, two-thirds could claim to have been Cipèrois 'since time immemorial'. Rather than the ravages of the *temps de malheur* and the break-up of large kinship systems, Cipières seems to have found ways of allowing them to evolve. So for Cipières it is not disruption but continuity that we prefer to stress, at least for the period leading up to the first cadastre in 1531. This persistence seems remarkable, even in the upland area of the Pré-alpes where similar continuities have been traced for at least the 16th century and beyond.[65] The implications of this kinship continuity in terms of property contiguities in the *quartiers* are explored in Chapter 8.

CHAPTER SEVEN

Medieval Agrarian Systems

Rosamond Faith

*By the 13th and 14th centuries, when our first documentary evidence begins, ameliorating climate conditions had led to the situation common to western Europe at the time: growth in population and increased pressure on land. Archaeological work on the Plateau de Calern shows that it was essentially by this time part of the farming system of Cipières as a whole which had been brought into cultivation by collective effort, possibly on the basis of the family, and not necessarily the result of a recent 'journey to the margin.' The land there was worked as version of 'sheep-corn husbandry'. Large numbers of sheep, the accumulation of many small peasant flocks, grazed a rocky landscape which nevertheless produced grain from small intensively manured areas, including the fissures in the limestone and, on a larger scale in the dolines – natural hollows – in which the individual flocks were folded at night. Land near the village was cleared for cultivation by repeated stone clearance, marked by the large cairns set in individual fields. In the 14th century the three villages of Raibaude de Caussols were run as an integrated estate. At Caussols a large demesne (reserve) profited from the much more extensive broad valley there, suitable for both arable and pasture, while her domestic establishments at Gréolières and Cipières benefited from the carrying services (*corvees*) owed by her tenants at Caussols. The plague of the mid-14th century depopulated Caussols and the land there was taken over and farmed by men from Cipières. By the end of the medieval period the common resource of the plateau grazing was beginning to come under pressure from the quasi-capitalist wool producers and merchants of Grasse, who entered into contracts with Cipières men to run larger flocks on the plateau.*

7.1. The wider geographical context: boundaries, zones and routes

Boundaries are sometimes seen as a product of the period in which lordship over land became more locally focussed, reflecting the divisions between the kind of lordships established in our region in the 13th century although even then they were far from stable. It is undoubtedly true that private property in land, and the boundaries which expressed it, were becoming more clearly articulated in the Middle Ages. But underlying these seigneurial divisions are boundaries which determined the access to resources claimed by different communities. Within this region boundaries developed in response to both political and social needs. The commune and canton boundaries of Caussols, Cipières and Gréolières run from the ridge of Cheiron to the lower ridge of La Malle. The river Loup is a natural boundary between the lands of Gréolières and Cipières, but it was also an important resource for both communities as a source of food and of power to drive their mills. To the south divisions along ridges were necessary to divide upland grazing between Cipières and Caussols.

We can see the process of making a boundary in the record of an agreement between Raibaude de Caussols and the people of Caussols on the one hand and the lord of the castrum of S Valery probably drawn up in 1321: *clapiers*, piles of stones or cairns combined with natural features were used to mark off a line which must often have been virtually invisible:

> '… and they have placed, fixed and marked the boundaries, marks and limits dividing and separating the said territories as has been set out and marked within the distance. Firstly a certain *claperum* newly placed next to the enclosure *day sebunda (?)* next to a certain stream bed (*vasilium*) as the water descends shall be the first boundary (*terminus*) And … there shall be at the other *claperum* marked with a cross on one stone fixed within the said *claperum*. Descending from *claperum* to *claperum* in a straight line to a certain great tree known as (?*Fcan ?ftan*) and a *claperum* at the Pounch de la vallet next to (*pratum?*) respecting the straight line towards the castrum of Barletto in which ? newly made ten … *claperia* without other bounds, and by which from now on shall be boundaries between the aforesaid parties and the said *claperia* shall always remain [ ] the said territories.'

But territory and rights could also be marked less formally: 'A simple mark, usually a heap of pebbles or turves (a *montjoie*) was all that was needed to warn off the herdsmen'.[1]

Within this broad area the different villages of Raibaude de Caussols' lordship have very different physical settings. The nature of their terrain determined the elongated shape of the Cipières and Gréolières territories. Cultivation of their steep slopes and the need to prevent the slippage of soil caused by deforestation demanded terraces. There may initially have been separate terrace systems around what are now outlying hamlets or farms at some distance from the present villages, perhaps remnants of the 'pre-castral' settlement phase described earlier. The medieval villages of Cipières and Gréolières-Basses were tightly huddled on protuberant shelves and remain so, but the commune of Caussols has a much more dispersed pattern with farms scattered along its gentler slopes and its broad open valley. While Cipières farmers had workable land near their village and on Le Plan, and meadow along the Loup, they also came to rely on using as well a much more intractable and remote area: the Plateau de Calern. Certainly by the 14th century, probably considerably earlier, the plateau had come under cultivation and was wholly integrated into the farming system of the villagers.

The *longue durée* in Cipières before the modern period was often referred to by its inhabitants, when it suited them, as 'time immemorial' as if the most significant part of human action was the product of a slow-moving continuous stream. Many responses might indeed seem to have been governed by the nature of what seems today to be an essentially marginal environment, with its barren plateau, its steep slopes, its thin, boulder-strewn limestone soils, its limited water supplies. Yet the mix of riverside meadow, hillsides and limestone uplands provided the resources for a poor but self-sufficient economy, as long as the balance of people and stock to land was maintained. Our first, firmly datable evidence of farming patterns comes from the mid-14th century, by which time they were evidently well established, but a suggested outline of the large-scale changes that had taken place before that date follows our suggested trajectory from a settlement pattern of hamlets and isolated farms to one of nucleation. The people who had farmed from the prehistoric and early medieval isolated farmsteads on remote defensible sites on crests and scarps had certainly been growing grain, for traces of their hand mills have been found, but meat was probably a very important element in their diet and they could well have run flocks and herds on the uplands.

Climatic conditions were improving at this time, making possible the cultivation of land formerly given over to rough grazing. Evidence from three sources: speleotherm history, the behaviour of glaciers and harvest dates show us quite dramatic changes in climate during the centuries of occupation of this environment. Although there is evidence of the occupation of these upland areas in the period before, during and after the Roman Empire (Chapter 2), it can be argued that the general amelioration in climatic conditions towards the end of what some call the 'Dark Age Cold' (AD 500–1000) created the circumstances for the first real expansion into the margins (Figure 186). This amelioration, which raised average decennial temperatures by more than a degree centigrade had created the environmental circumstances for the first surge in population in mountain areas which, we argue, enabled the establishment of family/clan groups in scattered homesteads in the area of spring-line effusions. A growing population needed more cereals and we suggest that this was the catalyst for the extension of cultivation onto the lower and more workable land now represented by the fields and terraces of topographic Zone 1 around the present village (see Figure 28). The water supply must have been crucial in siting these. The problem of permanent water supply was to bedevil the people of Cipières for centuries and access to reliable sources came to be rationed and the digging of a well (Rue des Puits) and the building of a fountain in the square in the 16th century must have been seen as vast improvements to the quality of life. The only consistently flowing water, whether from resurgence locations or simple run-off, lies below the village, where the *lavoir* was later sited and where the village washing was presumably traditionally done. The plateau has occasional natural cisterns which would have provided for the needs of the shepherds, their dogs, and lactating sheep and we must not forget the occasional huge rainfall in this area, especially in storms. David Austin suggests that most, later houses had cistern capacity in (and under them) for gathering water as well as ceramics and the like. The scattered farms of the pre-nucleation phase would have had to rely on small or intermittent streams, possibly storing water for the summer.

We can see from chance references in the notarial records of the mid-14th century the very distinct zones of the commune and their particular uses. The only option for communities that had to be self-sufficient in carbohydrates in an era when animal power provided the only form of traction was mixed farming, in which livestock husbandry was combined with the cultivation of food crops and vines. In the brief period in the mid-14th century that our medieval documents illuminate it is possible to see the demands of these different aspects of the peasant economy made on the landscape and on the social skills of the community.

7.2. Zones and their uses

1. Lands near the village (Zone I; Figure 28)

To make land fit for cultivation in this region meant a battle with stones as well as with trees: each new plot needed long hours of backbreaking stone clearing. And land once cleared did not stay cleared: the stones came back, brought to the surface by the action of animals and the weather and had to be removed over and over again. The massive cairns and walls of the terraced fields near the village and at La Combe may indicate an early area of cultivation, serving a community of scattered farms. The *mansus* or farm which Eldiardis gave to Lérins could have comprised all or part of this area, and it is significant that the bastide of Le Puy, probably a demesne home farm or bailiff's house, was here too: it may occupy the site of a substantial earlier farm (Figure 35).[2] In the 14th century the villagers held property divided among 'lands', *terrae,* whose size is seldom specified, but whose boundaries must have been known to all. Lands were identified as being 'in the place called …' and these place-names are very often the *quartier* names used in the later documents and mostly still in use today. Evidently by the 14th century the whole of the commune territory was mentally mapped. All are generally described as being 'next the land of X and next to the land of Y and face onto the 'public way', and each had another person's 'land', not waste land on either side. The 'lands' of a single property were not bunched together, but distributed over a wide area: the furthest from the village being those on the Calern plateau at l'Agremourie and Vaumeillane, Le Clapoua and Les Baumettes and at La Faye. The most common location was in *La Travessa* (Le Travers de Paraïre on Figure 31). From the later cadastral evidence there is a strong suggestion that 'lands' were commonly held in units of four, and this system may already have been in place by the 14th century, possibly dating from the first laying out of holdings. David Siddle provides evidence of the survival of this practice at least until the date of the first cadastre in 1531 (Chapter 8).

2. The plateau (Zones II–VI; Figure 28)

The archaeologists' view of the plateau as an area where enormous labour has cleared land for mixed farming is at odds with Bloch's pessimistic assessment of the limits which the Provençal landscape put on the extension of cultivation, with its 'waste land which was destined to remain permanently uncultivated ... *garrigue* covered with aromatic scrub dotted here and there with trees ... stretches of arid land where the top-soil was too poor to bear a crop ...'.[3] Two local studies have demonstrated farming on similar high plateaux in the region and in fact the concept of 'marginal' land has also itself been challenged for both France and Britain.[4] When necessity drove, careful husbandry could make even the most unpromising-looking land productive and the generally agreed cause for the extension of the cultivated area was the pressure to increase the food supply for an expanding population. That this was possible is due in no small part to the fact that with mean temperatures in the 12th–14th centuries equivalent to those in the period of the Roman Empire the conditions for peasant farming in these marginal areas were never better. The extension and re-organisation of the cultivated area in the Middle Ages is a Europe-wide phenomenon. It was achieved principally by bringing land previously considered marginal or intractable into cultivation, the 'conquest of the waste' of upland, fen and forest, bringing land into cultivation which had formerly been considered useful only as a source of rough grazing or raw materials. Not all land thus gained was kept permanently under the plough: Sclafert describes a stage of temporary cultivation in mountain regions by slash and burn of outlying woodland; a system which allowed the land to periodically recover its fertility.[5] Many descriptions of this process have evoked a kind of von Thunen-esque model, with cultivation gradually expanding piecemeal to take in areas further and further away from the core settlement, typically into forest or moorland.[6] By contrast, recent accounts of change in medieval English farming systems have tended away from a gradualist model to allow for rapid, planned, large scale and concerted change, both in settlement form and in field systems.[7] Andrew Fleming's suggestion that cultivation was established on the plateau as a single concerted campaign following a decision to upgrade the quality of a whole tract of land, rather than from casual, piecemeal actions by a few individuals' is very much in accord with this model (Chapter 4).

A long-running debate among British historians has centred on the question: was seigneurial planning at work in such change, or communal action? The fact that at Cipières an individual's lands, rather than clustered, were widely scattered over the whole cultivated area of the commune, just as in an open-field system, could be interpreted as the result of the sharing-out of cleared land among those who had contributed their labour to the common effort. Perhaps some kind of overall direction determined boundaries and made sure that the owners of each land kept up their frontage of the road, as was the case in the Vésubie valley.[8] Closely-set parcels laid out along the road could be interpreted as the product of planned and concerted communal landscape clearance, with holdings all laid off from a central 'spine' road and then distributed among the members of the community. The 'public way' itself may be an important clue. Andrew Fleming interprets the Cipières–Caussols road as an integral part of the terrace and plateau field system. It ran up to a gate in the castle wall at Cipières, so seems to have a strong link with the period of *incastellamento* and village nucleation (Chapter 4). The seigneur of the triple lordship ran the three villages as an integrated estate and from this perspective it could be seen as a 'seigneurial' road. But for the villagers whose lands abutted onto it, it was a 'public way'. And although it served the seigneur as a routeway for the mule trains transporting her goods from Caussols to Cipières it also reflects its strong function in the farming economy: it is walled where it runs through terraces, unwalled where it runs through open land: a sign that livestock were moving now through a densely cultivated landscape, now through pasture. Moreover the road would equally have served for local traffic of all kinds.

But a more individualistic scenario is equally credible, in which the road is still seen as the primary physical feature. The original clearances could have been the work of the individual 'family clans' each putting family labour to work to clear what became that family's parcels, and clearing and walling only its own land. David Siddle describes just such a 'land'. Such a heavy original investment of labour would surely have established a strong identification of a family with its particular lands, which they had literally 'made', as did the continuing care and cultivation of such scattered plots. We occasionally come across land described as 'dotal', implying that it was dowry, which played a traditional part in a family's inheritance strategy. As Siddle mentioned above, the earliest cadastre, from 1531, shows that a family's main property had a tendency to be geographically grouped, a tendency which diminished over time. The lands of the Borelli Marcons illustrate this well. Before the 16th century, when there are no comparable records, the tendency may have been much more pronounced.

3. *Terre gaste*

Although there were close-set farmlands on the plateau in the mid-14th century there was also *terre gaste*, waste, enough for a different kind of grazing practice, in which larger flocks ranged widely.[9] There may have been extensive area of waste elsewhere as well: at Le Plan, for instance, outside the protected areas. It seems as though the 'waste' was common property and that as in many pastoral areas, 'living in the central occupied zone gives rights over the vast territory surrounding it …'.[10] These common rights preserved the notion of the *castrum* as a territory, a notion which preceded the building of the castle itself: land anywhere within the whole commune of Cipières is described in the 14th century as 'within the territory of the said *castrum*'. It may be significant that there were no restrictions or stints for sheep mentioned in the communal pasturing agreements that have survived. But there were rules about pasturage nonetheless and these may have been incorporated in the yearly grants of common pasture for *toute l'annee*: that is to say for the two seasons from Epiphany to the first of May and from St Madeleine's Day until Michaelmas (29 September) which are found elsewhere in our region.[11] Anyone could pasture his own animals, but no-one else's, on the waste. Inhabitants who have no livestock of their own can sell their grazing for what they can get. This is part of a long conflict between 'outsider' graziers and the inhabitants. According to an agreement of 1357, 'The grass of land of *gaste* or *hermum* (waste) shall belong to the seigneur and he may sell it', but so could any villager who did not have livestock of his own.[12] Access to these areas of grazing was one of the few real assets of the poorer families of Cipières, and as we will see, it was to be the commercial exploitation of this common asset which was to bring large social and economic change.

4. Demesne land

Seigneurial agriculture in Cipières in the Middle Ages was entangled with peasant farming and had to accommodate to it. The situation would have been different in Caussols, where the demesne was more important, and the tenants more subordinated, but in Cipières Raibaude exploited the majority of her inhabitants by culling their surpluses through banal rights, charging for mills and so on, rather than by diverting their labour onto her demesne, which was probably worked by the *maleservi* and farm labourers. In the 14th century her demesne there included land scattered in parcels among the villagers' some of it on the plateau. She and her co-seigneur needed to bargain with her tenants to get land she wanted, to strike formal agreements with them about pasturing stock, access to water and so on. The inhabitants had grazing rights over demesne land (which suggests it may have been a relative innovation). In 1357, and probably for long before, they could pasture their animals in the fields sown for fodder (*campos ferragines)* and pastures of the demesne after the crops and hay had been carried and leave them there until they were sown, and in the pastures until March. There are signs that Raibaude was attempting to consolidate her land nearer the village by exchanges with the villagers and if pursued systematically this policy might have resulted by the sixteenth century in a consolidated block, reaching from the castle down to the river.[13] Le Puy, a large farmhouse or bastide, a remodelling of a much older building, stands a few hundred metres south east of the village in the largest level area of zone I, in the middle of its largest field. 'Probably seigneurial in origin' it could well have been the agricultural centre of the new demesne, possibly a bailiff's farmhouse.[14]

The larger and flatter terraced fields nearer the village were ploughed by oxen, probably drawing some kind of *araire* or scratch plough, the type most suited to thin and rocky soils and able to operate in smaller spaces than the *charrue* with a mouldboard (Figure 190).[15] Working animals needed water which meant that they could not be used far from the village streams or had to break off work to be taken to water: this was noted as a handicap in 1609: 'the waters are good: it is true that they are cisterns and far from the village which is inconvenient for the inhabitants'.[16] On the upper hillsides and on the plateau with its steep-sided dolines and narrow strips cleared between limestone ridges the soil was probably turned by hand, using hoes, picks or spades to turn and aereate it before sowing (Figure 191).[17] Land was worked on a rotation of grazing and arable, with a careful shifting of livestock onto fallows and stubbles to maintain fertility. As landholdings were widely scattered individual farmers must have planted their crops on a piecemeal basis, perhaps dividing each 'land' into cropping areas, perhaps devoting a single land to a single crop, or leaving it fallow, each year – our documents do not provide enough evidence to be sure. At any rate, whether a 'field' comprised an entire 'land', or part of it, the field was the unit of cropping. When the Argentin brothers hired two men in 1335 it was to plough and sow 'two fields'. In the 14th century the Cipièrois grew barley and wheat. The wheat needed an autumn sowing to give it enough daylight hours for ripening. A rotation was adopted (Figure 192) which rested the land completely every third year, and produced four crops every six years – these were the conditions laid down in one lease.[18] This system would have provided grazing on the stubbles in years 2, 3, 5 and 6 which would have compensated the land for the nitrogen taken out of it by the successive cropping of wheat and barley, and by the long growing season of wheat.

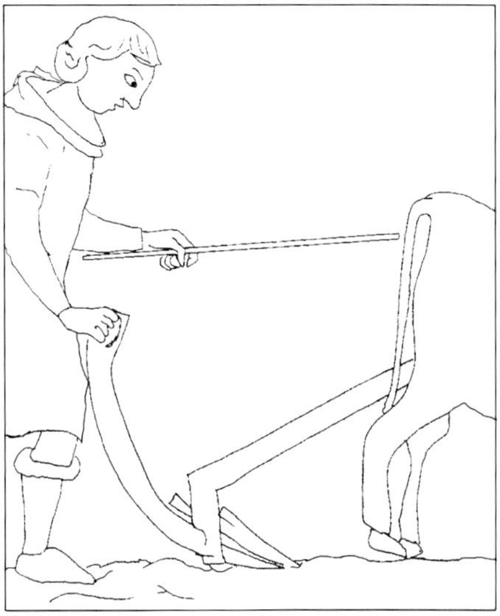

FIGURE 190. The ard *(araire)*, re-drawn from a medieval manuscript. Reproduced from Reigniez 2002, fig. 15 p. 86 with the kind permission of Editions Errance of Paris

Such a system worked the land very hard. It was much more intensive than that in use in 1609 and subsequently as David Siddle shows (Chapter 8). It would have depended on replenishing the land by the careful folding of stock on the fallows, a system which also entailed protection of the growing crops. This was achieved in different parts of the commune by different methods of stock management. On the larger terraces and fields near the village permanent walls and banks could keep animals off vines and growing crops, and the road through them to the plateau was engineered to prevent straying. Le Plan was well watered as cattle were grazed there, kept off the growing crops or grass by fences erected to protect land *in defensum*. On the dry pastures of the upper terraces and the plateau itself, sheep and goats which need very little water were the only animals which could have survived, and could have grazed there throughout the year, as it was stated in 1609 was the practice.[19] The sheep were essential in replenishing the fertility of the hard-worked plateau arables. As David Siddle shows, they were valued as much for their manure as for their

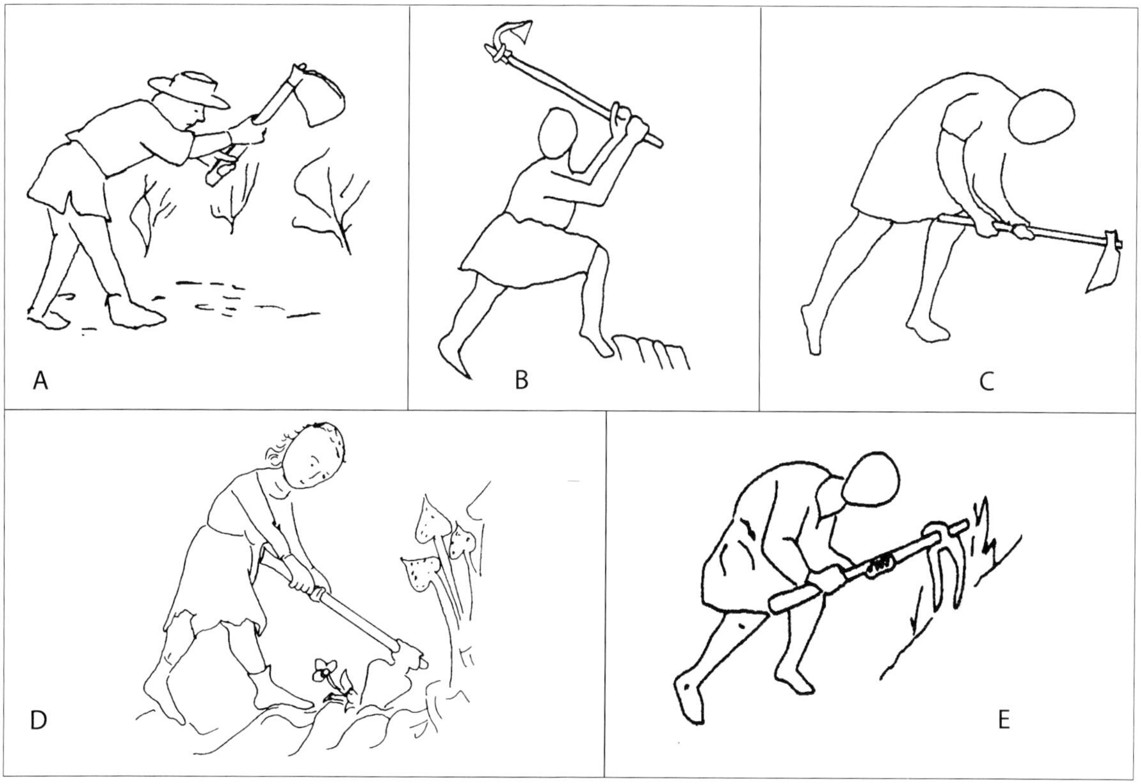

FIGURE 191. Illustrations of traditional farming showing a wide variety of hand-tools for clearing land and turning the soil, re-drawn from medieval manuscripts. Reproduced from Reigniez 2002, figs 61, 63–6 p. 122 with the kind permission of Editions Errance of Paris

products in the early modern period. Both the archaeology of enclosures on the plateau and what we know about the rotations practised support the idea that in the middle ages the smallish peasant flocks did not roam freely over the plateau but were fairly strictly confined, perhaps by moveable hurdles, at night 'close-folded' when they needed protecting from a range of predators – wolves and eagles in particular – on the stubbles and fallows of the cultivated dolines and *uvulae* to concentrate their manure there, grazing the surrounding uncleared land during the day (Andrew Fleming, Chapter 1). Other fodder

	Spring	*Summer*	*Autumn*	*Winter*
Year 1	barley sown	barley harvested	ploughed, wheat sown	wheat growing
Year 2	wheat harvested	grazing on fallow		
Year 3	grazing on fallow throughout year			
Year 4	barley sown	barley harvested	ploughed, wheat sown	wheat growing
Year 5	wheat harvested	grazing on fallow		
Year 6	grazing on fallow throughout year			

FIGURE 192. Seasonal rotation of crops on a 6-year cycle

crops than grass were available: the leaves of young trees and bushes, possibly holly, which today provide browsing for deer, but grass is the most plentiful and supports flocks today when their manure still produces a rich humus in some of the dolines. It is clear from John Crowther's work that the carbon content of the soil leached very quickly from the soils in the doline floors and would have needed the humic content topped up very frequently (Chapter 3). It would probably last for little more than a single year. A flock of 30, the standard *trentain* recorded in the documents of the 14th century, seems about right for this kind of system. A *trentain* of 1332 consisted of 21 ewes (*oves*) with fully-grown wool (*lanuti de capite*), seven young wethers, one old wether and one ram. This looks like a self-sufficient flock which could breed its own replacements. A pasturing agreement ruled that rams are allowed within the enclosures with a single wether but no other animal, perhaps an indication that breeding was regulated in order that the lambs could be born at a designated time, presumably in the spring. Some sheep were kept on land near the village during the winter and may have been moved up onto the plateau by stages if the practice in very similar areas of Provence in recent times may be taken as a guide, although the trip could equally well be easily taken in a day.[20]

There were attempts to control the numbers of goats, which will appear later as both an important resource and a threat to the environment (David Siddle, Chapter 8). By an agreement of 1334 each inhabitant of Cipières can pasture four goats in the upper protected areas of Le Plan (*in deffenso superiori de planis*), that is, from the road which goes from the *castrum* of Cipières towards the hill at Caillol by the ridge (*per brechum*) from the plain and from there to the said hill of Caillol' and only there. [21] Probably this is the road which leads from Cipières via lou Brech to the plateau of Cavillore and the bylaw would have limited the goats to a remote area beyond what is now the south-eastern boundary of the commune. This was the only enclosure in which goats were allowed and the goatherds in charge of them were liable to fines for infringements of the rules.

5. *Processing and storage*

The cereal crops were cut by sickles, probably high on the stalk in medieval fashion to catch every grain and leave long stalks for a separate harvest of the valuable straw (Figure 193). Threshing was done by leading mules or horses to trample over the sheaves laid on ground or a cobbled/paved threshing-floor to separate the heads from the stalks. Raibaude's tenants were obliged to use her private *aire*, and hire her animals for the job if they did not have enough of their own to thresh *lou siou en ben lou siou* (each his own).[22] This is a rare piece of medieval evidence for this practice used as an alternative to threshing with flails. The 1531 cadastre refers to stables near the castle which could have been successors to the range of farm buildings there must have been in the fourteenth century for the demesne livestock. Grain harvested under the bailiff's

FIGURE 193. Harvesting by sickle, re-drawn from a medieval manuscript. Reproduced from Reigniez 2002, fig. 269 p. 252 with the kind permission of Editions Errance of Paris

eye near the village would have been caught up, and taxed and tithed in this system, but up on the plateau where small threshing floors are found there were evidently ways to avoid this profitable monopoly and the grasp of the church. Grain there must have been threshed immediately after harvesting, probably by flails, and what was not ground and baked on the spot brought down in panniers on mules or the farmers' back. This was probably one of several ways in which working on the plateau was likely to have been a much more independent existence than down in the village under the eye of the seigneur.

Storage space was at a premium and grain was a precious and hard-won commodity so it was stored as near to the living quarters as possible, as was the straw and chaff produced by the energetic threshing on the *aire* which provided valuable feed for livestock, and firewood. A *casamentum* granted in 1337 consisted of a house (*domus*) between two others, two granaries or barns (*orrea),* four 'lands' and a meadow on the edge of waste land above Gréolières on Mont Cheiron, but there were also sheds (*casals*) These could be the unroofed *enclos* which are an important architectural horizon for this period (Figure 137) In the Vésubie region these dispersed barns were centres of cultivation, and that is a possibility at Cipières too, if some of the ostals remained dispersed.[23]

6. Permanent pasture

Not all clearances and fields were for arable. There was permanent pasture on Mont Cheiron and Le Plan as well as hay meadows by the Loup. The demesne had some fields sown for green fodder – *ferragine* – perhaps legumes of some kind. This careful production of fodder reflects the importance of cattle in the local economy. In 1471 the 34 households in Cipières had 90 head of cattle (40 cows and 50 bullocks) as against 1620 sheep and goats.[24] Oxen were used for ploughing on the lower fields, for threshing the corn by trampling the sheaves, as suppliers of milk, and when they were past work for meat, hides and bone products, tallow etc. Unlike sheep and goats, cattle need a regular water supply and the land on which they could pasture in summer must have been limited to that which was watered by streams or by artificial means such as irrigation channels of some kind. By arrangement with the seigneur the inhabitants had access to spring (or well?) water to irrigate their meadows five days a week; the water was reserved for the seigneur on Saturdays and Sundays. Caussols was much better supplied than Cipières in this respect: its broad valley had 'abundant and well-watered pasture' which must have been in short supply at the other two villages.[25]

Superior grazing was reserved for the plough beasts and protected. In a public assembly of 1334, 71 heads of households of Cipières approved a statute made by the Lady at the request of the inhabitants which laid down that each inhabitant may 'pasture a house-cow or cow in calf (*vacca domitatem vel turgam*) in the enclosed parts of the meadows of Syre and Le Plan (*in deffensa de pratis de syria… de planis*) and two other places equally with the oxen and plough beasts and the said cow (can remain) for all times of the year in all the places where the plough beasts are put.'[26] These restrictions applied equally to the Lady and the inhabitants and were drawn up jointly between them with an impressive show of legality, made in a 'public parliament in the enclosure of the court' of Raibaude de Caussols, properly summoned, and recorded by the notary, with the sworn witness of the entire community. They reflect a strongly established system of communal regulation of resources in which the Lady seems to have participated on a level footing with her tenants. The careful protection of certain areas from livestock, which was evidently well established by the time that these agreements were drawn up, may have represented a considerable limitation on what common pasture rights had been enjoyed previously and suggest that there was pressure on the available meadow land from cattle. Caussols, with its broad open valley providing meadow land and its more gentle slopes, was much better provided with both level grazing land and hay meadow than Cipières, but grazing there was also protected. From mid-March to Michaelmas (29 September) all livestock were kept out of the meadows (*prata*) entirely, and could not graze on the plain (*planum*) and from mid-April no draught stock (*avere*) 'may enter the banks (*ripas*) established and assigned within the enclosure (*deffensum*) of the said plain'. The slightly higher grazing land at Villevieille, where the grass perhaps started into growth later, was protected longer and from mid-April to All Saints (November) no animal may enter the protected stock area of the *castrum* . If the Lady's herdsman, or any other person, breaks the rules, all the rest are allowed to put their stock in once only and the culprit has to pay the fine. Draught oxen are allowed into the protected places only for are carrying out the hay, sowing corn, carrying out the sheaves or ploughing. Any infringement had to be paid for by the ploughman.[27]

8. Meadow

River meadows traditionally give the earliest and best hay and the valuable meadow land along the Loup which supplied hay for winter fodder was as important for livestock husbandry as was the availability of summer pasture. Some of the meadows along the Loup seem to have been individually, not communally, owned and appear as part of individual landholdings, like the 'land at the mills … next to the mill meadow' owned by Raymond Berand, a *maleservus*) in 1343 or, further down the river, land which Hugues Garin owned at Les Fontaniers (al Fontaynil) which the co-seigneur, Ferand Robion, was anxious to get his hands on.[28] The seigneur had important rights in the river, which were exploited through charges for milling. One of the *banalités* owned by Raibaude de Caussols was the power to compel the people of Cipières and Gréolières Hautes to use her fulling mill (*paratorium*) on the Loup. In the agreement of 1357 the seigneur agreed to build one mill or two at his own expense on the bank of the Loup and inhabitants of Cipières to construct a watercourse to it: perhaps an early version of the canal or leet which later served the mills along the bank. They were to pay multure for all the grain they ground there: in 1609 the Cipièrois were 'greatly oppressed and poor' because the mills belong to the seigneur to whom they pay multure at the rate of a thirtieth'.[29]

9. Woods

There was still enough woodland in the 14th century to give regular employment to a forester (*fustor*). Seigneurial woodlands were here, as elsewhere, a source of conflict which intensified as the tree cover was progressively cleared for cultivation. Trees became carefully protected: only the seigneur could cut wood from the trees in the protected area of Le Plan for building, plough timbers and so on (*scindere arbores a planta pedis usque ad caput* (*sic*)), while the inhabitants could only take dead wood, for firing.[30] Hunting – even keeping game acquired 'by chance and fortune' – without permission and putting poison in the river to kill the fish were forbidden.

10. Village, gardens and orchards

At Cipières (and at Gréolières-Hautes) Raibaude de Caussols had a *hospicium*, where her supplies were to be delivered, which must have had stabling and storage, a threshing floor and possibly workers' housing. Domestic buildings at Cipières included a kitchen, the 'second chamber' where the court was held, accommodation for the Lady's family and her domestic servants and for the notary during his visits. Within the walls there were open spaces, an orchard and chapel, and a courtyard where public meetings, assembled by the town crier, were held. In 1334, 71 inhabitants of were assembled *infra fortalicium curie*, in the fortification/bailey? of the court of the lady to agree to pasture regulations. In 1334 a similar meeting, described as a *parlhamentum* was summoned at a space described as 'in the castle' at Caussols, but another assembly there was held *in platea super peyronam* which sounds less formal.[31] Presumably the houses of Raibaude's co-seigneur, Fernand Robion, and the *domicellus* who worked for Raibaude as her bailiff were significantly superior to those of the villagers, either in position or size or both.

One result of nucleation into tightly packed houses, some back-to-back, along a street was that villagers now lived detached from the plots where they grew intensively cultivated crops for immediate household use, and perhaps kept fowl, even a pig. Improved climatic conditions now made it possible to grow nuts and vines and fruit trees: apples, pears, plums and possibly even figs: even on the plateau, *quartier* names show, one could find wild fruit trees. The villagers owned gardens, orchards and enclosed vineyards, probably terraced, ('a vineyard of four *fosserres*' – terraces?), hemp was cultivated and chestnut and oak trees individually owned. These small plots, gardens and orchards seem to have clung close to the village as they do today (and see Figure 72): 'a garden under the castle of Cipières next to the garden of William Lauger and next to the hemp plot of Ferand Robion' is one typical description. Their products must have provided an important supplement to the grain and livestock produced on the 'lands' and the pastures.

7.3. Inheritance, families and the land market

By the 14th century land always appears in the records as owned by individuals, or occasionally by brothers, not by an entire family. While transactions, notionally subject to the assent of the seigneur, were subject to the payment of *lods* and took place in her court, and alienation to 'outsiders' or the church was forbidden, the inhabitants seem to have treated their land as alienable, and the notarial registers contain many references to sales and exchanges.[32] Land could be lent to settle a debt, as when Jean and Rostaing Amadee lent a 'land' to the Argentin brothers for 15 years to pay off the 12 deniers they owed them.[33] It could be exchanged, as when Pons Argenti and Bartholemew Layet exchanged lands in La Travessa in 1332. There were added complications stemming from the fact that in that *quartier* there was both free land and land which was part of the *casamentum* of a *maleservus* holding, each carefully differentiated. The land which Bartholemew got was to be considered free, the *maleservus* land, which Pons got, would also be free but some other land which he had in the *quartier* would now be allotted to the *casamentum*.[34]

Marc Bloch associated the shift from family based to individualistic attitudes to land – or perhaps simply to more individualistic ways of describing it in official documents – with the persistent importance of Roman law in the Midi, but it is one experienced elsewhere in Europe. By the 14th century the family system which had strictly preserved the patrimony by constraining the marriage opportunities of the children, which we suggested was in force on the larger farms in Provence in the 9th century, were already changing. Many different influences were at work. More money and goods were circulating, so daughters could be dowered and sons provided for out of moveable wealth. The family land did not any longer have to support all the children: more opportunities were available for paid work outside the family, both locally, as farmhands or artisans, or in the growing towns. But land also remained heritable and was given in dowry. 'Dotal land' and land belonging to a group of heirs remained recognised categories: when Pierre Brotini and his aunt Beatrice sold Rostang Durant a land in La Faya in 1333 it was described as lying 'next to the dotal land (*terram dotalem*) of the said Rostang and next to the land of the children of Geoffrey Brotini'.[35] It is likely that peasant family strategies, here as elsewhere, worked on a balance between conserving the core of the property through descent, while allowing acquisitions and alienations to promote marriages and make provision for non-inheriting members.

The scattered 'lands' were farmed from houses closely packed into the village, the houses which were both living-space and farm buildings containing livestock and stored produce: this basic structure of farms in place by the 14th century continued into the early modern period and can still be seen in the 19th century. This structure, which emerged during the high-medieval expansion, had brought an entirely new way of life very different from the isolated existence on the large dispersed farms of an earlier era. In the terraced fields people now worked in close proximity, and even the plateau with people working its fields and tending its small flocks had plenty of life. In the village itself, with its tightly-packed and crowded houses the life of the street and the *place* has begun. The public assemblies and the seigneur's courts brought a new phenomenon to the countryside: the crowd. There were already – perhaps there had always been – the steep social and economic differentiation which appears in the later village. As examples of the Cipières villagers of the mid-14th century we can take two families of very different social standing. Pierre Leverii, son of James Leverii, was granted a *maleservus* holding in 1336. He had a house between two others on the public way, where one of his next-door neighbours was a *maleservus* also. He had six 'lands', two up on the plateau at L'Agrémourié, one at La Juillée, one on the *adrech*, the south-facing slope of La Combe. Two others were near Le Plan, at Les Pourcelles and the hill of Dilhole, and one at La Bovesc, as yet unidentified (Figure 31, but see Appendix 1). This was a small holding which had a heavy burden to sustain as well as feeding a family. The labour and livestock needed to work it would be at the call of the seigneur for *corvée* and probably some of its product went off (though this is not certain for Cipières) as rent in kind.

By contrast members of the Argentin family were employers of labour, money-lenders and purchasers of land. Three of them appear in the public assembly of 1334, and one acted as one of the village representatives in the purchase of a meadow in 1336. They entered into livestock contracts and agreements to rent land. Pons Argentin was an important figure in Gréolières-Hautes as well as at Cipières as a livestock contractor and money-lender: his grand-daughter Beatrice had a dowry of 53 gold florins when she married.[36]

7.4 The beginnings of capitalist pastoralism

The mixed farming system of the Middle Ages only continued under strains which ultimately transformed it. The cultivated area was probably at its greatest extent in the 13th and early 14th century, under pressure of population increase.

The scattered lands and intractable soils would have demanded large inputs of labour and the clearing of stones was a perennial burden. Even in the modern period Pierre Vial's land at Agrémourié, for instance, needed large inputs of labour to keep it in good heart.[37] The post-plague drop in population must have changed things in many ways. Families which lost men lost labour: hiring workers would have been an option only for some. Some families moved to Caussols, where farming was much easier and returns likely to be better. Land probably dropped out of cultivation as the balance of livestock and land shifted. The inhabitants' pasture rights – their hidden asset – begin to be exploited by a new kind of semi-capitalist professional pastoralism, controlled by merchant capital.

The rise of the Provençal cloth industry was making itself felt in this area probably well before the 14th century when there was a well-established community of weavers at Hautes-Gréolières which included a 'Master J A weaver'. One of the *banalités* owned by Raibaude de Caussol was the power to compel the people of Cipières and Gréolières (Upper) to use her fulling mill (*paratorium*) on the Loup.[38] Provence also became an important source of saffron as a dyestuff: there were saffron fields at Cipières and Caussols. Sclafert shows that very large-scale pastoralism based on long-distance transhumance virtually destroyed peasant livestock husbandry on St Victor's lands but although damage and strain were undoubtedly felt, the local picture at Cipières may well have involved much shorter distances and smaller flocks and herds than the long-distance large scale transhumance of the great estates (and Coste considers that Sclafert overestimated the extent of overstocking).[39]

In our area it seems as if it was the local towns, rather than a distant landowner, that made themselves felt. Flocks were smaller and moved over shorter distances than the great transhumances of the major religious houses. The Cipières farmers who raised sheep had always been involved in the market: there are references to them 'coming down from the mountains of Cipières' to sell their wool after the two yearly shearings, in May and at the end of the autumn, and like their English equivalents they entered into contracts with brokers who advanced them cash against the security of the wool to be delivered. This meant that they were not selling in an open market, and could not profit from changes in the price, but assured them a return in cash which could be spent in the town. These dealings with brokers also brought them under the influence of the urban merchant class and the plateau began to come under pressure from the increasingly capitalised economy of the rising nearby towns, in particular Grasse. Grasse had a considerable influence over a wide area, both as consumer and as a source of authority over local trading conditions. Its corn supplies came from the upland corn fields of Seranon and St Auban.[40] From the 13th century Grasse bourgeois were seeing the possibilities for profit in the burgeoning cloth and wool industry by more direct participation: they invested capital in flocks which grazed on the traditional grazing grounds of the neighbouring villages in summer. It may be part of this process that in 1244 La

Malle, the ridge south of Caussols, was given to Bertrand de Grasse. In winter flocks came down from the high mountains to pastures near the town at Opio, Cabris and Sartoux. The moving flocks were subject to the depredations of local castellans: this was already a problem in 1240 when the Statutes of Grasse were drawn up.[41] Capital from the prosperous citizens of Grasse was flowing into local livestock husbandry in the fourteenth century in the form of *gasaille* and *mergerie* contracts. These provided town-dwellers a chance of profitable investment which escaped the sin of usury in an increasingly important industry. They gained access to an important resource whose use was still confined legally to the village communities. From the villagers' point of view such contracts provided a source of cash and credit in an economy which was becoming increasingly cash-oriented. They enabled poor peasants to acquire flocks they could not otherwise afford and to increase their value by investing their labour and skill in their care, while using a free asset: their common rights on the pastures. The money such arrangements brought in enabled Cipières parents to provide dowries which were increasingly felt to demand bought, sometimes costly, materials. Under *mergerie* contracts the owner leased a flock to a local man who restored them at the end of the term, retaining half the capital and half of the increased value. Under some contracts the local man returned a sum of money which he had borrowed at the beginning, or repaid half the livestock and half the capital.[42] Much larger flocks were involved than the individual *trentain*: up to 200 are recorded. A contract drawn up in Cipières in 1334 related to a flock of five *trentains* of ewes, a third provided by the local man, the rest by the investor. The local man got rations and wages and could keep half the flock after the contact ended in five years. During that time he could sell lambs' wool and cheese, so the arrangement was not necessarily exploitative, but it represented a high risk if things went wrong. A contract between Pierre Agart and Pierre Flore, a prominent member of the community who was involved in several such transactions involved a total of 422 sheep. Flore put up 395 sheep and paid five-sixths of the expenses, including bread for the shepherds and their dogs. Agart put up the rest (just about a *trentain*), received a yearly wage, paid a sixth of the costs and was entitled to a sixth of the profits.[43] Cattle were also leased on similar contracts, as were bees, but the principal profits to be made were from wool, sold at the market in Grasse. Sclafert's maps show the importance of livestock in the local economy in the 15th century. There was overstocking at Mouans-Sartoux. The 1471 taxation records only 1620 sheep and goats at Cipières, but these were only those owned by the villagers and the surveys made for a *reaffouagement* in 1609 show the presence of considerable Grasse-owned flocks at Cipières.[44]

The villagers were thus already at the beginning of the processes which were to lead to the position in the 18th and 19th century described by David Siddle in which a minority of villagers had flocks, and full-time shepherds were employed. The contractual arrangements which brought urban bourgeois interests into the village introduced a new form of larger scale stock management, with a different kind of habitat for shepherds who were increasingly professionals and larger flocks which were no longer necessarily confined to the dolines of individual peasant farms. As long as cultivation continued on the plateau this must have led to conflict between the traditional small-scale sheep-corn husbandry, with its small fields and carefully managed small flocks, and the demands for space of the large flocks of the new entrepreneurs. The new larger flocks may have been managed and housed in a different way from the traditional practices. Some lessees (not specifically from Cipières) were allowed to burn woods and to use timber to build *granicas, curtes and jacinas* (*bergeries*).[45] Farmers now had to protect their fields against the passage of the larger flocks of the incomers, whose shepherds perhaps had less respect for the communally known and accepted boundaries. Andrew Fleming finds that 'the concept of the road as a walled corridor rather than a casual passage left between the fields developed and was taken more seriously as time went on' and that the Cipières–Caussols road was altered to allow 'a grudging acceptance of the right of passage through local fields' (Chapter 4). This kind of stockrearing was no longer part of mixed peasant husbandry but a specialised, and increasingly capitalised, occupation in the hands of a minority of villagers. It may also have undermined the mixed subsistence economy which had supported earlier generations. Duby considered that *mergerie* contracts, while bringing capital into the countryside, encouraged larger flocks, specialisation, enclosure and the undermining of the collective nature of earlier arrangements. Some certainly profited from the increasing market value of the common pastures. But these opportunities for individual enterprise must all the same have contributed to the engrossing of holdings and differentiation within the village which were to be important themes in the following centuries.

The plague virtually depopulated Mouans-Sartoux in 1351. Gréolières-Hautes was abandoned by the end of the 14th century and plague recurred to the end of the 14th century. But plague was not the only depopulator of villages: all over Europe people were moving away to better themselves in the towns. The seigneurial economy run by Raibaude in the mid-14th century depended on a full complement of tenant workers to provide her with rents and supplies, to transport her 'necessities' and to add to her income from their payments for mill, oven and workshop. The loss of tenants who moved to the towns was a threat to this. In 1337 Monnet Chamate, who had left Cipières and was living in Grasse, had to promise on oath that when his eldest son reached 14 he would return to Cipières, take on the family property there and remain as a resident.[46] The fall in population brought about a new balance of power in the countryside. One sign of this may be the fading away of official distinctions between classes: by the late 14th century we do not hear any longer of the distinction between *caslani* and *maleservi* and it is possible that the harsh conditions on which the *maleservi* held their little plots were relaxed. In a situation where the labour supply was shrinking tenants negotiated with lords on more favourable terms. *Chartes d'habitation* became common: these were formal agreements about the terms of tenure drawn up between lord and tenants. On the lords' part these were an attempt to retain people on the land by a formally recorded settlement.[47] On the tenants' part they were a chance to negotiate a better deal and reform abuses. In 1357 the inhabitants of Cipières were in dispute with their then lord Raymond d'Agout which was settled by a written agreement under which they paid 200 florins a year for their dwellings. The seigneur held on to his rents and his feudal rights: the inhabitants still paid the fine for selling land (*lods*), a twelfth of the value of inherited or acquired goods, a lamb each year for grazing the lord's meadows, and transport service to Nice. He agreed to build a mill on the Loup and an oven, for which they had to pay fees to use, while they were to build a watercourse and rebuild and enlarge the *castellum* if required. They were not to build their own houses higher than the castle, nor build a dovecote, nor take game. This sounds like a village community that was surviving, able to strike a bargain with a seigneur anxious to preserve his banal rights but not able to exploit the villagers' economy in any significant way.[48]

By contrast, by 1368 Caussols seems to have been virtually depopulated. The people of Cipières took advantage of the fact. Their representatives approached Raibaude and Reforciat d'Agout in Nice and requested permission to occupy the territory. While he reserved certain lands for himself Reforciat granted them rights of occupation there 'since the cause of habitation is for the procreation and raising of children'. The terms were that the present and future inhabitants of Caussols should divide the land between them, keep the cultivated land in cultivation and clear uncultivated land, paying a ninth of the crop of grain and vegetables. They owed a load of hay from the Caussols pastures and were forbidden to borrow each others' beasts for threshing but had to use the seigneurial stock if they had not enough of their own. They could build ovens and mills, owing multure and *fourrage*. Dovecotes and hunting were forbidden.[49] We do not know how many people actually moved from Cipières to repopulate Caussols, (*pace* Durbec 1972, 138 and Samaran 1957) but this repopulation was successful to the extent that corn was paid from Caussols in 1389 and the church there was still being kept in repair in the 15th century.[50] In later centuries Caussols would be dominated by 'outsiders', many from Grasse.

CHAPTER EIGHT

Agrarian Systems in the Post-Medieval Period

David Siddle

*New impulses followed the population traumas of the Black Death. These too left their marks on the landscape. As populations recovered there were changing opportunities for the Cipières peasantry. These opportunities involved the further development of individual property rights, and inheritance arrangements. Distinctions between caslani (*ostal?*) and maleservi families blurred and seems to have disappeared by the 16th century if not before. The association between* ostal *and* quartier *ended. There was further development of a farming landscape increasingly characterised by large flocks of sheep. As this sheep economy grew, obviously the demands for grazing land increased. This meant that fewer and fewer winter crops were sown. In this chapter the evidence in the cadastres is used to trace the evolution of peasant property rights from communal to individual proprietorship and the ways in which the grazing flocks of sheep and goats came to dominate both the economy and the farming landscape of the vast upland surfaces.*

8.1. Introduction

Population decline in the period from the onset of the Black Death to the mid-15th century changed the ways in which it was possible for family systems to operate. With the recovery of population in the following period, new commercial forces were at work. In these circumstances, large family holdings of land, which seem at least in part to have occupied particular *quartiers,* would have been less easy to maintain. How did this system change? The impetus was clearly much to do with the opportunities which emerged for profit from grazing both sheep and goats. It was perhaps this which helped peasants towards a definition of land rights based on exclusion as much as production. In the older world of *communauté* individual rights of ownership were blurred, but the Written Law, which characterised southern systems of jurisprudence, enshrined Roman principles. It encouraged the documenting of obligation: of marriage portions, loans, rental arrangements and, more significantly, of inheritance. So, once the system of patriarchal primogeniture enshrined in the *ostal* system began to disappear, the process of change seems to have been quite rapid. A significant impetus in this direction was the development of the cadastre, a record of individual holdings in specific places whose purpose was to introduce taxation based on property values rather than the services of labour and production. The closest the medieval system of taxation had come to this approach was a tax on the strictly regulated supplies of salt needed for peasants and their animals. (*gabelles de sel*). So the series of land tax registers that have been a feature of the taxation bureaucracy from the 16th century until the present day are crucial to understanding the emergence of individual property holdings and how this affected the landscape.[1]

8.2. Land 'use' in 1531

Before exploring evidence of proprietorship in the 1531 cadastre we will use it first to identify the main areas of what were, at least ostensibly, land use categories. These are offered with the *caveat* that what we are shown is tax value not actual use. Although this earliest cadastral document is not explicit enough to identify cropping and grazing practices, the new land holding and (putative) use system was clearly well in place by 1531. The ownership of each parcel was described sequentially by use, by *quartier* location (a term employed by the new bureaucracy to add specificity to vague place and space names) and by allocated tax revenue in terms of what it might be expected to produce. Surprisingly large areas of land were taxed as arable (*terre*), especially on the Plateau de Calern, while areas designated specifically as pasture for hay, on the other hand, were restricted to bottom lands. What is also surprising is the large number of very small domestic vineyard plots (over 80), though the *quartier* name by which they are identified (*vigno*) is not easy to identify in the modern landscape. It is evident from the listings in each subsequent cadastral document that the principles of land-holding classification and documentation, once established in 1531, pertained throughout much of the subsequent historical period, despite changes in the society and economy.

Land identified as hay pasture or vineyards may be accurate enough but all the members of the Cipières team question the designation of arable land (*terre*). The main reason is that the plateau carried very large numbers of sheep and goats (see Figure 202). The second is that by this time the older rotation systems described by Rosamond Faith were moving accordingly to a biennial system of crop and fallow (Chapter 7).

8.3. Individuation and the end of *ostal* land holding

All of the numerous taxation documents which span the years from 1531 to 1841 follow the pattern of describing the holdings of each individual 'proprietor,' its potential for use and its yield for tax. After 1531 there are fewer indications of brothers, fathers and sons sharing the same suite of land parcels, though David Austin has traced evidence for delayed inheritance in his analysis of parcel changes (Chapter 3). If at first the *ostal* system of kinship based on managed primogeniture (see Chapter 6) underpinned the way in which the cultural landscape emerged, what happened as the system of kinship collectivity broke down? The *ostal* families would obviously still attempt to hold land across a spread of ecologically different zones, but some individual proprietors, who were still identifiably part of an *ostal,* had already accumulated for themselves a significant portfolio of land parcels across a range of environments. What were the pressures as pastoralism expanded, particularly in the face of a system of individual family proprietorship?

One important element in this process was the pressure of population. The period embracing the last quarter of the 15th century and the first third of the 16th century saw the population of Cipières rising once again towards what was identified in the last chapter as a pre-Plague maximum. This trend was replicated throughout France. Although this '16th century spring' seems to have been slowing down by the 1520s in some areas, it was still on the march elsewhere. Indeed Le Roy Ladurie considers that in Languedoc, the boom in population in the period between 1500 and 1570 was 'the most striking fact about the sixteenth century'.[2] Gradually one can assume that a period of changing political and economic relations led to an ever more open land succession. Already apparent in the 14th century, the trend continued and it was this that had led to the appearance of 'proprietors' in the first cadastre of 1531. The first great cadastral document shows us a village whose population had achieved a new high point: a community fully occupied in farming in every *quartier* of its lands. It is reasonable to allow this new 'parcelised' view of farming opportunity and taxation to characterise the start of the modern period.

This quiet revolution saw the full emergence of legal inheritance and regulated transmission of property, orchestrated by the village notaries, principally, but not exclusively, the Lambert family who occupied a large house in the new Place (Figure 74). Land transactions were a clear feature of the 1531 cadastre and decorate the margins of a document that was not re-cast until 1610. This document also demonstrates the importance of well-established Cipières families in owning individual parcels of land and why, from the authorities' point of view, some much more focussed assessment of taxation may have appeared justified by this increasing level of economic differentiation and individuation. Taxation totals suggest at first sight that there was a considerable differentiation in crude wealth. Taxes varied from 3 florins (five entries) to 604 florins. Twenty-one individuals were rated for taxes of more than 200 florins. The graph of taxable property values then falls rapidly to a long tail. Half the entries show property valued at less than 50 florins.

David Austin (Chapter 2) has shown us how, in this period, the expansion of the medieval settlement of Cipières outside the old enclosures was marked by the creation of the new Place and soon the introduction of new streets southward (like the Bourgade) and westward (Le Caire) away from the new Place and along the edge of the gardens (*saffranier*). These streets were symbolic perhaps of this new style of expansion, the beginnings of an *embourgeoisement*, with new functionaries in crafts, shops and trades. It was also probably around this time that the village council formalised its proceedings, for it is from this period that the books of council *Délibérations* survive in an unbroken sequence, that is from 1537 to the present day.[3] This council was probably no longer convened under a tree on a casual basis, as happened for village assemblies in previous centuries, but in a room large enough to hold more than a dozen representatives, probably in the aforementioned notary's house opposite the church. It had a clear agenda of rights and responsibilities. There is also evidence that the last decades of the 16th century and the early years of the 17th marked a high point in the early modern mixed farming economy in which, as we will see later in this chapter, wool played an increasingly significant part.

What we seem to have is two competing models of social and economic relationships at this time. The first is the one presented by a primary reading of the cadastral document. This is of a society evolving towards individual proprietorship. Underlying this, however, is evidence of continuity of *ostal* social and economic relations, irrespective of the new bureaucratic order which defined 'proprietors'. This evidence suggests that an *ostal* ideology persisted for a while and indeed became part of the way in which kin accumulated assets during the period of recovery in the Renaissance.

We have all speculated, from our different disciplinary perspectives, about the relationship between family names (*ostals*/kin groups) and specific *quartiers*. Though some individual family names survived in the earliest cadastral registration of *quartiers* (Baume de Brun, Liere Daniele, Baume d'Ayaud, Plan d'Anlere) in these changing times, blocks of *ostal* 'family land' would be less likely to be associated with particular places, at least in the minds of the people in charge of naming *quartiers* for the cadastre. By this time population numbers had reached a new peak and *ostal* lineages were ramifying through a *cousinage*. These are identified in the 1531 document by the use of sobriquets. Though by no means consistent, we can identify some suites of 'same name' land parcels within particular *quartiers*, as we might have done, perhaps with much more assurance, two hundred years earlier. But by examining the patterns of ownership of land by *ostal* 'sobriquet' between 1531 and 1750 it is possible to provide evidence of individuation. How far, however, is it still possible to see traces of contiguities of *ostal* family lands in the 1531 cadastral record?

By 1531 there were so many branches within the expanding *ostal* lineages that sub-sets merited distinction by a sobriquet, a mechanism which allowed kin linkages to be overt, avoiding confusion. Assuming each sobriquet represents membership of one such loose relict *ostal* with between 20 and 30 people, we can begin to identify these contiguities as they appear in the record. Here we suggest that the juxtaposition of names sharing the same sobriquets in the sequential folio pages of the document indicate that, despite encroaching social and economic differentiation, kinship networks were still operating. These were at least in some ways *ostals* in the sense identified in Chapter 6. It is helpful to this argument to note that the term survives for at least the period of the first cadastre. At the same time there is also parallel evidence that, despite this level of continuity, in the two centuries after the *incastellamento* the mind set of the *ostal* had nonetheless begun to slip out of its original use. Certainly in the description of dwelling units in the 1531 cadastre there is some ambiguity of attribution. Each entry of land and property to be taxed was headed by the dwelling unit. There were a total of 231 such entries. Sixty-seven of these were described as *ostals* and 164 as *massons*. Twenty listed proprietors had no attributed dwelling and may be assumed to be living with relatives or renting rooms, though there was some absentee proprietorship. By the time of the next cadastration in 1610[4] the word *ostal* had disappeared almost entirely. So the 1531 cadastre provides us with a pivot to measure the change from older collective mind sets towards a slowly emerging sense of individuation. In this context, closer examination of particular name sets in this and subsequent cadastral records is revealing. If the use of term *ostal* survives in the document its meaning is best revealed in the contiguous or semi contiguous sequences of entries of proprietors with the same sobriquet. (Girard 'Blanchon' for example, with seven entries on ff. 87, 94, 94a, 95, 96b, 99a). To better illustrate this phenomenon and to see how things changed with the passage of time, attention is concentrated on two patronyms which appear in every listing of the community from 1334 until the present day: the Bourellys and the Florys.

8.4. The Bourellys

The Bourellys, appear as a single name in the 1334 assembly, where the family was represented by one Fulconis Borelli (Figure 187). Within the next two centuries numbers increased to make the Bourrellys one of the largest patronym groups in the village, with 37 household heads (possibly nearly 200 people) in 1531. Four main identifiable groupings emerge: eight proprietors under the sobriquet *Marcon* (one at least of the group is quite specifically identified as a mason); four proprietors with the sobriquet '*Magnan*', four with the sobriquet '*Baulhan*' and three belonging to the '*feu d'Antoine*'. Following the argument above it is no surprise to find that, although not exclusive, these sobriquet sub-sets are characterised by sequential folio entries in the Cipières cadastral register of 1531 (Figure 194).

Applying the Baratier household multiplier (5.0) each Bourelly sobriquet name would produce a target number for an *ostal* in the medieval period. The 'Marcon' Bourellys have six proprietors, with perhaps a total of 30 individual members. The rest may have had up to 20 members each.

If the 'Marcon' Bourellys were indeed masons, as the sobriquet suggests, they were among the first explicit specialist craft groups to emerge. They

Sobriquet	*First name*	*Folio no*	*Tax in florins*
Magnan	Louis	21	58
	Martin	21a	1
	Christol	38	1
	Peyre	49	115
			462
Baulhan	Honorat	69	111
	Marcon	70	63
	Rafou	28	99
	Guyon	86	99
			372
Marcon	Frans	115	93
	Jan	115a	138
	Jean Paul	127	135
	Manoel	127a	83
	Honorat	128	85
	Antoine	128a	103
	Estiene	153	109
			829
Feu d'Antoine	Mario	91b	74
	Beiton	92	38
	Calanque	92a	27
	Honorat	86	131
			270

FIGURE 194. Bourelly sobriquet sequences in Cadastre 1531

paid the most in taxes at this time (829 florins) and this specialist activity certainly coincided with a period when the fabric of the village was growing rapidly, Relative affluence is reflected in taxable property holdings in land and buildings and shows us how something of an open land market had already taken hold even by this time, even if land transfers may have mainly taken place within the framework of the ostal as a whole.

Assuming that the original distribution of lands for this *ostal* were in only four or five *quartiers*, as seems to have been the case (see Chapter 5), and assuming also a new movement of land between *ostals* through inheritance, dowries and land sales, can we still identify traces of a much earlier allocation in the distribution of parcels among the seven households within the *Marcon* sobriquet? The *ostal* members were certainly much more widely represented in the landscape of arable taxation in 1531 than they might have been in earlier times, but there is still some evidence of 'within *quartier*' spatial contiguities (Figure 195). In fact, of the 22 *quartiers* in which their lands were to be found, just over two-thirds (68%) also contained parcels of others with the same *Marcon* sobriquet. In eight cases there were three or even four other *Marcon* Bourellys with land in the same small area of a single *quartier*.

It is not difficult to postulate that at least the majority of these parcels, in at least eight of the *quartiers* above, were either part of the original holding of their ancestor in the period of the *incastallamento* (or indeed before) or perhaps from an expansion, driven by the *ostals*, during the 50 years or more before the cadastral record. In either case, the subsequent cadastres should reveal a further drift towards a spread of parcels reflecting individual proprietorship.

By 1610 (Figure 196), however, things were changing, although elements of the old system still remained. Folio page listings show that families were still occupying properties close to each other, but not in the same contiguities, with Bourelly names falling between folios 78 and 97.There were still 34 Bourelly heads of household. But by this time, two generations after the first cadastre, sequences of names in the folios are not so evident. Now less than a half (46%)

Quartier	*Estienne*	*Frans*	*Jean*	*Jean-Paul*	*Manoel*	*Honorat*	*Antoine*
	f.115	f.115a	f.127	f.127a	f.128	f.128a	f.143
Curnyario	2	2			3		8
Liero Danielo				8	8	8	
Libac desserand	2	1	1	2			
Mulieros	6	5		5			
Coulet	12s	17s		5s	5s	10s	
Libiero		26p		3p		11p	
Sous bari	3p		3p		10	10	
Vigno	4v		10v		4v	4v	
Messon*	45	45	25		30	35	
Carbonello					*5p*	*5p*	
Lumial	*2*	*2*					
Collo	*1*		*35s*				
St Claude						*4*	*4*
Calern	*10*		*10*				
Baudillons			10				
Clarion		5					
Clots			7				
Julho	1						
Plantados							4
Fayo				2			
Plan		10p					
Syno	5						
Valmeyano		23					

Figures represent tax value of land in florins; p =pasture o = ostal property (gardens) s = stable v= vineyard
Quartiers in bold = more than two Bourelly 'marcon' holdings
Quartiers in bold italics = two Bourelly 'marcon' holdings
Messon* (*maisons*) probably in Coulet close the stables of Jean-Paul in Collo

FIGURE 195. Bourelly *Marcon* distribution of land parcels 1531

of Bourelly *Marcons* had land close to their kinsmen in the same *quartier*. There were now nine *Marcon* household heads. This increase from 1531 was reflected in 17 acquisitions of land in what one might call 'non-Bourelly *Marcon*' *quartiers*. By this time they occupied land in twice as many *quartiers* (35 in total). Only Phillipe held all his lands in *quartier*s where *Marcon* land was held in 1531 (Figure 196).

So at the time of the second cadastre, three generations later, the word *ostal* had virtually disappeared from the record and new forms of land transmission by sale and dowry, already rather common in the 1531 cadastral period, are much more evident. It is in this period one might argue, that families really began to behave

Quartier	*Jehan*	*Mars*	*Phillipe*	*Augustin*	*Pierre*	*Manuel*	*Estenne*	*Pons*	*Jehan*	*Manuel*
	fo. 81	*fo. 82a*	*fo. 101*	*fo. 158*	*fo. 168*	*fo. 168a*	*fo. 172*	*fo. 195*	*fo. 196*	*fo.182*
Baumitos							2	27	27	
Cuniere	25	27	28		23			10		
Collet			35s					47s	30s	
Collo Basso	75m		65m		73m					
Vigne					18		60v	9v	9v	27v
Fayo						10	12			45
Baudillons	1		24							
Calern			27					10		
Combe			12	5						
Plan danlaire			24		24					
Plantades							35			75
Ribiere			35v		35					
Teils		1		34						
Caux				24						
Caugnier		27								
Clot de			6							
Barnoin							6			
Agremourie				22						
Frais			12							
Grateloup	14									
Laspe							23			
Graupollier			1							
Launotos		12								
Laire danelle			60							
Mouliere					24					
Plan							10			
Prat			54							
Sousbarri				20						
Sine					10					
Loup				20v						
Roure					35					
Lumial									22	
Font									3	
St Pons									m?	

Figures represent tax value of land
Quartiers in bold = more than two Bourelly 'marcon' holdings
Quartiers in bold italics = two Bourelly 'marcon', holdings
messon (*maisons*) probably in Coulet close to the stables. Jean-Paul in Collo?
p =pasture o = *ostal* property (gardens) s = stable v= vineyard, m = maison
35 *quartiers* 9 household head 45–50 people. The increase from 1531 represented by acquisitions of new land in new.
Non-Bourelly 'Marcon' *quartiers* now 35 in total, 17 of them new. Only Phillipe held all his lands in *quartiers* where 'Marcon' land was held in 1531
Houses: Augustin devant le chateau 4 : estene: ? jehan: Rue de St Pons 18 pons: Rue du Four

FIGURE 196. Bourelly *Marcon* distribution of land parcels 1610

differently. It is surely not coincidental that during this period (between 1531 and 1610) a new group of merchant houses appeared around the new Place and the Bourgade had also emerged as a focus for new property (see David Austin, Chapter 2). Rather than *quartiers* as in the 1531 cadastre, streets in the village (*rues*) were defined as such (Rue Droit, Rue de l'Adreche). In the village, the term *ostal* was now replaced by *maison,* as indeed it had been already for the Bourelly *Marcons* by 1531. Inheritance seems to have begun to focus on one or at the most two, male heirs and the rest probably had to work as *labourers* for them or their neighbours or, indeed, to find other work in the parish as *muletiers* or functionaries. The other alternative was to migrate to seek work elsewhere (Chapter 9). We argue then that a new, much more structured peasant society seems to have emerged during this period. By 1633 the use of sobriquets had also almost disappeared too. There were still clusterings of Bourellys (79%) in three named streets (L'Adrech, Colle and Bourgade), but land holding was much more diffuse.

8.5. The Florys

The Florys, a similarly long surviving family name in Cipières, are distinguished by five sobriquets in 1531 (Figure 197): *Garetto*, *Milan, Beaumon*, *Borrillon*, and *Garbo*. The *Garetto* Flory relict *ostal* alone had as many as nine named proprietors with households making a total of perhaps 50 people. Clearly through the exigencies of the demographic ebb and flow outlined above, the fortunes of all the longest settled families also oscillated, but not necessarily in tandem. The best evidence for this is to be found in the expansion and contraction of the Flory lineage. In 1334 there were five Flory names ostensibly in the same *ostal* (Figure 187). By 1531 there were 34 Flory entries and Louis Flory (no sobriquet) held the prestigious job of head bailiff for the seigneur, occupying a large house outside the village (Le Puy) overlooking the main arable land. This position stayed within the same family over the next three and a half centuries.

FIGURE 197. Flory sobriquet sequences in Cadastre 1531

Sobriquet	*First name*	*folio no*	*tax in florins*
Garetto	Andron	3	31
	Pyron	3a	44
	Jean	4	37
	Peyre	4a	35
	Jaume	51a	74
	Antony et Guyo	62	0
	Gerard (heirs)	77	0
	Claudon	140	28
	Mounet (heirs)	143	112
			361
Beaumon	Estene	22	188
	Martin	23	115
	Claudon	28	487
	Peyre	28a	507
			1297
Milan	Martin (et son souer)	8a	17.6
	Jan	8b	17.6
	Honore	8c	17.6
	Blaize	55a	17.6
			?
Borrillon	Jan	52a	66.0
	Jean	52b	7.6
			?
Garbo	Honorat	146a	38
	Heires de garbo	146	37
			?

The most significant branch of the original Flory *ostal* appears to have been the *Beaumons*. In 1531 (Figure 198) there were five *Beaumons*, four of them appearing in pairs in the record (ff. 22, 23, and 28/28a). Collectively they paid over 1404 florins in tax, the highest in the village after the Bourellys (1933 f.). At this date their lands were spread through 26 *quartiers*, but, with the exception of Peyre Flory *Beaumon* (*cap d'oustal*?) with lands in 14 *quartiers*, the others largely shared lands in the same *quartiers*, in eight cases with two other Flory *Beaumon* kinsmen.

At the time of the second cadastre (Figure 199), there were only eight Flory *Beaumon* heads of household in the cadastral document of that year and like the Bourelly *Marcon*s their lands were much more scattered through the *quartiers*. Few vestiges of kin coherence remained in the distribution of 38 parcels across the 27 *quartiers*, only six of which had two or more Flory *Beaumon* parcels. So only a third of the *quartiers* with Flory *Beaumon* land had more than one parcel (Figure 199). On the other hand, elements of the old system still remained with Flory *Beaumons* occupying houses in only four locations/streets in the village (Devant l'eglise, La Place, L'Adrech and Bourgade) as well as the bailiff's house (Charles Flory *Beaumon*) in Plan *quartier*. At the same time it is worthy of note that the Flory *Beaumons* had sizeable sheep flocks. In 1610 Charles the *seigneur*'s bailiff had an *étable de huit trenteniers* (240) sheep.

The Flory *Beaumons* still retained its sobriquet identity in the cadastre of 1633 and was among the last to do so. Charles the bailiff still held the house '*Sur le Plan*' and there are 11 entries in the folios. Most held substantial houses and paid a total of 1877 florins in tax, but their lands were very well scattered through the *quartiers*.

So from the sample evidence of these two family sub-lineages there were real signs of the development of a new set of property relations concentrating on individual household heads and stem family succession of a kind familiar throughout the region by the 18th century.[5] As we shall argue below, these changes were also accompanied by important shifts in regional economy

FIGURE 198. Flory *Baumon* distribution of land parcels 1531

Quartier	*Peyre*	*Estene*	*Martin*	*Claudon*
	fo. 22	*fo. 23*	*fo. 28a*	*fo. 28b*
Caulx	7	7	7	4
Glaudon	20pb	7	5	20
Graubello	8	4	4	4
Conbo Pons	3	2	1	
Fond	20p	2		35p
Coulet		2	20s	5
Laspe	10	4	4	
Syno	9	2	22	
Lono		*3*		*4p*
Combe		*2*	*1*	
Pre	*3*			*1*
Calern	*45*	*6*		
Collet		*20s*	*4j*	
Agremourie		*6*	*6*	
Fayo			3	
Mulieros	25p			
Maurenq	9			
Palme vignon	5			
Pessos	7			
Colle	24s			
Praon				6j
Sous bari				6j
Julho		10p		
Grangeon		1		
Malbosq		7		
Miraulx			3	

p = pasture s = stable v= vineyard, j = jardin
Quartiers in bold = more than two Flory 'Beaumon' holdings
Quartiers in bold italics = two Flory 'Beaumon', holdings
26 *quartiers*, 14 with two or more Flory 'Beaumon' land parcels

FIGURE 199. Flory *Baumon* distribution of land parcels 1610

Quartier	*Jean-Paul*	*Charles*	*Guilen*	*Antoine*	*Fouques*	*Martin*	*Jean*
Sous bari	*20pe*	*6*		*25s*	*33js*		*6*
Caulx	**24**			**38**	**24**	**36**	
Calern				**150**	**90**	**1**	
Agremourie	***22***	***2***					
Laone			***12***	***22***			
Vaumejane				***50***	***50***		
St Roche					10		
Valaune					40		
Barnoin						18	
Calancon						25m	
Teil						34	
Clot de Suer						14	
Graus							28
Bourgade							40s
Faye							12
Sine							36
Loup	20v						
Paraire		10					
Combe			70				
Pourcelles				55			
Safranier			3j				
Vigne			77				
Poumaires				8			
Roure				1	45		
St Claude				60b			

p = pasture s = stable v= vineyard, j = jardin
Quartiers in bold = more than two Flory 'Beaumon' holdings
Quartiers in bold italics = two Flory 'Beaumon', holdings Beaumons hold land in 27 *quartiers*, only three with three or more holdings, and three with two holdings

and land management. Pastoralism had taken over a dominant role in the economy and biennial rotation and reductions in land set aside for hay pasture characterised this new arable system.

8.6. Was there *morcellement* in Cipières?

In these circumstances of an increasingly open land market one would envisage a general increase in the level of sub-division of parcels, a proliferation of smaller and smaller units of land, both through population increases and through sales and endowments. Elsewhere in France *morcellement* proceeded apace during this period, encouraged by shifts in the economic balances in the country as a whole. The received wisdom among social and economic historians is that the improved food supplies in the later 15th century led to falling grain prices and that this encouraged the substitution of sheep for cereals. Le Roy Ladurie, for example, tells us that 'the peasant of Provence had abandoned marginal cultivation of mountain cereals and turned towards sheep rearing and transhumance, minimising losses by substituting animals for agriculture. In the *garrigue* it was a system of extensive rearing on wild thyme and low sparse vegetation'.[6] He argues that the recovery of population in the late 15th and early 16th centuries placed a burden on this arrangement. This was only solved by further marginalising the poor who responded by subdividing their arable parcels to the point of penury. We can also follow this argument in Neveux's use of what he calls the 'Poitrineau model', a similar explanation of sub-division leading to poverty in the Auvergne in the 18th century.[7] Conditions in Provence in the 16th century could only have been similar. We have argued above how the Cipières *ostal* system was being modified, that this process was well under way by the time of the first cadastre in 1531, and that it continued apace in the next 80 years during the period when Sclafert tells us that sheep numbers were at their highest. There is every reason to believe from subsequent inquests that they continued at this level in Cipières for much of the next 300 years (Figure 202).

What one might expect is that this process would indeed have opened the way to the kind of *morecellement* as grazing land increased at the expense of peasants with little land and only a few sheep. But whatever happened in Cipières, the cadastres provide us with no evidence that this led to a massive increase in numbers of small land parcels. Indeed David Austin has shown (Chapter 3) that while there is plenty of evidence of volatility in landholding boundaries there is actually little evidence for real bounded property spaces on the upland areas at all. The only markers he could detect were very small cairns on boundaries that could be seen to be there in 1841 and these were often placed in a superficial and temporary kind of way on the top of clearance cairns etc., i.e. stratigraphically at the end of the sequence of field monuments. How this relates to the issue of individuation is, at the very least, ambiguous.

One way of measuring the extent of the changes in use is to look at the number of arable parcels of land in representative *quartiers* both on the plateau (Figure 200), where the greatest competition for resources between pastoral and arable interests would be manifest, and *quartiers* below the plateau (Figure 201), where arable land was more likely to have been under the kind of pressures of subdivision outlined above. Here we are fortunate that the way in which the information was collected for the cadastres remained much the same between 1531 and 1727. The first cadastre of 1531 was at a fairly high point in the general process of pastoral advance mentioned above. We can only assume that Cipières was little different from other neighbouring communities in responding to the market demand for wool. The 1610 cadastre, however, coincided with a first actual assessment of grazing numbers.[8] These seem to represent something close to the maximum stocking rates both for the flocks of the Cipièrois and those of the seigneur and 'strangers' (Figure 202). Similarly, the 1750 *Declaration des*

Quartier	*1842 Section*	*Altitude (m)*	*1531*	*1610*	*1750*	*% Change*
Faye	E4	1266	81	71	37	- 53
Panagie	A5	1225	73	46	15	- 80
Serre	A4	1270	16	24	22	+ 27
Poumaris	F4	1200	26	32	24	- 8
Aspe	F4	1200	18	21	18	0
Agremourie	G1	1215	44	51	33	- 25
Baumitos	G3	1343	42	24	14	- 67
Roure	G3	1300	27	26	18	- 33
Teil	G5	1165	26	24	15	- 42
Clapoue	F2	1200	37	26	13	- 65
Totals			**390**	**345**	**208**	- 47

FIGURE 200. Plateau *Quartier* land parcels 1531, 1610, 1750

Quartier	*1842 Section*	*Altitude (m)*	*1531*	*1610*	*1750*	*% Change*
Camuero	E1	780	14	11	16	+ 13
Syno	B2	500	59	37	58	- 2
Fontaynos	B2	500	26	26	36	+ 18
Ribiero	B2	480	48	67	56	+ 14
Plantados	B2	720	15	18	8	- 53
Barnoin	D1	730	38	20	22	- 42
Carbounier	D2	800	14	11	10	- 29
Plan	D3	900	73	76	84	+ 13
Combes	D1	720	25	25	31	+ 19
Grabelle	D3	900	18	4	3	- 83
Totals			**330**	**285**	**324**	- 2

FIGURE 201. Lowland *Quartier* land parcels 1531, 1610, 1750

Biens[9] is close enough to the 1763 *Etat de Betail* (when goats were banned) to identify another time of maximised sheep rearing.[10]

In these circumstances, following the argument above, we would be looking for fragmentation of holdings through this period of 220 years, especially lands below the plateau, as population numbers were ostensibly maintained or increased and arable land came under pressure. Such trends could only have continued, one might argue through the period of overgrazing and the banning of goats (see below) in the early 18th century. Here we select for comparison, the numbers of land parcels within a set of sample *quartiers* from cadastres of 1531 and 1610 and the *Declaration de Biens* of 1750.

An increasing significance of grazing certainly seems to reveal itself in the overall reduction in the number of arable parcels of 47% over the period 1531–1750. But this masks considerable variety in the behaviour of individual *quartiers*, from Panagie which has 80% fewer parcels to a steady state in Aspe and even a 27% increase in Serre. Some of this variety may be explained by changes in the attribution of parcels to *quartiers* in the documents. They were afterall without mapped boundaries until 1841. Perhaps an explanation is that on the plateau there was no real contest between graziers and farmers within the village community, at least not those with sizeable flocks of sheep and goats. Whatever systems of grazing control had evolved they had been in place since 'time immemorial' and subject only to locally agreed adjustments. It was with foreign graziers, whose combined flocks were equivalent in size to those of local Cipièrois, that the problem lay. We will also raise the issue of out-migration which was certainly an important aspect of the Cipièrois economy by the 18th century (Chapter 9) and may already have come into play much earlier, making the competition for space between graziers and cultivators much less severe than it might have been.

Below the plateau, where we might assume competition for use was greater, according to the hypothesis presented above, more changes might have been anticipated. There is still evidence of startling variation in the number of parcels within *quartiers*, but in overall terms, with a dip of only 14% between 1531 and 1610, things appear to have altered very little over the whole period. Here things were perhaps managed in terms of the arable system with access for animals rather than a pastoral system with access to farmers, as on the plateau.

So, despite marked changes in the spread of holdings within families, what appears to happen in Cipières is a much more subtle competition for land between three groups: richer villagers with large sheep flocks, poorer villagers with few or no sheep and the *rentier* graziers from outside the community. This in itself did not lead to the kind of impoverishment of the poorest described elsewhere. It is best represented, perhaps, as a continual struggle between those who would cordon off 'their' land for their own use, both for pasture and arable crops, and those who invoked putative common grazing rights 'since time immemorial'. Almost certainly these were not mutually exclusive groups. Specific ownership of land would have complicated the issue of common pasturage and Bloch provides us with evidence that the erosion of these common pasture rights had begun as early as the 15th century if not before. So when the 1609 *Affouagement* observes that '*Cipières consiste de plusiers montagnes capable de donner herbages pour les bestiaux toute l'année ... quartier Calerne seulment reserve de seigneur ... tout la reste du terroir est commun...*' it may have been more than economical with the truth. In fact Calern had 69 parcels of arable land listed in the 1610 cadastre belonging to individual proprietors. Perhaps this was land dedicated to the seigneurial flocks in winter?

So what our findings above seem to confirm is that, by the early 16th century if not earlier, there were real signs of the development of a new set of property relations concentrating on individual household heads and stem family succession of a kind much closer to the *familles élargies* excellently described in a series of seminal papers by Collomp for Haute Provence in the 18th century.[11] At the same time, whatever the situation of arable parcels, pastoralism had assumed a dominant role in the economy; biennial crop rotation and reductions in land set aside for hay pasture characterised this new regime. It may also be that all this apparent ambiguity in the documentation represents a conscious or cultural ambivalence about rights of ownership and use which were in a constant process of negotiation and renegotiation between flock owners, farmers, external graziers and the seigneur, both in short and long-term cycles of use and change, as new patterns of behaviour evolved. Certainly on the plateau and perhaps elsewhere on the lower slopes, concentrating animals in a small space, especially at night, had its benefits for an arable system that placed a heavy reliance on manure from flocks. A rather extreme view of this dependence is provided by the 1750 *Declaration des Biens*[12] inquiry into land and property following the depredations of the War of the Austrian Succession. Respondents treated draught animals and sheep as if they were merely part of the agricultural rather than the pastoral economy. In fact, there are a number of entries which suggest that the sole purpose of keeping sheep was the fertilisation of the soil! These observations by larger property owners, however, give us a clear view of the integrated farming system in which arable farming and pastoralism were closely interlinked by dependence on controlled manuring by managed flocks. Several entries give us an indication as to the method by which this manure was concentrated. The entry for Pierre Vial the First Consul was more specific than most. He claimed that he kept '*7 trenteniers de moutons* [210 sheep] *que je tiens pour langrer (l'engrais) de mes mas*'.[13] Even more explicit was the *notaire,* Jean Baptiste Lambert, who reported a *bergerie* au Quartier de la Boual d'Aussel '*destinée a l'engrai de mes terres …*' and the subsequent special pleading that '*… ne donne autre profit que le peu de fumier de quelles troupeaux qui vont s'y reposer quelques fois par intervalles pendant la nuit ce que n'indemnise pas le taille et l'entretien*'. Similar entries are found for others with the same supplication that the sheep were *exclusively* for the purpose of fertilising the arable land. This must have appeared as nonsense to all but the most gullible taxation official but it signals the relative significance of activities.

It is clear from the shape of dolines and the positioning of shelters that animals were managed into these more cultivable places (see Chapters 3 and 6). In earlier times the smaller peasant flocks (*trenteniers*) would have been herded into smaller dolines for night-time protection, with shepherds and dogs occupying the peripheral shelters. Elsewhere some of the larger dolines and field areas had shelters nearby, but many did not and, as David Austin has shown (Chapter 3), the distribution of *bories* seems much more to do with emergency sheltering in storms or very temporary occupation when the shepherd was stranded by bad weather or darkness rather than anything more deliberate or systematic. The *bergeries* certainly had accommodation and many (but again not all) of the earlier *enclos* had *bories* integrated within them, as in our excavated example in Baoumes de Brun. It is also clear that animals would be likely to graze on the more open limestone landscapes, thereby adding to the quality of the soil developing there. This played an important part in the cropping practice even into the modern period. But the appearance of large *bergeries* coincides with increases in flock size and the appearance of wealthy individual grazier*s* in the 16th or 17th centuries. Some of these flock masters became part of the rural élite of their home villages, the focus for differences of wealth and occupational status which began to emerge within peasant communities throughout the region. Their *bergeries* certainly allowed for managed manure production on a bigger scale. The 1750 *Declaration Des Biens* gives us clear insight into the arable farming system operating at this time with its biennial rotation of parcels, although there were clear differences in the status of property holders (see Chapter 9) with many holdings of less than subistence size.

So the 'land question' in Cipières, which French social and economic historians make so much of elsewhere, even in the south, remained a trade-off between land for pasturing and winter feeding of sheep and goats and land for subsistence cereals. This seems to have applied even to plateau lands, if to a lesser extent, throughout the period. This was certainly not to do with any less pressure on resources from the pastoral sector as we shall now argue. Indeed the significance of this cannot be exaggerated. More significant in terms of the landscape history argument presented in this book it seems that the landscape of property division, terraces, walls and shelters which emerged in the period before and after the Black Death (1000–1531) seems to have remained little changed in subsequent centuries, despite the emergence of individual property rights. As both David Austin and Andrew Fleming make clear in their chapters, much of this early landscape remains as we see it today.

8.7. Pastoralism and animal husbandry in Cipières

Understanding the complex landscape archaeology of Cipières demands meticulous and subtle reading of the traces of at least 1000 years of surprisingly intensive grazing and farming, even on the plateau surfaces. Here, however, we examine the ways in which the grazing flocks of sheep and goats came to dominate both the economy of the two upland surfaces and what David Austin calls 'the architecture or workscape'. This was a dominance given further impetus in the case of our community, by the scale of opportunity created by the Plateau de Calern, an area of 24 km^2. We have presented above something of the ways in which individual property rights emerged to replace the collectivities of occupation implicit in the *ostal* system as described in Chapter 6 and in David Austin's reconstruction of the holdings in Baoume de Brun (Chapter 3). Now we look at the ways in which richer peasants responded to the commercial expansion of sheep rearing by acquiring large flocks themselves.

The ravaged and relatively barren landscapes of Cipières today are grazed by a flock of no more than 1000 sheep and perhaps 30 goats. There are no cattle, no horses, no mules. It is an effort of real imagination to envisage the area as pasturage for very large flocks of sheep and goats not to speak of hay pastures for a herd of browsing animals (cattle, donkeys, mules, horses). Sclafert tells us that by 1471[14] there were more sheep in this whole region than ever before *or since* (my italics)'. Yet there is evidence that for much of the historical period,

Date	*1609*	*1763*	*1791/3*	*1829*	*1838*	*1860*	*1902*
Cipèrois' sheep	9000	6240	4440	3000	5250	4950	1400
Seigneurial sheep	3000?	4000?	4110	–	–	–	–
Merchant graziers' sheep	8000	8550	?	3000	5000	–	–
Sheep (total)	20000	19085	8550	6000	12500	4950	1400
Goats	–	700	450	1829	2000	300	?
Cattle	150	9	–	–	2	1	–
Donkeys/mules	200	265	?	227	244	149	–

FIGURE 202. Numbers of animals in Cipières 1609–1902[15]

the number of sheep and goats within the territory of Cipières at any one time is likely to have exceeded 20,000 animals and that at the same time at least until the 17th century hay crops were taken (Figure 202) to feed perhaps 200 cows and oxen and similar numbers of mules, donkeys and horses.

It is also clear that restrictions were placed to hold down the numbers of grazing animals, particularly goats, from as early as the 14th century.[16] From the period of the earliest surviving records, as Rosamond Faith points out in Chapter 5, authorities restricted peasant families to flocks of no more than 30 animals (a *trententier*), and this may have been governed by the numbers easily managed by a dog and a shepherd at night time. It is possible that evidence of the management practices of this period are preserved in the doline walls, entrances, enclosures and corbelled shelters which characterise these upper surfaces.

The documentary evidence of the Cipières archives, together with regional sources, provides a real insight into the impact of animal husbandry and its effects on the environment. Four competing forces were at work here: first the demands of subsistence which were a product of the loose and often competitive aspirations of the poor majority; second the drive for profit on the part of seigneurs, the merchant graziers, some of whom were Cipièrois; third the interest of the seigneurs in protecting opportunities for commercial grazing and for hunting; and finally, there were the related interests of a nascent State, anxious to preserve the depleting assets of woodland, a conservationist urge which increased in proportion to the demand for marine timber to serve the needs of an expanding navy.

If at first the raising of sheep for wool went alongside those of the needs of the village society, the rapid growth described by some economic historians as 'the first commercial revolution' in the two centuries before the Black Death (in 1348) was very much driven by the trade in wool and cloth. Indeed the growth of towns and commercial interests in this early phase of the development was intimately related to this expanding market for wool. If a *trentenier* was at first a restriction, as the demand for wool pressed on supply, it later became merely a measure of flock size. Both Duby and Sclafert draw on early archival sources to make a case for the rapid overstocking of all southern upper pastures by sheep and goats by flocks belonging not only to local people but increasingly to nobles and merchants from lowlands who rented pasturage from them and their seigneurs.[17] By 1300, Duby quotes a figure of 20,000 sheep in the Provençale *bailliages* of St Maxime and Barjols and writes of communities 'groaning under the weight of the flocks of seigneurs and graziers', commenting that even by this time 'most upland pastures in the southern Alps were 'over-run and overgrazed'.[18]

Although we have no specific comparable figure for the Cipières plateau for this earliest period of expansion, it is unlikely to have been much different. Sclafert writes that 'the area behind Nice was noticeable for this expansion' and we assume Cipières to lie within this zone. This may have complemented the developments in Italy (Genoa, Milan and Florence). There is every likelihood that this earliest wool production in the thirteenth century, served the concentration of cloth manufacture focussed on Baucaire, just to the south-west of Cipières.

Using records from the 14th and 15th centuries Timbal[19] gives us our first real insight into the workings of the system in this region at this time. Within constraints on flock numbers supposedly imposed by the village councils regarding rights of common pasturage for village flocks, the heads of households (or *feu)* whose names appear in the first listings of inhabitants were able to take out contracts for pasturage '*toute l'annee*'. Two seasons were distinguished: summer and winter. *Hivernage* (*vuernalha)* extended from Epiphany until the first of May and *estivage* (*stivalha*) from the feast of St Madeleine to the Feast of St Michel. Dues were paid for pasturage of flocks of sheep at Christmas and for lambs and kids at either the beginning of Lent or at Easter. Clauses in agreements commonly forbade the introduction of transhumance flocks of strangers (***étrangères***). They also gave permission to shepherds to 'burn' (*incendie*) part of the pastures to improve them, and sometimes there were rights to use woods for firewood and buildings. Sometimes the village assembly approached the seigneur to establish the location of a pasturage. There seem to have been two shearings each year at the end of each of these periods of pasturage for there are specific references in these records to the number of ***éleveurs*** 'coming down from the mountains of Cipières' to sell their wool in Grasse both in May and at the end of autumn. Sometimes specific agreements were entered into for the purchase of wool in advance of shearing. These details give us a real sense of the pressure to produce as much wool as possible for the growing urban markets.

With lands throughout the plateau also open for arable farming the organisation of both activities must have taxed local ingenuities. If the testimony of subsequent bans and restrictions is to be believed, the struggle between the subsistence and semi-subsistence demands of poorer villagers and the growing commercial interests of the seigneurial flocks and those of graziers, both within and outside the community, is intimately connected to the ensuing overgrazing of this environment. It is a struggle which changed its character as more village families became involved in the production of woollen goods and their distribution. Despite persistent attempts by the authorities, both local and regional, to limit the overgrazing of pastures,[20] the complex six-year rotation of arable and fallow of the late Middle Ages, explained by Rosamond Faith in Chapter 5, had provided for a regime of both spring and autumn sowings of grains and pulses and production of the hay crops of winter feed for browsing animals. This had disappeared certainly by the late 16th century and probably much earlier, in favour of a biennial regime of spring-sown crops separated by fallow, a system which left half the arable lands of the community under fallow in any one year. In this way it was possible to further increase the size of sheep and goat flocks which grazed the plateau 'throughout the year'.[21]

It is testimony to the persistence of need, that a small area of hay pasture was still being specifically reserved to feed browsing animals which needed to be stalled in winter. Even as late as 1609, these lower pastures, were able to support a herd of up to 150 cows and oxen, particularly in the *quartier* Bourdelieres which is used as a '*pre de faucher d'un premier foin et la moisson de bled est permis respectivement aux habitants de introduire leur bétail même dans toutes les terres sauf le pred du seigneur*'.[22] In 1531, whatever the situation earlier, it was the *quartiers* mostly lower down in the parish, close to the village and down by the river Loup, which were specifically devoted to a hay crop. By the 18th century, however, while most families retained an ass or donkey, only the seigneur and one or two richer villagers kept larger browsers.

How was it possible for this increase in animal numbers without a concomitant pressure on arable land to the point of *morcellement* as seems to have been the case elsewhere? There was clearly a reduction in productivity as rotation practices moved from more complicated autumn and spring cropping below the plateau, to a biennial rotation everywhere. But we have argued earlier in this chapter that was not, it seems, a question of being starved onto smaller and smaller plots of land as the grazier-rich became richer and the grazier-poor became poorer. This may have been the case on the plateau but elsewhere the number of parcels seems to have remained much the same. We argue that the answer to this conundrum is to be sought in the social and economic ethos of the community. Early commerce in wool created options *within* the *ostal* system, both for raising capital and for migration through the networks of transhumance from early times (not unlike the Pyrenees). These options must have persisted and developed into more sophisticated commercial enterprises in later periods as markets expanded. What we find is that, although a considerable fraction of the proprietors in 1531 had not the means of subsistence from arable land, they could still rely on the support of senior kinsmen, enriched by their larger flocks, to work either on their lands or as shepherds, or in the expanding commerce of the region. So there is a strong case for arguing that for Cipières, sheep provided a way to instrument the expansion of population by moving to biennial rotations, leaving land for winter grazing, and by developing commercial links with the wider world to absorb the labour which was surplus to requirements. As time went on, the significance of the sheep-based economy was increasingly reflected in the social and economic structure of the rural community (see Chapter 9).

By 1763 the distinctions between those who had flocks and those with only a few animals were very clear. Almost all significant flocks of sheep were in the hands of a few individuals. All were from old-established Cipières families. In 1791 an Etat du Betail lists 4240 sheep and 199 goats. An Etat des Citoyens in 1793 registers 3590 sheep. They were owned by 30 flock masters with the largest flocks of more than 200 animals still owned by major families (Florys, Lamberts, Girards, Vials and Bourellys). In 1793 a Registre de Betail gives us 24 flock masters but now there were 8550 sheep grazing on what was now redefined as the common lands (*communuaux*)[23] of Cipières. For the first time there is a record of pasture land held by 'Panisse à Aix' the seigneur and some indication as to where flocks were being pastured (Sections A–F on the 1841 cadastre) with the area of pasture calculated in *cannes*. The Panisse pastures in sections ABE comprised 190,919 *cannes*. His flock is not specified (presumably incorporated into the communal flock) but comparing other pasture areas and associated flock sizes specified in the return, his flock almost certainly exceeded a thousand animals. There is some evidence from a listing of shepherds in 1794 that these were driven off to the south to form what was called a 'national flock'.

The Revolution released the Cipièrois still labouring under the constraints of ancient privilege and increasing taxation. But the respite was quite temporary. With the Restoration, the noble family Panisse was again represented as major flock owners, and by the 1830s it had the largest flocks, once more occupying 190,000 *cannes* of pasture. This represented an opportunity to graze over a 1000 sheep at a time when the total village flock was 5272 sheep and 1829 goats! Pasturing numbers were maintained at similar levels in the early years of the 19th century, but goat numbers began to dominate with the decline in the demand for wool. Although the grazing economy persisted through much of the rest of the 19th century, the numbers of animals and those involved in managing them declined rapidly thereafter. By the end of the century there were only around 1000 sheep and 200 goats in Cipières, and numbers have not increased since that time, a far cry from 'time immemorial' with flocks of over 20,000 animals grazing the lands of the community.

A few farmers continued to grow grain crops into the 20th century, but the decline of the old system of occupation based on biennial fallows, seems to trace a similar line. In 1793 there were still 180 *cultivateurs* who claimed to be growing crops, the same number as half a century earlier. They still produced 9835 *quintaux* of grain, mainly the old faithfuls of *froment* (53%) and *meteil* (40%) with the rest comprising a little oats, barley and rye as it always had done over the previous millennium. And at this point the landscape must have looked much the same as it had in earlier centuries. Indeed, even the returns for the 1841 *cadastre* reveal much the same picture, despite the growing evidence of decline and absentee proprietorship. After this time, however, the decline in both pastoral and arable farming was exponential. In the early 20th century only 364 hectares of land were farmed for cereals. In the 1920s a third of this acreage survived, concentrated on the best and most easily worked lowlands. By this time, the remaining population lived in a relict landscape of deserted parcels and what was effectively a token flock of sheep and goats. The slow and tentative revival of population in the last few decades has depended on the forces released by a post-industrialising society with the affluence and leisure to spend on second homes and on increasingly rapid transportation to take people in search of wildscapes.

CHAPTER NINE

Population, Economy and Society 1531–1900

David Siddle

This chapter points to increasing social and economic differentiation in the early modern period. For the 18th century, detailed demographic evidence, elicited from vital event records of the village and the cadastral inventories, are used to make the case for a differentiated social and economic structure. By this time a core population of permanent resident families of ménagers, *merchants and craftsmen married early and raised large families. They formed about a third of those listed in the taxation documents. The remaining two thirds were either temporary or semi-permanent migrants.*

9.1. Introduction

The changes outlined in the previous chapter were taking place against a background of social and economic disturbance which was reflected in the general slowing down in population growth that characterised much of the 17th century, a period of economic decline in France as a whole. It was reflected in the inflated grain prices and the anarchy which accompanied the wars of the Fronde in the mid-century.[1] This was also the period of the Little Ice Age (see Figure 186) and there were famines throughout the middle years of the century: in 1630 and then in 1649–52, 1661–62 and again in 1693–94.[2] At this time there were revisitations of the Plague. Infant mortality in France rose to 50%, and life expectancy was no higher than 30 years.

Given these circumstances it is not surprising to find that in Cipières, as in many of the villages of the region, the expansion of the society in the 16th century (perhaps still reflected in the numbers of *feu* in the 1610 cadastre), had also effectively ended by that time. Indeed in the cadastres which survive for 1633 and 1640 there is no evidence of any effective increase in population. The changes that were taking place were to do with a lessening of the constraints of feudal society. The restrictive laws governing textile work, relaxed in the

15th century, allowed the class of merchants and drapers which had established themselves in the village in the 16th century to develop further. Such people were clearly evident in the social and economic class structure of Cipières in the seventeenth century. In 1633 there were 252 proprietors, but a number of them were identified as outsiders (from Vence, Biot and Grasse for example) and a clear village élite seems to have been emerging. This consisted of powerful and more affluent villagers from the old *ostal* structures, like the Flory *Beaumons* who, as we have seen in Chapter 8, had already begun to separate themselves from the others as reflected in the hierarchy of taxation in 1531. There were also notaries like the Lamberts who had settled in the village in the 15th century and prospered thereafter as well as some other newcomers. In 1633 total taxes ranged from a single florin to 2051 florins. The top three quintiles, above 820 florins, were occupied by a composite group of locals and incomers: officials, notaries and merchants from nearby towns. There was an expatriate Cipièrois, Raymond Giraud, who was now a '*bourgeois d'Antibes*' and who had two houses in the Place and '*un pigeonnier au jardin*'. In this group there were also two court officials (*roufoulgiers de la cour de Grasse*) all living in either the prestigious new Place or the new street (the Bourgade) leading southwards from it (see Chapter 2). Their precise functions in the village are not always clear from the cadastral survey, but we may assume they were managing the burgeoning wool and textile economy (see Chapter 8). There are also two villagers in this category living in houses 'outside the castrum', one of whom, as we have seen, was a Flory *Beaumon,* the seigneurial bailiff. Twelve others from the village paid between 400 and 800 florins, a 'middling sort' which included a shop keeper and two lawyers. Five of them had the title 'Monsieur'.

Despite the demographic crises of the last half of the century in France as a whole there is some evidence that economic conditions in the south stabilised. It seems that by the end of the century the population of Cipières had risen again to reach levels achieved some two centuries earlier. An *Affouagement* for 1698 indicates that at this time there were 267 '*chefs de maison*' living in or occupying 188 inhabited houses. This would yield a population of perhaps 1300 (close to the medieval maximum). If they were all present at any one time it would certainly have placed some pressure on the housing stock, leading to the apartment sub-divisions which were a feature of the next century, if not already part of the response before this time. Apartments were certainly much in evidence in the first 18th-century cadastre of 1727 and the *Declaration des Biens* of 1750. In both documents neighbours are frequently identified as living not only '*a côte*' but '*dessus*' and '*dessous*', clear indications of occupancy by rooms and the addition of floors identified by architectural survey in the Rue Longue (see Figure 68).

The step I am taking here is to identify a last stage in the process, which must also have been replicated in other areas sharing a similar experience of settlement evolution, namely the final moves from the mind-set of collective occupation to individual property rights. As I have argued in Chapter 8 this was a transition from *ostal* modes of thinking and behaviour to patrilineal inheritance systems and eventually to the well-documented evolution from stem family to modern nuclear family which was a feature of life in the uplands of Provence by the same period.[3] What I propose here is that our sources can only allow us to envisage an often uneasy and uneven evolution. Wool provided a chance for richer peasants to step away from subsistence and into a life of commerce and proto-industrialisation with the emergence and gradual dominance of three associated developments: a more open market for land, the growth of a culture of economic migration and the marketing and manufacturing opportunities provided by sheep ownership. Cadastral records reveal that, by the 18th century, a system had fully evolved in which land and title to taxable property passed between families through a variety of operands, including dowries, sales and even rental arrangements. There was much for the village notaries to do. If in earlier periods before and even after *incastellamento,* families maintained land in the same *quartiers* through generations to the point of 'time immemorial,' in the last chapter we saw the ways in which relict features of this behaviour still manifested themselves. David Austin has shown for a particular *quartier* (Chapter 3) the process by which older *ostal* contiguities disappeared and land changed hands so frequently that a *quartier* map of land owners was completely altered over two or three generations. This may also be reflected in the considerable changes in the number of parcels in each *quartier* over a similar period (see Chapter 8).

So at the end of the 17th century we find a community going through important social changes and already showing some marked differentiation in status and wealth. It would also seem to be bursting at the seams at a time when economic opportunities, within the wider economy, were opening in the towns and cities of southern France. At the dawn of the 18th century Cipières, with its developing sheep and textile economy, was poised to become part of a rapidly modernising world.

9.2. The 18th century: an early modern economy and society

As we reach towards the richer records of the first half of the 18th century, we approach a society of apparently quite puzzling contradictions. On the one hand we can discern a community in which main core families appeared to survive and prosper. We have also seen that in the 17th century, despite economic and social malaise elsewhere, Cipières showed some evidence of growing prosperity. Alongside this prosperity one can also see some evidence of social and economic instability in the rest of the village society. Of the 32 family names which appeared in listings after the Plague period and which persisted until 1840, 23 (72%) appeared after 1600 (see Figure 188). This new injection seems to be reflected in rising fertility in the region as a whole, where upland areas in particular showed persistently higher birth and survival rates than in the lowlands.[4] It also signalled the end of the dominant influence of the older extended kinship families, because the changing character of family names reflected not just an influx of newcomers, but a much more fluid society

If some new families came into the village and stayed, others seem to have been in Cipières for no more than a generation or two, rather as they did in the less stable villages of the lowland areas. In fact a significant proportion (28% of incomers), appear in the cadastral record after 1531 only to disappear again within the period of 200 years. It seems that by the 18th century, this was a new and much more open society and one which was expanding rapidly. Indeed, the first 18th-century cadastre[5] for Cipières in 1727 seems to point to a settlement which was bursting at the seams. The document lists 293 *propriétaires* occupying land and buildings in Cipières. Only 75 of them (26%) were listed as single house owners, the rest were occupying either parts of houses, rooms or apartments or had no independent dwelling indicated at all! If the '*propriétaire*' entry in the register was equivalent to a stem or nuclear family, in the sense of the now more relevant coefficient of around 5 per household (see Chapter 6) this would give us a total population of over 1450! So an initially pessimistic view would be that, in a period when the old family coherences were breaking down, the 18th-century village appeared to have become, in large measure, a community of impoverished apartment dwellers.

Certainly the village accounts and council minutes throughout the 18th century present a community apparently living largely on credit and close to penury (Figure 203). This is not surprising, as French historians point to this whole period as one of particular distress throughout the region. Again it is Le Roy Ladurie[6] who presents us with the best account of the difficult years of the early 18th century, a period of longer winters and harvest failures which characterised the surge in the Little Ice Age (see Figure 186). The natural

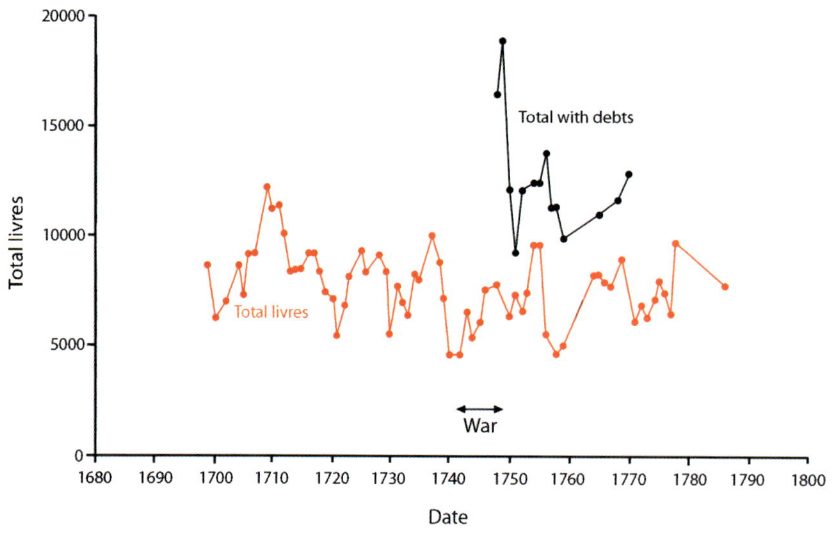

FIGURE 203. Cipières during the War of Succession: graph of tax indebtedness and total tax revenue

response to these forces in mountain areas was crisis out-migration. Indeed Braudel refers to these Alpine regions as 'human factories pouring out their penurious excess populations each winter' onto the plains.[7]

Cipières was ostensibly no different to many other alpine and sub-alpine communities in this regard. The pages of the council *Délibérations* in this period would seem to confirm a perception of a famine-threatened community. A record of 1719, for example, claims that two-thirds of the village population 'left each winter to seek sustenance elsewhere'.[8] Winter out-migration was certainly a tradition among textile workers in this region, men and women ('*les gavots*'), from at least the 13th century, and was part of the long and changing response as opportunities for work in towns developed whether in trade, services or crafts.[9] But this was nonetheless a sizeable proportion of the Cipières population even allowing for a measure of exaggeration.

During this period there were certainly incentives to migrate. Despite apparent economic hardship, the tax burden, based on property and land (used or unused) remained constant. With fewer people around to pay taxes on a regular basis, the burden fell on residents and the level of borrowing increased exponentially over the eighteenth century. Community debts, which were large at the beginning of the century,[10] were still large by its close. Economic distress among the poorest was not likely to have been improved by the ban on goat keeping in the 1730s, which was not lifted until 1770. The community also had to face the depredations of the War of the Austrian Succession (1741–48) which resulted in the billeting in Cipières of the armies of several states over a 6-year period.[11] It was during this period, in the middle years of the century, that village records are explicit in claiming a community in the last stages of penury. When the War of the Austrian Succession drew to a close, it was claimed that Cipières was left in a state '*ruinée par l'enemi de l'état soumise dans une bananité ... subsiter a son affouagement ...*' with debts of 15,679 *livres* (twice the annual total budget) and facing the first of three major demographic crises which occurred in 1747, 1750 and 1763, as a side effect of penury and army occupations.[12]

I would argue, however, that this sorry story presents a very partial picture of life in Cipières at this time. Indeed there are clear signs of an over-egged pudding! First, the archival record is rich in evidence of opportunities for work in commerce, trade, services and industry within and outside the village. I have pointed in the introduction to this chapter to evidence of social and economic change in the 17th century. By the 18th century a new proto-industrial society was much more clearly evident, as urban markets developed for more sophisticated fabrics and work was put out for winter activity in many villages and small towns in the region. There were demands for carders, spinners and weavers to keep pace with changes. Setting aside those who called themselves *travailleurs* (day labourers, journeymen) who numbered 135 in the 1727 cadastre, the number of *propriétaires* with designated crafts and trades (carders, weavers, spinners, cloth makers, tailors, glove makers, carpenters, shepherds, merchants) and professions (notaries, surgeons, bourgeois) increased from 33 in 1727 to 47 by the first effective census in 1806[13] (Figure 204). It is also likely that some failed to identify themselves for tax collection purposes. A further indication of the significance of these changes is that in the vital event registers of the turn of the 18th century[14] occupational identifiers of this kind were rare, yet by the mid-century and beyond they were commonplace.

So changes in the character of the economy both seem to have led to, and been made possible by, quite complex demographic responses. To unravel this story it is necessary to reach beyond the accepted methodologies of family and demographic history to explore some of the character of the vital event registers of this period.

Occupations	*1727*	*1750*	*1806*
Travailleurs	135	?	58
Ménagers	39	?	40
Bergers	13	14	27
Tisseurs de toile	4	4	1
Tisserands	6	–	–
Tailleurs des habits	1	5	2
Cardeurs de laine	6	2	2
Facturiers de laine	–	2	–
Faisseur d'etoffe	–	1	–
Marchands	2	1	–
Marachals de fer	2	2	3
Menuisiers	–	–	3
Macons	2	1	2
Cordonnier	1	–	–
Chirurgiens	2	2	3
Notaires	2	2	5

FIGURE 204. Designated crafts trades and professions 1727, 1750, 1806

9.3. Economic migration and its impact on fertility

Using and adapting techniques pioneered by Michel Fleury and Louis Henri in the late 1950s, historical demographers have been working on European vital event registers for more than 50 years.[15] After numerous reconstitutions of community populations, they have revealed the character of what they have termed the 'normal' European marriage pattern. This generalises fertility behaviour over much of north-western Europe in the pre-industrial period.[16] The main demographic feature associated with this phenomenon was a slow population increase, managed by intermittent, but often persistent, restrictions on the age of marriage (normally around 25–6 for women) and by birth spacing which was controlled by poor diet and breast feeding (lactational amenorrhoea). This gave an average of only approximately 15 fertile years of marriage to a woman who survived the rigours of childbirth and infectious diseases. If we add to this picture the declining natural fertility as women

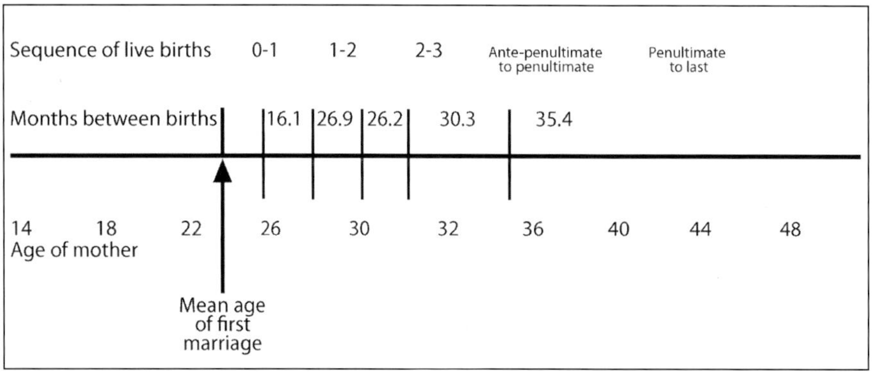

FIGURE 205. Norms of fertility in 18th century France

moved towards (in modern terms) a relatively early menopause at around 40 years old, this left a maximum potential number of about seven or eight live births over a fertile married period of 15 years. Evidence from a wide range of French reconstitutions, which show extending periods between penultimate and last birth, the realistic expectation would be around five live births (Figure 205). With infant mortality at close to 50% in this period there was a good chance that only half of these offspring would survive. In other words, most semi-subsistent families of this largely rural society might sustain four or five offspring, but would be seriously embarrassed by seven or eight. Infant mortality rates for those that did so were exacerbated by a frequently inadequate diet. But new impulses in the economy (especially involving proto-industries associated with wool, as in Cipières) provided work even for small fingers, and with this, and a cash income, there was earlier marriage and therefore rising fertility in societies with a proto-industrial dimension.[17]

The evidence from which these deductions emerge is the product of long and painstaking re-constitutions of demographic behaviour from good sequences of vital event registrations for whole communities. It is these data which provide the averages and percentages of statistical analysis. As a way of pointing to trends it is useful enough, as I will now show, but unfortunately they reveal very little about migrant behaviour.[18] Yet as I have argued above, in any period of rising birth rates and better survival and with increasing opportunity for work in the urban sector as in the 18th century, the impulse to migrate was obviously strong.[19] The answer seems to be that migration in some mountain areas was not merely a response to local food crises, as it was as late as the 17th century in some areas, but became part of a quite diverse pattern of social and economic behaviour involving manufacture, services, trade and commerce.[20] The character of these rural societies was further altered by money coming back from members of families working 'abroad'. Dowries and marriage portions became available to those who would otherwise have had to delay or indefinitely postpone marriage.[21] So the overall effect would have been to reduce the average age of first marriage, even for those with no other strings to the bow. Finding ways of exposing this potential set of demographic responses became the key to understanding migration behaviour in Cipières.

By concentrating attention on migration, analysis of even patchy vital event registers (as in the case of Cipières) proved instructive. Family reconstructions (rather than a full reconstitution) were undertaken for the whole of the period 1691–1772, the period for which vital event registers survive. Here attention is directed to fertility behaviour by focusing on 800 marriages and records of subsequent births. With all the frustrations of broken sequences in the records, particularly of marriages, analysis nonetheless revealed something of the diverse demographic behaviour posited above and provided some interesting insights into what at first might appear to be the rather curious demographic responses of the Cipières community. To set against any estimates based on household multipliers using tax returns (which, as I have pointed out above, suggest a

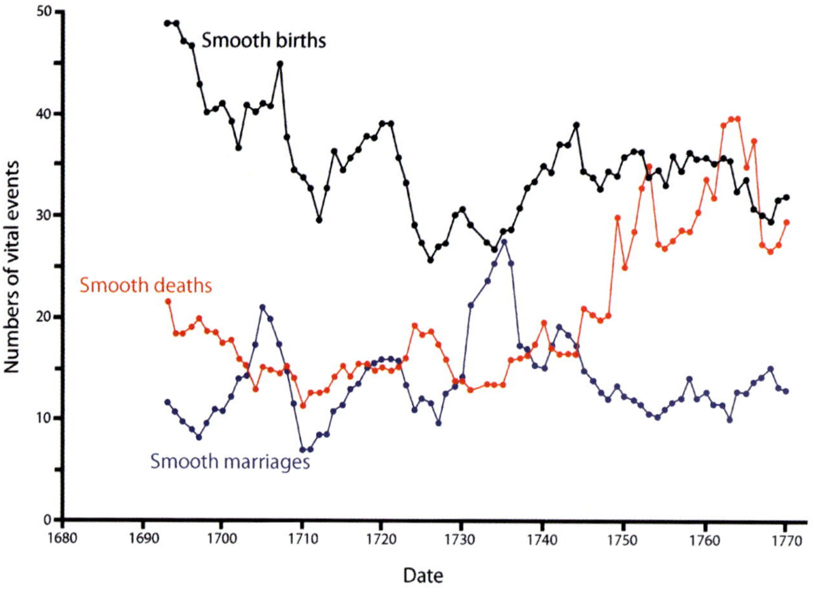

FIGURE 206. Cipières: vital events 1692–1772

buoyant population during this period), this examination and analysis of the registers of births reveals an apparent overall *decline* in fertility between 1691 and 1740. This is, of course, the usual indicator of a falling population (Figure 206). From a high point of between 47 and 60 births per annum at the end of the 17th century, the trend of the graph, despite some recoveries, persisted downwards towards a minimum of around 30 births per annum in the period between 1725 and 1740. After this there is another recovery to an average of around 35 births per annum until the late 1760s. At the same time the mean age of first marriages (MAFM) was lower than European norms, a characteristic which should produce rising fertility. With admittedly rather few records to rely on in the earlier period, because of missing marriage records, we can see the mean age of first marriage for women drifts upwards from a low 17.5 years old in the 1720s to just under 22 in the period between 1740 and 1772 (Figure 207). This was still low by the measure of the European marriage pattern but closer to the behaviour of other groups in the region.[22] How far is this phenomenon attributable to out-migration?

What is clear is that, while recorded marriages fluctuated around an average of 12 *per annum* and the overall trend in fertility showed marked variation over the period 1691–1772, the pattern of conceptions was more surprising. Working with the initial hypothesis that migration was, as stated above, characterised by

FIGURE 207. Cipières: Mean Age at First Marriage 1720–1772

	Men			*Women*	
Period	*Mean age at marriage*	*Total Births to marriages*		*Mean age at marriage*	*Total Births to marriages*
1720–1725	17.75	8		17.5	19
1733–1742	24.6	30		20.5	44
1743–1752	23.6	42		21.5	60
1753–1762	26.7	70		21.8	77
1763–1772	25.1	70		21.7	76

crisis out-migration in winter and a return for spring and summer agricultural activity, it was surprising to find that over the period 1691–1735 the general trend in the number of conceptions in the periods from April–September was, in fact, actually falling from a more expected near 30 *per annum* in 1691 to only 10 *per annum* in the early 1730s. So when the received wisdom (supported by the village council!) would have us assume that most people were occupying their marriage beds as returning summer migrants they were, in fact, still out and about. During the same period of years, winter conceptions (October–March) remained relatively consistent. So after a period in the late seventeenth and early 18th centuries when summer conceptions exceeded those of the winter (as one might expect of a society whose inhabitants were expected to de-camp for winter work), the trend is replaced by a marked preponderance of *winter* conceptions which persisted through the period 1715–1750. In other words, for a significant cumulative period of the record (1715–1748; 1757–1761) autumn and winter conceptions actually *exceeded* those for the summer months. It seems, therefore, that migrants who, according to village administrators in 1719, 'normally' returned in May or June[23] were not doing so in any numbers during this period. Clearly the pattern of migration was more complicated, although village officials may have been reporting what was more common behaviour in the 17th century and as part of a plea for reductions in taxation (Figure 208).

Against a generally downward movement in births, this trend line also seems to show us that it was perhaps the group of permanent residents of the village who maintained the population (and who, for those without remittances, struggled to pay taxes!) during this period. This would certainly be true when those who went away for work did not return on a regular basis in either spring

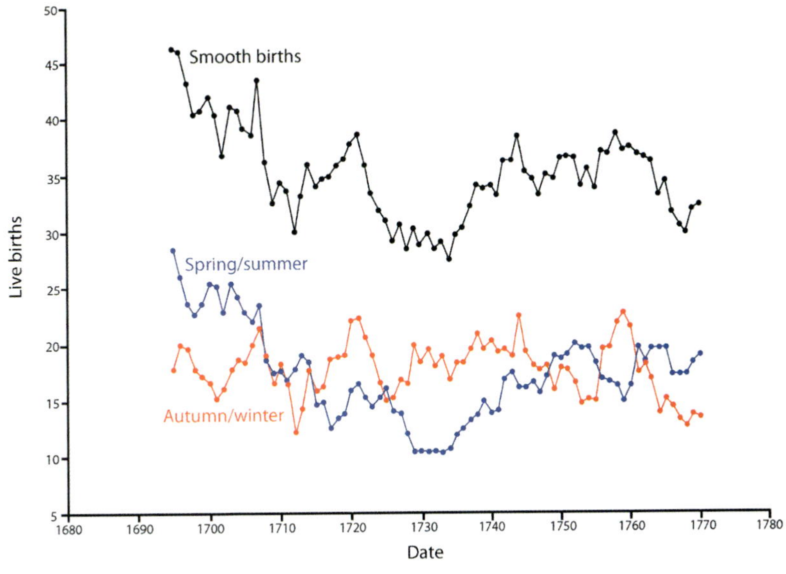

FIGURE 208. Cipières: seasonal conceptions and births 1692–1772

or summer, as their antecedents may have been doing in the late 17th and early 18th centuries. What we may be identifying is a period when circular, or seasonal, migration turned into something else and that this 'something else' reflected changing opportunities for permanent work. If this was the case then we might expect this behaviour to change again during and after the War of Austrian Succession in the 1740s and through the middle decades of the century when a more economically variable situation developed and there were fewer opportunities for work away from the village.

What we seem to be identifying is the development of at least two broad groups of families: a group who basically were resident in the village throughout their fertile lives, but who might also be absent for short periods of time. They conceived their children at no particular time of the year and provided the framework of the village society. A second group was responding to, or devising, dynamic migration strategies and followed the call of different social and economic opportunities. These opportunities varied according to family status, age, point in the life cycle, and economic and political circumstances of the wider world. Closer examination of the family reconstructions for Cipières revealed just how diverse this economic and social behaviour might be, both between families and over time.

In the light of this distinction between stayers and movers we can begin to distinguish whole categories of behaviour from the family reconstructions. This evidence allows comparison between the 'normal' birth spacings within the fertile marriages of the group of permanent or semi-permanent residents, and those marriages which show a much more diverse pattern of fertility.

Working from 807 family reconstructions, 10-year cohorts were assembled first of those brides who went on to complete a full fertility cycle, from menarche to menopause, with regular live births to signal persistent presence in the village of both partners. Then the fertility behaviour of individual women who appeared in our records less regularly or more briefly was examined. This group included a sizable fraction whose marriages appear to have been at least technically 'infertile', in that they make no further appearance in records.[24]

This approach is admittedly most useful in capturing the behaviour of the first broad group, those who regularly appear in the birth records in a full fertility cycle of 20 or more years. But by assuming unrestricted opportunity for conception when the marriage bed was occupied, it is possible to examine these fertility profiles as a surrogate for migration behaviour of one or even both partners.

We can further refine the second of these two groups, (the more frequent migrants) by making a somewhat arbitrary division between periodic short term migrants whose offspring appear in our records at least every 3 years and those demonstrating longer apparent absences. It is possible in this way to divide fertility behaviour into four categories representing degrees of presence or absence in the community (Figure 209). These are:

i) *permanent and semi-permanent residents* with normal or fairly normal birth spacing throughout fertile period, and to these can be added periodic shorter term migrants with more patchy, but nonetheless persistent, fertility;
ii) *longer-term periodic migrants* who demonstrate more intermittent fertility and lengthy periods of apparent 'sterility';
ii) *semi-permanent* migrants whose unions produce one offspring soon after marriage only to disappear from subsequent records; and
iv) the *apparently sterile marriages* with no recorded offspring. This category remains rather more uncertain as a surrogate for migration, as indeed does the previous category of marriages, some of whom may have proved their fertility on only one occasion but remained in the village. Nevertheless, the broad parameters of these figures are revealing.

While admitting that the margin for error of interpretation increases with the number of years between recorded births (and is obviously highest for those marriages which record no births at all!), analysis of 10-year cohorts for the years between 1691 and 1750 reveals something of the character of this population during the years when migration behaviour may have changed most radically (Figure 209).

The group of long-term residents who formed the core of the village (category 1) are thus seen to have represented 16–35% of unions in particular cohort periods, with the highest number (34.7%) during the years when I have already postulated that migration was curtailed by war (1741–1750). The

Category	**Attributes**
1. Consistent fertility **or** broken birth spacing	**Permanent resident** cohabitation: full fertile period. Intermittent but persistent fertility, with periodic absences if one or two years or less = **short-term periodic migration.**
2. Inconsistent fertility	Birth spacing of three years or more through full fertile period =**long-absence cyclic migration.**
3. Marriages with only one recorded child.	Early death of one or both spouses or **permanent migration.**
4. Marriages with no recorded births	Infertile marriages **or** death of one spouse **or permanent migration** of one or both spouses

Number of marriages in each category

	1691-1700	1701-1710	1711-1720	1721-1730	1731-1740	1741-1750
1.	**23 (22.9)**	**34 (24.7)**	**42 (36.6)**	**19 (15.8)**	**46 (26.6)**	**55 (34.7)**
2.	**39 (37.1)**	**57 (41.3)**	**24 (20.9)**	**33 (27.5)**	**40 (23.1)**	**29 (18.4)**
3.	**11 (10.2)**	**22 (16.0)**	**33 (28.7)**	**38 (32.0)**	**60 (34.7**	**(35 (22.3)**
4.	**31 (29.5)**	**25 (18.1)**	**16 (13.9)**	**30 (25.0)**	**27 (15.6)**	**38 (24.2)**
Totals	**105**	**138**	**115**	**120**	**173**	**157**

Figures in brackets = percentages

FIGURE 209. Cipières: fertility behaviour and long-term residents

groups (categories 3 and 4) whose marriages were followed by longer periods of apparent absence (infertility or sterility), comprised never less than a third of those who married in Cipières, and for one cohort in the particularly difficult years 1721–1730 and 1731–1740 57% and 50% respectively. One can only assume that a very considerable proportion of these marriages were between people for whom the village was a very temporary base for one or both partners: that any children they may have had were raised outside Cipières and did not return to marry in the village.

Having established the parameters of our approach, it is the purpose here to use sample demographic and cadastral records of the individual families taken from the first two of these categories to shed light on the character of this increasingly differentiated society. In what follows, this analysis is allowed to colour our view of a community which was deeply influenced, from the mid seventeenth century if not before, by the changing opportunities for manufacture, trade and commerce both in the village and in the wider world. We are thus able to examine the evidence of the tidal wash of these elements as they created a village society with increasingly permeable strata.

At the head of village society was the seigneur and his family (the Panisses in the 18th century) and their retainers: a bailiff, forest and game guards. In the absence of accessible archives this family and any insight into the way they managed their lands and animals remained hidden from our view until we have a glimpse of their affairs in the Revolutionary period and in the nineteenth century. These records confirmed what we suspected: a persistent absence from the village. It seemed that by the 18th century, if not before, the château had long been more or less deserted with the seigneur living in Aix-en-Provence close to the princely court.

Below the *seigneur* there was a village élite: a group made up of the permanently resident families identified in the analysis above and first and foremost comprising those *ménagers* from ancient *ostals* who had large flocks of sheep and many land parcels. To these must be added the *notaires* who had been resident accumulators in the village for at least 200 years of managed property transfers and their own accumulating assets in land and property. Finally in this group were the incomers with their interests in trade, commerce and the professions. They all tended to hold one or more substantial houses in the village and also to rent apartments to others.

Below them in the hierarchy were a 'middling sort', who occupied niches in craft occupations, held some land and animals but who were drawn into trading activities outside the village. Many aspired to become members of the permanently resident élite as they slipped into the shoes of their fathers or uncles or made good marriages. They occupied either smaller houses or parts of houses and they merged at critical times, when things were tight, with the lowest group, the itinerant labourers (*travailleurs*) who sometimes made it into the class above them. It was they who rented apartments consisting of one or two rooms and served in any capacity for which cash or kind might change hands. They were lucky to hold more than a parcel or two of land. This group included junior cadets and their partners, third and fourth sons and daughters, or the children of poorer parents: collectively they were those who left little mark in the record of fertility, but some of these families were day labourers, workmen, peddlers, poorer shepherds, muletiers and servants in the village. It was this group of the village poor which comprised around half the taxable population in the 18th century and it was they who seem to have been in the village only rarely and briefly, summer or winter, spring or autumn, with seldom enough time to conceive children there.

9.4. Permanent residents: the village élite

A fair number of the 219 unions which formed during the study period above (1691–1750) certainly did not conform to the norms of the European marriage pattern. Indeed a significant number seem to have married much earlier, even

FIGURE 210. Fertility behaviour of long stay residents

f.530 Girard, Pierre: b. 5.10.1718; m. Gras, Mariane (ndb) on 19.12.1741; *chirurgien* 1751; *mr. chirurgien*, 1752; 5 children 1746–1755; signing often as godparents after 1750.
f.535 Seitre, Jean: b. 9.5.1717; m. Pons, Mariane (b. 1.10.22) on 6.2.1741; *ménager* 1751; 9 children 1744–1765; signing godparents after 1749.
f.571 Seitre, Jean: b. 19.4.1719; m. Girard, Margaton (b. 1.12.1719) on 8.7.1743; *tailleur d'habits* 1754, 1760, 1763: 8 children 1744–63; all godparents sign after 1749.
f.576 Aussel, Pierre: b. 4.10.1719; m. Trestour, Marie (b. 28.5.1724) on 8.10.1743; *tisseur de toile*, 1751, 1754, 1756; *faisseur de toile*; *mr. tisseur de toile* 1765; 9 children 1745–1765; some godparents sign.
f.577 Maurel, Pierre: b. 16.9.1719; m. Pons, Clere (b. 29.9.1724) on 26.10.1743; *ménager* 1752, 1763; 8 children 1744–1766; *bourgeois*; signing as godparents after 1752.
f.584 Maurel, Louis (ndb or ff); m. Seitre, Isabeau (ndb or ff) ndm (possibly married in Magagnosc); *ménager* 1751, 1755, 1761; 8 children after 1744; godparents sign after 1749.
f.589 Bourel, Pierre Joseph (ndb); m. Seitre, Anne Marie (ndb) on 10.8.1744; *faturier d'étoffe* 1749, *faisseur d'étoffe*, 1752, 1757, 1761; 7 children 1746–1764; Some evidence of absences in spacing and location of godparents: Biot, Gréolières, most of whom sign after 1750.
f.591 Malet, Jean Baptisite (ndb); m. Seitre, Mariane (ndb) on 21.9.1744; *ménager*, 1754; 11 children 1746–1765; godparents, mainly *ménagers*, sign after 1747, possible link with Valbonne early on.
f. 598 Flory, Jean Joseph (ndb); (mother from Gourdon); m. Maurel, Janne (b. 14.4.1718) on 19.7.1745; *ménager* 1754; most godparents sign after 1750, links with Gréolières, St Jean
f.601 Flory, Claude b. 18.9.1718; m. Lautier, Marie (b. 3.9.1725) on 3.9.1745; *ménager* 1750, *travailleur* 1755; 8 children but more absences after 1752, no signers; marginal long stay ability.
f. 631 Lambert, François b. 10.5.1727; m. Court, Mariane (ndb) on.19.2. 1748; *bourgeois* and *notaire* 1751, 1753, *notaire royale* 1763; 7 children 1751–1771; all godparents sign.
f.631 Giraud, Honoré b. 2.9.1722; m. Pons, Françoise (ndb) on 20.2.1748; *ménager*, 1751, 1752, 1767; 8 children 1749–1767.
f. 637 Lambert, Jean b. 2.9.1715; m. Pons, Angele (b. 5.3.1727) on 14.10.1748; *ménager* 1753; 8 children 1749–1765; all godparents sign after 1751.

before puberty, and it is these better-off families that had numerous children. This seems to have happened especially in the earlier years of the vital event record, drawing down the mean age of first marriage for all girls to 17.6. So there is evidence here of marriage arrangements (and alliances) preceding a consummation, allowing young men a place in the society of the village while going away for the experience of commerce or training.

These are the families which, together with those who were absent only intermittently, made up the warp and weft of the village community. Their numbers seem to have varied from decade to decade: from just under 16% between 1721 and 1730, the 'period of distress' noted in the village archive (above), to nearly 35% during the period of the War of the Austrian Succession (1741–1750) when it is natural to assume that the opportunities to find outside work would have been reduced. On average they represented just over a quarter of the potential number of inhabitants of fertile years (Figure 210). Increasingly by mid-century, men showed an ability to sign their names in the registers both as parents or god parents, as indicated in Figure 210.

At the top end of Cipières village society in the 18th century were the lawyers, surgeons, tailors and *ménagers* most with sizable flocks of sheep and/or many land parcels. The village notary (or notaries, for there were increasingly more than one family) was a very necessary agent in this process of commoditising property relations. It is useful, therefore, to reconstruct the life story of the main notarial family, the Lamberts, in the village through the centuries of change.

9.5. **The Lambert family** (Figure 211)

The Lamberts were the first and most important family of notaries and tax collectors who dominated the transactional life of the village from a date somewhere between 1471 and 1531 until the present day. They appear in the records of the first cadastre of 1531, where Messire Peyre Lambert[25] has sizable landholdings in 16 *quartiers* worth a total of 451 florins in tax. He also owned the largest house (*messon)* in the village (tax value 170 florins): almost certainly this is the prestigious four-storey house that still stands facing the main door of the church (*devant l'eglise*) and which remained in the family over the next five centuries (Figure 78). This might provide the best socio-economic indicator that we have of the beginnings of a shift that had been made towards commerce and an open property market. A notary could only operate if there were enough taxes to pay and domestic, commercial and other legal contracts to write. This was also the period of the creation of the new Place and the appearance of the substantial merchant houses on the eastern flank of the square. By 1610 there were two Lambert property owning families: Antoine Lambert[26] and Messire Alexandre Lambert.

Sixteenth-century French lawyers were usually 'untroubled by scruples and with a full knowledge of the sovereign power of money'.[27] So, in Cipières, the Lamberts were well established to provide the grease for a rural society

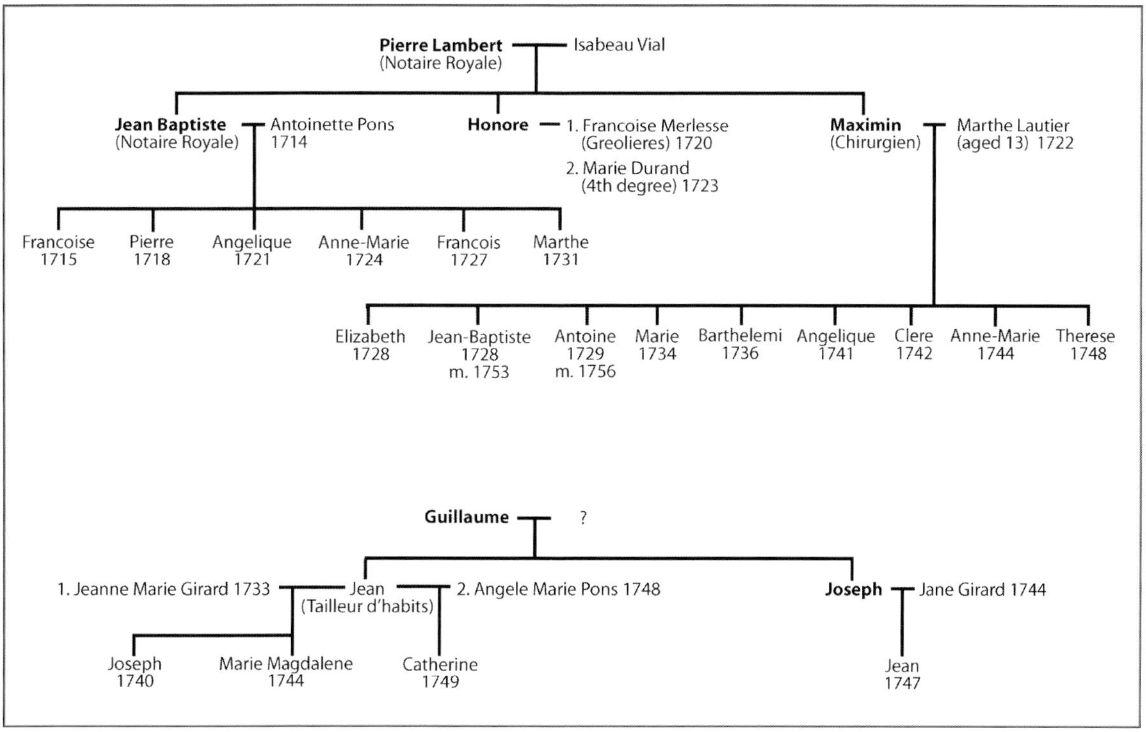

FIGURE 211. Lamberts' family tree 1700–1750

experiencing a developing rural economy. It was they who managed the affairs of both the merchants and the usurers as well as accumulating their own land, animals and capital for themselves. The Lamberts of 1610 had houses 'at a distance from Cipières village' worth 400 florins (the highest tax value) in Rue de Calern, as well as the main family house *devant l'eglise*. They also had stables and gardens in the Bourgade. With the exception of two areas of arable land in *quartiers* Font and Gardette registered under other names, they had also managed to keep their land holdings under the single name.[28]

By 1633 there were five Lambert household heads, Antoine Lambert who lived in the house ('*avec cinq membres*') in front of the church and maintained another house in the Bourgade. The tax assessor appointed by the court, had the house in the Bourgade and a personal tax assessment of 950 florins.[29] Charles Lambert was another court official with a house in the Bourgade and a personal tax assessment of 950 florins. Together with another notary, M. Jehan Pons, their taxes indicate that they were the richest men in the village. Allagrad Lambert and Antoine Lambert 'of Grasse' had no property in the village but paid taxes on lands worth 493 florins. Altogether the Lambert family paid 2053 florins in tax at this time. Together with Raymond Giraud 'bourgeois of Antibes' they give some indication of the importance of outside connections.

By the 18th century our family reconstruction provides us with a clearer view of the networked relationships of good marriage alliances which underpinned this and other emergent bourgeois families in Cipières. A reconstruction of the family tree for the 18th-century Lamberts helps us to identify the behaviour most revealing of their success, even in a community apparently ravaged by war and penury (Figure 211). In 1750 there were two senior brothers in Cipières. Jean Baptiste was the notary and his sibling Maximin was the *chirurgien,* already referred to above. Jean Baptiste occupied the family house already described, '*devant l'eglise*' held in succession to his father Pierre and his brother Honoré (who appears to have been living elsewhere). Maximin was living not far away in the Rue de la Place in a house which belonged to his father-in-law and which was in process of renovation in 1750.[30] In addition to their professional activities the family were flock masters, with sizable numbers of sheep. In 1763 for example Francois Lambert, son of Jean Baptiste, had over 400 animals, the third largest flock in the village.[31] They also owned *bergeries* in Boual d'Aussel, to the west of the village, which were designed specifically to provide 'both manure from the flocks of his own and other flocks which stayed in them overnight but did not pay the tax', a fascinating insight into land management and the use of sheep folds to accumulate manure from both one's own and other animals belonging to the poor.[32] One also assumes that they employed day labour to manage both their lands and their flocks.

In 1750 Jean Baptiste also had an irrigable pasture with a day's worth of scythable hay in Pre Long (down by the river) which served to feed his plough animals (unspecified but assumed to be mules), some fruit trees and a little garden growing spring and summer herbs for the pot. Beside the meadow he had land with five *panneaux* of seed corn and 15 fruit trees with some small oaks. This land, like all others in the parish whether on the plateau or elsewhere, was sown biennially. His other lands included some in La Caux (on the terraces just south-west of Cipières) with a few nut trees and also another one in Gremollière (Agrémourié) at the far end of the plateau (where the family had held land since at least 1531), taking three *panneaux* of seed but two-thirds of which was 'uncultivated for many years'.[33] Maximin, with his role as surgeon, seems to have been more of the farmer than the grazier. The sons of Guillaume were a distinctively junior branch of the family who took up the respectable craft of tailor.

The spacing of their offspring reveals them all as living together in the village for most of their lives. For example, Maximin Lambert, the village surgeon in the mid-18th century, was the brother of the notary. He married Marthe Lautier in October 1722 when she was only 13. Their physical union was clearly delayed until she reached puberty and she had her first child in August 1726. She then had ten further children over the next 25 years and in almost every month of the year (Figure 211). This behaviour is a reflection of the continuity of opportunity for permanency provided by the notarial and commercial families. It was these first incomers, like the Lamberts, Mallets, Funels and Ricords, who had arrived in the village after 1471 and before 1531, who tended to appear at a higher point in the emergent social and economic structure, with new functional roles: as notaries, traders and craftsmen.

This enhancement through mixing activities of agriculture, craft, trade and professional expertise was even truer of later incomers: new professionals like the Dedoues (also notaries) and those with commercial connections like the Vials who appear in the late 17th and 18th centuries. Their very appearance in the village suggests an expansion of commercial and social functions involving more formal transactions. The expansion of the village and its *embourgeoisement* in the 16th century reflect these changing circumstances. Even by the 1630s higher status people with titles, usually the notaries, are appearing among the oldest Cipèrois families (e.g. Jehan Pons, worth 809 florins) reflecting the growth of commercial functions in the region. One expatriate Giraud, for example, lived in Antibes but maintained a house in the Place and paid 2051 florins in tax. Other incoming families in the 17th century seem to have had their roots in the wool trading families of Provence. Most significant of these was the Vial family.

9.6. The Vial family (Figure 212)

Pierre Vial, First Consul of the parish council of Cipières in 1750, came from a family of merchants probably from Grasse, who settled in Cipières in the mid-17th century. There were no Vials in the cadastral record of 1610, but in 1633 Antoine Vial held a house and stable in the 'new street' of la Bourgade and he paid for land and property to the tax value of 192 *livres*, which placed him straightaway in the top third of the village society as measured by the tax on land and property (but not, at this time, of animals).[34] By the early years of the 18th century the Vials had married into the older but smaller *ostal–ménager* flock master families, the Isnards, the Seitres and also into the Pons.[35] In 1750 there were two branches of the family, both identified as *bourgeois* in the 1750 *Declaration*, mainly living in the Rue du Four. Pierre lived in a house he inherited from his father, Guillaume, with whom he lived until his father's death in the 1740s.[36] Guillaume (*ménager* and merchant in 1727) had married Marie Pons in 1707. Pierre was born in 1710, the second of his five children. There are indications of Pierre's first (very early) marriage in 1726 or thereabouts

FIGURE 212. Vials' family tree 1700–1750

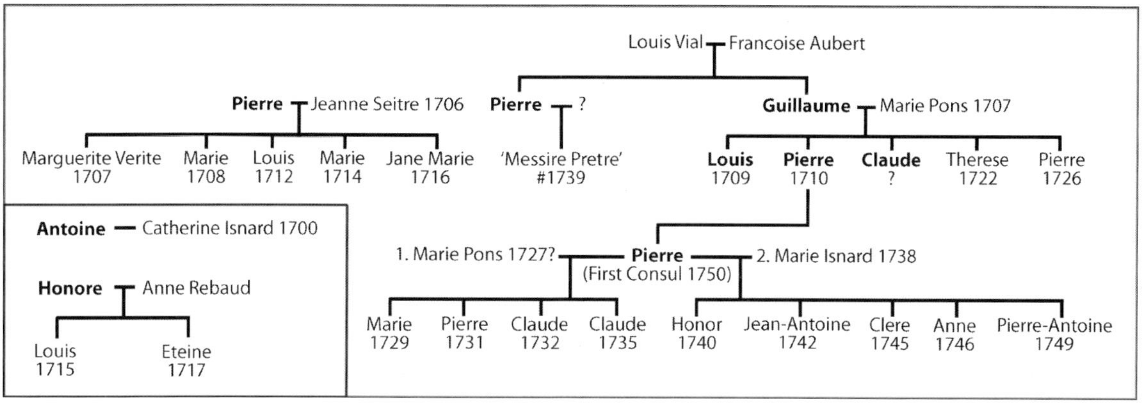

to another Marie Pons. Though no record exists of a marriage in the Cipières registers, a first child, Marie, was born there in 1729[37] and there were three other children born before the death of this first wife in 1736. A subsequent re-marriage to Marie Isnard in 1738[38] produced five further children before the upwardly mobile Pierre was made First Consul in 1749. By this time he too had also become a well-established merchant (*négotiant*). Given the size of his flock, his interests certainly included cloth and wool.[39] In 1750 he had 210 sheep (or seven *trenteniers*). He and other major flock owners ostensibly kept these flocks for the sole purpose of 'fertilising his arable land'. By 1763 this flock had increased to 536, the largest in the village.[40] He also had two mules and a mare '*pour la culture de mes terres*'. At this time he was living in a house in Rue du Four acquired from his brother Claude Vial (a priest)[41] which had three rooms, a stable and loft barn of a type which characterised the village then and still does today. He held land in six *quartiers*.

Below Pierre Vial in the economic system, in terms of individual taxed wealth, were ten *propriétaires* with taxes of over 100 *livres*. Seven of them carried the title of 'Sieur' or 'Mr', one of whom was also entitled *bourgeois*. Four were *ménagers*. There were also a *marchant*, a *négotiant* and another who was a *chirurgien*. All these main property owners, except the Vials, were part of families with a long heritage in the village except the new men of the weaving trade. Among this group were the Ricords.

9.7. **The Ricord family** (Figure 213)

The Ricords appear in the medieval records for Grasse as 'inhabitants of Cipières' but seem to have only a toe-hold in the community in 1531, with two bits of land and no other property.[42] They emerge sporadically in village records but make no specific appearance in the 17th century cadastres. But Louis Ricord, who appears regularly in our 18th century records, both in cadastres, vital event registers and as a functionary was by then a significant craftsman and trader. He seems to have married into Cipières in the last decade of the 17th century, coming from a family with Cipières roots and with interests in woollens, based in Bar near Tulle. He married[43] Jeanne Lauthier on 6 December 1693. No dates of birth of the bride and groom were recorded, but the spacing of births suggests that it was an early marriage[44] (Figure 213). His first child, Marguerite, was born in February three years after the marriage and thereafter his six subsequent children were born with metronomic regularity at just around three yearly intervals, all of them conceived in the summer and spring months of the previous year. In

FIGURE 213. Children of Louis Ricord and Jeanne Lauthier with intervals between births

Child's name	*Birth interval*	*Interval between births in months*	*Date of birth*
Marguerite	0–1st	37.7	February, 1696
Marie	1st–2nd	37.2	March, 1699
Claude	2nd–3rd	36.5	March, 1702
Marie	3rd–4th	38.1	May, 1705
Marguerite	4th–5th	44.4	February, 1709
Jacques	5th–6th	37.6	May, 1715
Anne	6th–7th	37.1	March, 1717
Françoise	7th–8th	33.7	January, 1718

these circumstances we may be safe in assuming that any absences for commercial purposes were clearly timed for the winter slack period.

The godfather of his first child Marguerite was Jean Mas, also from Bar near Tulle in the Dordogne and at the time of the marriage of his son Claude, another Ricord from Bar married into a Cipières family.[45] This kind of wide family linkage may not have been unusual, but this is the only specific case I found.

Strictly speaking this experience places the family (just) in the category of *longer absence cyclical migrants*, but their position in village society was clearly more significant than this classification would imply. In 1727 Louis occupied a large house with four rooms, a stable and a small garden, a significantly placed house on the junction between the Bourgade and the Place and he is identified in the cadastre of that date as a *tisserand de laine*.[46] There is little doubt that he also maintained a flock of sheep and that a considerable and predictable proportion of his time was spent in commerce to do with the wool and cloth trade, with perhaps stretches of 18 months away at a time.

9.8. The middling sort: longer-absence migrants, periodic returners and the upwardly mobile

Below the upper level in village society, there seems to have been a group of families whose lives were certainly dominated by circular migration. The pattern of birth spacings indicated, in some cases, very frequent and, in others, quite lengthy absences from the village by either the husbands or by all the family. Claude Ricord, the son of Louis, who was born in 1702 (see above) married at the young age of 19 in January 1721.[47] His bride, Anne Marie Girarde, was 16. This behaviour was characteristic everywhere among proto-industrial families with interests in spinning and weaving. At first he lived in a '*part maison*' next to his father's house in the Bourgade and still under his father's name. In 1727 he occupied an apartment property in a house he shared with André Suque and with Guillaume Aubin[48] at a time when he had only two children. The spacing of his six children born between 1722 and 1740[49] did not quite follow that of his father. The first child was born after 17.5 months. Four children were born in August and September (winter conceptions) and two in January (spring conceptions). We may assume a lifestyle, perhaps dominated by his father's outside interests, which, during these years of his early maturity, placed him more closely within the middling sort.

He stepped up quickly into the élite group when his father died. At the time of the 1750 cadastre, Claude, was now '*Messire*' Claude, a flock master of 50 years old who also had commercial links with relatives elsewhere[50] and occupied the big house 'on the square' which had belonged to his father. He had quite a sizable land holding (nine parcels in nine *quartiers*, one of which contained a share in a *bergerie*) and a daughter who had married one of the village tailors (Joseph Pons).[51]

Among this group were the longer-term migrating sons of *ménagers* who also eventually returned to take over from their fathers. Because their intermittent re-appearance was in itself a check on fertility, their marriages too tended to take place much earlier (16–18 years old) than the European marriage pattern, as in the case of the Giraud's quoted below, without the detrimental effect of over-reproduction. The new opportunities in commerce also manifested themselves to those from smaller families who nonetheless owned sheep flocks, especially if a good marriage could be made.

Joseph Guizol was born in 1705 to a reasonably well-off flock master, also called Joseph and by 1727 he was a 22 year old joiner (*menuisier).*[52] He was the only son (he had two much younger sisters). In 1723, at the age of 18, he married another 18 year old, Marie Ricord, the daughter of Louis the well placed proto-industrialist described above.[53] Over the next decade he became a *periodic returner*, but unlike his father-in-law he was largely absent from the village. Two children were born to this union in Cipières in 1737 and 1739 in an apartment in the Rue l'Église, where he was a near neighbour of the Lamberts in 1727.[54] It was owned and also occupied by his father, also called Joseph Guizol, a joiner (*menuisier*) who, with only three recorded offspring, may also have spent most of his time plying his craft outside the village.[55] By 1750 the young Joseph had changed his designation to *ménager*, following the death of his father, and by this time he occupied the whole of a prestigious house 'in front of the church', in succession from his father Joseph consisting of 'six small rooms a stable and a hay loft' (bought from Pierre Flory). This house was appropriate for a family which was quite well placed in the upper quartile of wealth and related to the Ricord family. At the end of the 1740s Joseph Guizol had 13 pieces of arable land in 11 *quartiers* spread throughout the parish but mainly on the plateau. He also had his own *bergerie*, reflecting a sizeable flock of sheep.[56]

One effect of a large family group, what one might call a 'relict *ostal*', is that it provided an opportunity to step up the family economic structure. While on the one hand, as we have seen, the Bourelly numbers declined, the progress of families within the structure of these long settled family groups sometimes followed a trajectory which took them from itinerant labourers (*travailleurs*, semi-permanent migrants) to *bourgeois ménagers* (permanent residents) in the space of a generation.

On the other hand, records for individual women show us that for a significant number there were gaps in conceptions, often of a number of years rather than seasons, punctuated by what seem otherwise to be quite normal responses of birth spacing. This seems to reflect a rather different experience of migration.

Jean Baptisite Giraud, for example, seems at first to identify himself as a potential long-term stayer. He married Jane Pons in October 1719,[57] when she was 25 years old, a perfectly normal age for marriage by western European standards of the time. She had two children quite quickly (after 20.9 months and 18.3 months). Then there was a gap of eight years (98.1 months) before the next child, Anne, was born in March 1731.[58] These were the years when migration behaviour may have changed for others too as economic and environmental conditions worsened. It is also possible that both partners moved away together, raising other children outside, but I find no reference to them in subsequent records of marriage or death. So let us assume that Jean Baptiste returned to family life from 'abroad' in the early 1730s, for there were three more children in quick succession (16, 15 and 11 months). Finally there was another period of absence for at least three years, before two further births. The final child was born in Jane Pons's 46th year. There is no evidence of either predominant winter or summer conceptions in this record. By 1750, Jean Baptisite is listed as a *ménager* living in the house he inherited from his father in Rue de la Baumette. Significantly he is also noted as having 'many lands' and owning part (a third) of a *bergerie* making him a well-placed member of the community, 13th in the tax ranking.[59] Here we see someone who is probably an employer of labour as well as an entrepreneur with out-of-village interests.

Jean and Jean Joseph Giraud represent another emergent successful stem family, marrying within the *ostal* family nexus and which passed through stages from itinerancy to permanent residence. Jean Giraud was the son of Claude Giraud and Jane Flory. He too married a Flory, Jeanne the daughter of Guillaume, in August 1706.[60] He was identified in the register of births as a *travailleur* and his occupation left him time, in the pattern of his life, to father only three children in Cipières; a daughter, Honoré in 1709, a son Jean Joseph in 1713 and another daughter Clere in 1720. Then the family fortunes began to change. In 1733, the younger brother Jean Joseph, then aged 20, married Françoise the 18 year old daughter of Jean Baptisite Lambert, the notary (see above).[61] This was a very good marriage and the family had clearly made considerable progress in the preceding decade. In the years between 1733 and 1759 nine children were born to this union and the status of their godparents (*notaires*, *bourgeois*) reflected the increasing position of the family. By the 1740s these godparents were all *bourgeois* or cloth merchants, as indeed Jean was himself, with links outside the community. In 1750 he was living in one of the larger houses in Rue Bourgade, which he still shared with his aged father and very definitely part of the village élite.[62] For this branch of the family birth spacing (an average of 2.9 years) shows us a family quite clearly in permanent residence. He (together with his brother in this case) was paying taxes of 225 *livres* which placed them in the top quartile of the community at this time.

9.9. The lesser sort: day labourers and the itinerant, semi-permanent migrants

At a lower level in the structure were the junior or apparently less successful members of families, who occupied rooms or part dwellings rather than dwellings and had access to only a few parcels of land. It was in this group that we find the irregular returners and semi-permanent migrants.

One of our first recorded marriages in the vital event registers of the period was between Christophe Pons and Marie Girard, in October 1691.[63] Their children were born in the autumn months of 1698, 1703, 1708, 1712 and 1715. Was this one of a number of cases of a winter migrant returning in the spring but not always managing a conception? On the other hand, records for individual women show us that, for a significant number, there were gaps in conceptions often of a number of years rather than seasons, punctuated by what seem otherwise to be quite normal responses of birth spacing. Perhaps they too were absent from the village in service or working with their husbands.

A less tangible group technically held land and property in the village, but their appearances in the vital event records are quite transitory. Of course, there are some of the couples who marry in Cipières who make no further appearance in the registers at all. They will have been those who were either childless or whose marriages ended in the death of one or both partners without subsequent remarriage of a widow. Others seem to marry very young and then disappear either immediately or after having spent some time in the community and raising one or perhaps two children. It is among this group, with its patchy ambivalent record, that we find the day labourers, road makers, harvesters, muletiers, soldiers, seamen, who form the flotsam of itinerant labour so common in Alpine regions, especially during periods of environmental stress.[64] If this is so, then they rarely seem to have returned to their home village except when they were forced back by circumstances.

The question we might ask is how far did this movement represent crisis out-migration, or was it merely part of a kinship strategy in which younger and junior members of families went away to ease the burden on those who remained, as seems to have occurred elsewhere in the Préalpes?

As we have seen, our demographic analysis shows that there were a lot of them and that their numbers varied according to pressures and opportunities, averaging 45% of recorded marriages and ranging from 34% early in the century to 58% in the 1730s. There are those, like Jean Baptisite Giraud (above), who seem to return for periods of a year or two at a time. His identity was 'of the village' but his occupation clearly took him out of the community for long periods. During the first half of the 18th century it becomes ever more difficult to distinguish between, and to categorise, these periodic short-term migrants. As time went on, many more tailors, carders, dealers in cloth are specified as fathers, husbands and godparents in the vital event registers. *Travailleurs* directly associated with these activities seem to choose artisans as godparents. More usually those people who carried the title *travailleur* were at the lower end of the scale,[65] though as perhaps the sons of better placed fathers they were not necessarily always to remain so. As we have indicated earlier, perhaps some of this apparent poverty may have been a feature of family taxation strategies, but the demographic crises of 1747, 1751 and 1763[66] and the migration behaviour of the community as a whole suggests otherwise. Many others (58%) were not exclusively, but mainly, in the poorer category and had no title or designated occupation. The vast majority of these families lived in one or two rooms in the 18th century, with perhaps an access to a stable or a loft. This was exacerbated when soldiery were billeted during the War of the Austrian Succession. The cramped conditions of many ostensible inhabitants are also signalled by the fact that at least one family (Emmanuel Aussel a shepherd) lived in 'two small rooms under the roof' of a house in the Bourgade.[67] This was elsewhere in the record designated as 'the hay loft'. On the other hand, the 1750 *Declaration des Biens* rarely reveals the true nature of the potential position of those who have other interests outside farming.

Let us look at Etienne and Charles Aubin, the sons of Adam Aubin.[68] Etienne Aubin was 28 years old in 1750.[69] A simple ranking based largely on his six parcels of arable land puts him well down the hierarchy, but he also held two properties in the village, one in succession to his father valued at 100 *livres* and another worth 100 *livres* also which he had as a dowry from his wife, Honorade Flory, whom he had married in 1746.[70] In addition he had also purchased a stable from Girard Boniface for 120 *livres*. The clue as to his real status is in the titles *berger* as well as *travailleur* in the entries in the vital event registers.[71] His older brother, Charles Aubin,[72] was 38 years old in 1750. His situation seemed very similar (seven arable parcels with a tax value of 16 *livres* and a house in la Placette worth 100 *livres* which was the product of an inheritance partition and also a sizable stable). Almost uniquely (and certainly beyond the demands of the recording official), he also reveals that he had four *trenteniers* (120) of sheep! It is this pastoral dimension in the life of this family and, no doubt, many others, which better characterises their condition. It was those with no sheep (58%) and with no goats either, between the ban in 1731 and the repeal in 1770, who were pushed closest to the margins of subsistence as day labourers, whatever support their kinship network might be able to provide.

9.10. Conclusion

The opportunity to use demographic sources to unravel the social and economic structure of Cipières in the 18th century has revealed the potential significance of both short and longer term migrations and their contribution to maintaining a core village society. I hope to have shown that the village society and economy in Cipières was maintained by a variable group of permanent residents of probably no more than between 150 people in the 1720s and 350 in the 1740s, out of a 'potential' population of around 1000 according to the cadastres. From this group came the heads of farming families, craftsmen, traders and professionals, most of who carried out several functions within the society. As is so often the case, the part played by women in this society remains largely hidden from view in the official records. I can only assume that in both farm work and woollen crafts, as well as in the day-to-day decision making, they played an important role, as they certainly did elsewhere in alpine societies. This would have been especially true when men were away for protracted periods. Older continuities of kith and kin and the practices of 'time immemorial', though much diminished in status, were probably still the glue that bound the village society together in the difficult times of the 17th and 18th centuries, but they manifested themselves in new ways. They provided the emotional capital for those who were to leave the village in search of work elsewhere and, at the same time, the moral incentive to repay, in one form or another, that debt of support. If there was an initial first phase, dominated by seasonal migration, as happened throughout the alpine region, it seems gradually to have developed other characteristics as burgeoning urban markets created new agendas. Opportunities for peddlers, tinkers, traders, itinerant craftsmen, servants and tradesmen in the late 17th and 18th centuries promoted what Fontaine calls 'a culture of itinerancy' in which families provided emotional backing for their travelling relatives whose remittances eased the burden of their more frequent and often lengthy absences.[73] Family members established themselves as merchants in local towns and acted as bankers and facilitators.[74] At the same time Cipières' resident traders, merchants and craftsmen and workmen came to reflect what was happening economically outside the community as much as within it.

On the other hand the demographic study has also shown us that the landscapes of Cipières were no longer so full of folk as they had been in previous centuries, especially in the period before the Plague when peasants shaped the landscape of what was then the mixed farming economy described by Rosamond Faith in Chapter 5. There is a clear sense that although subsistence cultivation of cereals, vines and fruit was still important, the massive investment in labour needed to shift the stone unearthed by ploughing or in maintaining the systems of walls, terraces enclosures and boundaries was no longer available by the 18th century, even if it had been deemed necessary. The land was gradually running down to pasture and what remains to us today is a landscape of the past, but one that gives us a sense of the investment of energy which is a testament to the skills and perseverance of the first Cipèrois.

During the last half of the 18th century the community continued to struggle to survive against a tide of debts[75] plus an annual pension for the seigneur of 280 *livres*. Despite repeal of the sanction against goat keeping, the poorer people were often hungry and 'seeking out land elsewhere' and the poorer lands were no longer able to support cultivation. Nevertheless, there is some evidence that despite continuing difficulties, by the end of the 18th century, Cipières had managed to return to at least a putative population close to early 18th century levels. The name was still being maintained 'on the land'. In 1795 there were 998 people (plus 40 *soldats*) = 1038 official inhabitants. But a decade later in 1806 the *recensement* shows that the population had declined by nearly 10% to 941.[76] This trend continued until the permanent collapse of population in the second half of the 19th century. Beyond this time the community maintained its character and its hold on its primary resources with an increasingly uneasy balance between 'time immemorial' and modernising forces.

CHAPTER TEN

Les Baumes in the Modern Era

Andrew Fleming

It is argued that the corbelled stone shelters (the bories), *and the substantial* enclos *with which some of them are associated, date mostly from the early post-medieval period. The* bories *are regularly spaced, but otherwise display no recognisable recurring relationships with the main agrarian landscape. They are best seen as* imposed *upon the latter – shepherds' shelters dating from the time when the economy of the plateau and the region had come to be dominated by large commercial flocks and the activities of share-croppers. This dating is also suggested by the degree of degradation of the* bories *and the likelihood that, with the development of shelters and* bergeries *roofed with tiles, these corbelled structures would have become devalued as shelters. These arguments, based on archaeological observations and on the known economic history of the commune, concur with those recently made by Thiery for upland communes to the south of the Plateau de Calern, on the basis of both documentary information and fieldwork. A comparison is made between the parcel boundaries marked on the 1842 cadastral map and the field evidence; some stretches of the parcel boundaries followed well-marked archaeological or geological 'edges', whilst others do not correspond to any features visible on the ground.*

10.1. Introduction

Within an essentially archaeological framework, there are two obvious ways of achieving some understanding of the post-medieval exploitation of the Plateau de Calern. One is to consult the cadastral survey of 1842 – the first in which parcels of land are marked on a surveyed map – and try to match their boundaries with physiographic and/or archaeological features visible on the ground. The other is to study the distribution of the obvious post-medieval structures, which in this case means the definite *bories,* enclosures with standing walls and associated shelters of various kinds (including *bories*), and *bergeries.*

Probably these two approaches are largely relevant to different chronological horizons, in the sense that virtually all of these structures were *installed* well before 1842, probably within patterns of occupancy and ownership of land parcels which were rather different from those which obtained then (cf. Austin's analysis of the fluid situation at Baoume de Brun, Chapter 3). On the other hand, the *use* of some of these structures, perhaps the majority, intermittent and casual though it may have been in many cases, probably continued well into the 19th century.

10.2. Post-medieval structures: *bories*, enclosures and *bergeries*

I suspect that the *quartier* of Les Baumes, which is relatively distant from the village of Cipières, came to be regarded as relatively marginal by the 19th century; there are few post-medieval enclosures here, and only one example of a large rectilinear *bergerie* with a tiled roof, on the northern edge of the area. But there are numerous *bories* (Figure 214), spaced with a considerable degree of regularity across the research area. *Bories* are not, of course, confined to the plateau; they seem to have been in use all over the commune, as general-purpose sheds and shelters. In principle, it would be interesting to apply techniques of locational geography to their distribution, using Thiessen polygons or nearest neighbour analysis, but there are one or two enumeration problems. In general, *bories* have distinctive architectural characteristics. Usually it is not hard to distinguish them from other types of shelter, although it has to be said that there are one or two structures which seem to be heavily robbed or unfinished *bories*, and also a few large piles of stone, revetted at least in part, which may represent collapsed *bories,* some of which may have been added to by stones cleared from nearby land (Figure 215).

That said, the spacing of *bories* is as regular as one is entitled to expect, given the vagaries of the terrain. They are marked on Figure 223. There are evidently

FIGURE 214. Les Baumes: typical corbelled shelters (*bories*)
PHOTOGRAPH: ANDREW FLEMING

FIGURE 215. Les Baumes: a collapsed *borie* or perhaps a large clearance cairn
PHOTOGRAPH: ANDREW FLEMING

'push' and 'pull' factors; *bories* do seem to be slightly thinner on the ground in the relatively high, thin-soiled land in the south-west part of the research area, and conversely it seems that the value of some extensive and/or deep-soiled dolines and uvulas is such that they tend to be supplied with *bories*, though whether these should be regarded as representing proprietorial claims or simply convenient control stations cannot be determined by archaeological inspection. The regular spacing of the *bories* implies quite strongly that, around the period of their construction, the Plateau de Calern was grazed systematically and in a disciplined fashion (see Chapter 8), with the shepherds probably needing to keep one eye on their flocks and the other on those of their competitors.

The *bories* would have provided shepherds with shelters in which to spend the night, avoid the sun in the middle of the day, store equipment, and reduce the risk of being struck by lightning, (no mean hazard in this environment). A reasonably fit shepherd would rarely have been more than two minutes' walk from a large corbelled shelter. In the state in which we see them today, *bories* are not rainproof. Their roofs were originally supplied with beds of turf, secured with pegs or ropes, which would have made them much more waterproof, and probably slowed the destructive effects of freeze–thaw processes. Arguably, once tiles became available, the custom of repairing these turf roof-covers would have been less diligently observed (see below). The distinctiveness of *borie* architecture, and the regularity of *borie* spacing, strongly suggests that these structures belong to a relatively limited chronological horizon. Certainly it would be wrong to regard the *bories* as in any sense 'timeless', especially in the climatic conditions of the Plateau de Calern; the vicissitudes of economic and agrarian history at Cipières suggest that we would be most unwise to assume continuous maintenance of their turf roof-covers.

The location preferences of the *bories* are variable. One or two stand at the edge of uvulas or dolines, at floor level. But a *borie* may also be found on the sloping side of a doline, or overlooking a doline from its upper edge. All these cases seem to represent, in part at least, a 'proprietorial' or 'controlling' attitude to more valued parcels of land. A few *bories* are to be found in the kind of high-lying positions from which shepherds could watch over a large area of pasture – or be seen to 'control' such a zone by other graziers. One or two *bories* lie within medieval 'fields'. A few are located quite close to roads, but there is no suggestion that *bories* were placed preferentially in relation to the road network. It is sometimes possible to pick out an area of stone-quarrying

which is clearly associated with the construction of a *borie* (Figure 216). The floor of such a quarry would have provided a 'yard' adjacent to the shelter, an area which could have been enclosed by a dead hedge and which might have provided a rough threshing-floor on occasion, and perhaps a sheep-milking zone. At one site in Les Baumes, the walls of *borie* quarry have been excavated in such a way as to leave a small yard with high rock walls, presumably used as a stock pen, approached by going past the entrance of the *borie* (Figure 217). In Les Baumes, the small, not very numerous roughly rectangular enclosures, with high, quite well-preserved walls, often measuring perhaps 20–30 m 'along' the contour and *c.* 5–10 m 'across' it (though some are on ground which barely slopes) usually incorporate a *borie* (Figure 218). There is one case where the enclosure has no *bori*, but there is one only *c.* 100 m away. In two places, *bories* stand near other structures which have had tiled roofs – one a large *bergerie,* the other a much smaller rectangular building. The relationship between *bories* and places where sheep could be penned seems to have been a loose one. Many *bories* are free-standing, and many walled dolines, where sheep were presumably often encouraged to spend the night when crops were not growing there, do

left: FIGURE 216. Les Baumes: a ruined *borie* and its quarry. Note the line of stones in the foreground, suggesting that the quarry floor may have been used as a 'yard' or working area
PHOTOGRAPH: ANDREW FLEMING

right: FIGURE 217. Les Baumes: a *borie* (right) has been built next to its quarry (left), providing a probable stock enclosure which is entered by going past the *borie*
PHOTOGRAPH: ANDREW FLEMING

FIGURE 218. Les Baumes: a *borie* with adjacent enclosure
PHOTOGRAPH: ANDREW FLEMING

not possess their own *bories*. Finally, there is no suggestion of any systematic correlation between the distribution of *bories* and the parcels of land marked on the 1842 cadastral map. Whether the duties of a shepherd involved exploiting solely his family's (or master's) land, or whether at certain seasons (notably after the harvest) he had the right to use the plateau as a large upland common, presumably he would have had, or used, a shelter or shelters on just one or two of the more valued parcels among a scattered portfolio of land. From an archaeological perspective, the main conclusions from Les Baumes are that, in terms of spatial distribution, the *bories* repel rather than attract one other, that together they achieve an even coverage of the land, that they have a wide range of locational preferences, and that their association with the practice of penning flocks in purpose-built walled enclosures is demonstrable only to a certain extent. If one may extrapolate from the situation at Les Baumes, the *bories* represent a serious economic investment in, and engagement with, all parts of the Calern terrain – probably in a context of emulation or competition. Such an economic investment probably represents not a wave of agricultural innovation, but rather a determination to exploit existing productive capacity to the full, for economic and/or fiscal reasons, during a relatively brief chronological horizon in which, for a time at least, the importance attached by numerous active stakeholders to the exploitation of the plateau was considerable.

10.3. Evidence from elsewhere

Daniel Thiery[1] has developed a productive dialogue between archaeological and documentary evidence which has shed considerable light on the historical context of *borie*-building. He has shown how, in the post-medieval era, the uplands to the south of Cipières – the Plateau du Caussols, the Plaine de la Malle and Le Ferrier – were extensively exploited for agrarian and pastoral purposes by the residents of hill-foot communities like Châteauneuf, Magagnosc, Grasse, St Vallier de Thiey, and St Cézaire. In 1774, only four out of 14 *bastides* at Caussols were inhabited all the year round, and in 1834 every single one of 327 owners of land there had their principal residence elsewhere. Yet this was a productive place, with no less than 104 threshing-floors being recorded in 1834. Thiery records that in the late 18th century the pastures at Caussols were thrown open to common grazing after the first hay harvest and after sowing time, and that they were used between May and October by transhumant flocks from Basse Provence. The land supported 60 *trenteniers (1800)* sheep, the ratio between ewe and lamb flocks and those containing wethers being 2:1. I include here a photograph of a transhumant flock of 1500 sheep, to indicate the space they occupy; it was taken at La Vialasse, on Mont Lozère, in June 2010 (Figure 219).

The investments made by outsiders are symbolised archaeologically by the so-called *voie romaine,* a well-engineered road which has been driven northwards through some very rocky terrain to bring it to the edge of the fertile northern half of the Plateau de Caussols. Its cobbled surface and carefully walled edges

FIGURE 219. La Vialasse, Mont Lozère: the space occupied by 1500 transhumant sheep (June 2010)
PHOTOGRAPH: ANDREW FLEMING

are beautifully preserved in places to this day (Figure 220). According to de Beauchamp[2] roads like this are old transhumance routes of medieval origin which were substantially improved in the 17th and 18th centuries. These road-surfacing methods involved cobbled surfaces and, on rising ground, transverse stone sills, effectively acting like steps, which stabilised individual compartments of metalling and were evidently intended to confine the effects of damage and consequent erosion within such compartments. The fragmentary remains of such road surfaces may be seen on the road leading from Caussols up to the Col du Clapier (Figure 221), a road which continues to Grasse and Magagnosc. According to Thiery this route was used 'between the 15th and the 19th centuries by the inhabitants of Magaganosc and Châteauneuf when fetching cereals produced at Caussols and on Calern'.[3] Much more heavily damaged remains of carefully constructed surfaces may be seen, for example, on the road leading up to the southern edge of Calern from the Chapelle de St Vincent near Gourdon, and also on the Cipières–Caussols road

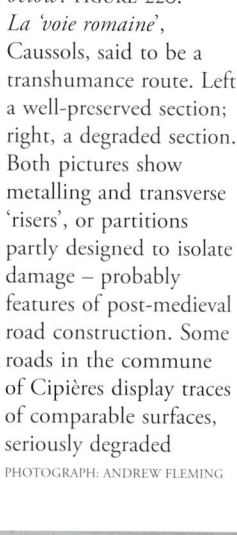

below: FIGURE 220. *La 'voie romaine'*, Caussols, said to be a transhumance route. Left: a well-preserved section; right, a degraded section. Both pictures show metalling and transverse 'risers', or partitions partly designed to isolate damage – probably features of post-medieval road construction. Some roads in the commune of Cipières display traces of comparable surfaces, seriously degraded
PHOTOGRAPH: ANDREW FLEMING

FIGURE 221. The road from Caussols over the Col du Clapier to Grasse and Magaganosc. Left, climbing towards the pass; right, descending from the pass towards Caussols
PHOTOGRAPH: ANDREW FLEMING

already described, in the stretch where it breasts the slope from La Combe to the Vaumeillane bench and higher up where it climbs to the northern edge of Calern proper.

Linking the *bories* and rectangular buildings with sloping (tiled) roofs visible in the field at Caussols with the *bastides* and *cabanons* mentioned in the 1834 cadastre, Thiery has argued that most of these dry-stone walled structures were put up by '*colons*' from Magagnosc, Grasse and Châteauneuf in the 16th and 17th centuries.[4] He obtained closer chronological control, however, from his study of the communes of St Vallier de Thiey and St Cézaire (1992). The 1657 cadastre records many *clots* (enclosures) '*entourés de pierre sèche*' and also the fact that many of them had been quite recently constructed. As he says [my translation]: 'taking possession of a piece of land on the common waste and surrounding it with a drystone wall established ownership. Paying tax on this enclosed land reinforced this claim, especially if the commune and the chapter turned a blind eye to the takeover'.[5] A *clot* was often accompanied by a *courtil de pierre sèche* or a *courtil tout couvert de pierres* – both of which designations Thiery takes to mean a *borie* (though, confusingly, a *courtil* could also mean an enclosure). There were also *cabanons tout couverts de tuiles,* however, and the 17th century mentions of '*un grand courtil pour y enclore l'average* [flock of sheep]' and '*un courtil et un cabanon joignant couvert de tuiles*' could be archaeological descriptions of the structures which we have encountered on the Plateau de Calern. Both tiled roofs and cisterns, then, are mentioned in this 17th century context. Thiery's earlier study of the uplands of Le Ferrier[6] showed how, in the mid-17th century, people from Magagnosc owned 75% of the land here, to which they went in summer only – traversing a distance of 8 km and climbing some 400 m to do so. Thiery has argued that every family from Magagnosc with land on the plateau would have needed a *borie* (unlike the inhabitants of St Vallier, who could have commuted on a daily basis). Of 18 *bories* found through fieldwork, 12 could be identified as *bastidons* mentioned in the 1817 cadastre; nine of them were seasonally occupied. Using data from cadastres dated 1657, 1742 and 1817, Thiery argues that the construction of these *bories* can be dated between the beginning of the 17th century and the end of the 18th. In the 17th century, their use was associated with productive agriculture, which included the cultivation of beans, chick peas, lentils, haricot beans, and fruit trees; but from the beginning of the 19th century, the use of this area switched sharply to pastoralism, with only five shepherds controlling *c.* 900 sheep and *c.* 100 goats in 1832, and only one shepherd with 270 sheep in 1878.

10.4. Cipières

How may we relate these findings to the situation at Cipières? According to Siddle (Chapter 6) after the *temps de malheur* (*c.* 1340–1440) the population gradually recovered, reaching virtually medieval levels – *c.* 1050 in 1471, *c.* 1350 in 1531 and *c.* 1300 in 1610 and in 1698. By 1806, however, the population had declined to 941. But as Siddle has also shown, the population figures for the early modern period are mostly of legal and fiscal significance, since many Cipièrois were now leaving the commune for long periods to work and make money (Chapter 9). In the 1720s the group of permanent residents was no more than 150; it was *c.* 350 in the 1740s. Most of these people were labourers and artisans of one sort or another, including shepherds and weavers, many living in apartments in the village. And it seems that outsiders who had accumulated capital elsewhere must have helped to create and stimulate the increasing land market of the later 16th century. By 1633 there was a village elite consisting of powerful outsiders from places like Vence, Biot and Grasse, and the more affluent villagers (Siddle, Chapter 9). Of the 32 Cipières family names known for the period between the Black Death and 1840, 23 made their first appearance after 1600. In the 18th century there were also substantial flock-masters here – *menagers* from ancient *ostals*, but also men from families which had come from elsewhere – the Lamberts, the Vials and the Ricords. In 1609 the 'village flock' of *c.* 20,000 sheep included 8,000 owned by merchant graziers, and the situation was much the same in 1763 (Chapter 8). These flock-masters were concerned not merely with pastoral production; they evidently had considerable control and influence in the wool market too.

10.5. Dating the *bories*

As we have seen, fieldwork on the Plateau de Calern suggests that classic *bories* are numerous, regularly spaced and comprehensively distributed; some are associated with stock enclosures, others are not. Archaeologically, they look as if they should have been constructed over a rather limited time horizon, a period when the plateau was heavily implicated in a form of economic activity which was productive and lucrative enough for every stakeholder to require one or more of these solidly-built corbelled shelters – a time when motive and opportunity coincided and for those with the capacity for vigourous economic action there was money to be made. As Thiery has shown (see above), in this region *bories* were evidently being constructed in numbers in the first half of the 17th century, and it would not be unreasonable to extend this period of construction backwards into the second half of the 16th century. The confident, repetitive architectural style of the *bories* suggests that they were constructed by professionals. As we have seen, by this time the requirement for efficient, relatively large-scale shepherding coincided with the availability of labour, as individuals had to sell their stake in the land and could no longer call on the support system represented by the large traditional families. Arguably the 'complete' coverage of the Plateau de Calern by *bories* would have been achieved when the 'village flock' had itself arrived at something of a plateau, the maximum size permitted by contemporary practice, which could well be the figure of around 20,000 achieved by the early 17th century. By extension, this general dating is extended to those *enclos* which incorporate *bories*. Walls and *bories* are generally linked by the character of their masonry and the degree of degradation which they have suffered (the walls being more vulnerable than the *borie* itself as long as the latter's corbelled roof holds up).

Thiery[7] is clearly willing to countenance the construction of classical corbelled *bories* both later and earlier, even much earlier, than this period of *c.* 1550–1650, but I am sceptical about both of these propositions. Let us take the later period first. After 1650 or so, the use of tiles for roofing would presumably be on the increase. Unlike the roofs of corbelled shelters, tiles helped to channel rainwater into cisterns (Figure 222) or tubs and thus satisfy the drinking requirements of increased numbers of sheep; they were much more effective at keeping out rain; they were much less vulnerable to freeze–thaw processes; they were available to roof relatively large enclosures if required. Being totally interchangeable, they could be readily re-used. Tiles may well have become cheaper over time; every new batch arriving in an area increased the stock available for re-cycling. Between 1763 and 1791 the number of sheep recorded for Cipières declined by some 55% (Siddle, Chapter 8) and the trauma of the War of Austrian Succession (1740–1747) (Chapter 9) would not have been conducive to investment. Even in an area where the transportation costs for tiles may have been relatively high, and the use of old-fashioned building methods may therefore have persisted longer, it is hard to believe that many new *bories* were constructed in the 18th century. Of course, these shelters continued in use, as our excavations at Baoume de Brun have demonstrated.

FIGURE 222. Plateau de Calern: mouth of a cistern. This one is apparently isolated; others are placed where they can catch water from an adjacent tiled roof. Some still have wooden drinking-troughs in the vicinity
PHOTOGRAPH: ANDREW FLEMING

I do not think it likely that classic *bories* go back in general to the Middle Ages (though the earliest ones *might* pre-date the mid-16th century by some decades). The *bories* have no integral, detectably recurrent relationship with the primary clearance landscape nor with its dendritic pattern of roads. In the early modern period many of the products of pastoralism in any case would probably have been taken *south*, towards the markets, rather than into Cipières. If it is accepted that the roofs of many of these structures built *c.* 1600 have collapsed within 400 years, owing to freeze–thaw processes, it is hard to believe that substantial numbers of them are virtually twice as old; there are very few large piles of stone which might represent 700 or 800 year old collapsed *bories*. Moreover it seems clear that the circumstances obtaining *c.* 1600 were very different from those of *c.* 1300, in relation to the pastoral regime and the basis of economic and social control. In the Middle Ages, any owners of relatively large, market-oriented flocks would have had to operate within constraints which resulted from the extensive agrarian interests and communitarian traditions of large *ostal* families. Once these constraints had been substantially diminished, the way was open for a regime which led to the spread and even distribution of professionally built shepherds' shelters and temporary cool-stores across all the seriously usable parts of the plateau. Sheep were now much more frequently kept overnight in walled enclosures (and eventually under tiled roofs) and the resultant manure was now brought under control, either for direct use by its owner, or for sale to, or negotiated exchange with, others who had cereals or pulses to grow on the plateau (see Siddle, Chapter 8). Insofar as dolines could now be used less frequently as overnight stock pounds, hay crops may now have become larger and of better quality. The growing importance of market-oriented pastoralism in the early modern period led inevitably to closer surveillance and management of livestock, greater control of the products of pastoralism, and a more professional approach to the provision of infrastructure. We may observe the archaeological effects of these changes on and around the Plateau de Calern. They manifest themselves in the form of *bories,* shelters with tiled roofs, walled enclosures and roofed *bergeries*, cisterns and certain sections of roads, now heavily degraded for the most part, which have once been embellished with metalled surfaces.

10.6. The 1842 cadastre

The boundaries of the parcels of land marked on the 1842 cadastral map can be identified in relation to various features on the ground. Figure 223 shows the aerial photograph of much of the *quartier* of Les Baumes, with the cadastral map for comparison. A close comparison of the map and the photograph shows clearly how some lengths of property boundary followed archaeologically and/ or geologically defined 'edges', whilst others consisted of apparently arbitrary lines across the land (though they may of course have been marked by stones or posts at the time when the map was drawn). The mapped boundaries may follow medieval parcel boundaries, which may be continuous and conspicuous stretches of walling; the edges of zones of clearance, indicated variously by the cessation of clearance cairns or the ends of terraces; or fragmentary lines of piled or placed stones. Some of these medieval boundaries follow the edges of rock outcrops or other geological features which may have piles of stone or low terraces placed along them. But sometimes they are more tenuous – or may consist of imaginary lines between two marked points. The most obvious illustration of this variability lies near the north-west corner of the Les Baumes *quartier*. Here, the northern boundary of the *quartier*, and hence also of the parcels which adjoin this boundary, is formed by the Chemin des Baumettes, which is marked on the 1842 map as if it were a continuous walled road. Archaeologically speaking, however, this is not the case. To the west, only one side of the road is marked by a continuous wall, as the road passes through a relatively distinct parcel of cleared land and feeds into a conspicuous gateway; the other side of the road is more tenuous. Further east, there is no structural trace of the road, though it is obvious from surface wear on the rock – its 'polished' appearance – that this easy passage along the grain of the geology must have been a routeway along which livestock were frequently driven (and probably still are). Thus in 1842 the parcels of land along the northern edge of the *quartier* (and also along the southern edge of the neighbouring Le Rouré *quartier*) were bounded in some places by a structurally defined roadway, in others by the line of a routeway which was not precisely defined on the ground at all. It is striking that one of the less archaeologically-conspicuous boundaries, a thin meandering wall already mentioned in Chapter 4, and illustrated (Figure 168) was still a boundary in 1842, where it forms the northern edge of parcels 569 and 571. The same could be said of the southern boundary of parcel 442 (near the south-west corner of the map). This boundary too has already been illustrated (Figure 167). It consists of an intermittent straggle of stones running through a zone where the slight terraces (which are based on natural geological 'ribs') stop. This 'field edge' is more of an archaeological feature than a prominent boundary, and its continuing recognition into the 19th century must say quite a lot about the continuity of recognised parcel edges over the centuries.

The 1842 cadastre demonstrates that the relative value of different kinds of land on the plateau was still recognised in the early 19th century, though seemingly less meticulously than in the later Middle Ages. In the commune as a whole, there are numerous small *quartiers* in the area around the village; on the plateau there are fewer, larger *quartiers* (see Figure 31). The tendency for the land near the village to be divided into relatively small *quartiers* may be partly a function of greater time-depth (this zone presumably having been claimed and occupied for longer, and perhaps more continuously). But it must also indicate the *value* of the land relative to that on the plateau and further away from the village. A comparable tendency can be seen on the plateau, in the *quartier* of Les Baumes. On Figure 223 it can be seen that there were more, and smaller, parcels of land in the zone of large uvulas to the north-west of the Chemin des Baumes and in a narrow north–south band running up the centre of the area. Conversely, in much of the western part of the area, where the ground rises and there are only a few, small dolines, land parcels were relatively large. In Chapter 4, it was suggested that in the late Middle Ages many dolines were accompanied or partly surrounded by zones of clearance cairns, which seem, in archaeological

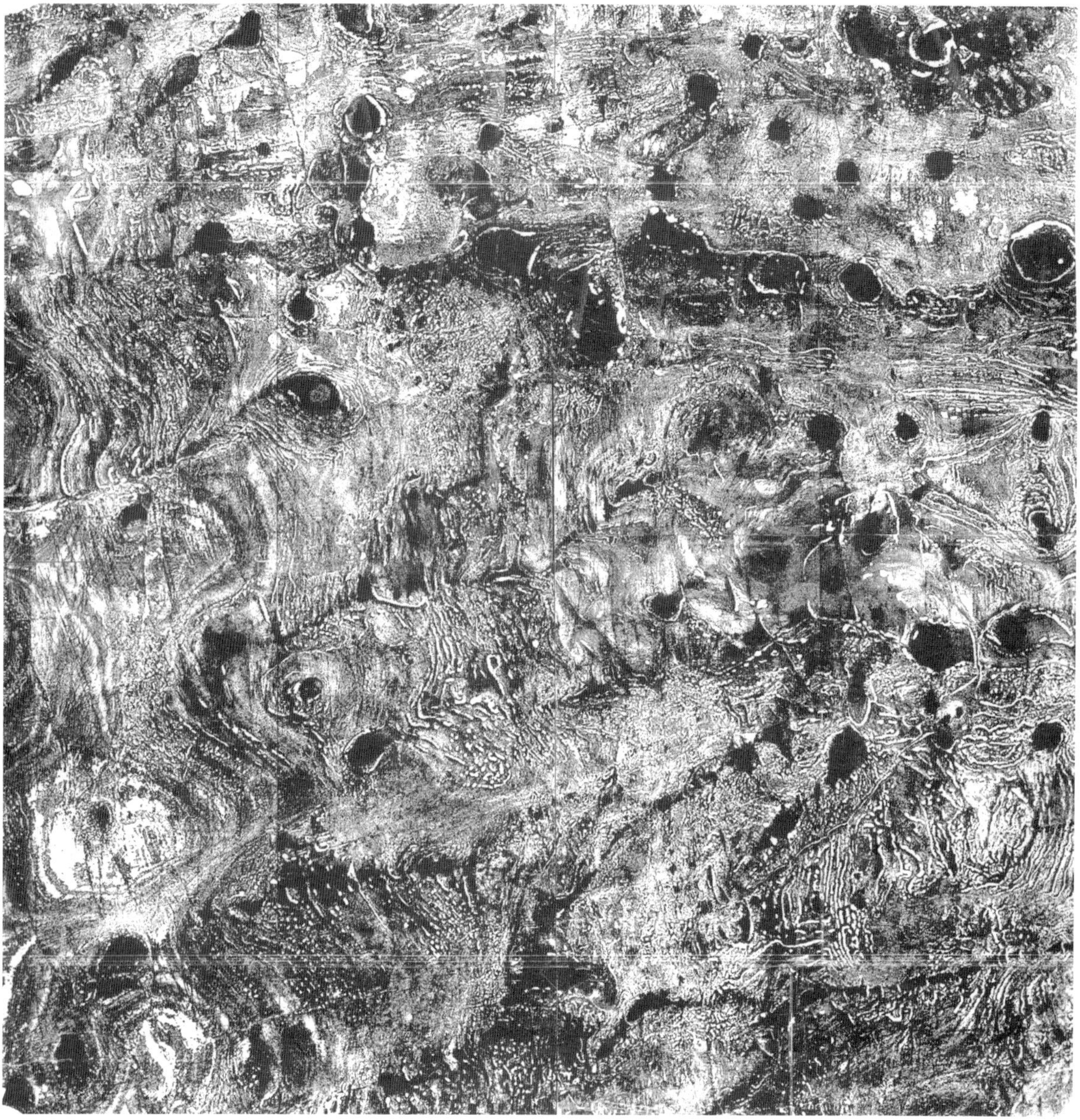

FIGURE 223. a) Air photograph of most of the Les Baumes *quartier*; b) (on facing page) the same area on the cadastral map of 1842. The black spots indicate *bories* (which were not marked on the 1842 map)
AIR PHOTOGRAPH REPRODUCED BY KIND PERMISSION OF THE IGN

terms, to have 'belonged' to their dolines. Whether this was the case or not, such perceptions had vanished by the 19th century. As can be seen from Figure 223, the edge of a land parcel which was also a doline was effectively the edge of the doline itself, often marked by a revetment wall. Usually, individual dolines are claimed as individual parcels of land, and the land which surrounds them is part of another, often much larger parcel. This tendency is best demonstrated near the north-east corner of Figure 223, where the very large parcel 589 is the land which surrounds no less than seven doline-parcels, whilst parcel 585, just to the east, plays much the same role. Almost all dolines are claimed as individual

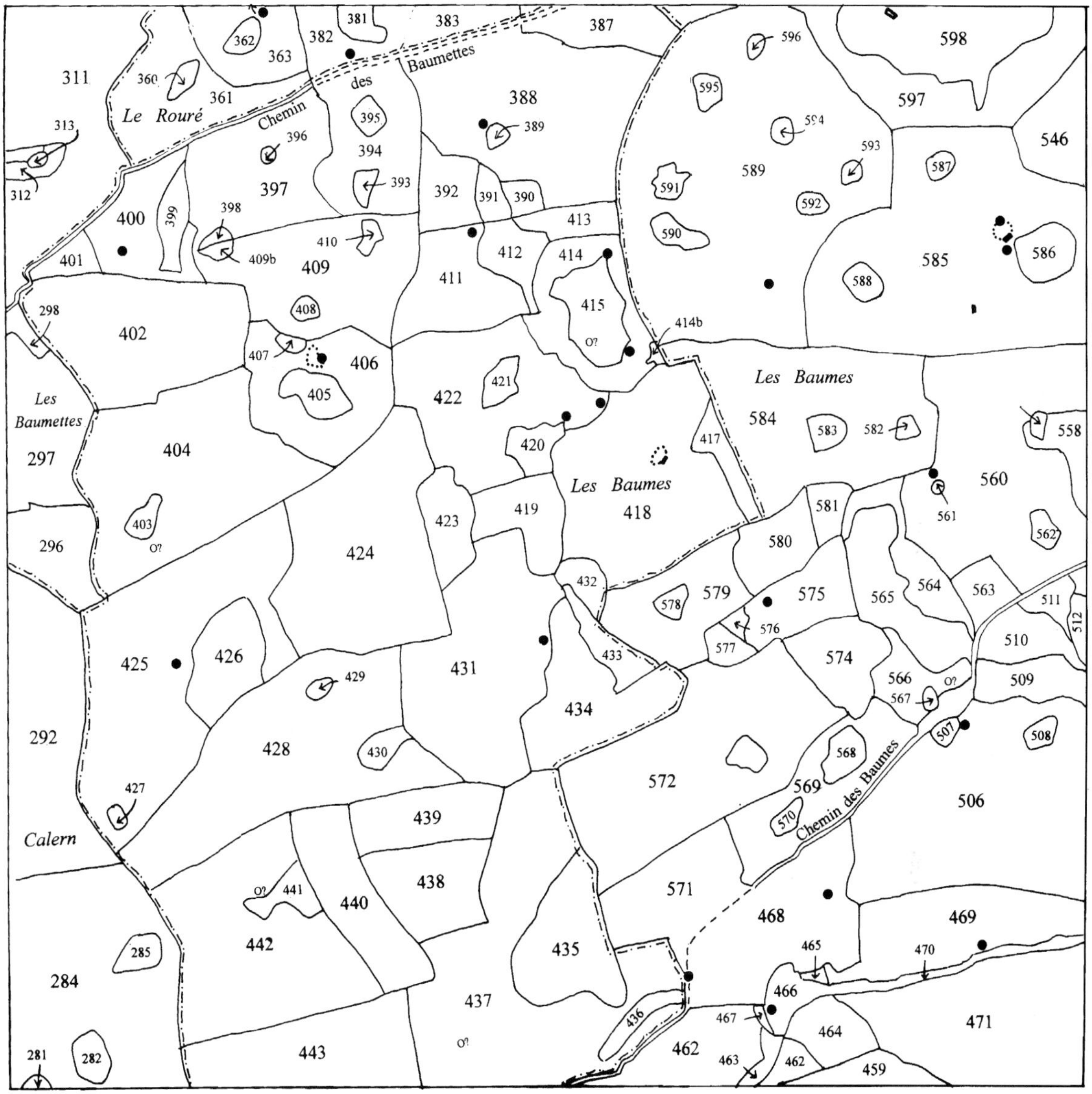

land parcels, even quite small, shallow ones such as 313, 396, 427 and 429, and there is one case where a small, shallow doline is actually divided into two parcels (398 and 409b, near the north-west corner of the map). It seems that the particular value of dolines, even quite small ones, was widely acknowledged, and the appropriate property rights maintained, at least in legal and fiscal terms. It is interesting that the 1842 cadastral map recognises just one doline cascade as a land parcel (470, near the south-east corner of the map) but ignores all others, such as the one in parcel 404, for example. This suggests that such cascades were now much less valued than they had been when work parties went to the considerable trouble of quarrying stone and building terrace walls along them.

It cannot be established by archaeological inspection how far the parcels represented on the 1842 cadastral map reflect actively and regularly used parcels of land, as opposed to legally and fiscally defined entities. The act of surveying and mapping itself, which involved visiting the terrain with a knowledgeable local informant – if not several – eliminated, by definition, any actual or pretended vagueness on the part of land-holders. The latter were evidently concerned to see that the dolines, the most valued bits of land, were put on the map; but the intricacy of some of the other boundaries suggests a complex history of the definition of property. Several centuries of inheritance, exchange and purchase of land may have left those who continued to actively use the land out here with quite complex portfolios of dispersed property. In 1842 the definition of boundaries varied, as it must have done in the Middle Ages, along a continuum, from the long stretch of prominent walling to the imaginary line, not marked on the ground – a situation not dissimilar, apparently, to that of the late medieval agrarian landscape on the plateau; there is no particular reason to expect such arrangements to have changed over the centuries. The important point is that the modes of defining boundaries which seem likely to have obtained in the Middle Ages, on the basis of purely archaeological reasoning, can be shown to have obtained in the 19th century on the basis of cartographic evidence.

Self-evidently, the 1842 cadastre represents the advent of a 'Cartesian' approach to the landscape of Calern, exemplified by accurate survey and mapping, and the need for every parcel to be treated as a legal and fiscal entity – whether it was actually claimed by an owner, and taxed, or not – to be precisely defined and bounded by continuous lines on a map. Yet this must have been a time when the application of more efficient and comprehensive administrative and legal instruments to the Plateau de Calern can scarcely have seemed more absurd. Long ago, the extended families of the later Middle Ages had left no stone unturned, almost literally, in their quest to improve the land they occupied. Yet in this highly competitive, explosive situation, with the potential for so many problematic social encounters and ways of (mis)behaving almost on a daily basis, they must have sorted out most of their disputes without recourse to maps or lawyers, talking matters through at the village *parlement*, establishing norms and customs relating to the occupancy and use of land through their daily practices and social strategies. Later, with many of the Cipièrois seeking work elsewhere, rich merchant graziers exploited summer pastures on the plateau, in more extensive and lucrative operations. In behavioural terms, the situation was surely simpler; yet clearly lawyers flourished now, as housing provision in the village testifies. Ultimately, the flowering of cultural practices and norms which paid homage to rationality and the principles of science coincided with a period of agrarian and demographic decadence which has essentially persisted until recent times.

CHAPTER ELEVEN

Reflections

11.1. Reflections 1

Andrew Fleming

A. The archaeology and history of landscape; holism and interdependence

My work at Cipières has been mainly concerned with the archaeology of the Plateau de Calern, and my reading of the primary clearance landscape on the plateau and its interpretation as an artefact of the later Middle Ages apparently represents a new insight in this region. This has involved the importation of classical approaches of British landscape archaeologists to the upstanding archaeological features which are so frequently encountered in our upland regions.[1] My interpretation, derived largely but not exclusively from the greater part of the large *quartier* of Les Baumes, has been based on field observations and associated modes of argument, centring around the taxonomy of ruined stone-built structures and the morphology of land parcels and roads, as well as the use of horizontal stratigraphy. A road, and then by extension a dendritic network of roads, has been taken to represent a particular chronological horizon. Part of my assessment of the relative age of stone-built structures has been based on the extent of their physical degradation, and I have thus had to consider the impact of climatic factors upon their current state of preservation. The work has involved the selection of a study area large enough to offer a representative range of land parcels, built structures and geological characteristics, and thus the observation of recurrent and thus representative patterns in the field data. In principle, the relative chronological sequence is derived purely from archaeological argument; if these structures were all prehistoric, the *sequence* would be essentially unchanged. The creation of an absolute chronology, however, has involved the importation of other forms of information, including the presence in one corner of the commune of a large nucleated village dating from the later Middle Ages, the persistence over time of *quartier* names from that epoch, the document-based population estimates made by David Siddle (this volume), Daniel Thiery's work on the dating of stone structures in neighbouring communes, the existence of the 1842 cadastral map, and a general understanding, based on the work of colleagues in the project team and others, of the economic and social history of Cipières within a regional framework.

Thus archaeological observations and arguments have established the *relative* sequence of structures and cleared land parcels on the Plateau de Calern, whilst a largely document-based history has made a major contribution to the understanding of absolute chronology. But it is important not to downplay the role of arguments and observations which attempt to build bridges between these very different sources of information. Whether one is in the field, trying to make sense of particular structures, or at the word-processor, attempting to write about the social and economic history of this upland community through the eyes of a landscape archaeologist, one soon finds oneself asking questions about the practice of farming. For example: what were the flock sizes, how were livestock moved around, how were they kept away from growing crops, how were they watered, what happened to their manure, and how was produce stored, processed and moved off the plateau? What crops were grown, and where, how were they watered, fertilised, protected and eventually processed and stored? And how did all these matters work out in terms of the seasons of the year? Equally pressing, if not more so, are questions involving the socio-economic context of production. What was the potential size of the labour force available for clearance, field work and livestock supervision? What were the seasonal pinch-points and bottle-necks, if any, in terms of labour availability? How were managerial decisions made, in the short and longer term? How were land and labour controlled, and how far did market conditions and various fiscal obligations influence agrarian strategies? How far did what we might call communitarian values and practice constrain or enable the economic ambitions of particular individuals and families? What categories of people travelled outside or through the commune? Where were they going, what was their business, how frequently did they travel and at what season? What was the relationship between the various 'infrastructural' facilities in the village – the threshing floors and the basement byres, for example – and economic activity on the plateau? And as land was gradually cleared, how should we picture the changing physical appearance of the landscape, and how did the presence of trees, undergrowth and various potentially useful plant and shrub species relate to agrarian practice?

These and numerous related concerns have of course been the staple fare of economic and agricultural historians for many years. I list just a few of these questions here not in order identify any limitation in the nature of the progress we have made during our studies at Cipières, but rather to point out how closely daily and seasonal agrarian practice, indeed most recurrent human action and behaviour, intersect with the archaeology of landscape. There may be some justification for the view that fieldwork in the landscape should be regarded as a specialised craft, probably best maintained as a closed shop for archaeologists who have received a particular kind of training. But at the same time, as the Cipières Project (among comparable studies) shows, the practice of landscape archaeology can never be hermetically sealed within its own classical concerns. To label a narrow linear stone pile which exhibits traces of facing on both sides a 'wall' is only to make a beginning. Where do the stones come from, and how were they won? Was the wall built according to some kind of mental template, by people accustomed to building such walls and attempting to standardise their practice, or not? What was the function(s) of the wall? How high did it need to stand? Was it simply a base for a more perishable superstructure, or did it need to be supplemented *along its length* by organic materials? How far was the wall a barrier to physical movement, and how and why did people move from one side of the barrier to the other? Again, this list of questions could be extended. But the point I am making here is that interpretive questions involving daily human practice are integral to the practice of the landscape archaeologist from the outset. And this is why I have not hesitated to ask such questions, and indeed to provide tentative and sometimes evidently speculative answers to some of them during my discussion of the basic archaeological sequence on the Plateau de Calern.

The consequences of asking such questions within this overtly interdisciplinary project have been chastening to some extent, in the sense that the project's historians have not necessarily been able to answer my questions about socio-economic and agrarian conditions and practices, and I have frequently been unable to answer theirs. In mutual dialogue, we may sometimes make a little progress with some of these issues. The point I am making here, however, is that to study the archaeology of landscape is to engage in a discipline which is holistic in more than one sense. As I have noted elsewhere,[2] landscape archaeology is a multidisciplinary endeavour, involving specialist methodologies and ancillary disciplines; for instance, it may be necessary to work with environmental archaeologists or historians, to find someone who is knowledgeable about local vernacular architecture or the technology of extracting and processing metal ores, and so on. But above all the *arguments* which landscape archaeologists use to support their narratives are also necessarily holistic; ideally, interpretations based on different categories of evidence, and arguments starting from largely independent premises, are brought into convergence. This is an essential, non-negotiable condition of working in landscape archaeology. In the case of the history of the high limestone plateau which forms the major part of the land of the commune of Cipières, the outcome of such an approach, as we have seen, is essentially dichotomous. On the one hand, it is possible to create a narrative of the history of the landscape which implicates various categories of evidence and argument. But there is also a large residual agenda, in the form of debates which may never find closure; it involves other specialists – especially historians – and topics which link our disciplines. Put more simply, there is much about the history of Cipières that we do not yet know. But the good news – which is inherent in the nature of the discipline of landscape archaeology – is that there are often several modes of investigation, more than one route by which we may investigate a particular problem – as I hope our work at Cipières has demonstrated.

B. Approaching the long-term history of the uplands

The second point which I wish to make here concerns perceptions of the history of upland areas like the Plateau de Calern and indeed the entire commune of Cipières. Influenced by masters such as Braudel and W. G. Hoskins, in the early years of our work here we had a strong sense of *la longue durée* – or perhaps to put it more accurately, a feeling that the patterns of walls and terraces and stone-piles which we were observing must have been created *gradually*, over long periods of time. The visible archaeology – of which there is so much – almost came to symbolise the essential 'timelessness' of peasant lifeways, worked out in close adaptation to the constraints imposed by an upland ('marginal') landscape which has always been demanding and recalcitrant. In part, such an insight was essentially poetic. We empathised with the English poet A. E. Housman, who felt that the wind on Wenlock Edge was the very same wind which had blown when 'the Roman and his trouble' were at large in the area; or with the landscape historian W. G. Hoskins, who wrote in a memorable passage in *The Midland Peasant:*[3]

> 'if the peasant of Henry VIII's day could have returned to the streets and lanes and fields to visit his great-grandson, he would have felt at home, back in a timeless world in which all the fields had their familiar names ... in which all the familiar boundaries and landmarks were still to be found as he had always known them … the smells alone, most nostalgic and evocative of all our senses … would have told him that nothing had really changed ...This was the ancient, unchanging life of the village, whatever else had happened in the meantime ...'

Our frequent encounters with such a heavily worked agrarian landscape also led us to regard Cipières as a 'taskscape' or a 'workscape'[4] and hence to visualise those aspects of peasant experience which *are* almost timeless – the heat of the sun on the back of the neck, the swirling clouds of dust and chaff at threshing time, the slow pace of a limping, heavily laden mule on a narrow pathway over the plateau, and so on.[5]

We should not lose sight of these perceptions of *la longue durée* in historical landscape studies. However, if one considers the creation of the infrastructures of living and working at Cipières, the temporal rhythms are rather different. I have suggested above that the landscape of primary clearance on the Plateau de Calern was probably the creation of two or three centuries, and that individual components of the agrarian landscape – the field of clearance cairns attached to a doline, for example – was mostly the work of a few short seasons, perhaps a few weeks – or even a few days, if we envisage the labour available to the head of a large *ostal* family, or a group of such families if we postulate the collaboration of neighbours. The argument is based on the often visibly similar character and state of degradation of cairns on a given parcel of land, and also on an understanding that to *claim* a piece of rough land and bring it into effective production is not something which can be approached in a casual or piecemeal fashion (the same is true for the study of the resultant archaeological landscapes, see above). The need to take in land outside the uvulas and dolines by digging trenches and clearing stones, creating cairns of different forms which suited the nature of the local geology, and constructing suites of terraces, both as doline cascades and on dry hillsides, must have arisen in economic, social and demographic circumstances which also afforded corresponding *opportunities* for putting such extensive and intelligently constructed infrastructural facilities in place. This must have involved not only the availability of adequate labour but also an atmosphere of vigorous competition, even a spirit of emulation, and the presence of particular incentives and rewards for participants. In other words, the phase of primary clearance, as I have called it, must have been very much of its time. The picture sketched by David Siddle elsewhere in this volume, of large, expansive and expanding *ostal* families at Cipières in the centuries between *incastellamento* and the Black Death, fits this scenario very well. It is also reminiscent of the model put forward by Friedman and Rowlands for prehistoric Europe.[6] Here, if I may oversimplify the model, certain families, having gained a slight demographic edge and obtained access to more labour, are able to arrange more elaborate and successful feasts and ceremonies, attract more followers, become the best families to marry into, and eventually have access to even more productive labour, so that the cycle may start again, at a higher level of inclusiveness, social power and productivity. Agrarian production and social reproduction thus develop a relationship of mutual feedback. In a more universal context, the differences between the organisation of this familiar pattern of socio-political and economic action under hereditary chiefs and under Big Man systems is not a topic which can be pursued here; indeed such differences seem relatively immaterial.

Arguably the scenario of intensive and relatively rapid social and material investment which I believe we have to confront in order to understand the primary clearance phase on the plateau is also applicable to the planned village at Cipières itself. Virtually by definition, the planning and construction of the village was not a piecemeal or gradual process. The fact that it must surely have involved at least three phases of expansion (see Austin, Chapter 2) – the eastern sector, the western sector, and the *place* together with La Bourgade – demonstrates the village's *recurrent* capacity to act effectively and collectively – whatever the detailed structures of organisation and the incentives – when circumstances required or dictated. Arguably the creation of the planned, nucleated village would have necessitated and inculcated certain patterns of organisation and modes of thought and action, family rooted and yet also communitarian in some sense, which would have been largely novel in this countryside of dispersed farms and hamlets (if our model is broadly accurate). Arguably too it was this new *mentalité*, along with the new demographic circumstances, which enabled and inspired the rapid colonisation of the plateau and its less obviously productive expanses of terrain.

In their seminal work *The Corrupting Sea*,[7] Hordern and Purcell have argued that most Mediterranean societies have had to cope with environments best described not as marginal but rather as exposed to recurrent risk; their strategies for dealing with such environments can be summarised under the headings of diversification, storage and redistribution. Undoubtedly elements of all three strategies will have been present at Cipières in the later Middle Ages. The intricate and intelligent development of the agrarian landscape of the Plateau de Calern outside the 'honey-pots' of the uvulas and the dolines, and the consequent expansion of its productive capacity, represents a rather obvious case of diversification. Although there is no space to elaborate here, one might also argue that it was the *interdependence* of the specialist knowledges, skills and agrarian practices, whose effects are to some extent still visible in the Calern landscape, which constituted an even more significant adaptation to the risk-prone environments which form the subject of Hordern and Purcell's thesis. Such interdependence, of course, would have made communities like Cipières particularly vulnerable to major regional crises when they occurred – as in the mid-14th century.

In the light of this kind of analysis, it is thus particularly interesting that when demographic and economic recovery occurred in the Cipières region, in the 16th and 17th centuries, the new colonisation of the plateau, expressed archaeologically by the regular pattern of *bories* and largely associated stock enclosures in most corners of the Calern plateau, seems to display much the same pattern as the earlier clearance episode – a rapid investment in necessary infrastructural facilities, if my reading of the archaeological landscape is correct. Obviously, by the early modern period the social, economic and demographic circumstances had changed considerably, as David Siddle has so ably demonstrated (Chapter 9). Nevertheless, given the will to exploit certain new economic opportunities, it was evidently possible to put the necessary physical facilities in place and to re-organise the application of labour and the conversion of agrarian practice, and to do this rapidly. If the property boundaries which become visible at Les Baumes with the production of the 1842 cadastral map are any guide, in the early modern period the late medieval pattern of agrarian parcels was in part respected, in part repudiated. And perhaps we should take this as a potent symbol of the change within continuity (or continuity within change?) which we perceive, however imperfectly, when we consider the question of Cipières and *la longue durée.*

11.2. Reflections 2

David Siddle

Andrew Fleming (above) has addressed some of the shortcomings of our interchanges, mainly deriving from the tangential nature of our research strategies, which emerged over such a long period of time. Perhaps we cast our nets somewhat independently and from the perspectives of our individual research experiences. My own background, working with documentary evidence from the archives of Haute Savoie, was particularly beneficial in leading towards interpretation of social structures and in using the taxation driven sources (inquests, land tax registers, surveys, deliberations). My progress was defined by the lengthy period, sometimes years, between phases or 'seasons' of archaeological work. This turned me towards the rich seam of sources where my previous French research experience was strongest: the interactive use of taxation and demographic evidence. The result was that, in many ways I ploughed my own furrow, working evidence already collated by Anthony Lewison and his field assistants alongside the rich resources of the archive in the basement of the Cipières Mairie. This is not to say that whenever we were all together in the field it was not the richest of experiences. It was always a pleasure to follow David Austin across seemingly randomised pediments of stone fragments and hollows to have them revealed as real features of the farming landscape, or to trace Andrew Fleming's eye along a previously indiscernible trackway or boundary to have it leap out like a stereoscopic image as he led the way towards a break or turn of direction. Both were a delight and an inspiration. Later in the research experience it has been an equal pleasure to work alongside Rosamond Faith and find a scholar made sympathetic by her previous experience of documentary evidence from the Midi to the idea of large kinship associations both in dwellings and in the workscape.

Together we all began to see this apparently barren landscape of neglect as a living and breathing medieval and post medieval world, densely populated and living within the sound of the persistent bleating of large flocks of sheep and goats. It was also possible to envisage a village community through its phases of rapid medieval expansion as its inhabitants came to live in apartments above some of their animals and below their store of hay or grain. It was a regret that with a continuing and necessary pre-occupation with plateau landscapes we could not really explore together the bench with its massive stone piles, the accumulation of generations of field clearances, the lower tree covered terraces towards the river Loup with its seigneurial woods and vineyards, fulling mill and cow pastures. Nor has it been possible, in the absence of seigneurial papers, to establish with any certainty exactly where the seigneurial lands were. Although the large field below the village, dominated by the bailiff's house, is a clear candidate for demesne land, the extent of seigneurial rights over grazing on the plateau remains a mystery. Over much of this lower area we had no other opportunity but to stand and stare and speculate.

The main advantage of the *longeurs* between field work phases was that it allowed me the opportunity, and more importantly the time, to use the 18th century vital event records photocopied by Lewison (births, marriages and deaths) alongside the rich trove of inquests and cadastres of the period. I was thereby able to offer a much fuller explanation of demographic, social and economic behaviour of the periods of very rapid social an economic change in the medieval and then again in the early modern period than a shorter time scale for our research would otherwise have made possible. Admittedly the conclusions for the early modern period are offered with more confidence than those for earlier periods, where sources were patchier and interpretations inevitably more speculative. Ironically it was in precisely this period of early population expansion before the Black Death that work by David Austin, Andrew Fleming and Rosamond Faith came together with my own speculations to allow richer and hopefully more accurate landscape interpretations as well as a deeper understanding of the social and economic life of the community. Their findings certainly emboldened me to carry my own thoughts forward towards an interpretation of social structures relating to extended families.

There are clear risks of course in making links with the insights of other scholars in a team. The danger is always of mutually reinforcing shaky hypotheses. As Andrew Fleming has pointed out, we could not always ask each other questions for which answers were available, sometimes because our research trajectories had diverged and sometimes because the evidence was just not there. If our periodic interchanges were unlikely to produce truly collaborative work, as time passed our insights improved and I truly believe that with all our caveats and reservations did make rope bridges across seemingly unbridgeable chasms in our understanding. Indeed, using different parameters we have often surprised ourselves by coming to conclusions, which were pleasingly conversant.

11.3. Reflections 3

Rosamond Faith

Joining the Cipières project at a comparatively late stage was to find myself in a landscape, metaphorically and literally, which was strange to me but familiar to my colleagues. I had more in common with the young archaeology students from Lampeter University, there for training in field work, and I learned alongside them to use my eyes: even a modern construction of corrugated iron and plastic string could have something to teach about its function and history – that is where the sheep had gathered, that is where a repair had been made. Speedily my perspectives changed by simply being in the landscape. On the Plateau de Calern, initially nothing but a barren wilderness of grass and rocks, farms and fields and roads began to emerge. Our daily journey to the plateau by a roundabout road trip in a Landrover, turned out to be a much shorter walk from the village by a handmade road used by the Cipièrois for generations. Riding a horse up from Caussols brought home how ideal sure-footed mules must have been as pack-animals on these steep and winding ways. In David Siddle's words it is the archaeology of the plateau that reveals, 'the investment of energy which is a testament to the skills and perseverance of the first Cipèrois' in creating the environment which made farming possible there. It is this appreciation of the 'buildedness' of the farming environment that is one of the most important things that the medieval historian can take from the archaeologist.

And if this was in so many ways a built environment, who built it? David Siddle and I have both been led by our work to question an orthodoxy of European demography: the European Marriage Pattern model. My work on the peasant families on the estates of S Victor de Marseille, had already led me to appreciate the importance of extended families as the 'work-group' which made life possible in upland landscapes where pastoralism was the mainstay. I met them in David Siddle's *ostal* families who were the backbone of Cipières society, and among the builders of the roads and walls, the patches of arable hard-won from the stony upland. He has provided names and dwellings for a form of social organisation, once common across Europe, whose slow decay he is able to show from the demographic record.

Another orthodoxy now became open to challenge: that of the 'Tragedy of the Commons', which argues that communal systems collapse because the participants will be dominated by greedy individuals. The plateau farming infrastructure could only have been formed, and farmed and regulated, on the basis of, in Andrew Fleming's words, the 'communitarian traditions of large *ostal* families'. It was more the intrusion of merchant capital that began the end of peasant sheep farming, and that was only possible because the Grasse merchants could exploit the peasants' common rights.

A third orthodoxy which it became possible to question was that of the effects of *incastellamento* on the peasantry. The 'feudalisation' of the landscape classically proposed by Duby here worked not to the suppression of peasant rights but to the advantage of a group, the *caslani*. They too were, in effect, shapers of the built environment, shown by David Austin's analysis of the evolution of the village plan. That peasant *agency* has been a theme throughout encourages the shift, still rather tentative among English medievalists, away from the view that developments in peasant settlement patterns and farming practice were landlord-driven.

The landscape and people of Cipières in the past have continued to inform my own subsequent work, and working with a group of colleagues who are also friends on a well-loved place has become an image to me of the good academic life.

11.4. Reflections 4

David Austin

When I was first asked to go to Cipières by Anthony Lewison, I had no notion that it would be an engagement that would last the best part of 25 years and involve me in a working relationship with so many people. If I had known that, I might have done things differently and spent my time more wisely. The landscape that I encountered, as an archaeologist trained and experienced in the British topographic tradition, was so alien to me that a lot of time was spent trying to find the right questions to ask and then to develop methodologies which might begin to answer them. In hindsight this turned out to be an endlessly repetitive process both in the field and in discussion with my colleagues. Time and again we would find ourselves addressing the same issues and engaging with the same questions, often standing in the same place in the landscape. However, in spite of this, we made significant progress and the time spent in debate and argument was in the end worth it. So often these days, there is simply not enough time in research projects just to talk and reflect. Our professional worlds require targeted outcomes to be identified from the start and we must drive towards them with utmost efficiency. This is not the topographic tradition: the mechanical exercises of data retrieval and analysis do not always allow the equally important growth of familiarity with place, the observation of peripheral things which might have meaning in ways that are unexpected and revealing, and the emotional connection with real people, experiences and feelings. These contribute to the complex and holistic understanding of place and locality that is so bred into the bone of the topographer. One of the things we have tried to bring to our text at the end is some sense of both the intellectual and the sentimental journey we have made and the connection and engagement we came to have with the landscapes of Cipières.

What we have achieved is a contribution to the history of the Alpine and Mediterranean regions of Europe from a particularly British perspective which has allowed us to ask some very basic questions and get some very surprising answers, without the baggage of presumption drawn from the acceptance of long-established authority. Rosamond Faith and David Siddle have already drawn attention to the challenges we have made to the understanding of some of the large historical processes of the last 1000 years and Andrew Fleming to the broad sweep of material chronology and social change which give a new kind of narrative to these upland landscapes. I, like my colleagues, take great pride in our achievement, although painfully aware, as all scholars are at the end, of those things we failed to understand or the trails we followed with no final destination. We are immensely grateful for the opportunities which this project have given us to develop both this knowledge and our friendships and we are in eternal debt to the people of Cipières and to the many colleagues we met and who gave us a hand along the way.

APPENDIX ONE

Information on *Quartier* Names drawn from Key Documentary Sources

David Austin

1842	*1750*	*1610*	*1531*	*1332–52*	*Translation*
L'Agrémourié	Gremol(l)iere	Lagremolier	Lagremoulier (Alagre-moulyer Alagremollier)	Agremeliar (Agrarmenc')	*Gooseberry bush*
L'Aire d'Annelle As place-name only on map in La Combe – not a quartier	L'Aire Danelle	Liere Danelle	Leiro Danello		*The threshing-floor* + personal name
L'Armas	L'Armas (Ma(r)s)	Larmarr (Mar)	Lamar (La Mar) [Lybac de la mas]		*Fallow or waste land, desert, uncultivated land*
L'Aspé	L'Aspe	Laspe Laspest	Laspe		*Aspen*
				Le Play de Blaciarias	
La Baisse de Calern		(La Baisse de) Laurier La Baisse de Campanier (?) Dessus de Calern	Baisso de ?lenrur?		*The base of (the Plateau de Calern)*
Les Baudillons	Ba(u)dillons	Baudillons Boudillone	Baudilhons		Poss. personal name or *the place of the box-trees*
Les Baumes	B(e)aume (Baumo)	B(e)aume (Baumo)	Baumo		*Caves*
La Beaume d'Ayaud	Baume d'Aillau(d)	Baume d'Aillaud	Baume d'Aillaud (d'Alhaud)		*The cave* + personal name
Les Baumettes	Baumettes	Beaumette (Beaumit(t)os)	Baumitos	Las Balmetas	*Small caves*

1842	*1750*	*1610*	*1531*	*1332–52*	*Translation*
La Baoumo de Brun L'Avenc et Baomo de Brun	Baume de Brun	Beaum de Brun Combo de Brun	Baume de Brun Clapiers de Brun		*Cave, rock shelter, rock face* + personal name? *Stone piles* + personal name? *Small valley* + personal name?
Le Baou d'Aussel	Le Bau(d) (Boual) d'Aussel	La Boal Daussel La Font Daussel	Prat Daussel (Dausuels, Dausulhet		*Cliff* + personal name
Le Bausset	Bausset (Bou(i) sset)	Boisset (Baus(s)et)	Boisset Bausset		*Box [tree]*
			Bes(s)ono		?
	Baud de la Guelle	Baux de Julian	Bosq de Gilly	Le Bovesc (?)	? *Cliff* or *wood* + personal name
	Blaus				?
			Boudrano		?
	Boullegue	Boligo (Boulegne Bolleile Bollene)	Boul(i)ego		?
			Bramefam (Bramo Fam)		Small hamlet on E side of R. Loup now in Courmes.
		Broque(t)	Broquet (Bronguet)		?
Le Calern		Calern Plus sault Calern Vinq de Calern	Calern	Calern	Very early form con-taining element meaning *mountain* 1539: 54 = Calern & Calernet together
		Cabanon Cabanos	Cabanos		*Huts, cabins*
Le Calernet	Calernet	Calernet Calsernet	Calernet (Qualernet)		See Calern

1842	*1750*	*1610*	*1531*	*1332–52*	*Translation*
Le Camp de l'Hosté					*The camp of the army*
		Camp de Nouelle (Nouille)	Camp denovillo		*The new field*
			Camp dau tormand?		
Camuéro	Camio(l)le (Camilotte)	Camiolle (Camiole)	Camiollo (Camiello)		?
		Cavilcolle (Cavilocille)	Cavilho (Canilhollo)	Cavillore(?)	*Horse hill*
Les Carbonelles	Carbonelle (s)	Carbonelle	Carbonello		*Charcoal (lands)*
Les Carbouniers		Carbonier	Carbounyer		*The charcoal burners*
La Caou	(La) Caux (La Couche?)	Caux Caus	Caulx [Val de] Causso		*'Causse' or limestone plateau or upland*
		Caupré	Caucans (Cauquans, Calquan)		
		Caucadi(e)s	Cauquadis (Quauquadis)		
La Chapelle	Dessus la Chapelle de Penitens		Saint Cappello		*The (holy) chapel* *Chapel of Penitence*
La Clapoua	Clapoue	Clapoue(t)	Clappou(et)	Clapoua	*The rock*
Clarréou	Clarieou (Clorreou, Clot Reou, Rier)	Clauriou (Clot riou, Cloreon)	Clarriou		*The hollow or flat land* + personal name?
Les Pesses de Clarréou					*The parcels or pieces of (arable) ground* + Clarréou
Le Clauvas L'Hubac de Clauvas	Clauvan (Claucan, Clauna(n)	Clauvau (Claunau)	Clauvan (Claunan, Lauvau)		Personal name? Or if orig. lauvan = *thin flat rock or slab*

1842	*1750*	*1610*	*1531*	*1332–52*	*Translation*
	Cluetes		Clots		*Flat, cultivated hollows or*
			Clot de Saint		*flat areas*
			Mayol		
			Clot dan quat		
			Clot Dessane		
			Clot dau Prieure		
		Clot de Pesier			
		(Peosoir)			
		Clot de Girard	Clot de Girard		
	Clot de Gras	Clot de Gras	Clot de Gras		
		Clot dan Bouis	Clot dau Bois		
		Clot de Four	Clot de Furo		
	Clap de Furi	(Cloit de Fure,			
	(Feuve)	Clout de Fure)			
		Clot de Sine	Clot de Sino		
		Clot de Codino	Clot de Codeno		
		(Coudene,			
		Coudere)			
	danlaire	Clot dan laire			
	Clot de Sueil	Clot Dansuels,	Lou Clot		
		(du suel)	Dausnels		(cf. Le Baou
			(Daugnels, Dau		d'Aussel)
			Suels)		
		Clot de Galine	Clot de Galine	Lo Clot de	
			(Gallyno)	Gallinis Calerno	
		Clot de Rostan	Clot de		
			Roustang		
			Drago de		
		Lis cle de	Roustang		
		Blanche	Lis Clo de		
			Blanche	Le Prat dels	
	Liscle	Clot Besson		Blancs iuxta	
		Clot de	Clot Besson	Ban' Lupi	
		Baumon			
	Clot Besson	Clot de			
		Lanelau			
		Clot de			
		Lortiquier			
		Clot Margue			
		Clot de Pairol			
	Clot de Peirol				
	Clot de Mouriers				
	en Plan				
Colle Basse	Colle Basse	Collo Basso	Collo Basso		*Low pass or low hill*
		(Colle, Colo)			
L'Hubac de					*Shady side of*
Colle Basse					*low pass/hill*

1842	*1750*	*1610*	*1531*	*1332–52*	*Translation*
				Lo Colla day?llo	
La Colle de Rougiés	Col de Rougies	 Colle de Calern	Colle de Rougies Collo de Calern	 La Cella de Calern	*Pass or hill* + personal name?
Collet du Lumiaou	Lumian (Lumiau)	Lumial (Lumeal)	Lumial (Lumeal, Lamehl)		*Small hill, mountain* + personal name
Les Collets	Col(l)ets	Collets	Col(l)et (Coletz)		*The small hills/mountains*
Collet de la Croix		 Colet de Cana[n]gne Colet de Rimongili Colet de lau Fouquet Colet de Baumon Tour de la Colette	 Collet de Ca(n)va(i)gno Colet de Raymond Gilly Colet de Sors Colet de Groutin (Broteu)		*Small hill of the cross* *Small hill* + personal names
Collet d'Embarnoui Embarnoui Les Graoux d'Embarnoui	 Barnoin (Bernoin)	 Barno(u)in (Barmoin,	 Barnoin		*Small hill* + enclitic 'en' as locative, i.e. *house of* or *place of* + personal name (Barnoin)
La Combe L'Adrech de la Combe L'Hubac de la Combe	La Combe	Combe (Combos)	Conbo(s)		*The (deep) valley* *The sunny (north) side of La Combe* *The shady (south) side of La Combe*

1842	*1750*	*1610*	*1531*	*1332–52*	*Translation*
La Plus Haute Combe L'Hubac de la Combe la plus haute					*The highest part of La Combe*
	Combe d'Andon (d'Auban) Combal de Bouda(s) Combe des Guignues (Combes de Gaigoun) Combe de Richard Combal de Bigarotte	Combe dau Pons Combe Dambau Combe de Domergo Combe dau Pomier) Combal de Baudair Combau de Tuigs (Thuie) Combe de Barnoin Combe daux Guigoes Combe du Puit Combe dau Raiol Combe de Richard Rachert	Combe de Monsen Auban Combo di Bumi (Bumy) Conbo de Marcon Conbo Magnet(t)o Conbo dau Poule Conbo dau Pres Combe dau Pons Conbe dau Bou Conbo de dou Mergou Conbo dau Poumyer Conbal Daubert	Bunoy	*(Deep) valley* + personal names
Les Combes	Combes				*The (deep) valleys*

1842	*1750*	*1610*	*1531*	*1332–52*	*Translation*
Les Costes	Cuse (?)	Coste de Serisse (Serraye) Coste dau Colet	Costos (Costso, Caussto, Causse)		*The sides, flanks (of the mountain, gorge)*
Les Coulets	Coul(l)ets	Coulet	Coulet(z)		*The small hills*
La Courneirée	Curnairee	Cournairie	Curnayrio (Cur Noyer)		*The dogwood* or possibly *the dogwood cutter*
	Cauregniere (Courigniere)	Caurignier	Caurignere (Cauregneyro)		*Vallon de Coourignère* As place-name only for one of the dry valleys crossing low-land between, e.g., Pas de Bouis & Collet de la Croix
	La Croiree	Croirie			?
La Croix	(La) Croix	Croix	[see Cros below]		*The cross*
La Croux La Croux de Coulets	(La) Croux (Craux, Couze)	Croux (Crous)	CRosamond (Cuos, Ruos) (are some entries Croix?) Vallon de la CRosamond(Cos, Ruos)		*The cross*
		Culalasse de Ricord			?
	Elucttes				
Embouisset					Locative enclitic + personal name, *Bouisset's place*
Entre Four	Trefour	L'entrefour (Lantrefour)	Lantrefour		Puzzling, but seems to con-tain element 'four' *oven*

1842	*1750*	*1610*	*1531*	*1332–52*	*Translation*
Entros L'Hubac d'Entros	Trou L'Adrech de Trou (?) Libac de Trou	Trahou (Trabou)	Tra(h)ou (Tragou) Colle de Trahou	Trahoy	Locative enclitic + *hole*
L'Eouvé	Leouze (Leauze, Leoye)		Leu Hyve		*Evergreen oak*
			Fade		?
			Lou Fal	Le Fualh (?)	?
La Fatime	Fatime(s)	Fatime (Fatimo)			
La Faye Le Faye et Colle de Rougiés	(La) Faye	Faye	La Fayo	La Faya	*Beech-tree*
La Coste de la Faye		Combau de la Faye	Coste de la Faye		*The side of La Faye*
	Fousses	Faisse (Faissos)	Fayssos Faissos de Brun Plus luenge Fayo		Strips of cultivated land retained by walls *(Both terraces and long strips)*
Les Ferrages			Ferraye Garnyero (Fayes gar nyro, Frayo gar nyro) Feulier(r)e (Fuliero)?		*Areas for growing cattle fodder or vegetables*
Les Ferrages Le Desport	Desport (Despres)	Desport, (Despor)	Desport (Dos Pors)		?
Le Puits			Puy Manuy(s) (Marniyo, Maurier, Mauris)		*Well of the seigneur*
		Figure de Ricord			?*Fig*

1842	*1750*	*1610*	*1531*	*1332–52*	*Translation*
Le Ribas de la Font (v.Les Prés de la Lone et de la Font)	(La) Fontain (i) e(s) (but hard to distinguish from Fontainiers)	Font	Font (Fond)		*The river-side at the spring, well*
		Font de Calern	Fond de Calern	La Font de Calern	*The spring/ well on Calern*
			Font Aymente		
			Font St Mayol		
La Font de la Sine	Font de la Sine	Val de la Sine	Val de la Sine		*Valley(spring) of the hawthorn*
Les Fontainiers Les Fontaniers de la Ribière	Fontainiers (Fonteinieres)	Fontanier (Fontanios, Fontaynier) Vallon de la Fontaynor	Fontaynyos Vallon de la Fontaynos		*The water diviners* or *carriers.* Also a Provençal family name
Le Fraï	Frei (Fray)	Frais (Fray)	Frais (Frait)		*The ash*
Gache		Colet de Gache	Coulet de Gacho		*Sentry hill*
	Galis (Garis)		Gallies (Galiz)		?
	Gardettes (Leigardettes)	Gardette	Gardetos (Gardillos)		*The boundary stones* (of reserved pasture)
		La Gast	La Gast		*The waste*
La Gaou de Pounchon	Cau de Ponchon (Poujou, Pounjou)				Prob. caus, *limestone upland of the Pounch*
Les Gipières	Gipieres	Gipiere	Gip(p)ieros		*Lime quarries*
	La Glaire				?
La Gorge de Puits					*The gorge of the wells/ springs*
Grabelle	Grabelle	Grabelle	Grau (Grao) Bello		*The beautiful, large, flat rock/rocky eminence, tor*
La Grangoue	Grangeou	Grango(a)ue (Grangoane)	Grangouo		*The grange (monastic farm)*

1842	*1750*	*1610*	*1531*	*1332–52*	*Translation*
Graou de Paillier	Gra(u)d de Paillier	Grau de Pallier	Grau de Pailler		*Straw (maker's) crag* or *Crag* + personal name
Les Graous de Pons Les Graous de Pons et Coste de la Faye	Grau de Guillon Pons	Grau de Guilhon Pons (Pons de Gras)	Grau de Guilhon Pons		*The crags* + personal name
Les Graoux	Grau(s)	Graus (Graos, Grao)	Graud (Graos)	Las Grasas	*The crags*
	Gratte Loups	Grate Loup	Gratto Loups		*Crags of the (river) Loup*
			GravierRosamond (Grav(l)-inos)		
Le Gros Pounch L'Hubac du Gros Pounch	Grepon (Greman)	Gripon	Greppon, Grep		Mod. *The great Pounch mountain,* but earlier ?
L'Hubac du Château	Libac	Libac	Ly Baq		*The shady side of the Chateau*
	Jas Couvert				?
La Juillée	Juillee (Juillie)	Jullie (Juliet)	Jullee		*The rose* Jullee & Julhio hard to distinguish in 1539 and 1750
Les Juillos	Juille	Jullo	Julhio		*The roses* see Jullee above
Les Lebourières	(La) Bouiriere	Bo(u)riere (Boinere)	Borriero Borrino		?perhaps derived from Prov. Bousset, *box(tree),* poss. *Box-maker*
		La Loge			*The hut*
		Loup	Loup (Louppe)		*(River) Loup (wolf)*
Matheron	Matheron (Mattel(l)on)	Mataron	Malheron (Malharan, Malsaran)		Personal name, *'the bad heron'*
Le Maupas	Mau Pas	Maubo(u)sc	Mal Bosq		*The bad wood* (perhaps a family name)

1842	1750	1610	1531	1332–52	Translation
Maurenc	Ma(u)renc (Marenne, Marron)	Maurenc	Maurinq (Maureng)		Personal name?
Meynard	Mainard	Mainard			Personal name
		Coste de Mangarido	Coste de Mangarydo		
		Baume de Mainard			
		Font de Meinard			
Les Miraous	Miraux (Moraux)	Mirau(l)x	Miraulx		? Poss. derived from mouret, *wall of rock*
			Coste de Myroland?		
		Baume de Merle	Clapiers de Myroland		
	Mottes				*Mounds*
Les Moulières	Mo(u)l(l)ieres	Mouliere (Moliniere, Moliner)	Moulier(r)os (Moulier)		*The boggy (lit. soft) lands*
Les Moulins	Moulin	Moulin	Moulin	Mollenas	*The mills*
	(La) Mellou(x) (Malloui, Miou)	Miloue (Melous)	Melou (Melhout, Melouo, Milou)		*?*
Les Moures	Mour(r)es	Mouret (Moures)	Mourres		*The rock-walls*
			Le Noyer (Lerenoer)		*The nut-tree*
		Laupachiere	Pachriros		*?*
Les Panégières	Panagiere(s)	Panagiere (Bois de)	Panagieros		*The basket-makers (or poss. pig-grazers, given the wood name in 17th C.)*
L'Hubac des Panégiéres	Adret Panagier(e)s			Adrech de Panagenis	
Le Travers de Paraïre		Paraire Paraire de la Four	Paraire	La Travessa	*The great slope of the place for fulling (wet-pressing) cloth*

1842	*1750*	*1610*	*1531*	*1332–52*	*Translation*
Pas de Bouis	Pas d'Aubuis (D'Aubari) Par (Pas)	 Pal (Par)	 Pal (Pas)		*The path* + personal name
	Pas Destrugue (de Trugue)	Prats Dastouego (Destruigere)	Pasdastroigou (Pad Dastrigo)		*The path* + personal name *Vallon du Pas d'Estrugue* is a place-name for the dry valley between La Croux and Les Graoux d'Embarnoui
			Paume de Vignan Pausso de Veyan		*Rock of the vines?*
Les Pesses	Les Pesses L'adrech de Pesse	Pessou (Pesse, Pessoir)	Pesso(z)	Les Pesses	*The pieces of (arable) ground*
La Pinée	 Pinede	Pinee Pinetos (Pentet)	Pynee Penetos (Penitos)		*The pine*
Plan d'Anlaïre	Plan danlaire	Plan danlaire Libe danlaire	Plan danlaire		*Plain, flat area at the aire* + personal name?
Le Plan de la Faye Le Plan des Costes Les Graous du Plan	(La) Plans au devant Plans	Pla(u)n Plan au puit Pons de Plan	Plan(e) (Pland, Planz) Plan la plus luegno Pons de Plan	Plans Terra Planorum Pratum de Planis	*Plain, flat area* Plan may be an area on the southern part of the lowland, but it has several houses in 1610 and may also be part of the village
Les Plantades	Plantades	Plantades	Plantados		*The planta-tions (of trees)*
		Pons de Guiou Guigeul (Guigoue)	Pons de Guillol		? Personal names

1842	*1750*	*1610*	*1531*	*1332–52*	*Translation*
Le Pouirac	(Pouirac) Poiurac	Poirac (Pou(i)rac)	Poyiraq		*Bucket water-wheel (an irrigation device)*
Les Poumeirés	Poumaires	Poumeyrer (Poumairier , Pomairet)	Poumaires		*The apple orchards/trees* Poumaires & Poumayris hard to distinguish in 1539
Le Poumeiris	Poumieres (Poumaris)	Poumieris	Poumayris (Poumarris, Poumarriz)		*The apple orchard* see Poumaires
Les Pourcelles	Pourcelles	Pourcellos (Poureillos, Poureillet, Pareillet)	Pour Cellos (Pous Sellos, Pour Sellos)	Las Porcela Las Porcellas	*The pig(let)s*
La Barre Pousse		Pouse du Serilet	Pouss, Perse Baumo Rousso		*The mountain ridge* + ?
Les Prés	Pred(s) (Prets)	Pres (Prat, Pras) Prat dau Clapier Prat Daubert (Prats dau Bouier) Pratz Redon	Prat(s) Pres de Bumis Pras de Guyol Prat Danastant Prat Daussels Prat dau Clapier Prat Daubert Prat Ridon		*Meadows* + personal names
	Pre Long	Prat Long (Pralong)	Pra Long		*The long meadow*
Les Prés de la Lone et de la Font	Preds de la Fontaine	Prat de la Lone	Lons Pras		*The meadow of the pool* or *the bend of the river*
	Laun(n)et(t)es (Loune)	Leaunne, (Lianne Launiet Launitos, Launnette)	La Lono (Lonne, Leuni) Colet de Lon	Campum day Layne	*The pool* or *the bend of the river*
	Prouourt				?
Le Revest		Revest Lairete	Layretos ? (Lauzetos)		*The shady side*

1842	*1750*	*1610*	*1531*	*1332–52*	*Translation*
La Ribière La Ribière des Costes	Ribiere(s)	Ribiere	Rybiero		*The river side/bank*
	Roc Egrege				
Le Rouré	Rour(r)e Libac de Roure	Roure	Roure(t)		*The oak* (quercus robur)
Le Sabouarat L'Avenc et Le Sabouarat	Sabarat (Sabarot, Saborot)	Sabaro(u)t	Sabarot		?
Le Saffranier	Safranier	Safranier			*Mollasse,* i.e. *compacted sand* or *the saffron ground* (doubts as to whether this plant would grow at this altitude)
	Sambourettes	Sambourettes	San Borreloz		?, but prob. not a saint's name
Saint Claude	St Claude	Saint Claude	Saint Claudon (Glaudou)		*St Claude*
Saint Roch	St Roc	Saint Roch Ribau de St Roch	St Roq		*St Roche*
		Roche de Teyt (Test)	Rocqo de Tyt (Syt)		?
	St Antoine	Saint Anthoni	Saint Anthoni		*St Anthony*
L'Adrech de San Meya	Saumejan (Saumeyan) Libac de Saumeyan	Saumeyan (Saumeian, Sanmaian)	Sullmiyan (Suels Meyan)		*The middle summit*
Le Serre L'Hubac du Serre	Serre	Serre (Serreye Serisse)	Serre Lybaq Desserane (Deserand)	Pratum de Syria	*The crest*

1842	*1750*	*1610*	*1531*	*1332–52*	*Translation*
La Sine	(La) Sine	Sine (Sino) Sine de Laugrier	Syno		*The hawthorn*
Le Teil	Teil Libac de Teil	Teil (Thel, Theil)	Teil (Tels)		*The lime-tree*
Les Termes		Tormes Aulsommet			*The boundaries*
	Tousque (La Tourque)	Tousque			? *the tusk*
		Tranquat (Trenquat)	Trenquat		?
		Valalaune (Valalanne)	Valalaune (Valalanno)		*The valley of the river bend/pool*
Valaraouvo	Valalause	Valalausso Combe de Valalausso	Vala Lauss(o) Lousse (Leus(s)e) Combe de Valalausso		*The valley of the thin rock slabs*
		Vallon dan Bout	Vallon dan bout, Vallon de bou dan		? *The valley at the end*
Vaumeillane	Val(e)mejan (Valmeyan)	Vaumeiane (Vaumeyane)	Valmiyano (Vau Myane)	Vilmeyana	*The middle valley*
			Vanado da Laz		?
Le Verger		Verger	Verger (Vergner)		*The orchard*
			Vilanayryo (Valon dau guynyer)		?
		Veilho	Vrihol, Vilho	Vielle Ville ?	*The old town* or ? *the (night) watch*
	Vignasse	Vignasse	Vignasse		*The vineyard*
	(La) Vigne(s)	Vignos	Vignes		*The vines*
		Vignondrado	Vigno Ondrado		*The vine* + personal name

VILLAGE					
1842	*1750*	*1610*	*1531*	*1332–52*	*Translation*
			Castel		*Castle*
		Praon	Pra(h)on		? village edge somewhere?
		Devant le Chateau			*In front of the castle*
			alla Plasse		*In the Place*
		Rue du Four	Rue du Fourt		*Street of the oven*
			Souto Loustal		*Under the ostal*
	Sous le Barry	Soubo le Barry	Souto Lou Barry		*Under le Barry*
			Souto la Font		*Under the spring*
			Souto la Combe		*Under the valley*
			Souto Mess Reynaud		*Under the house of Reynaud*
	Soulte	Soulz lou Coulet			*Under le Coulet*
		Soulz la Pla(i)n			*Under le Plan*
			Sous la Colle		*Under La Colle*
			Souto loussolur, Souto lou Soulier		
			Maison		
			Ostal		
			Peseng		
			Boutiqo		
			Cazal		
			Stables		
		Bourgade			
		Calancon (Calanquon, Calailcon)	Calancon (Calanquo)		

1842	*1750*	*1610*	*1531*	*1332–52*	*Translation*
		Colle (Col(l)o)	Collo		2 maisons, 3 ostals, 1cazal, 7 gardens, 8 stables
		Collet(s) Coulet	Collet(s) Coulet		Coulet, Collet – 2 quartiers in lowland and a part of the village – v. hard to disentangle in 1531 & 1610
		Porte de Libac	Porto de ly baq		*Gate on the shady side*
		Pre de l'Eglise			*Near the church*
		St Pons	St Pons		*St Pons*
		Rue du St Pons			*St Pons Street*
	L'Adrech	Rue de Ladrech	Ladrech Ladrech messen veilho		*Street on the sunny side*
		Rue de la Boucherie			*Butcher Street*
		Devant l'Eglise			*In front of the church*
		La Bourgier			
		Plan			Plan is an area on the S part of the lowland, but may also be part of the village ?Place?
		Derriere la Confrerie			*Behind the Brotherhood*

Notes

Preface

1 Allen 1983; Ede 1983; Pirie 1985; Canti 1985a and b
2 Lewison 1985
3 Allen and Lewison 1987
4 Lewison and Ungar 1986
5 Lewison 1986a
6 Lewison 1987
7 Lewison 1992
8 Crowther 1996
9 Hepper 1996 and 2001
10 Lewison *et al.* 1993
11 Austin *et al.* 1993, 1994 and 1995
12 Bone and Trethowan 1994

Chapter 1 – Setting the scene

1 In landscape archaeology, landscape history, historical geography, vernacular building, palaeo-environmental research and botany
2 Dauzat and Rostaing 1983, 132
3 Climatic data provided by the Observatoire du CERGA (Centre d'Etudes et de Recherches Géodynamiques et Astronomiques) with the kind assistance of the Director
4 Hepper 1996 and 2001
5 Compared with the evidence for earlier centuries, the Cipières archive for the 18th century is a cornucopia. Part of the reason for this change is the improving quality of records and their preservation (Figure 56). The council minutes and accounts and various inquisitions and cadastres provide us with fresh insights into long-held ways of doing things. They also give us a rich view of a society which, despite its apparent isolation, was poised on the edge of the modern world. Alongside the steady tread of parish bureaucracy and the demands of tax collections there were two dramatic events: the War of the Austrian Succession and the French Revolution. Compared with the regular records of the life of the community, which always hide as much as they show, both these events reveal something of the underbelly of the community. For the first time, perhaps, we feel the escaping steam of real life rather than the regulated engine beat of officialdom.

Chapter 2 – An outline early chronology and an account of the village's morphology

1 See *Mémoires de L'Institut de Préhistoire et d'Archéologies Alpes Mediterranée.* 46, 2004, 5–6
2 Brétaudeau 1996, 36; Salicis 2002; Del Fabbro 1998
3 Brétaudeau 1996, Gazenbeek 2004
4 Brétaudeau 1996, pls 118, 119
5 Brétaudeau 1996, pls 136–8
6 del Fabbro 1998
7 Brétaudeau 1991
8 Buchet 2001
9 Gazenbeek 2004, 102, my translation
10 Salicis 2004; Salicis in Gazenbeek 2004, 79–84
11 Salicis 2004
12 Dauzat and Rostaing 1983
13 Baratier 1969
14 Ungar and Allemand 1984
15 Bourin 1996, 20
16 Lagrue 1996
17 Poly 1977
18 Planel 1980,12, citing Poly 1977
19 Poteur 1976
20 Moris and Blanc 1883, 114
21 Latouche 1955, Duby 1976, 28; Liautaud 1971, 81
22 Lagrue 1996
23 Poly 1977, 125–8

24 Planel 1980, 24
25 Baratier 1969, 111
26 Durbec 1971
27 Gonnet-Roanne 1984
28 Demians D'Archimbaud 1981
29 Planel 1980, 26
30 Durbec 1965, 31 & 84
31 see Bourin 1996, 28–9 for a similar list of questions
32 Taylor 1983; Austin 1990
33 Pesez 1992
34 See, e.g. Dyer 1985
35 Austin 1985
36 Lagrue 1996, 110
37 Hodges 1997
38 Rippon 2004
39 E.g. Uhlig 1972; Roberts 1987; Toubert 1973; Göranson 1977
40 Roberts and Wrathmell 2000
41 Fabre *et al.* 1996 for an overview
42 Austin 1985
43 Poteur 1994
44 Baratier 1961
45 Lewison 1986

Chapter 3 – The archaeology of the central part of the Plâteau de Calern

1 Poteur 1994
2 Hepper 1994a
3 Crowther 1994 & 1997
4 Crowther 1997
5 Crowther 1997
6 Ingold 1993
7 Goody 1983
8 Lewison 1987
9 Roc 1995
10 Bone and Trethowan 1994
11 Bretaudeau 1991
12 Gazenbeek 2004
13 Poteur 1994, 23–4

Chapter 4 – The Les Baumes landscape survey: dating the basic agrarian landscape of the Plâteau de Calern

1 Poteur 1994, 3
2 Poteur 1994, 26
3 Lewison 1992
4 Poteur, 1994, 26
5 Poteur, 1994, 2, 3
6 Faith, R. *pers. comm.*
7 ABdR 396 E18
8 R. Faith, *pers. comm.*
9 Faith, R., *pers. comm.*
10 Bretaudeau 1996, pls 118, 136–8
11 ADdBR 396 E17 (1332–3), E18 (1335–1352) and see Appendix 1
12 Siddle, D., *pers. comm.* and see Appendix 1
13 Faith, R., *pers. comm.*
14 Siddle, D., *pers. comm.*
15 Dauzat and Rostaing 1983, 132
16 Faith, R., *pers. comm.*
17 Lewison 1992
18 Rendu 2003, fig. 56.
19 *Ibid.*, 405–6
20 Rendu 2004, 148
21 Rendu 2003, 496
22 *Ibid.*, photos 22, 26; figs 13, 23
23 *Ibid.*, 346

Chapter 5 – Settlement, social structure and politics from the 5th to the 14th century

1 Gazenbeek 2004,102–3,121–2 & fig. on 123
2 Bodard 1985, 61–8
3 Bange 1984; Favory and Fiches 1994; Dubled 1953; Parodi *et al.* 1987, 24
4 Geary 1985; Poly 1976, 104
5 Chiche-Aubrun 1985; Cru 1985; Bange 1984
6 Faith forthcoming
7 Viazzo 1989, 107ff
8 Toubert 1983, 324; Le Roy Ladurie 1974, 33–5
9 for an excellent survey see Poteur and Salch 1999; Bouchard 1999
10 Weinburger 1990
11 Poly *et al.* in Zimmerman 1992, 360
12 *Cart. Lerins* cclviiiix, cccxix
13 Gourdon, n.d. 71
14 *Cart. Lerins* lxxxviii; Cais de Pierlais 1889, 67
15 Poteur and Salch 1999, 19; Latouche 1955; Tits-Dieuade 1985, 40
16 *Cart. Lerins.* cxiv, 104; Poly 1976, 355–7; Poly *et al.* 1992, 360
17 Cais de Pierlais 1899, 48–55

18 *Cart. Lerins* cxxii–cxxx
19 *Cart. Lerins* lxxxvi, lxxxviii
20 Poteur 1981,30–3
21 Demians D'Archimbaud 1980, i. 57; Higounet 1992, 109–17
22 Boyer 1990, 418; Demians d'Archimbaud 1977
23 Guerard 1857, 788
24 Thevenon 1996, 135; Gazenbeek 2004, 123
25 Froeschle-Chopard 1996, 112
26 Institut des Fouilles 1955–6, 40–42, 109–115; *Inventaire: Coursegoule* 2000, 21 for 'churches of first parochial network'
27 Froeschle-Chopard 1996, 116
28 Froeschle-Chopard 1996, 112; Durbec 1972, 135, 140, 146
29 Poly 1976, 111; Baratier 1971, 124
30 Poly *et al.* in Zimmerman 1992, 327ff; Poly 1976, 112
31 Giordanengo 198, 4
32 Duby 1953; Fossier 1982; Bisson 1991; Toubert 1983; Wickham 1988; Parodi *et al.* 1987; Faith 1997; Poly 1986; Poly and Bournazel 1991
33 Planel 1980, 14ff; Poly 1976, 318ff
34 Giordanengo 1988, 29
35 Samaran 1957a, 18; Archives des Bouches du Rhone 396 E17
36 Guerard 1857, 788. For the details of the descents of these four fees see Durbec 1972, 146–7
37 Benoit 1925, 432–6
38 Poteur 1996, 42; Benoit 1925, no. 78; Durbec 1972, 135
39 Durbec 1972, 141
40 Durbec 1972, 141; Froeschle-Chopard 1996, 113
41 Giordanengo 1988, 223
42 Durbec 1972, 148–52; Baratier 1969, 52–77. The entries for our area are nos 186, 191, 141, 133; Samaran 1957a, 21. In 1252 Cipières paid *quistas, alberga* for 29 hearths at 12 *deniers* a hearth, and owed 100 *sous* for *cavalcata.* The Statutes of Frejus of 1235 reveal that it had then jointly with Caussols owed one armed and mounted fighting man. *Quistas, 6 livres alberga* and an unarmed man were owed at Caussols, *quistas,* 75 *sous alberga* and a mounted man at Gréolières-Basses, *quistas,* 50 *sous alberga* and 50 *sous* for *cavalcata* at Gréolières-Hautes
43 Samaran 1957a, 25
44 ABdR 396 E17 (1332–3), 396E18 (1335–1352); Samaran 1957a, 1957b
45 Giordanengo 1988, 36–7; Sauze and Senac 1986, 106; Boyer 1990, 358; Bonnassie 1991, 312 n 100; Poly, Aurell and Iogna-Prat in Zimmerman, 1992, 339–40; Baratier, 1969, 70–4
46 Giordanengo 1988, 4; Samaran 1957a, 25–6
47 Samaran 1957a, 112–4
48 *pace* Samaran 1957a, 25
49 Samaran 1957a, 89–90; 113–5
50 Derouet 1995, 651–3
51 Samaran 1957a, 27–8
52 Sauze and Senac 1986, 112–3
53 Samaran 1957a, 30–7 at 32; 1957b; Charles-Edwards 1979
54 Samaran 1957b, 232
55 Samaran 1957b, 235 n. 31
56 Samaran 1957a, 112–3, 1957b, 232
57 Samaran 1957a, 36–7, 65
58 Faith 1997
59 Samaran 1957a, 33–7, 1957b
60 Samaran 1957a, 113–6
61 Faith 1997
62 Benoit 1949,162; Marchandiau 1984, 113–21; Archives A-M G 0698 (1368)
63 Samaran 1957a, 87–8; e.g. B du R 396 E17 no. 39 for Jacobus *textor* and Raymunda *textoricis alias gibelina* of Gréolières-Hautes
64 Samaran 1957a, 84–5
65 Samaran 1957a, 30

Chapter 6 – Population, economy and society, 1050–1531

1 Braudel 1990; Duby 1968; Le Roy Ladurie 1974, Bloch 1966
2 Bryson and Padoch 1981, 3–19
3 Moberg *et al.* 2005, 403, 613–7
4 Bloch 1966, 1–20; Braudel 1990, 137–54; Smith 1978, 163–88; Burke 1972; Le Roy Ladurie 1972; Dupaquier 1988, vol. 1
5 Postan 1973; Bartlett 1993; Glacken 1967; Sclafert 1933; 1959, 6; Williams 2000
6 Le Roy Ladurie 1972
7 Lamb 1977; Appleby 1980; Moberg *et al.* 2005; Wanner *et al.* 2000

8 Slicher van Bath, 1963
9 Duby 1968, 118–19
10 Braudel 1990, 137
11 Smith 1968, chap. 3
12 Bloch 1966, 5–15
13 Baratier 1961; Sclafert 1959, 10–11
14 Sclafert 1959, 62–96
15 Smith 1968, chap. 3
16 Du Parc 1962
17 Binz 1963
18 Brondy *et al.* 1984, 183
19 Baratier 1969, 185; Baratier 1961, 92; see also Duby 1968, 119
20 Nabholz (1967, 500) argues that the cultivated area of Europe did not increase beyond the level that it reached in 1300
21 see Sclafert 1963 (for Dauphiné), 181 *et seq*
22 Baratier 1961, 58–61
23 Baratier 1961, 58
24 Baratier 1961, 61
25 Baratier 1969, 184
26 *Op. cit*
27 Durbec 1971; ABdR, 396 & 200
28 Timbal 1969
29 Flandrin 1979, 80–88; Mitterauer and Seider 1982; Seccomb 1992; Le Roy Ladurie 1974, 31, 1987
30 Hammel 1972
31 Mitterauer and Seider 1982, 30; Wall *et al.* 1972; Goubert 1977
32 Le Roy Ladurie 1974, 31–9; Goubert 1977; Flandrin 1979, 81–5; Siddle 1983, 1986a, b & c
33 Poitrineau 1981
34 Le Roy Ladurie 1987, 84–8
35 Le Roy Ladurie 1974, 31–9
36 *Op. cit.*, 36
37 Cheveneau 1965, 33
38 Jones and Siddle 1983
39 Le Play 1851
40 Fauve Chamoux 1987
41 Flandrin 1979, 80–8
42 Rodgers 1992
43 Rodgers 1992, 21
44 In 1334 something just over 300 persons
45 Durbec 1971
46 ABdR 1031 fo.7
47 Thiery 1994, 137–8
48 Durbec 1971, 123; Bertrand, Cresp, Gautier, Isnard, Lambert, Ricord, Camatte, Tombarel, Girard
49 Durbec 1972,144
50 ABdR, Nov, 1334: 396E17 & 18
51 Samaran 1957a, 107–29
52 Lamb 1982; Appleby 1980
53 Nerveux 1968, 41–87
54 Fossier 1982, 21
55 Braudel 1990, 158–72
56 Baratier 1969, 191–2
57 Le Roy Ladurie 1987, 26
58 Le Roy Ladurie 1974, 29–31; 1987, 21–94
59 Durbec 1971 ; Thiery 1994
60 Le Roy Ladurie 1974, 30–2
61 Braudel 1990, 164
62 ACC Cad 2, 1531
63 Ligurian immigrants
64 ABdR; Durbec 1971
65 Siddle 1983

Chapter 7 – Medieval agrarian systems

1 ABdR 396E 18 no. 320; Bloch 1961, 201
2 Poteur 1994, 68
3 Bloch 1966, 202
4 Planel 1980, 39; Boyer 1990, 159ff; Bailey 1989
5 Sclafert 1959
6 E.g. Fourquier 1975
7 Dyer *et al.* 2001, 191; Austin 1990
8 Boyer 1990, 169
9 ABdR 396 E18 no. 277
10 Boyer 1990, 167
11 Timbal 1969, 140–53
12 *Acte d'habitation* of 1357
13 ABdR 396 E 18, no. 373
14 *Inventaire* 67–8 and fig. 42
15 Reigniez 2002, 2180–7; Samaran 1957, 119, 62ff
16 ABdR B1326
17 Reigniez 2002,100
18 Samaran 1957a, 65, 55
19 see note 16
20 Samaran 1957a, 125
21 Samaran 1957a, 118–23
22 Acte d'habitation of 1357
23 Samaran 1957a, 83; Boyer 1990, 93. The cadastre of 1531 records *ostals* in Julho, Fontaynyos and *cabanes* in Poumieres

24 Sclafert 1957, 141
25 *Actes* of 1357, 1368
26 Samaran 1957, 118–23
27 Samaran 1957, 123–6
28 ABdR 396 E18,nos. 224, 320
29 Acte of 1357; Arch.de B du R. b1326, fo.225v
30 Acte of 1357: A D A-M E103/2/FF 3
31 Samaran 1957a, 118, 123, 116
32 Samaran 1957a, 27
33 Samaran 1957a, 65
34 ABdR 396E 17 118 April 1332
35 Samaran 1957a, 95
36 ABdR 396E18 fos 68,215v, 224; Samaran 1957a, 47, 60, 65, 90, 91, 120
37 *Declaration* of 1750: see Appendix
38 Above, p. 28
39 Sclafert 1959; Coste 1976, 113ff; Timbal 1969, 140–53
40 Planel 1980, 37
41 Malaussena 1969, 155–7; Benoit 1925, 432–6
42 Samaran 1957a 65–73; Duby 1968, 148–50
43 Samaran 1957a, 72
44 Gourdon 81–2; ABdR B1326
45 Sclafert 1959
46 Samaran 1957a, 26, 111
47 Aubenas 1943
48 *Acte* of 1357
49 *Acte d'habitation* of 1368
50 AAM G0467, G 1102

Chapter 8 – Agrarian systems in the post-medieval period

1 ACC Cads 1–8; 1531; 1610; 1633; 1640; 1727; 1750; 1791; 1841
2 Le Roy Ladurie 1974
3 ACC Deliberations 1537–2005
4 ACC Cad 2
5 Collomp 1972
6 Le Roy Ladurie 1987, 47
7 Neveux, in Duby 1968; Poitrineau 1981
8 ABdR, *Affouagement* 1609
9 ACC, Cad 8 1750
10 ACC, *Etat de betail* 1763
11 Collomp 1972a, 1972b, 1977, 1983, 1988
12 ACC Cad 8
13 ACC Cad 8 f.2
14 Sclafert 1959, 140; *Arch de Bouches de Rhone*, B200 *Affouagement* 1471
15 *Affouagement*, 1609; ACC: *Etats de Betails*, 1763, 1791, 1838 *et seq.*
16 Sclafert 1959, 177, 178, 182, 228
17 Duby 1968, 147; Sclafert 1934
18 *Op.cit.* 147
19 Timbal 1969
20 Baratier 1961, 43; Sclafert 1959, 140
21 ABdR, 1609, B1326, f225
22 *ibid.*
23 ACC Admin 7 No. 15, 1793

Chapter 9 – Population, economy and society, 1531–1900

1 Le Roy Ladurie, 1972
2 *Ibid.* p. 272
3 Collomp 1972; 1977; 1983; 1988
4 Flinn 1981
5 ACC Cad 7 1727
6 Le Roy Ladurie 1972
7 Braudel 1966, 42; Poitrineau 1981
8 ACC Délibérations, 1719
9 Roux (nd); Poitrineau 1981; Fontaine 1996 ; Viazzo 1989; Siddle 1983
10 In 1718 they were listed as 33,724 *livres 6 sols 9 deniers*: ACC Compte 37 f.5
11 Lewison 1992; Siddle 1996
12 Siddle 1996
13 ACC Cad 7, 1727; Cad 8,1750; *Registre Civique* 1806
14 ACC Births marriages and deaths (VE) 1992–1772
15 Fleury 1956; Henri 1965 & 1980; Wrigley 1973; Wrigley & Schofield 1981, and numerous examples published in journals of family history and population history; *Annales de Demographie Historique*; *Journal of Family History,Continuity and Change*; *Annales: economies societes,civilisations; Demographie Historique*, etc
16 Medick 1976; Kreidte *et al.* 1981; Clarkson 1985
17 Medick 1976; Kriedte *et al.* 1981; Clarkson 1985
18 Ruggles 1992; Wrigley 1994
19 Poitrineau 1981
20 Siddle 2000
21 Siddle 1986a–c; 1997

22 Jones, A.M. Mean Age of first marriage: Montmin (Haute Savoie):

	M	F
1658–1702	25.2	22.7
1703–1747	25.3	24.3
1748–1792	23.7	23.4

23 ACC Ad.2/1719
24 Wrigley 1969 has argued that, for all sorts of reasons, 20% of all unions were naturally infertile. In this case we must assume an unknown proportion of marriages in which both partners left the village together in the early years of marriage and did not return for any significant period in their fertile years
25 ACC Cad 2 1531, ff.83, 84
26 ACC Cad 3 1610, f.155
27 Bloch 1966, 137. He identifies notaries as a step above village craftsmen in the emerging social hierarchy
28 ACC Cad 3. f.155
29 ACC Cad 5 f.
30 ACC Cad 8 f.156
31 ACC *Etat de Betail* 1763
32 ACC Cad 8 1750 f.15
33 ACC Cad 8 1750 f.16
34 ACC Cad 5 1633
35 ACC VE Registers 1700 f.135
36 ACC Cad 7 1727 f.174
37 ACC VE Reg 1729 f.218
38 ACC VE Reg.1738 f.520
39 ACC Cad 8. ff.1–2
40 ACC Etat de Betail 1763
41 ACC Cad 8 f.4
42 ACC Cad 2 1531 ff.68 and 77
43 ACC VE Reg 1693, f.36
44 ACC VE Reg ff.66, 127, 157, 191, 259, 339, 348, 359
45 ACC VE Reg. 1721, f.288
46 ACC Cad 7 1727, f. 605
47 ACC VE 1721, f.287
48 ACC Cad 7 1727, f.155
49 ACC VE ff.298, 316, 410, 458, 495, 518
50 ACC Cad 8 1750, f.155
51 ACC Cad 8 f.224
52 ACC Cad 7
53 ACC VE 1723, f.308
54 ACC Cad 7
55 ACC VE f.136
56 ACC Cad 8, f.49
57 ACC VE 1719
58 ACC VE 290, 306, 413, 456, 460, 462, 507, 523
59 ACC Cad 8 f.45
60 ACC VE 1705, f.208
61 ACC VE 1733, f.361
62 ACC Cad 8, 1750, f.
63 ACC VE 1691, f.10
64 Poitrineau 1981; Braudel 1990 ; Viazzo 1990
65 In 1750, 46 designated *travailleurs* had revenues of between 1 and 50 *livres per annum*
66 Siddle 1996
67 ACC Cad 8 1750, f.164
68 ACC VE f.351
69 ACC Cad 8 1750, f.164
70 ACC VE 1746, f.
71 ACC VE 1712, f.
72 ACC Cad 8 f.221
73 Fontaine 1996
74 Fontaine and Siddle 2000
75 ACC Admin 7 1779
76 ACC *Registre d'Etat Civil* 1806

Chapter 10 – Les Baumes in the modern era

1 Thiery 1990, 1991, 1992, 1994
2 de Beauchamp 1994, 153
3 Thiery 1994, 132 (my translation)
4 Thiery 1994
5 Thiery 1992, 7
6 Thiery 1990
7 Thiery 1994, 141

Chapter 11 – Reflections

1 see, for instance, Fleming and Ralph 1982
2 Fleming 1996
3 Hoskins 1957, 190
4 Ingold 1993
5 See Given (2004) for brief but effective evocations of Mediterranean peasant life
6 Friedman and Rowlands 1978
7 Hordern and Purcell 2000

Bibliography

Abbreviations for Primary Sources

AAM Archives Departmentales des Alpes-Maritimes, Nice

ABdR Archives Departmentales des Bouches du Rhone, Marseille

ACC Archives de Commune de Cipières

Primary and Secondary Sources

Allen, M.J. & Lewison, A. (1987) 'Reconstructing an agrarian system in the Alpes-Maritimes, France, *Antiquity*, **61**, no. **123**, 364–9.

Anon (2000) *Inventaire du Canton de Coursegoules. Recherches Alpes-Maritimes et contrées limitrophes régionales*, Conseil Général des Alpes-Maritimes, **153**, Nice.

Appleby, A.B. (1980) 'Epidemics and famine in the Little Ice Age', *Journal of Interdisciplinary History*, **10.4**, 643–63.

Assier-Andrieu, L. (1981) *Coutume et rapports sociaux: étude anthropologique des communautés paysannes du Capcir*, Paris.

Aubenas, R. (1943) *Chartes de Franchise et Actes d'Habitation: documents, textes et mémoires pour servir à l'histoire de Cannes et de sa region* Cannes.

Austin, D. (1985) 'Doubts about morphogenesis', *Journal Historical Geography*, **11.2**, 201–9.

Austin, D. (1990) 'The 'proper study' of medieval archaeology', in Austin, D. & Alcock, L.W. (eds) *From the Baltic to the Black Sea*, London, 9–42.

Bailey, M. (1989) *A Marginal Economy? East Anglian Breckland in the later middle ages*, Cambridge.

Bange, F. (1984) 'L'ager et la *villa*: structures du paysage et du peuplement dans la region Mâconnaise à la fin du haut moyen âge (IXe–XIe siècles)', *Annales*, **39**, 529–69.

Baratier, E. (ed) (1969) *Enquêtes sur les droits et revenues de Charles I d'Anjou en Provence (1252 et 1278)* Paris.

Baratier, E. (1961) *La Démographie Provençale du XIIe au XVIe Siècles*, Paris.

Baratier, E. (1969) *Histoire de La Provence*, Toulouse.

Baratier, E. (1971) 'Les communautés de haute Provence au Moyen Âge: problémes d'habitat et de population', *Provence Historique*, **85**, 237–48.

Baratier, E., Duby, G. & Hildesheimer, E. (1969) *Atlas Historique: Provence, Comtat Orange, Nice, Monaco*, Paris.

Barroul, J. (1971) 'L'évolution de l'habitat dans les anciens évêches de Sisteron et d'Apt' *Provence Historique*, **85**, 316–21.

Bartlet, R. (1993) *The Making of Europe: Conquest, Colonisation and Cultural Change 950–1350*, London.

Benoit, F. (1925) *Recueil des actes des Comtes de Provence appartenant à la maison de Barcelone. Alphonse II et Raymond- Berenger V (1196–1245)* 2 vols, Monaco-Pris.

Binz, L. (1963) 'La population du diocèse de Genève à la fin de Moyen Âge', *Mélanges d'Histoire Èconomique et Sociale en Hommage au Professeur A. Babel*, Geneva, 145–96.

Bloch, M. (1961) (trans. L.A. Manyon) *Feudal Society*, London.

Bloch, M. (1968) (trans. J. Sondheimer) *French Rural Society: an essay on its basic characteristics*, Berkeley and Los Angeles.

Bodard, P. (1979) 'Le Plâteau de Calern et ses abords. Étude de géographie physique et humaine', *Annales de la Société Scientifique et Littéraire de Cannes et de l'Arrondissement de Grasse*, **29**, 89–101.

Bodard, P. (1985) 'Soixante-quinze sites inédits où peu connus du départements des Alpes-Maritimes: contribution à la connaissance des populations de l'ancien Comté de Nice dans l'antiquité et le haut Moyen Âge', *Mémoires de L'Institut de Préhistoire et d'Archéologie Alpes Mediterranée*. **18**, 83–91.

Bodard, P. (1986) 'La notion de territoire au temps de castellaras et des premiers villages de la Provence romaine des Alpes-Maritimes' in *Territoires, seigneuries, communes: les limites de territoires en Provence*', Actes des Troisièmes Journées d'Histoire de l'Espace Provençal, Mouans-Sartoux, 9–19.

Bonnassie, P. (1991) 'The formation of Catalan feudalism and its early expansion' in Bonnassie, P. (ed.), *From Slavery to Feudalism in South-Western Europe*, 149–69 Cambridge.

Bourdieu, P. (1962) 'Célibat et condition paysanne', *Études Rurales*, **5–6**, 32–135.

Bourin, M. (1996) 'Introduction de la problématique du colloque', in Fabre *et al.* (eds) (1996) 17–30

Boyer, J-P. (1990) *Hommes et communautés du haut pays Niçois médiévale: la Vésubie (XIIIe–XVe siécles)*, Nice.

Braudel, F. (1966) *La Méditerranée et le monde Mediterranée à l'époque de Phillipe II*, Paris.

Braudel, F. (1979) (trans. Sion Reynolds), *Civilisation and Capitalism, Vol. I: The Structures of Everyday Life*, London.

Braudel, F. (1990) (trans. Sion Reynolds), *The Identity of France, Vol. II: People and Production*, London.

Brétaudeau, G. (1991) 'Un important village gallo-romain découvert dans la commune de Gourdon', *Mémoires de L'Institut de Préhistoire et d'Archéologie Alpes Mediterranée*, **33**, 19–30.

Brétaudeau, G. (1996) *Les enceintes des Alpes-Maritimes. Mémoires de L'Institut de Préhistoire et d'Archéologie Alpes Mediterranée*, (hors série) **2**, 203–20.

Brondy, R., Demotz, B. & Leguay, J-P. (1984) *La Savoie de l'an mil a la Réforme*, Rennes.

Bryson, R.A. & Padoch, C. (1981) 'On the climates of History', in Rotberg & Rabb (1981) 3–17.

Buchet, L. (2001) 'Le village de la "Bergerie du Montet" (Gourdon) de la protohistoire à la fin d'Antiquité.' *Mémoires de L'Institut de Préhistoire et d'Archéologie Alpes Mediterranée*, **43**, 33–57.

Burke, P. (1972) *Economy and Society in Early Modern Europe*, London.

Cais de Pierlais, E. (1989) *Le XIe siècle dans les Alpes-Maritimes*, Turin.

Cartulaire de l'Abbaye de Lérins (1883) eds Moris, H. & Blanc, E., Paris.

Castex, J.M. (1980) *L'Aménagement des pentes et des sols dans les Alpes-Maritimes et le Var*, Nice.

Chevalier, M. (1956) *La Vie Humaine dans les Pyrènées Ariégeoises*, Paris.

Cheveneau, R. (1965) 'Villages pré et protohistoriques des Alpes-Maritimes', *Mémoires de l'Institut de Préhistoire et de l'Archéologie Alpes Mediterranée*, **9.1**, 21–45.

Chiche-Aubrun, M. (1986) '"L'ager" de Seillans du IXeme siècle à nos jours' in *Bastides, bories, hameaux: l'habitat disperse en Provence.* Actes des 21èmes Journées d'Histoire Régionales Mouans-Sartoux, 15–16 Mars 1985, 7–15.

Clarkson, L.A. (ed.) (1985) *Proto-industrialization: the first phase of industrialization?* London.

Collomp, A. (1972) 'Famille nucléaire et élargie en Provence au XVIIIème siècle', *Annales Économies, Sociétés et Civilisations*, **27**, 969–75.

Collomp, A. (1977) 'Alliance et filiation en Haute-Provence au XVIIIème siècle', *Annales Économies, Sociétés et Civilisations*, **32.3**, 29–53.

Collomp, A. (1983) *La Maison du Pére: famille et village en Provence au XVIIIème siècle*, Paris.

Collomp, A. (1988) 'From stem family to nuclear family: changes in the co-resident domestic group in Haute Provence between the end of the eighteenth century and the middle of the nineteenth century', *Continuity and Change*, **3**, 65 –81.

Coste, P. (1976) 'L'origine de la transhumance en Provence: enseignement d'une enquête sur les pâturages comtaux de 1345', in *L'Élevage en Mediterranée Occidentale*, Paris, 113–9.

Cru, J. (1986) 'Le polyptyque de Wadalde (813–814) et l'occupation du sol, l'exemple de la villa Rovagonis', in *Bastides, bories, hameaux: l'habitat disperse en Provence.* Actes des 21èmes Journées d'Histoire Régionales Mouans-Sartoux 15–16 Mars 1985, 75–96.

Dauzat, A. & Rostaing, C. (1983) *Dictionnaire étymologique des noms de lieux en France.* Paris: Librairie Guénégaud (2nd edition).

De Beauchamp, P. (1994) *La Provence et le Corse préromaines et romaines*, Privately printed.

Del Fabbro, L. (1998) 'Un ensemble protohistorique en bordure orientale du plâteau de Caussols: Troubade (06)', *Mémoires de L'Institut de Préhistoire et d'Archéologie Alpes Mediterranée*, **40**, 67–83.

Delano-Smith, C. (1979) *Western Mediterranean Europe: a Historical Geography of Italy, Spain and southern France since the Neolithic*, London.

Demians D'Archimbaud, G. (1977) 'L'organisation de la campagne en Provence occidentale: indices archéologiques et aspects démographiques', *Provence Historique*, **27 fasc. 107**, 3–23.

Démians d'Archimbaud, G. (1980) *Les Fouilles de Rougiers (Var): contribution à l'archéologie de l'habitat rural médiéval en pays Méditerranean*, Paris.

Demians d'Archimbaud, G. (1981) *Rougiers, village médiévale. Approche d'une société rurale méditerranéenne* Paris.

Derouet, B. (1995) 'Terroir et parente: pour une mise en perspective de la communauté rurale et des formes de reproduction familiale', *Annales*, **25**, 645–86.

Desaulle, P. (1976) *Les Bories de Vaucluse*, Paris.

Dubled, H. (1953) 'Quelques observations sur le sens du mot *villa*', *Le Moyen Âge*, **59**, 1–9

Duby, G. (1953) *La société aux XIe et XIIe siècles dans la région Mâconnaise*, Paris.

Duby, G. (1968) (trans. Cynthia Postan), *Rural Economy and Country life in the Medieval West*, Columbia.

Duby, G. & Wallon, A. (1976) *Histoire de la France Rurale*, 4 vols, Paris.

Dunbabin, J. (1998) *Charles d'Anjou: power, kingship and state-making in thirteenth century Europe*, London.

Dupaquier, J. (1988) *Histoire de la population Française*, 2 vols, Paris.

Duparc, C. (1962) 'Évolution démographique de quelques paroisses de Savoie depuis la fin du XIIIe siècle', *Bulletin Philologique et Historique*, 247–74.

Durbec, J-A (1968) 'Les villages du Val du Chanan du XIe au XVe siècles', *Bulletin philologique et historique du Comité des Travaux Historiques et Scientifiques. Année 1965 (actes du 90e congrès national des Sociétés Savantes tenu à Nice)*. Paris, 37–150.

Durbec, J-A. (1971) 'Les villes et les villages de la région de Grasse au Moyen Âge: Caussols, Cipières, Gréolières', *Annales de la Société Scientifique et Littéraire et arrondissement de Grasse*, **23**, 134–46.

Dyer, C. (1985) 'Power and conflict in the medieval village', in Hooke, D. *Medieval Villages*, Oxford, 27–32.

Fabre, G., Bourin, M., Caille, J. & Debord, A. (eds) (1996) *Morphogenèse du Village Médiéval (IXe–XIIe siècles)*, Montpellier.

Faith, R. J, (1966) 'Peasant families and inheritance customs', *Agricultural History Review*, **14**, 77–95.

Faith, R. J. (1997) *The English Peasantry and the Growth of Lordship*, Leicester.

Fauve-Chamoux A. (1987) 'Fonctionnement de la famille souche dans les Baronnies des Pyrénées avant 1914', *Annales de Démographie Historique*, Paris, 241– 262.

Favory, F. and Fiches, J-L. (eds) (1994) *Les Campagnes de la France mediterrannées dans l'antiquité et dans le haut moyen âge*, Paris.

Flandrin, J-L. (1979) *Families in Former Times: kinship, household and sexuality*, Cambridge.

Fleming, A. (1996) 'Total landscape archaeology: dream or necessity?' in Aalen, F. (ed.) *Landscape Study and Management*, Dublin, 81–92.

Fleming, A. & Ralph, N. (1982) 'Medieval settlement and land use on Holne Moor, Dartmoor: the landscape evidence', *Medieval Archaeology* **26**, 101–37.

Flinn, M.W. (1981) *The European Demographic System 1500–1820*, Brighton.

Fontaine, L. (1996) *History of Peddlers in Europe*, Oxford.

Fontaine, L. & Siddle, D.J. (2000) 'Mobility, kinship and commerce in the Alps 1500–1800', in Fontaine, L. & Siddle, D.J. (eds) *Migration, mobility and modernization*, Liverpool, 47–69.

Fossier, R. (1982) *L'Enfance de l'Europe: Xe–XIIIe siècles, aspects économiques et sociaux*, Paris.

Friedman, J. & Rowlands, M. (1978) 'Notes towards an epigenetic model of the evolution of "civilization"'. In Friedman, J. & Rowlands, M.J. (eds) *The Evolution of Social Systems*, London.

Gazenbeek, M. (2004) *Enceintes et habitats perchés des Alpes-Maritimes.* Association pour la promotion et la diffusion des connaissances archéologiques, Antibes.

Geary, P. (1985) *Aristocracy in Provence: the Rhône basin at the dawn of the Carolingian age*, Stuttgart.

Gimpel, J. (1977) *The Medieval Machine; the industrial revolution of the middle ages*, London.

Giordanengo, G. (1988) *Le droit féodale dans le pays de droit écrit*, Rome.

Given, M. (2004) *The archaeology of the colonized*, London & New York.

Glacken, C. J. (1967) *Traces on the Rhodian Shore: nature and culture in western thought from ancient times and the end of the eighteenth century*, Berkeley.

Gonnet-Roanne, P. (ed.) (1984) *Histoire de Grasse et de sa Région (Collection Histoire des villes de France)*, Lyons.

Goody, J. (1983) *The Development of the Family and Marriage in Europe*, Cambridge.

Göranson, U. (1977) *Kulturlandskap och samhällsutveckling*, Stockholm.

Goubert, P. (1970) 'Le tragique XVIIe siècle', in Braudel, F. & Labrousse, E. (eds) *Histoire Sociale et Économique de France, Tm. II*, Paris, 329–65.

Goubert, P. (1977) 'Family and province: a contribution to the knowledge of family structure in early modern France', *Journal of Family History*, **2**, 179–95.

Gourdon, M. (ed.) (n.d.) *Mouans et Sartoux: histoire de deux communautés*, Mouans-Sartoux.

Guerard, B. (ed.) (1857) *Cartulaire de l'Abbaye de S. Victor de Marseille*, 2 vols. Collection des documents inédits sur l'histoire de France: Collection des cartulaires de France, 8 & 9 Paris.

Hammel, E.A. (1972) 'The zadruga as process', in Laslett & Wall 1972, 335–73.

Henri, M. & Fleury M. (1965) *Nouveau manuel de dèpouilement et l'exploitation de l'Ètat civil ancient*, Paris.

Henri, M. (1980) *Techniques d'anaylse en dèmographie historique*, Paris.

Hepper, N. (1996) 'Plants of the Plâteau de Calern, Alpes-Maritimes (France): the vegetation of a doline and its karst surroundings', *Biocosme Mésogéen, Revue d'Histoire Naturelle*, **13**, 69–85.

Higounet, C. (1980) 'Structures sociales, *castra* et castelnaux dans le Sud-Ouest Aquitain (Xe–XIIIe siècles)' in *Structures* Féodales *et* Féodalisme dans l'Occident Mediterranéen (Xe–*XIIIe siècles)*, Ecole Francais de Rome, 109–17.

Hodges, R. (1997) *Light in the Dark Ages. The Rise and Fall of San Vincenzo al Volturno*, London.

Hodges, R. (2003) *Villa to Village*, London.

Hodgett, G.A.J. (1972) *A Social and Economic History of Medieval Europe*, London.

Homans, G.C. (1960) *English Villagers in the Thirteenth Century*, New York.

Hordern, P. & Purcell, N. (2000) *The corrupting sea: a study of Mediterranean history*, Oxford.

Hoskins, W.G. (1957) *The Midland peasant*, London.

Hyams, P. (1980) *King, Lords and Peasants in Medieval England: the common law of villeinage in the twelfth and thirteenth centuries*, Oxford.

Ingold, T. (1993) 'The temporality of landscape', *World Archaeology*, **25**, 152–74.

Jones, A. M. (1986) 'Mean age at first marriage: Montmin (Haute Savoie)', unpublished paper.

Kellenbenz, H. (1978) 'The economic organisation of early modern Europe', in Mathias, P. & Postan, M. M. (eds) *Cambridge Economic History of Europe*, vol. VII, Cambridge, 462–547.

Kreidte, P. (1981) *Industrialisation before Industrialisation: Rural Industry in the Genesis of Capitalism*. Cambridge.

La Polyptyque, Delisle, L. & Marion, A. (eds) (1857) in Guerard, B. (ed) *Cartulaire de l'Abbaye de Saint-Victor de Marseille*, (2 vols), Appendix 10, 633–56.

Labrousse, E. & Braudel, F. (1970) *Histoire Économique et Sociale de la France*, vol. 2, Paris.

Lagrue, J-P. (1996) 'Les bourgs castraux en Basse-Provence occidentale: Genèse et organisation', in Fabre *et al.* (eds), 97–111.

Lamb, H.H. (1982) *Climate, History and the Modern World*, London.

Laslett, P. & Wall, R. (eds) (1972) *Household and Family in Past Time*, Cambridge.

Latouche, R, (1955) 'Quelques aperçus sur le manse en Provence au Xe et au XIe siècles' in *Receuil de travaux offerts a M Clovis Brunel*, 2 vols. Societé de l' École de Chartes, **1**, 104–6.

Le Play, F. (1871) *L'organisation de la famille selon le vrai modèle signalé par l'histoire de toutes les races et de tous les temps*, Paris.

Le Roy Ladurie, E. (1972) *Times of Feast, Times of Famine: A history of climate since the year 1000*, London.

Le Roy Ladurie, E. (1974) *Les Paysannes de Languedoc*, Illinois.

Le Roy Ladurie, E. (1987) *The French Peasantry 1450–1660*, Aldershot.

Lewis C., Mitchell-Fox P. and Dyer C. (1977) *Village, Hamlet and Field: changing medieval settlements in central England*, Manchester.

Lewison, A. & Ungar, C. (1986) 'Le Plâteau de Calern: un exemple d'habitat dispersé dans un système agro-pastoral', in *Bastides, bories, hameaux, Actes des Deuxièmes Journées d'Histoire Régionales*, Mouans-Sartoux, 141–50.

Lewison, A. (1985) 'Constructions en pierre sèche sur le Plâteau de Calern, Cipières, Alpes-Maritimes', *Mémoires de l'Institut de Préhistoire et d'Archéologie des Alpes-Maritimes*, **27**, 59–73.

Lewison, A. (1986) 'Une analyse systèmatique du territoire de Cipières (Alpes-Maritimes)', *Mémoires de l'Institut de Préhistoire et d'Archéologie des Alpes-Maritimes*, **28**, 117–131.

Lewison, A. (1987) 'Creating a cadastre in the Alpes-Maritimes 1831–1842', *Landscape History*, **9**, 65–76.

Lewison, A. (1992) 'A village and its territory in southern France: a study in upland archaeology and history', unpublished M.Phil. Dissertation, Department of Archaeology, University of Wales Lampeter.

Liautaud, R. (1971) *Histoire du Pays Niçois*, Paris.

Liber feudorum major (1945–7) Miquel Rosell, F. (ed.), 2 vols, Barcelona.

Lopez, R.S. (1976a) *The Birth of Europe*, London.

Lopez, R.S. (1976b) *The Commercial Revolution of the Middle Ages, 950–1350*, Cambridge.

Magnou-Nortier, E. & Magnon, A. (eds), (1966) *Receuil des chartes de l'abbaye de la Grasse*, Paris.

Malaussena, P-L. (1969) *La Vie en Provence Orientale aux XIVe et XVe siècles*, Paris.

Medick, H. (1984) *Interest and Emotion: Essays on the study of family and kinship*, London.

Miskimin, H.A. (1977) *The Economy of Early Renaissance Europe 1460–1600*, Cambridge.

Mitterauer, M. & Seider, R. (1982) *The European Family*, Oxford.

Moberg, A., Sonechkin, D.M., Holmgren, K., Datsenko, N.M. & Karlén, W. (2005) 'Highly variable Northern hemisphere temperatures reconstructed from low and high-resolution proxy data', *Nature*, **433**, 613–17.

Nabholz, H. (1967) *The Cambridge Economic History of Europe*, vol. I, Cambridge.

Netting, R. M. (1981) *Balancing on an Alp*, Cambridge.

Parodi, A., Raynaud, C. & Roger, J. M. (1987) 'La Vaunage du IIIe siècle au milieu du XIIe siècle: habitat et occupation des sols', *Archéologie du Midi Médiévale*, **5**, 3–59.

Pesez, J-M. (1992) 'The emergence of the village in France and the west', *Landscape History*, **14**, 31–35.

Planel P.G. (1980) 'Settlement and economy in the northern part of the viguerie of Grasse in the central middle ages', unpublished MA Dissertation, Department of History, University of Southampton, Jan. 1980.

Poitrineau, A. (1981) *Remues d'hommes: les migrations montagnardes en France au XVIIe et XVIIIe siècles*, Paris.

Poly, J-P., Aurell, M. & Iogna-Prat, D. (1992) 'La Provence', in Zimmerman, M. (ed.), *Les Sociétés méridionales autour de l'an mil: répertoire des sources et documents commentés par M Zimmerman*, 327–60.

Poly, J-P. & Bournazel, E. (1991) (trans. C. Higit), *The Feudal Transformation 900–1200*, New York.

Poly, J-P. (1976) *La Provence et la société féodale 879–1166*, Paris.

Postan, M. M. (1973) *Essays on medieval Agriculture and General Problems of the Medieval Economy*, Cambridge.

Poteur, J-C. (1976) 'Origine et évolution de l'habitat médiéval en Provence orientale', *Atti del Colloquio Internazionale di Archeologia Medievale, 1974*, Palermo: Institute of Medieval History, University of Palermo.

Poteur, J-C. (1984) 'Résau paroissale et implantations castrales du Xe au XIIIe siècle: l'exemple de l'évêche de Grasse-Antibes', in *109e Congrés National des Sociétés Savantes, Dijon 1984*, 66–92.

Poteur, J-C. (1986) 'Les limites des seigneuries du diocése de Vence entre le XIe et le XIIIe siècles', in *Territoires, seigneuries, communes: les limites de territoires en Provence'*, Actes des Troisièmes Journées d'Histoire de l'Espace Provençal, Mouans-Sartoux, 29–53.

Poteur, J-C. (1994) *Inventaire général du patrimoine culturel: Cipières: Conseil Général des Alpes-Maritimes*, Nice.

Pounds, N.J. (1990) *An Historical Geography of Europe*, Cambridge.

Reigniez, P. (2002) *L'Outil en France au Moyen Âge*, Paris.

Rendu, C. (1998) 'La question des *orris* à partir des fouilles archéologiques de la Montagne d'Enveig (Cerdagne): état des recherches et elements de reflexion', in Rousselle, A. & Marandet, M-C. (eds) *Le paysage rural et ses acteurs*, Perpignan, 245–75.

Rendu, C. (2003) *La montagne d'Enveig: une estive pyrénéenne dans la longue durée*, Canet.

Rendu, C. (2004) 'Des cabanes aux maisons: les transformations d'une estive pyrénéenne du Moyen Âge aux temps modernes', in Cursente, B. (ed.) *Habitats et territories du Sud.* Comité des Travaux Historiques et Scientifiques, 147–63.

Rich, E.E. & Wilson, C.H. (1967) *The Cambridge Economic History of Europe, Vol. 4. The Economy of Expanding Europe in the Sixteenth and Seventeenth Centuries*, Cambridge.

Rippon, S. (2004) *Historic Landscape Analysis*, York.

Roberts, B.K. (1987) *The Making of the English Village: A Study in Historical Geography*, London.

Roberts, B. K. & Wrathmell, S. (2000) *An Atlas of Rural Settlement in England*, London.

Roc, I. (1995) 'Une Bergerie sur la Commune de Cipières. Étude Architecturale et Ethnographique: La Jassa de la Caus', unpublished MA Dissertation Dept of Socio-Ethnology, University of Nice.

Rogers, S.C. (1992) 'When the shoe fits: census data, oral history and stem families in south-west France', *Historical Methods*, **25.1**, 20–27.

Rotberg, R.I. & Rabb, T.H. (eds) (1981) *Climate in History*, New Jersey.

Ruggles, S. (1992) 'Migration, marriage and mortality: correcting sources of bias in English Family reconstitutions' *Population Studies*, **46**, 507–22.

Salicis, C. (2002) 'Du Néolithique au Moyen Age au pied du plâteau de Cavillore à Gourdon (06)', *Mémoires de l'Institut de Préhistoire et d'Archéologie Alpes Mediterranée*, **44**, 147–60.

Salicis, C. (2004) 'Les structures quadrangulaires sommitales des Alpes-Maritimes (SQS 06)', *Mémoires de l'Institut de Préhistoire et d'Archéologie Alpes Mediterranée*, **46**, 11–46.

Samaran, C. (1957a) 'Étude sur la Vie Rurale en Haute Provence Orientale au Debut du Quatorzieme Siècle d'après le Témoinage de Deux Registres Notariaux', Diplome d'études supérieures d'histoire du moyen âge, Université d'Aix.

Samaran, C. (1957b) 'Note sur la dependance personelle en haut-provence au XIVe siècle, *Annales du Midi*, **69**, 229–36.

Sauze, E. & Senac, P. (1986) *Un Pays Provençal: le Freinet de l'an mil au milieu du XIIIe siècle*, Paris.

Sclafert, T. (1934) 'Le déboisement des Alpes du Sud: ii, le rôle des troupeaux' *Annales de Géographie*, **43**, 126–45.

Sclafert, T. (1933) 'À propos du déboisement des Alpes de Sud', *Annales de Géographie*, **42**, 266–360.

Sclafert, T. (1959) 'Cultures en Haute Provence: déboisements et pâturages au Moyen Âge', *L'Homme et la terre*, **4**, Paris.

Sclafert, T. (1963) *Le haut Dauphiné au Moyen Âge*, Paris.

Seccomb, W. (1992) *A Millennium of family Change: from Feudalism to Capitalism in North-western Europe*, London.

Segui, E. (1946) 'La guerre aux chèvres sous l'Ancien Régime, *Cahiers d'Histoire et d'Archéologie*, **16**, 11–21.

Siddle, D.J. (1986a) 'The transmission of wealth in peasant Savoy', *Itinera*, **5/6**, 123–182.

Siddle, D.J. (1986b) 'Inheritance strategies and lineage development in a peasant society', *Continuity and Change*, **3**, 333–61.

Siddle, D.J. (1996) (trans. Ungar, C), 'Cipières et la Guerre de Succession: repercussions démographiques, *Centre Régional de Documentation Occitane*, Mouans Sartoux.

Siddle, D.J. (1997) 'Migration as a strategy of accumulation: social and economic change in eighteenth century Savoy', *Economic History Review*, **50.1**, 1–19.

Siddle, D.J.(2000) *Migration Mobility and Modernisation*, Liverpool.

Siddle, D.J. & Jones A.M. (1983) *Family Household Structures and Inheritance in Savoy, 1561–1975*, Liverpool Papers in Human Geography: Department of Geography, University of Liverpool.

Slicher van Bath, B.H. (1963) *The Agrarian History of Western Europe 500–1850*, London.

Smith, C.T. (1978) *Historical Geography of Western Europe before 1800*, London

Taylor, C.C. (1983) *Village and Farmstead: a history of rural settlement in England*, London

Thiery, D. (1990) 'Le terroir du Ferrier, commune de Saint-Vallier-de-Thiey (A-M); étude des constructions en pierre sèche', *Mémoires de l'Institut de Préhistoire et d'Archéologie Alpes Mediterranée*, **32**, 71–87.

Thiery, D. (1991) 'Le terroir du Ferrier (commune de Saint-Vallier-de-Thiey (A-M)', *Mémoires de l'Institut de Préhistoire et d'Archéologie Alpes Mediterranée*, **33**, 59–94.

Thiery, D. (1992) 'Le pierre sèche et le milieu rural dans les textes anciens: communes de Saint-Vallier et de Saint-Cézaire (A-M)', *Mémoires de l'Institut de Préhistoire et d'Archéologie Alpes Mediterranée*, **34**, 3–16.

Thiery, D. (1994) 'Caussols en 1834: étude du milieu rural des constructions en pierre sèche', *Mémoires de l'Institut de Préhistoire et d'Archéologie Alpes Mediterranée*, **36**, 131–142.

Timbal, P.C. (ed.) (1969) *La Vie en Provence Orientale aux 14e et 15e Siècles, bibliotheque d'histoire du droit et droit romain*, Paris.

Tits-Dieuade, M-J. (1985) 'Grands domaines, grands et petits exploitations en Gaule mérovingienne', in Verhulst, A. (ed.), *La Grande Domaine aux époques mérovingienne et carolingienne*, Gent 1985.

Toubert, P. (1973) *Les Structures du Latium médiéval: Le Latium méridiona et al Sabine du IXe siècle à la fin du XIIe siècle*, 2 vols. Rome: École Française du Rome.

Uhlig, H. (1972) *Die Siedlungen des Landlichen Raumes*, Giessen.

Ungar, C. & Allemand, D. (1984) 'Deux exemples de forteresses en falaise dans les Préalpes de Grasse: Gars et Gourdon', *Mémoires de l'Institut de Préhistoire et d'Archéologie Alpes Mediterranée*, **26**, 77–86.

Viazzo, P. (1989) *Upland Communities, Population and Social Structure in the Alps since the Sixteenth Century*, Cambridge.

Walter, J. & Schofield, R. (1989) *Famine, Disease and the Social Order in Early Modern Society*, Cambridge.

Weinburger, S. (1990) 'La transformation de la société paysanne en Provence médiévale', *Annales*, **45.1**, 3–21.

Wickham, C, (1980) *The Mountains and the City: the Tuscan Apennines in the early middle ages*, Oxford.

Williams. M. (2000) 'Dark ages and dark areas: global deforestation in the deep past', *Journal of Historical Geography*, **26.1**, 28–46.

Williamson, T. (2003) *Shaping Medieval Landscapes: settlement, society, environment*, Macclesfield.

Wrigley, E.A. (1969) *Population and History*, London.

Wrigley, E.A. (1994) 'The effect of migration on the estimation of marriage age in family reconstitution', *Population Studies*, **48**, 81–97.

Wrigley, E.A. & Schofield, R.S (1981) *The Population History of England, 1541–1871: a reconstruction.* London.

Zerner-Chardavoine, M. (1968) 'Enfants et jeunes au IXe siècle: la démographie du polyptyque du Marseille 813–814' *Provence Historique*, **126**, 355–84.

Unpublished Material in Project Archives

Allen, M.J. (1983) 'A cursory study of the environment and palaeo-environments of the Plâteau de Calern near Cipières (A-M), via pedological examination', unpublished report, project archives.

Austin, D. (1987) 'The Upper Loup Valley Historic Landscape Project', unpublished (first) application to the Leverhulme Trust, project archives.

Austin, D., Crowther, J., Fleming, A., Garfi, S., Hepper, N., Johnson, M., Lewison, A., Siddle, D. & Ungar, C. (1993) 'Le Projet Cipières, 1993', unpublished report to the Ministère de la Culture, Préfecture de la Région de Provence-Alpes-Côtes d'Azur, Direction Régionale des Affaires Culturelles, Service Régionale de l'Archéologie, project archives.

Austin, D., Crowther, J., Fleming, A., Garfi, S., Hepper, N., Johnson, M., Lewison, A., Siddle, D. & Ungar, C. (1994) 'Le Projet Cipières, 1994', unpublished report to the Ministère de la Culture, Préfecture de la Région de Provence-Alpes-Côtes d'Azur, Direction Régionale des Affaires Culturelles, Service Régionale de l'Archéologie, project archives.

Austin, D., Crowther, J., Fleming, A., Garfi, S., Hepper, N., Johnson, M., Lewison, A., Siddle, D. & Ungar, C. (1995) 'Le Projet Cipières, 1995', unpublished report to the Ministère de la Culture, Préfecture de la Région de Provence-Alpes-Côtes d'Azur, Direction Régionale des Affaires Culturelles, Service Régionale de l'Archéologie, project archives.

Austin, D., Crowther, J., Fleming, A., Hepper, N., Johnson, M., Lewison, A., Siddle, D. & van Rose, S. (1993) 'The Cipières Project', unpublished (second) application to the Leverhulme Trust, vol. 1: Project Statement; vol. 2: Detailed Statement, project archives.

Bone, J. & Trethowan, T. (1994) 'Cipières 1994: excavation report', unpublished report, project archives.

Canti, M. (1985a) 'Nineteenth-century agricultural land classification at Cipières, France' unpublished report, project archives.

Canti, M. (1985b) 'Aspects of physical geography at Cipières, France', unpublished report, project archives.

Crowther, J. (1994) 'La Combe soil analyses', unpublished report, project archives.

Crowther, J. (1996) 'Soil and sediment studies at Cipières: further report on work undertaken in September 1994', unpublished report, project archives.

Crowther, J. (1997) 'Cipières: soils investigations', unpublished report, project archives.

Ede, J. (1983) 'An examination of a terrace on the Plâteau de Calern, near Cipières (A-M)', unpublished report, project archives.

Hammond, I. (1986) 'A critique of land use and land use change in Cipières Commune, France: 1844 to the present day', unpublished BA dissertation, School of Geography, University of Oxford.

Hepper, N. (1994a) 'Cipières Project: Plâteau de Calern: plant ecology: the vegetation of doline 163 and its karst surroundings', unpublished report, project archives.

Hepper, N. (1994b) 'Cipières Project botanical study 1–15 June 1994', unpublished report, project archives.

Hepper, N. (2001) 'Botanical and ecological survey of Cipières Commune, Alpes-Maritimes, France', unpublished paper, project archives.

Johnson, M. (1994) 'Understanding upland landscapes: the Cipières Project', unpublished draft paper, project archives.

Lewison, A. (1983) 'Archaeological field walk in Alpes-Maritimes, France 1983', unpublished report, project archives.

Lewison, A. (1986b) 'Cipières. A village in the war-zone: 1742–1748', unpublished paper, project archives.

Lewison, A., Siddle, D. & Ungar, C. (1993) 'De temps immemorial – Les Cipièrois', unpublished introduction to the exhibition in the Chapel of St Lambert, Cipières, project archives.

Siddle, D. (1991) 'Cognitive space: the mental landscape/template of the Community and territory of Cipières in the pre-industrial period', unpublished paper, project archives.

Siddle, D. (1992) 'Managing a Malthusian crisis: a mountain village during the War of the Austrian Succession', unpublished paper, project archives.

Siddle, D. & Ungar, C. (1995) 'Évolution du complexe agro-pastoral dans une commune de moyenne montagne: un volet du "Projet Cipières"', unpublished paper, project archives.